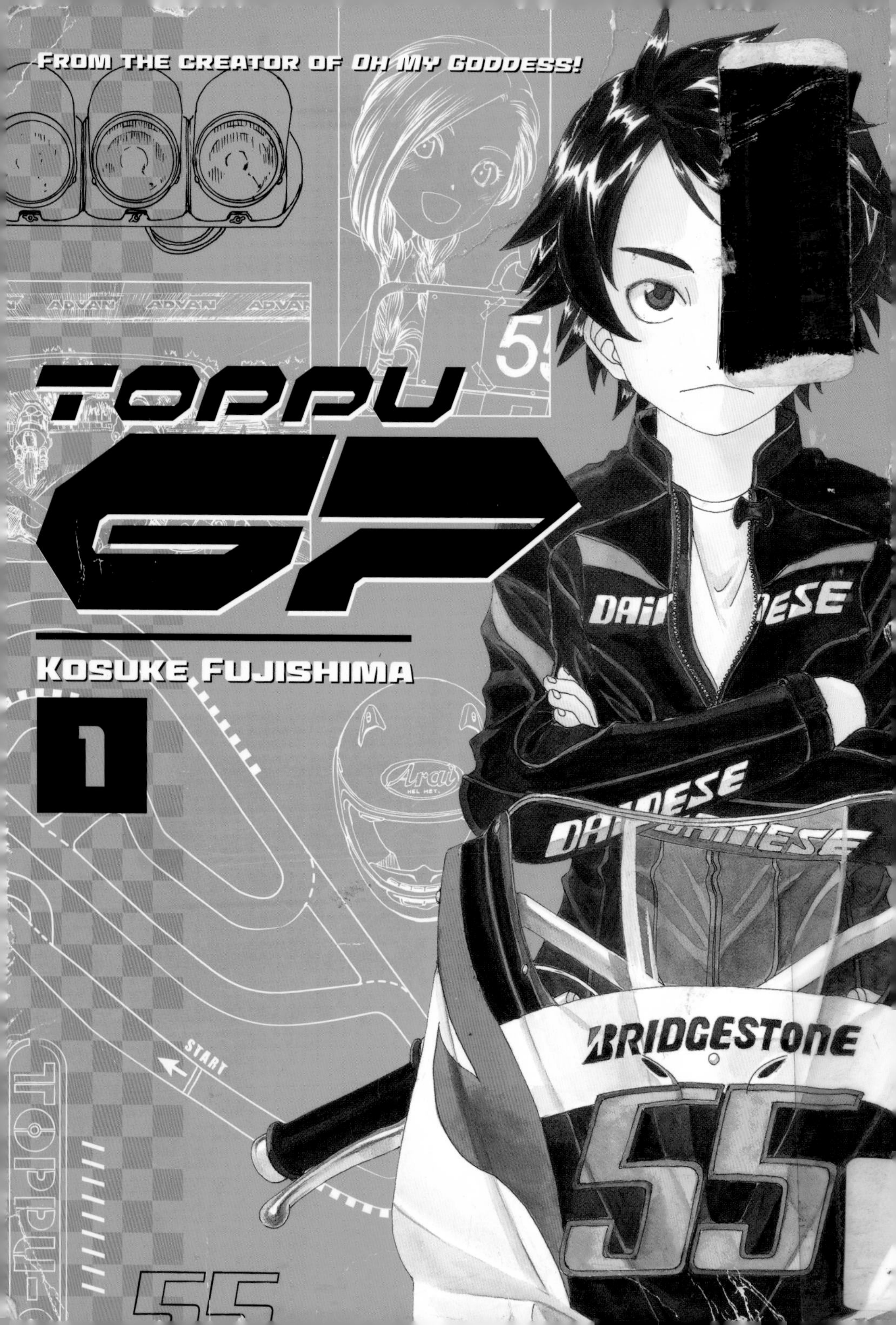
FROM THE CREATOR OF OH MY GODDESS!
TOPPU GP
KOSUKE FUJISHIMA
1
ADVAN
55
Arai
START
BRIDGESTONE
55

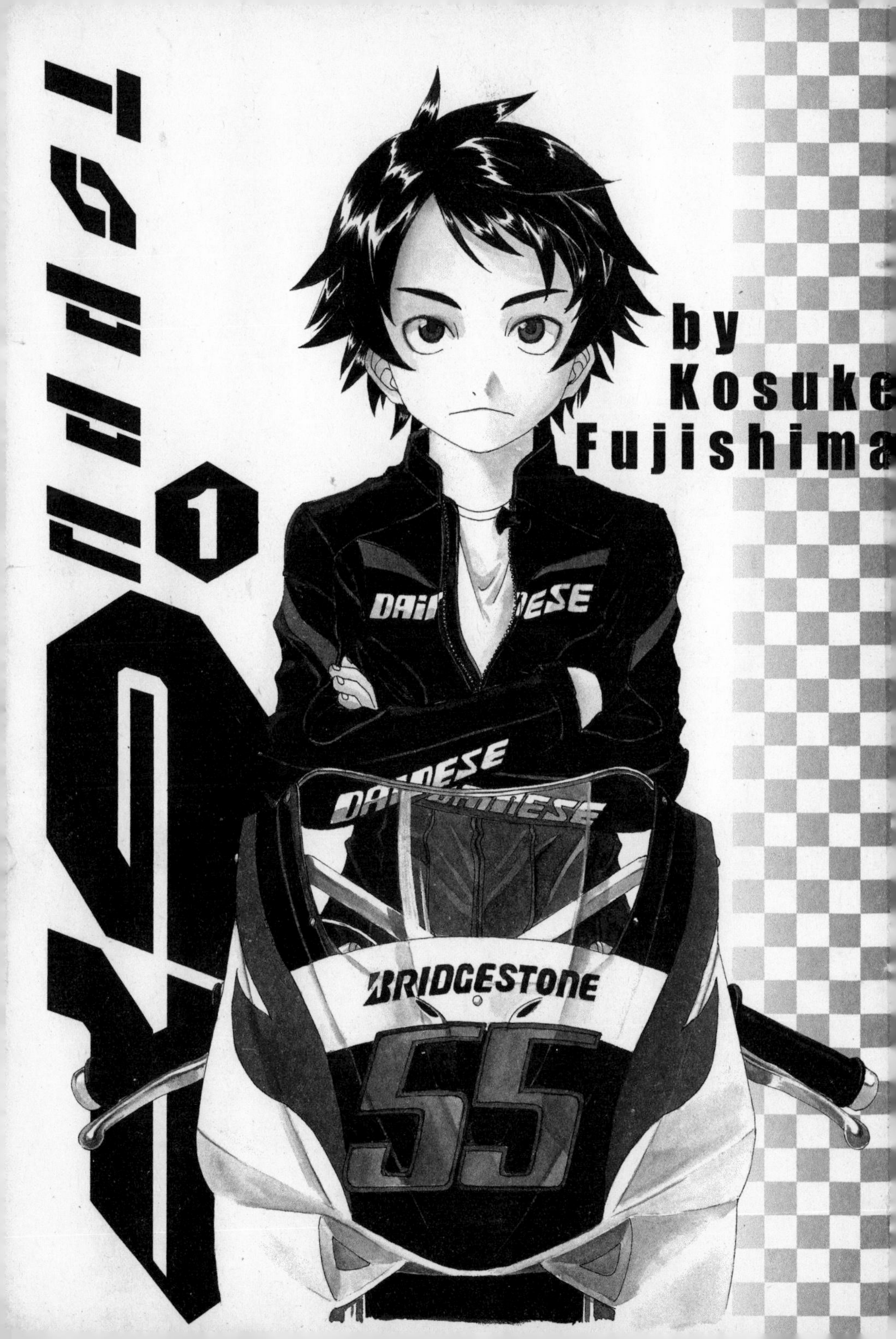
1
by
Kosuke
Fujishima
DAINESE
BRIDGESTONE
55

[TOPPU GP]

Presented by

Kosuke Fujishima

In cooperation with
Honda Motor Co., Ltd.
DAINESE JAPAN
JAPAN AUTO SPORTS CENTER

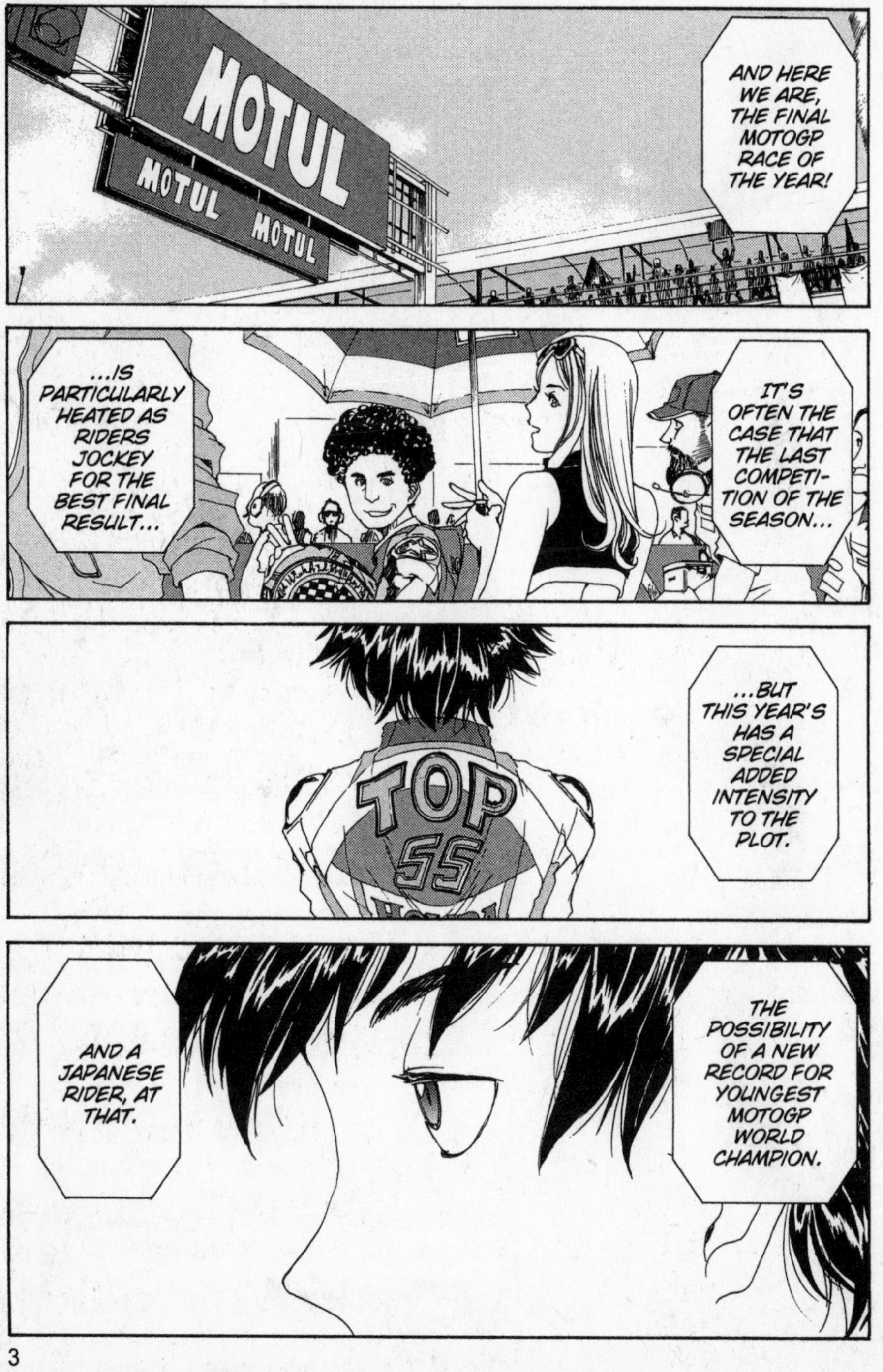
AND HERE WE ARE, THE FINAL MOTOGP RACE OF THE YEAR!
MOTUL
MOTUL
MOTUL
IT'S OFTEN THE CASE THAT THE LAST COMPETITION OF THE SEASON...
...IS PARTICULARLY HEATED AS RIDERS JOCKEY FOR THE BEST FINAL RESULT...
...BUT THIS YEAR'S HAS A SPECIAL ADDED INTENSITY TO THE PLOT.
TOP
55
THE POSSIBILITY OF A NEW RECORD FOR YOUNGEST MOTOGP WORLD CHAMPION.
AND A JAPANESE RIDER, AT THAT.

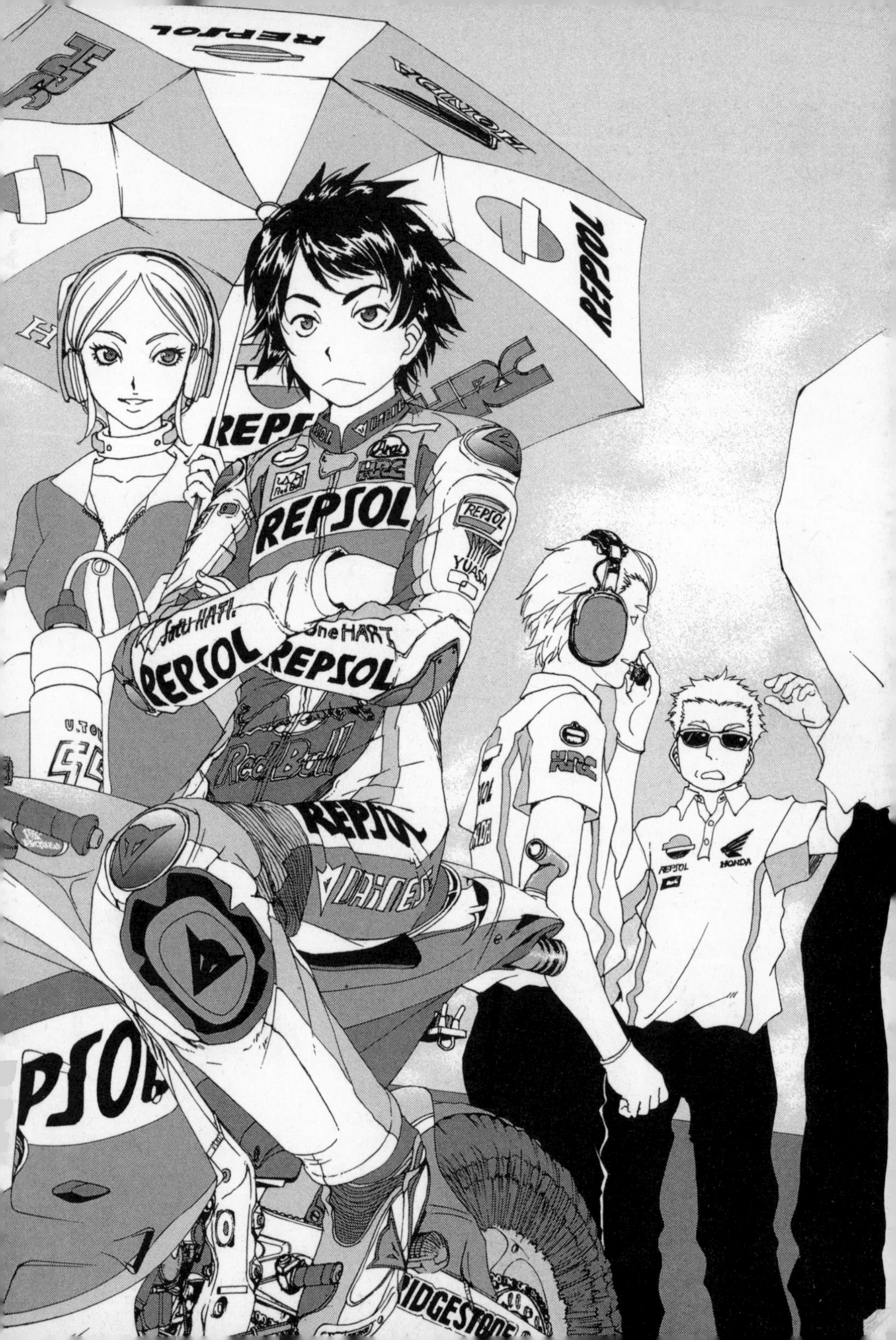
REPSOL
REPSOL
Satu-HATI.
REPSOL
One HART
REPSOL
YUASA
Red Bull
REPSOL
REPSOL
HONDA
BRIDGESTONE

Lap 1:
TOPPU UNO

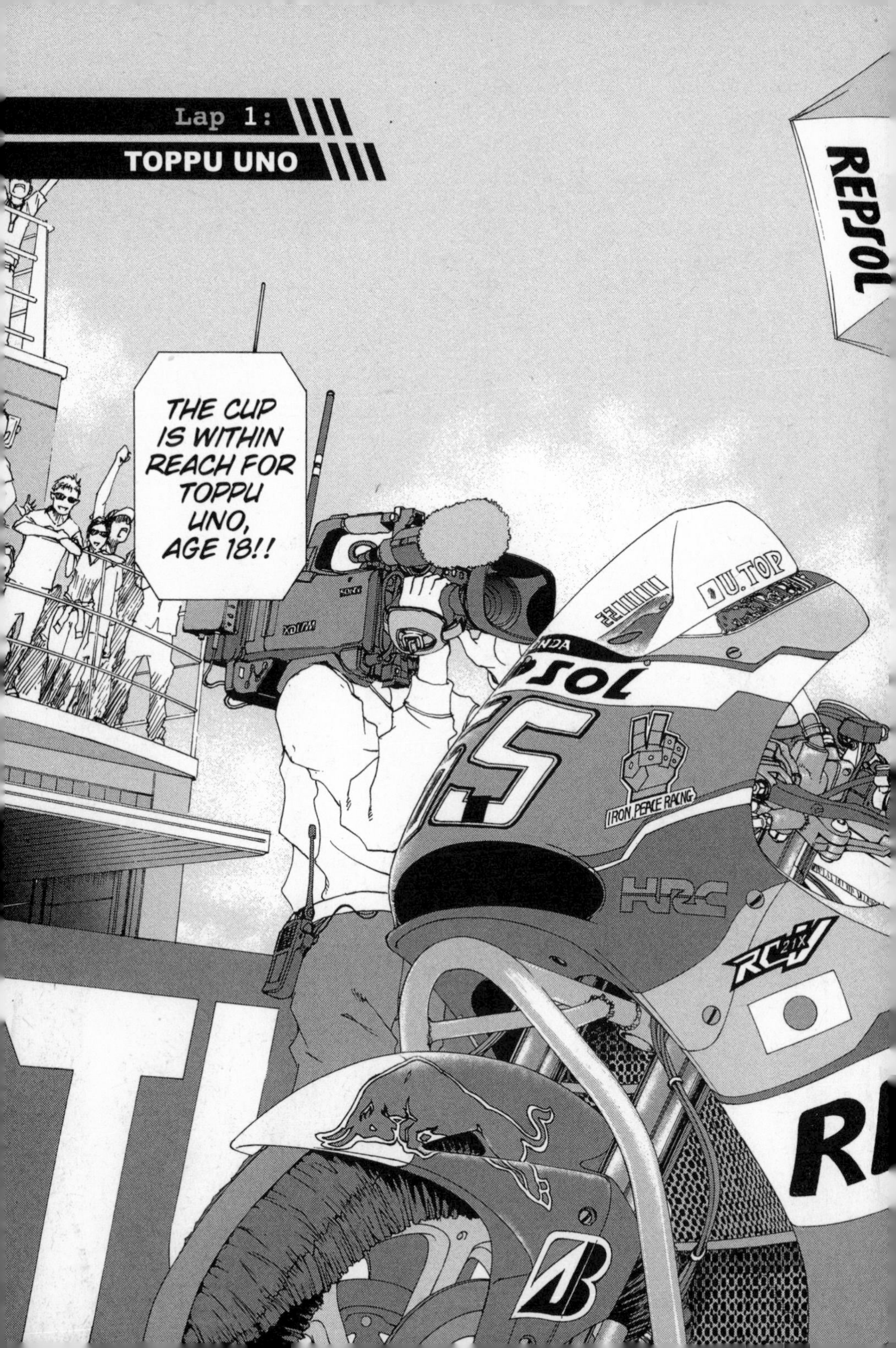
REPSOL
THE CUP IS WITHIN REACH FOR TOPPU UNO, AGE 18!!
DU.TOP
IRON PEACE RACING

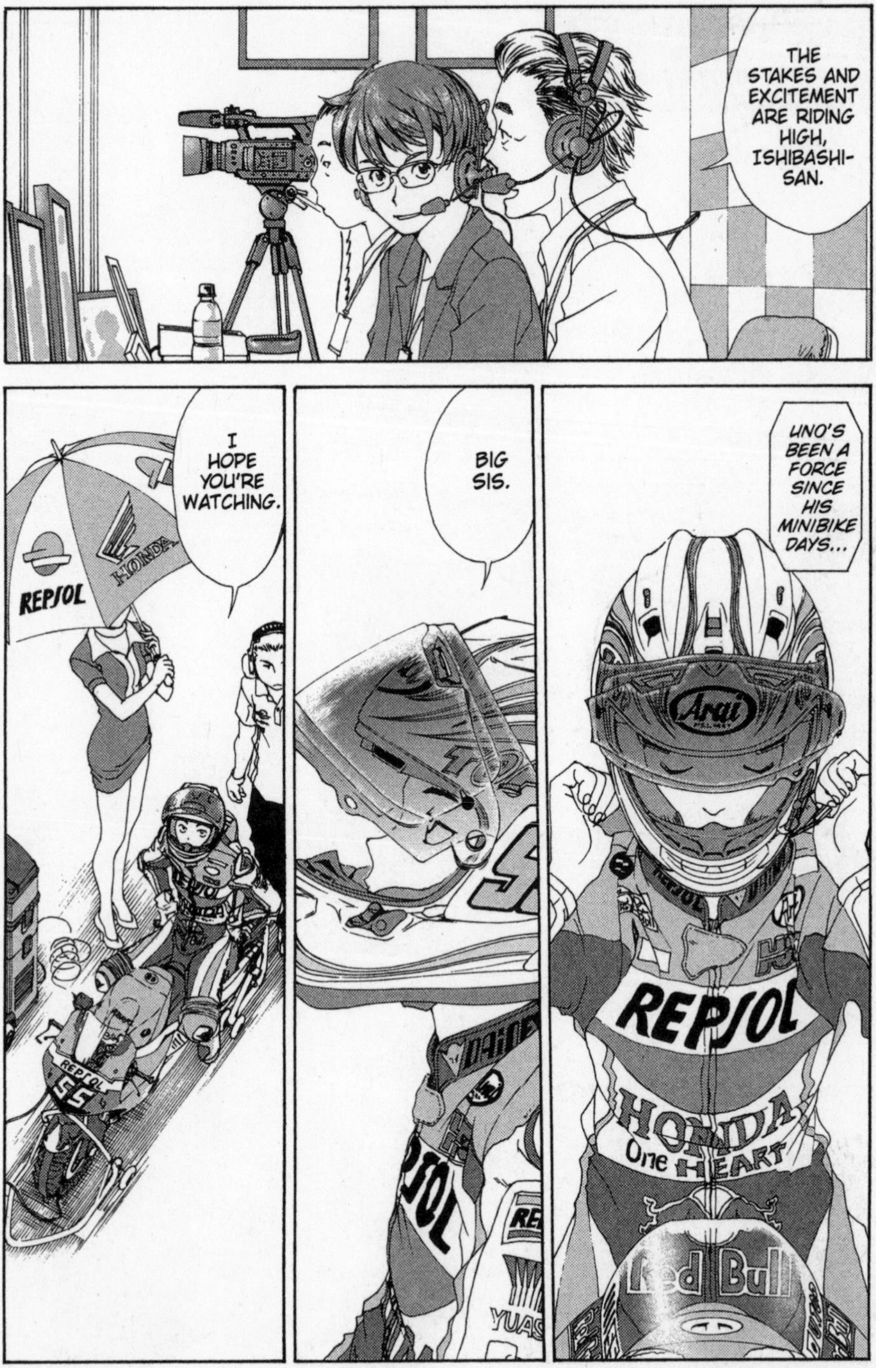
THE STAKES AND EXCITEMENT ARE RIDING HIGH, ISHIBASHI-SAN.
I HOPE YOU'RE WATCHING.
BIG SIS.
UNO'S BEEN A FORCE SINCE HIS MINIBIKE DAYS...

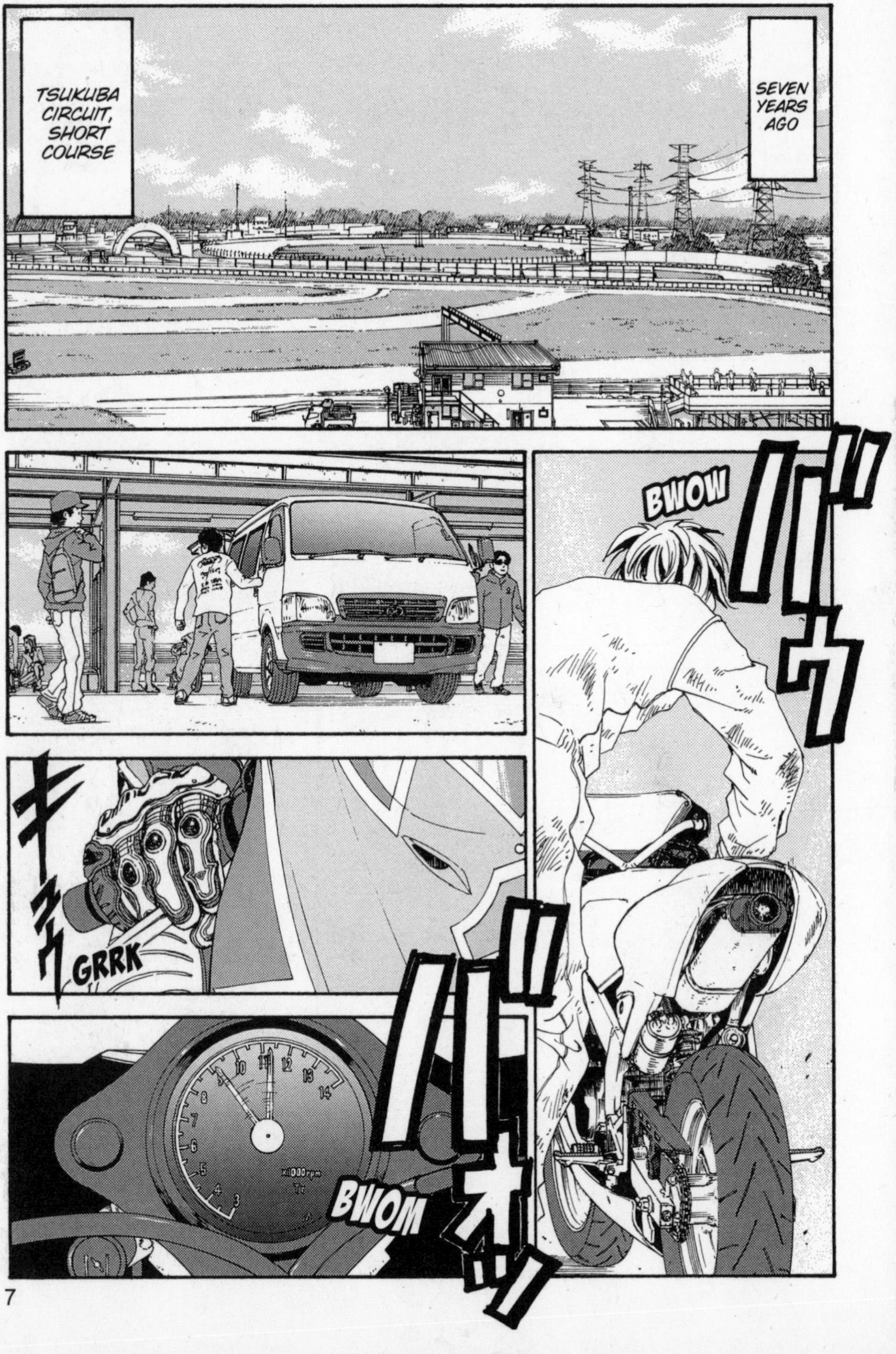
SEVEN YEARS AGO
TSUKUBA CIRCUIT, SHORT COURSE
BWOW
バウ
GRRK
BWOM
バオッ

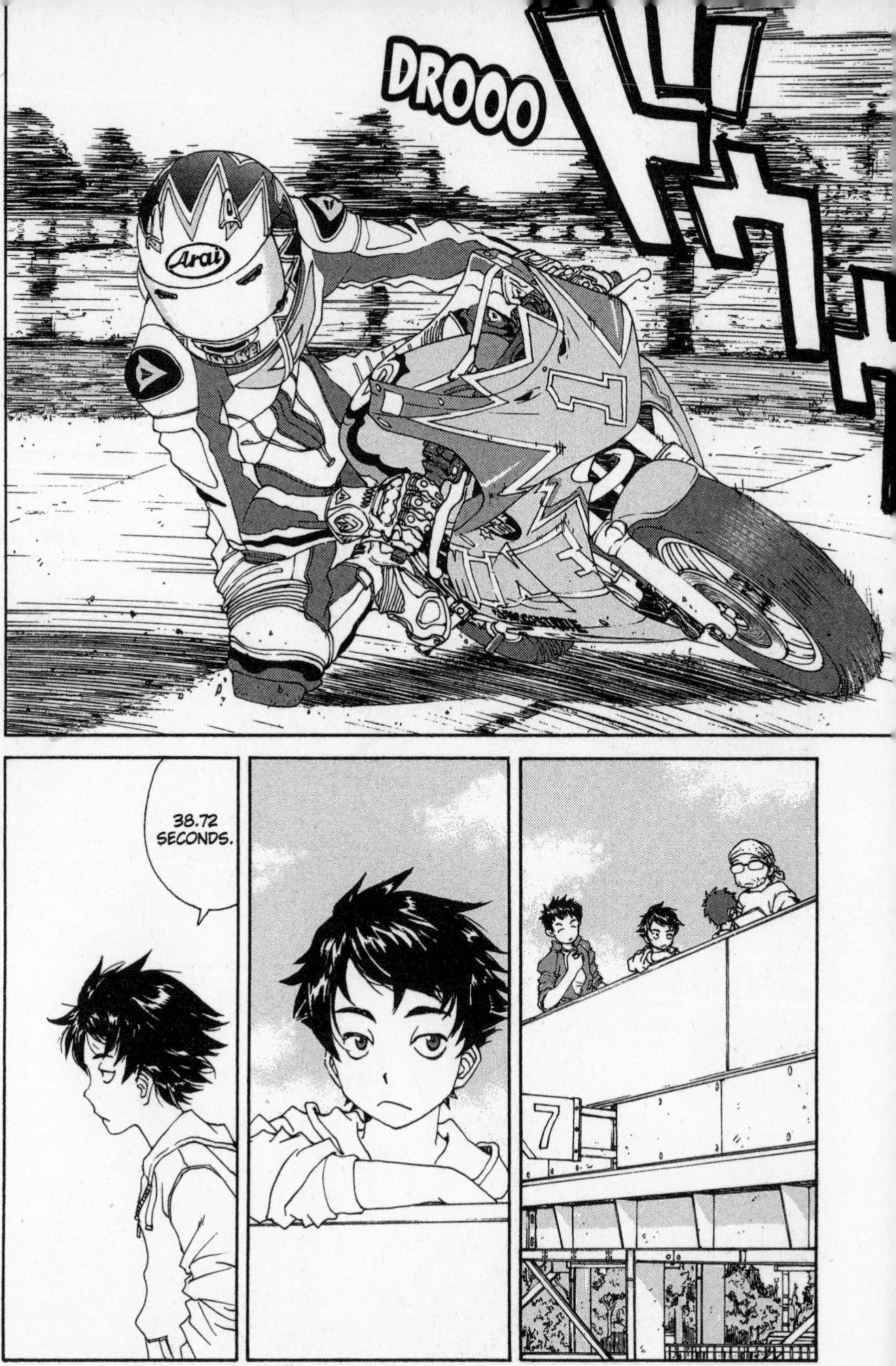
DROOO
38.72 SECONDS.

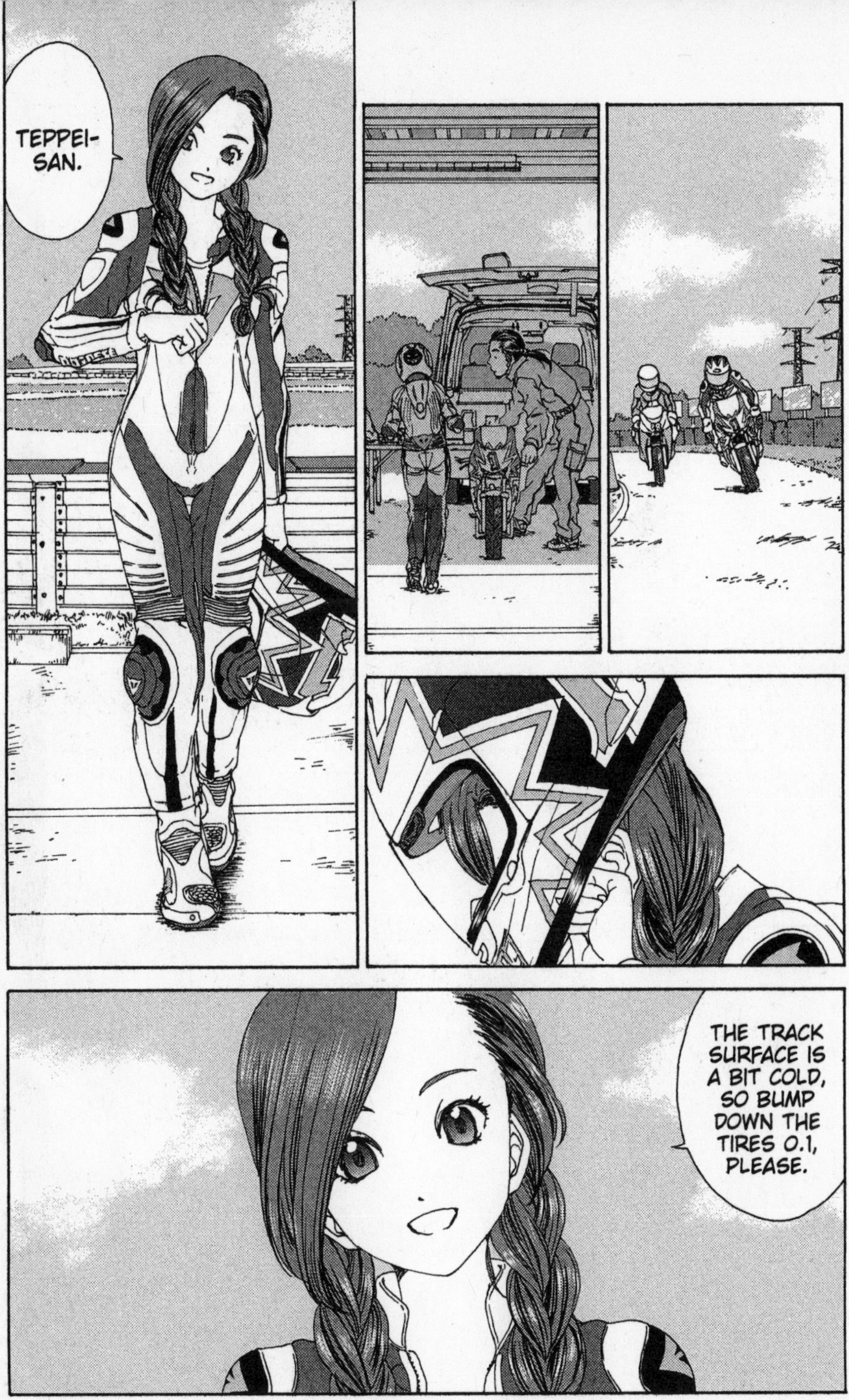
TEPPEI-SAN.
THE TRACK SURFACE IS A BIT COLD, SO BUMP DOWN THE TIRES 0.1, PLEASE.

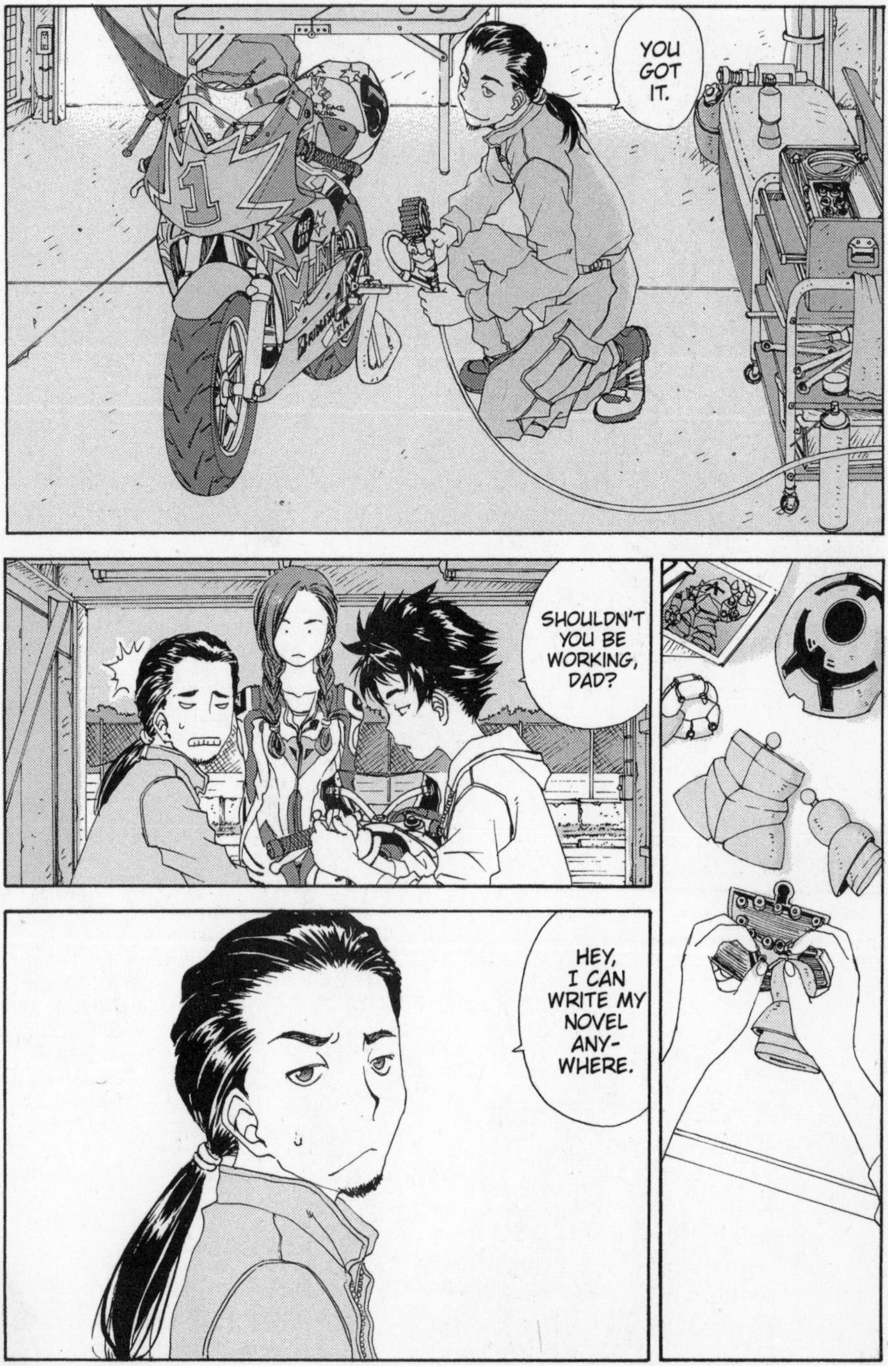
YOU GOT IT.
SHOULDN'T YOU BE WORKING, DAD?
HEY, I CAN WRITE MY NOVEL ANYWHERE.

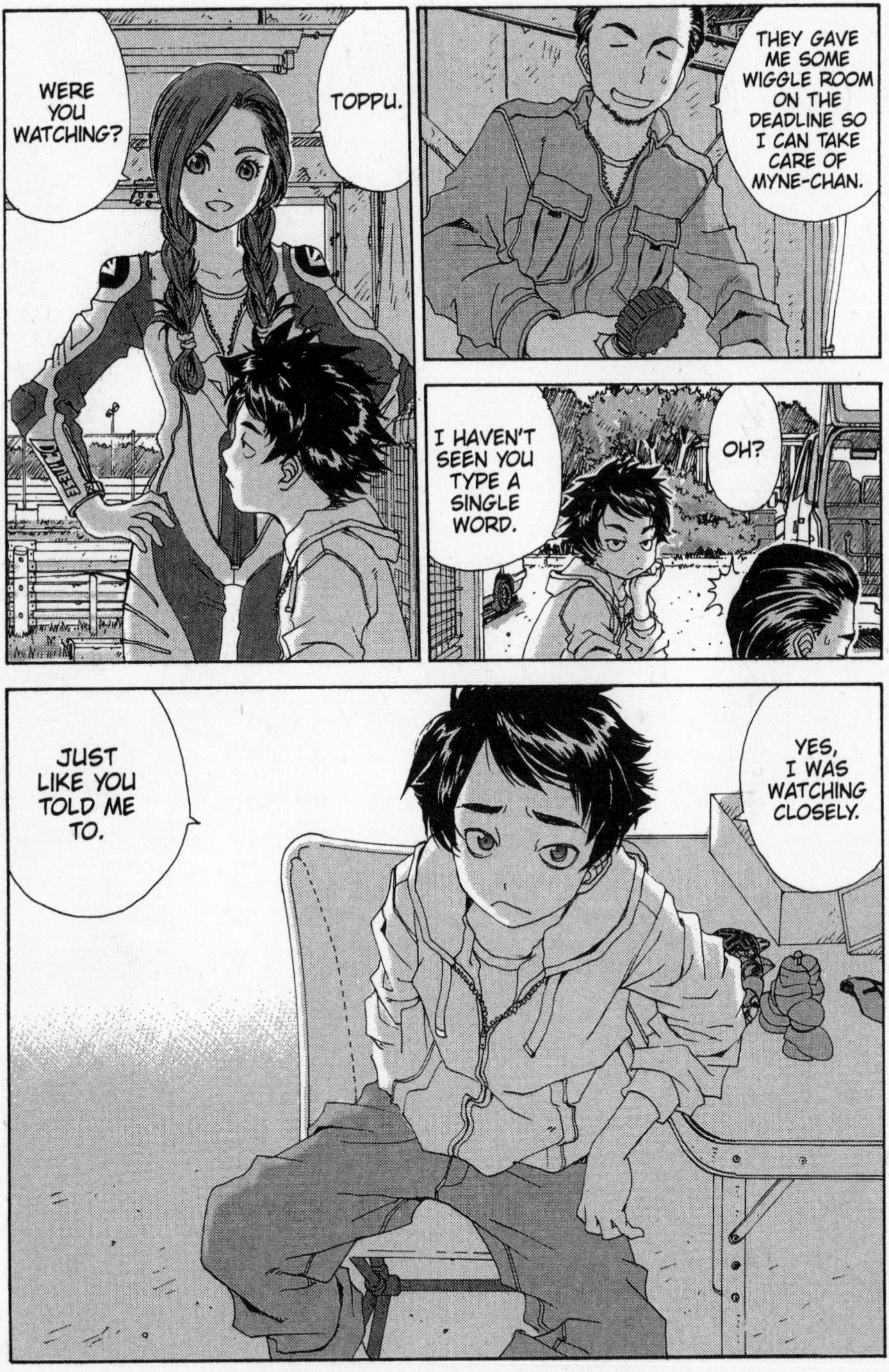

THEY GAVE ME SOME WIGGLE ROOM ON THE DEADLINE SO I CAN TAKE CARE OF MYNE-CHAN.
I HAVEN'T SEEN YOU TYPE A SINGLE WORD.
OH?
TOPPU.
WERE YOU WATCHING?
YES, I WAS WATCHING CLOSELY.
JUST LIKE YOU TOLD ME TO.

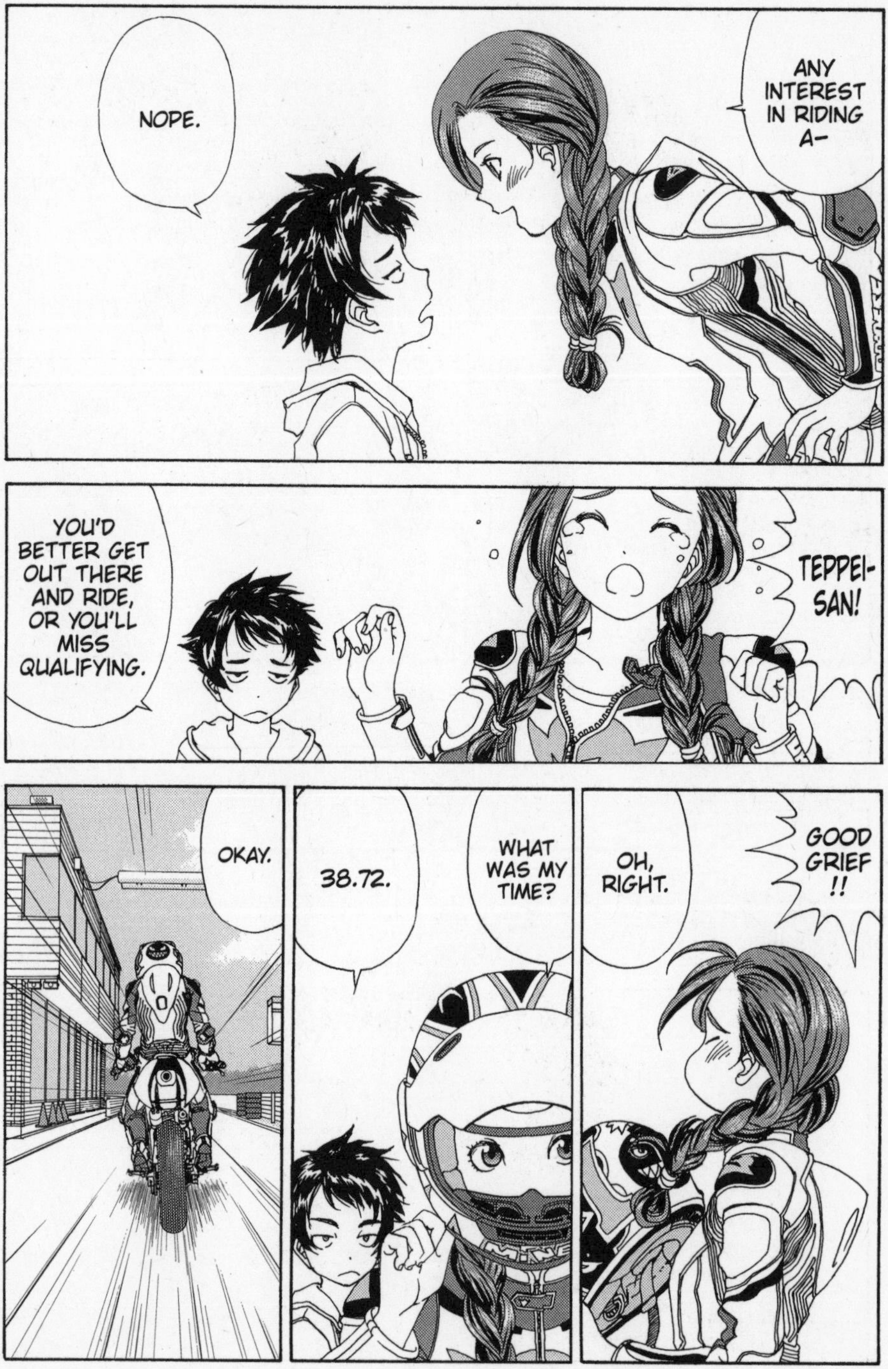
ANY INTEREST IN RIDING A–
NOPE.
TEPPEI-SAN!
YOU'D BETTER GET OUT THERE AND RIDE, OR YOU'LL MISS QUALIFYING.
GOOD GRIEF !!
OH, RIGHT.
WHAT WAS MY TIME?
38.72.
OKAY.

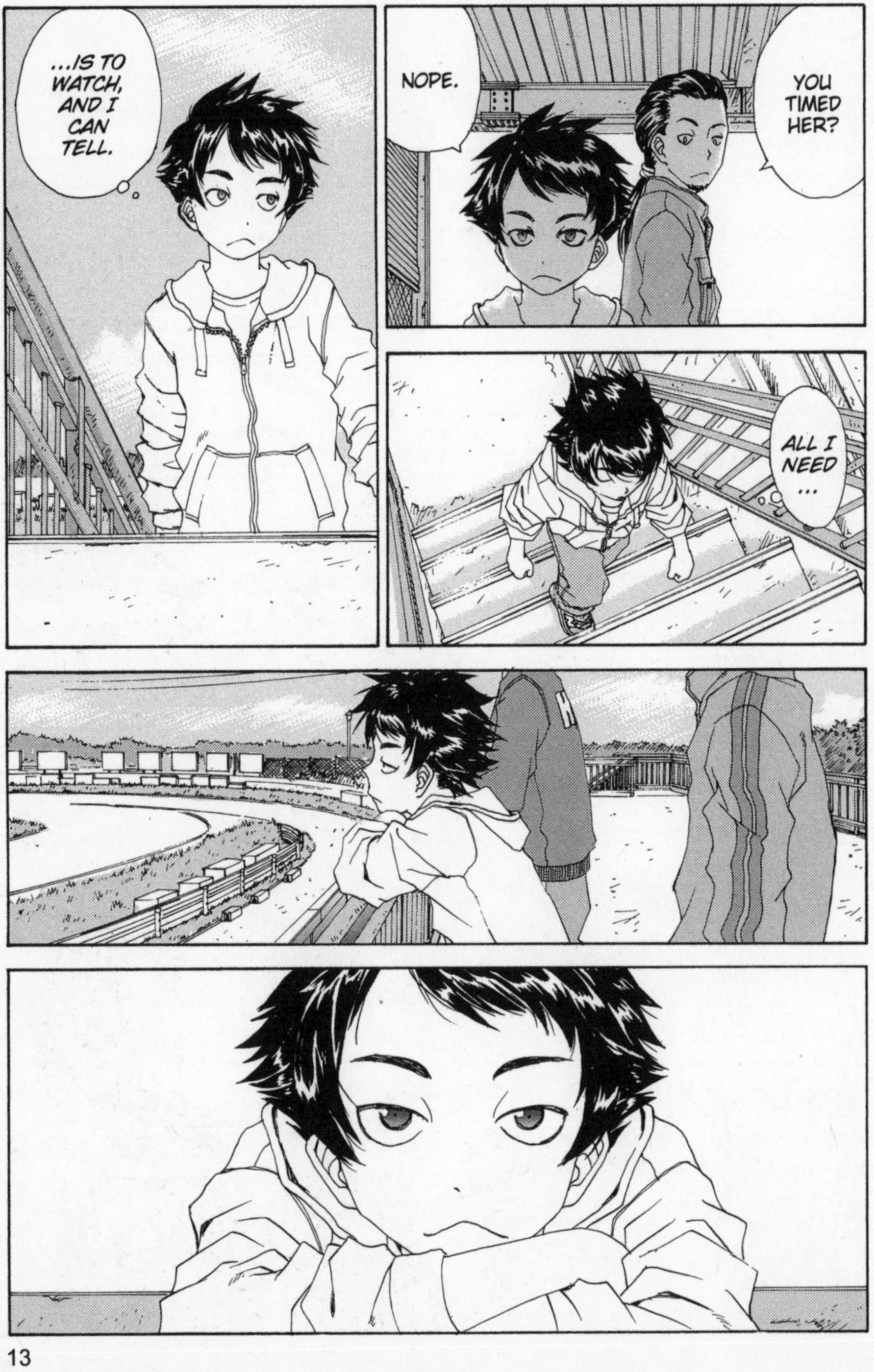
YOU TIMED HER?
NOPE.
ALL I NEED ...
...IS TO WATCH, AND I CAN TELL.

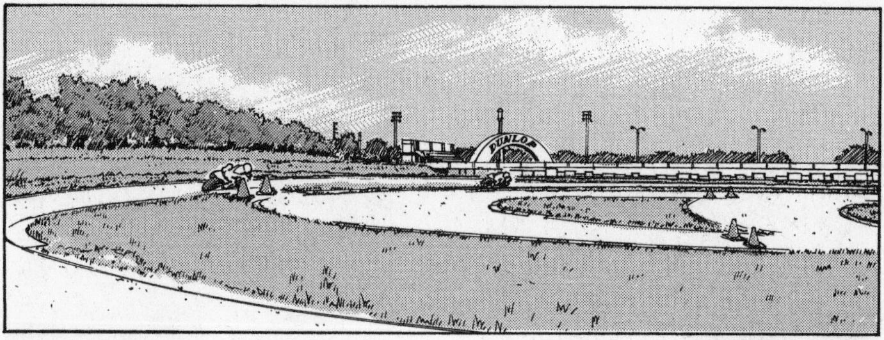
DUNLOP
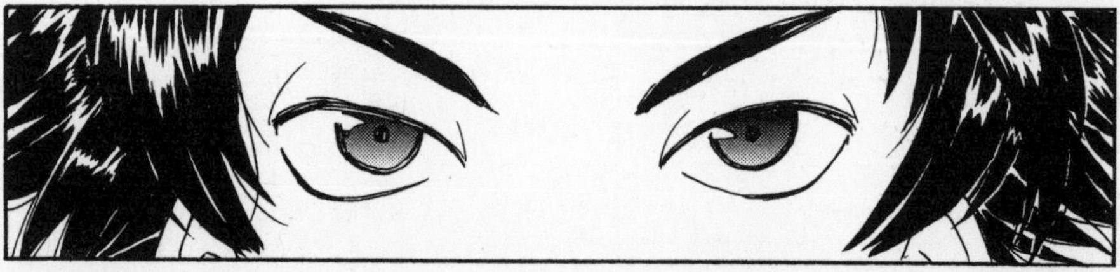
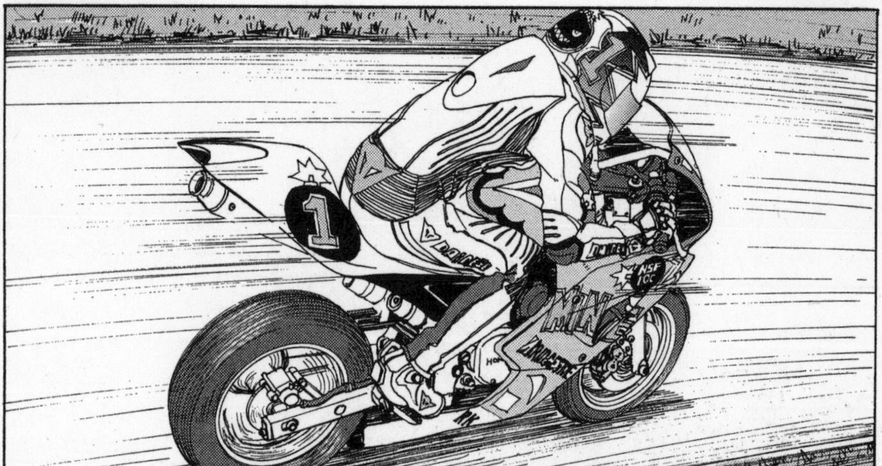
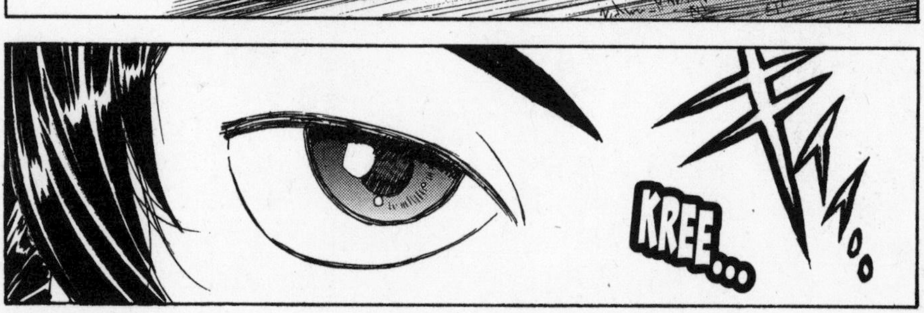
KREE...

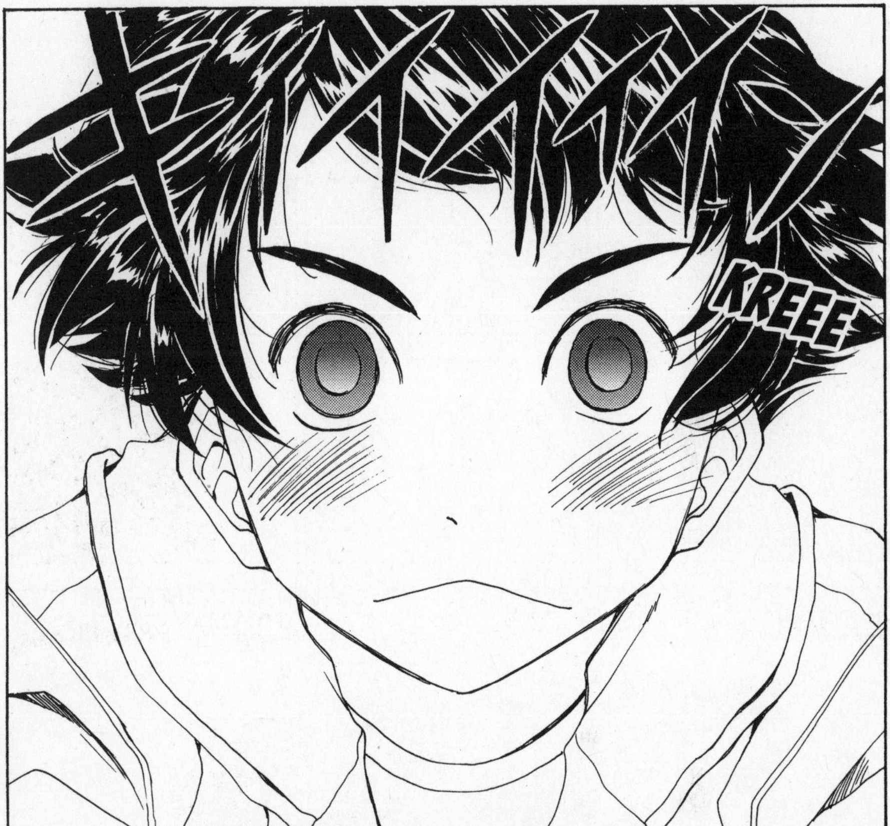
KREEE

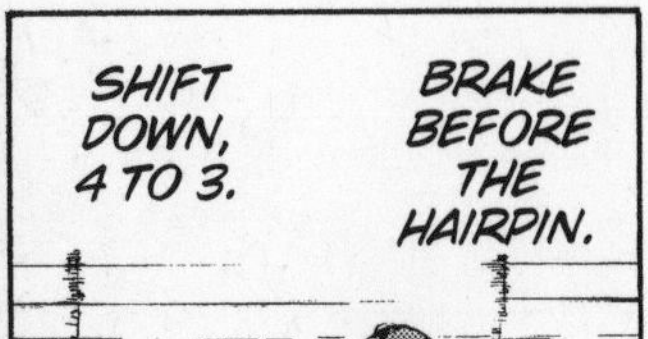
BRAKE BEFORE THE HAIRPIN.
SHIFT DOWN, 4 TO 3.

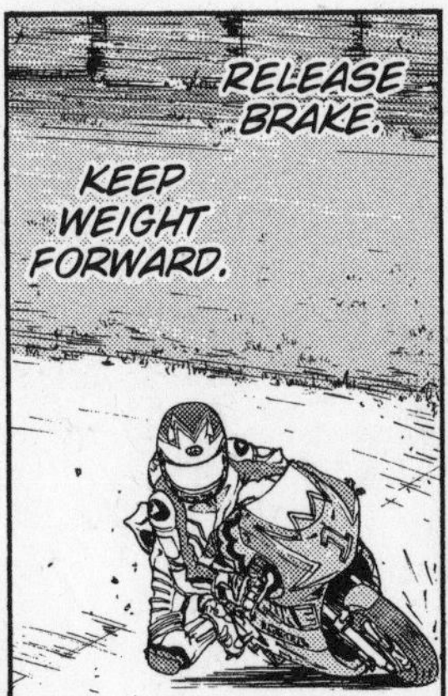
RELEASE BRAKE.
KEEP WEIGHT FORWARD.

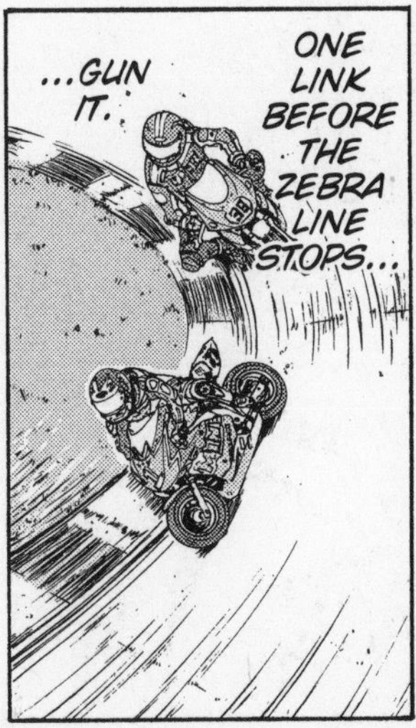
ONE LINK BEFORE THE ZEBRA LINE STOPS...
...GUN IT.

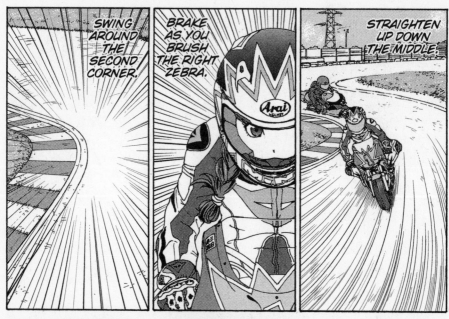

SWING AROUND THE SECOND CORNER.

BRAKE AS YOU BRUSH THE RIGHT ZEBRA.

STRAIGHTEN UP DOWN THE MIDDLE.

JUST LIKE THE FIRST HAIRPIN.

THEN FULL SPEED.

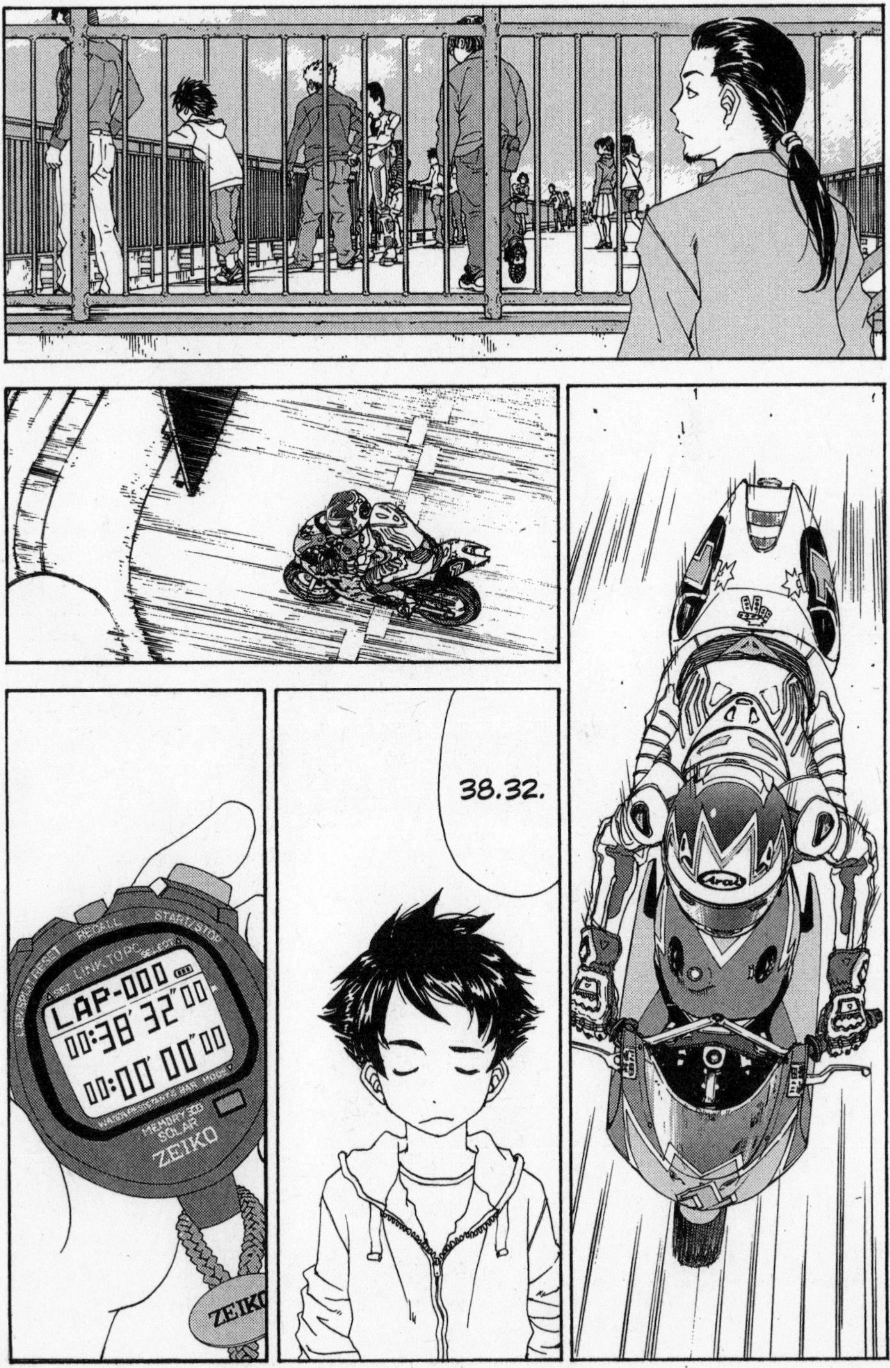
38.32.
START/STOP
RECALL
LAP-000
00:38'32"00
00:00'00"00
SOLAR
ZEIKO
ZEIKO

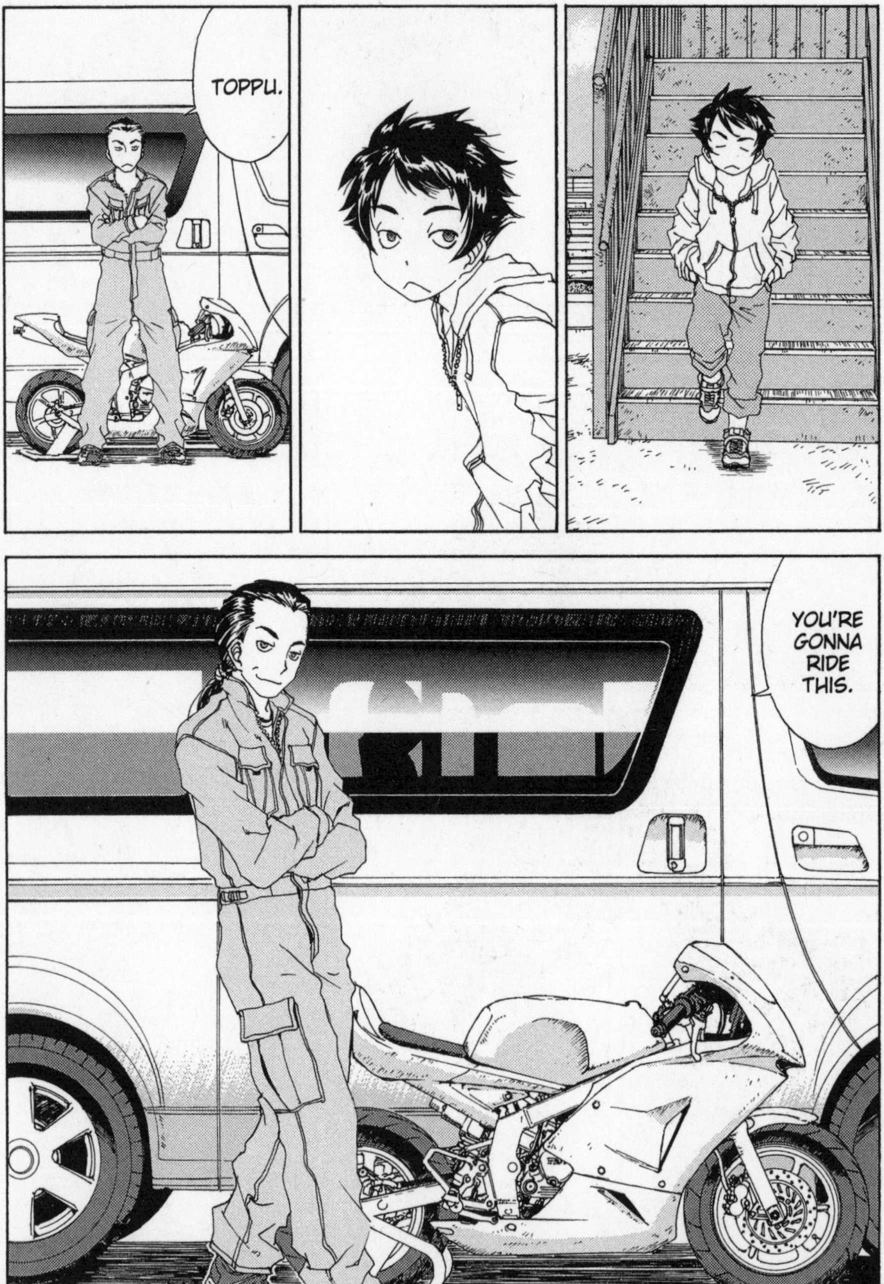
TOPPU.
YOU'RE GONNA RIDE THIS.

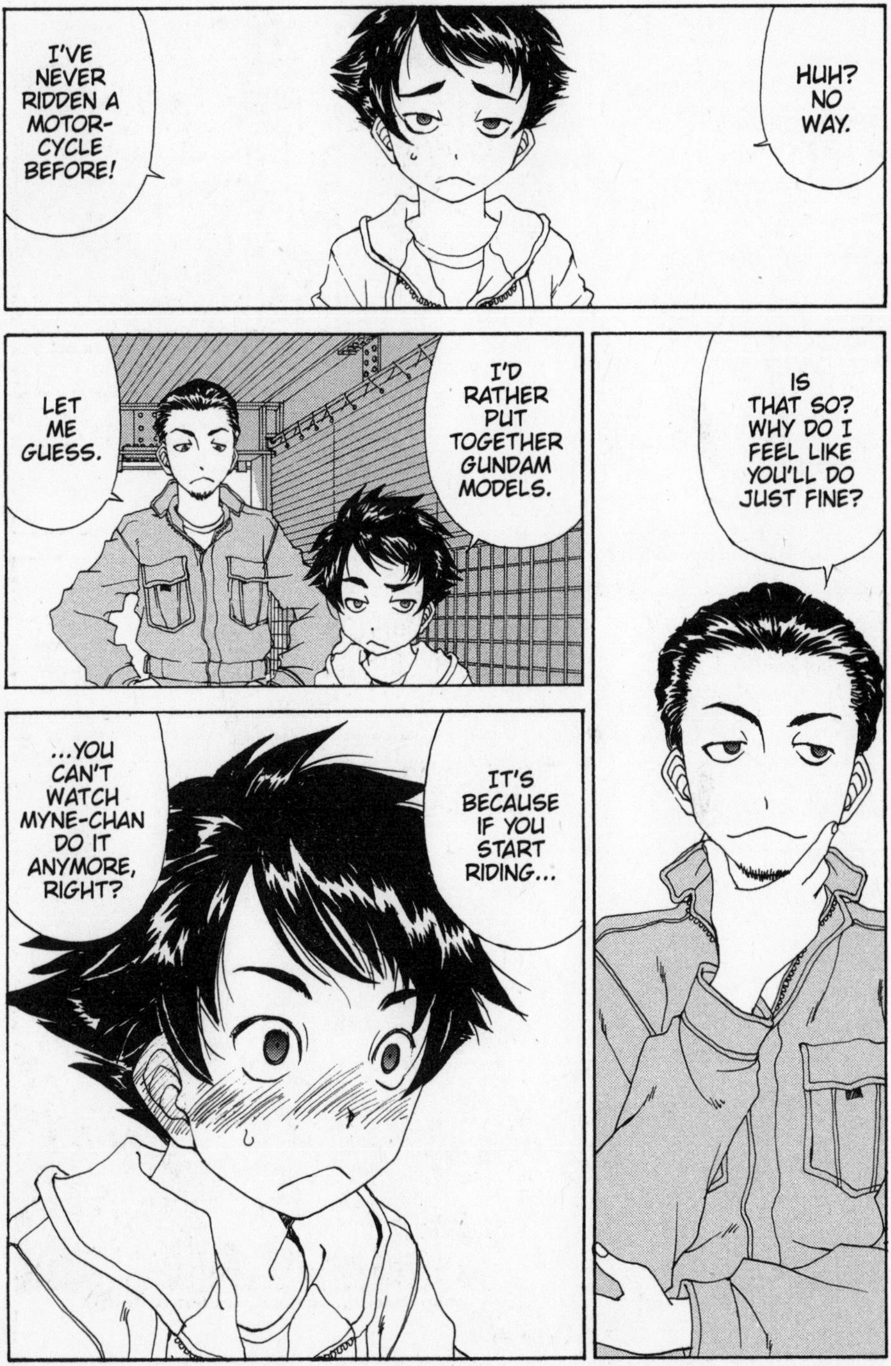
HUH? NO WAY.
I'VE NEVER RIDDEN A MOTOR-CYCLE BEFORE!
IS THAT SO? WHY DO I FEEL LIKE YOU'LL DO JUST FINE?
I'D RATHER PUT TOGETHER GUNDAM MODELS.
LET ME GUESS.
IT'S BECAUSE IF YOU START RIDING...
...YOU CAN'T WATCH MYNE-CHAN DO IT ANYMORE, RIGHT?

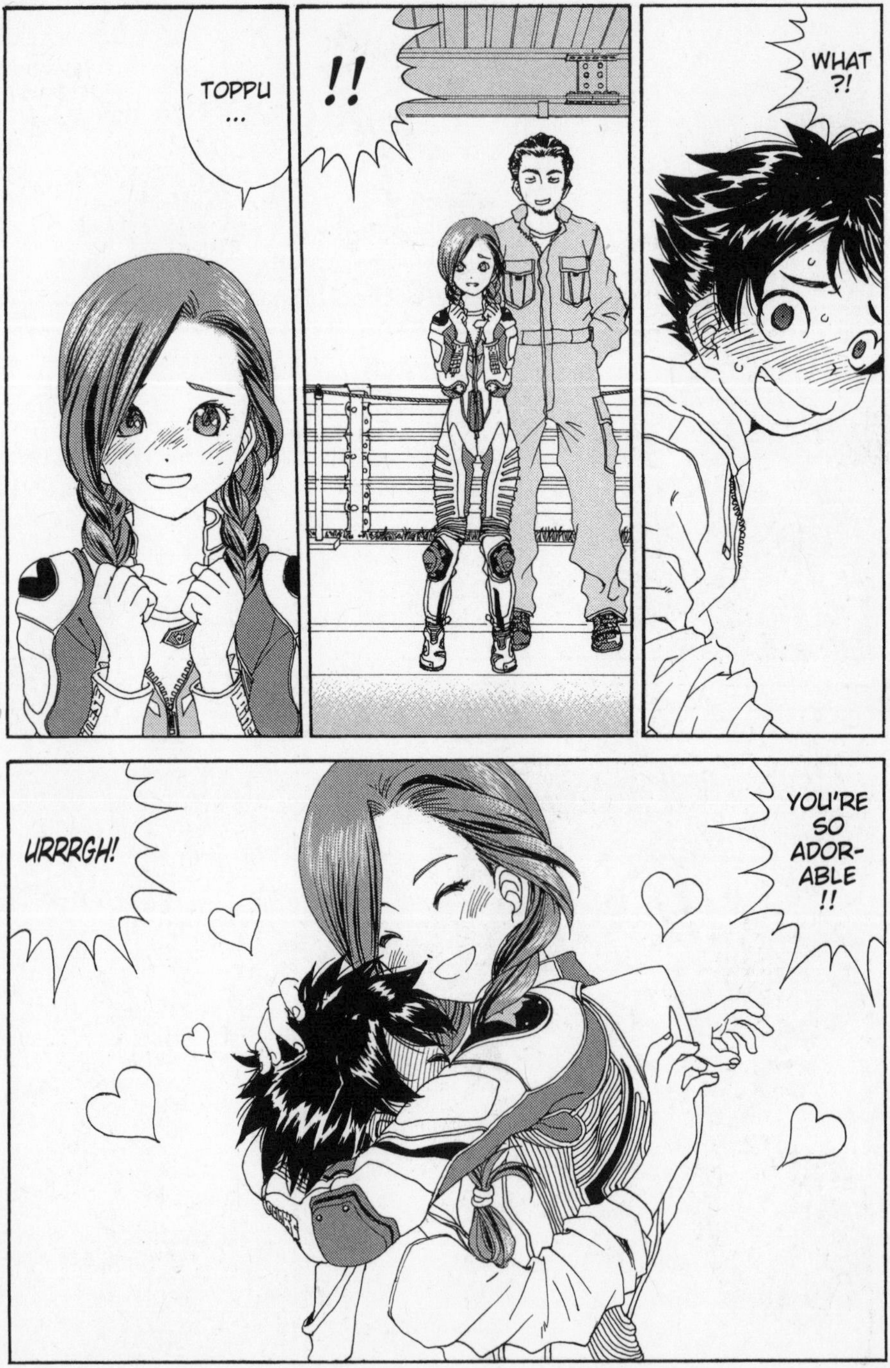
WHAT ?!
!!
TOPPU ...
YOU'RE SO ADOR- ABLE !!
URRRGH!

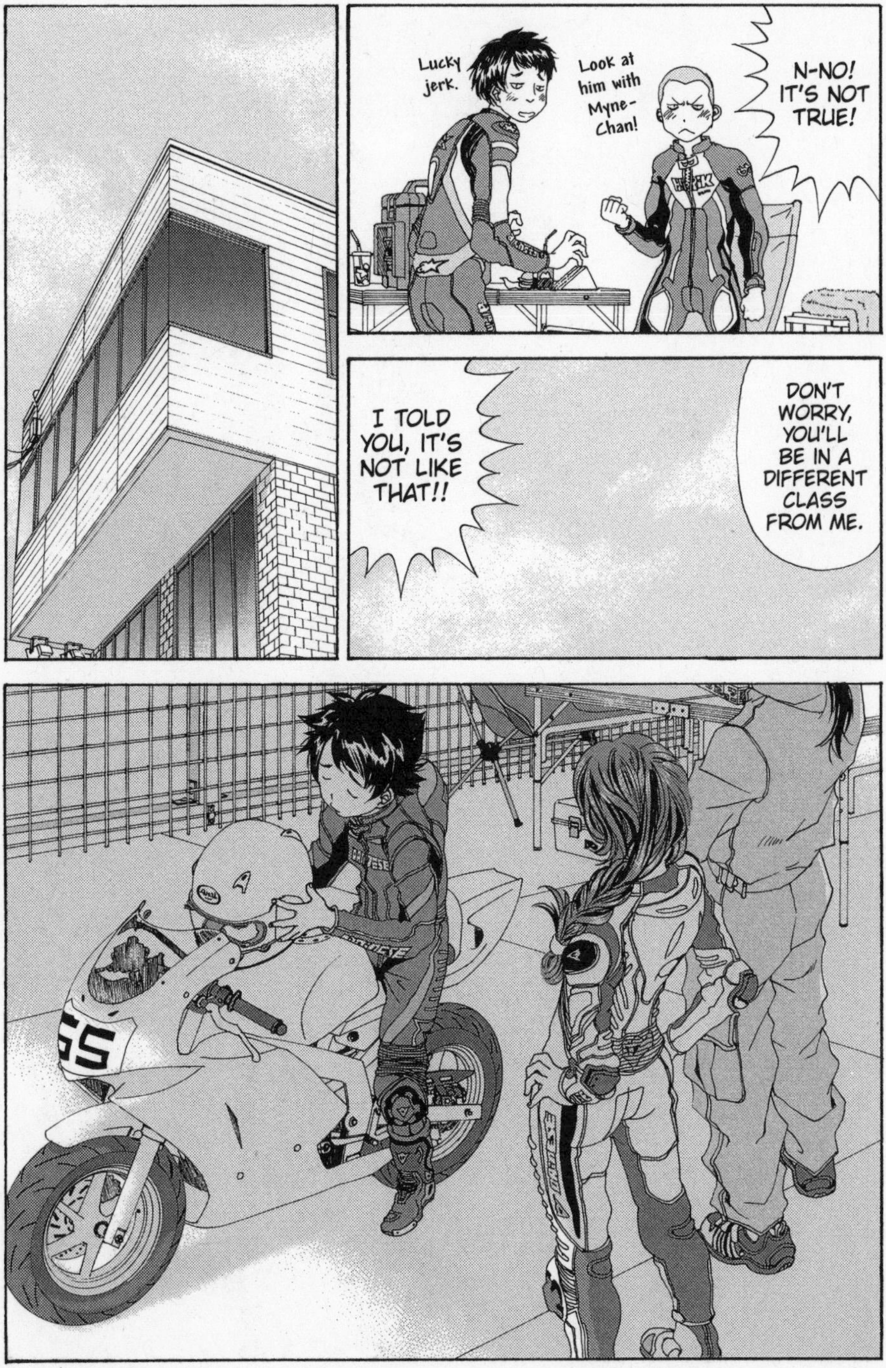
N-NO! IT'S NOT TRUE!
Look at him with Myne-Chan!
Lucky jerk.
DON'T WORRY, YOU'LL BE IN A DIFFERENT CLASS FROM ME.
I TOLD YOU, IT'S NOT LIKE THAT!!

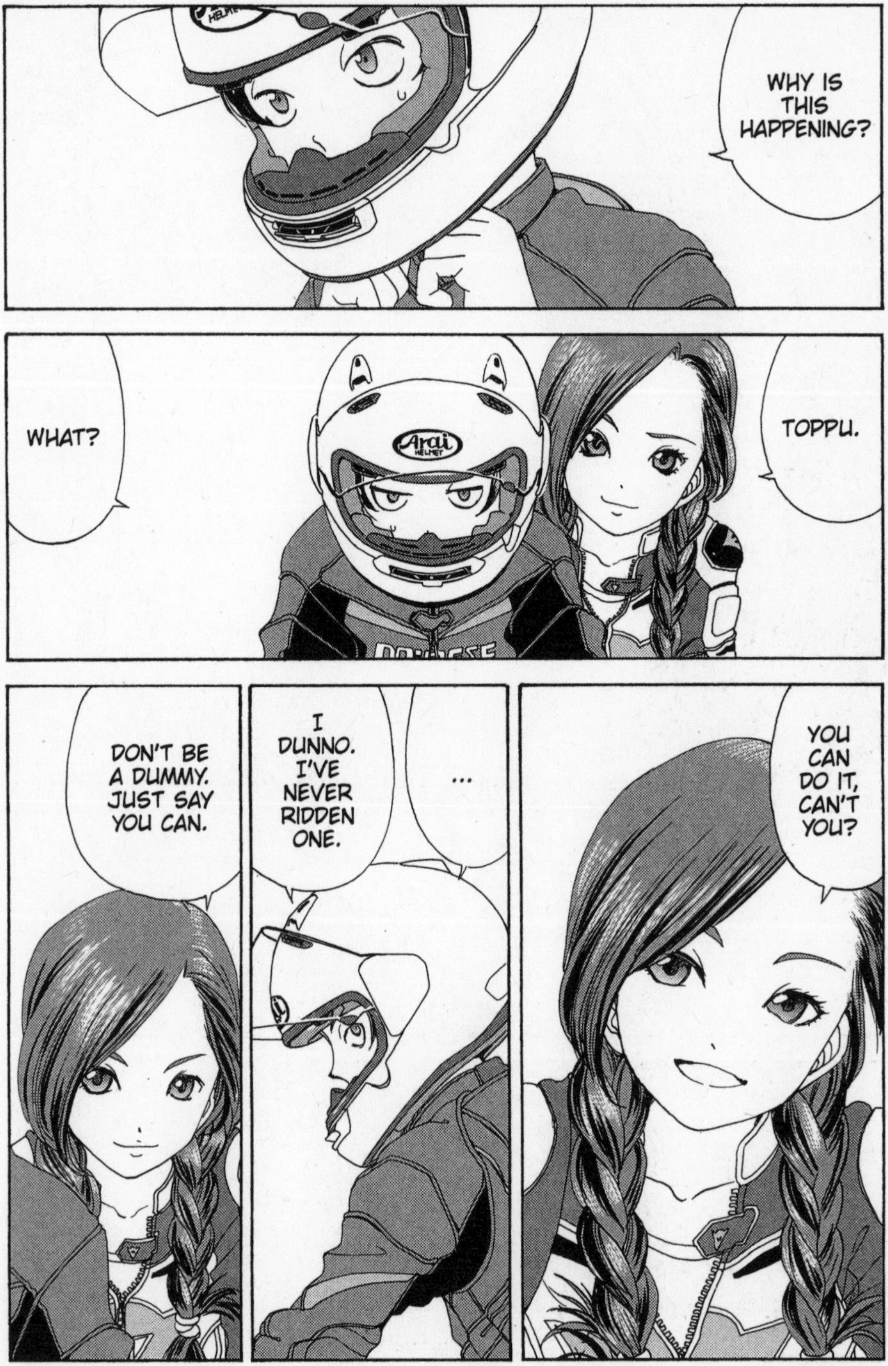
WHY IS THIS HAPPENING?
TOPPU.
WHAT?
YOU CAN DO IT, CAN'T YOU?
...
I DUNNO. I'VE NEVER RIDDEN ONE.
DON'T BE A DUMMY. JUST SAY YOU CAN.

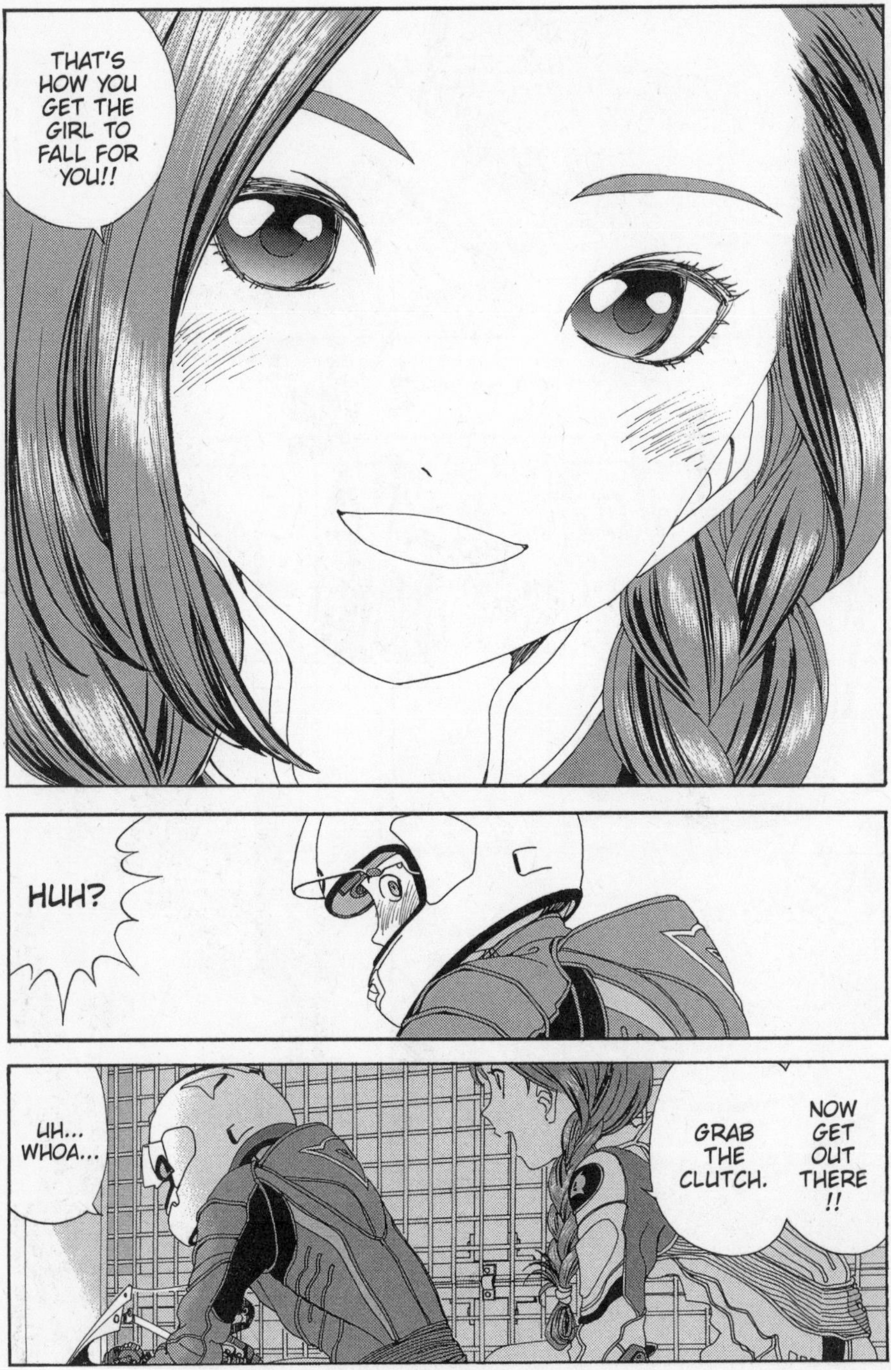
THAT'S HOW YOU GET THE GIRL TO FALL FOR YOU!!
HUH?
NOW GET OUT THERE !!
GRAB THE CLUTCH.
UH... WHOA...

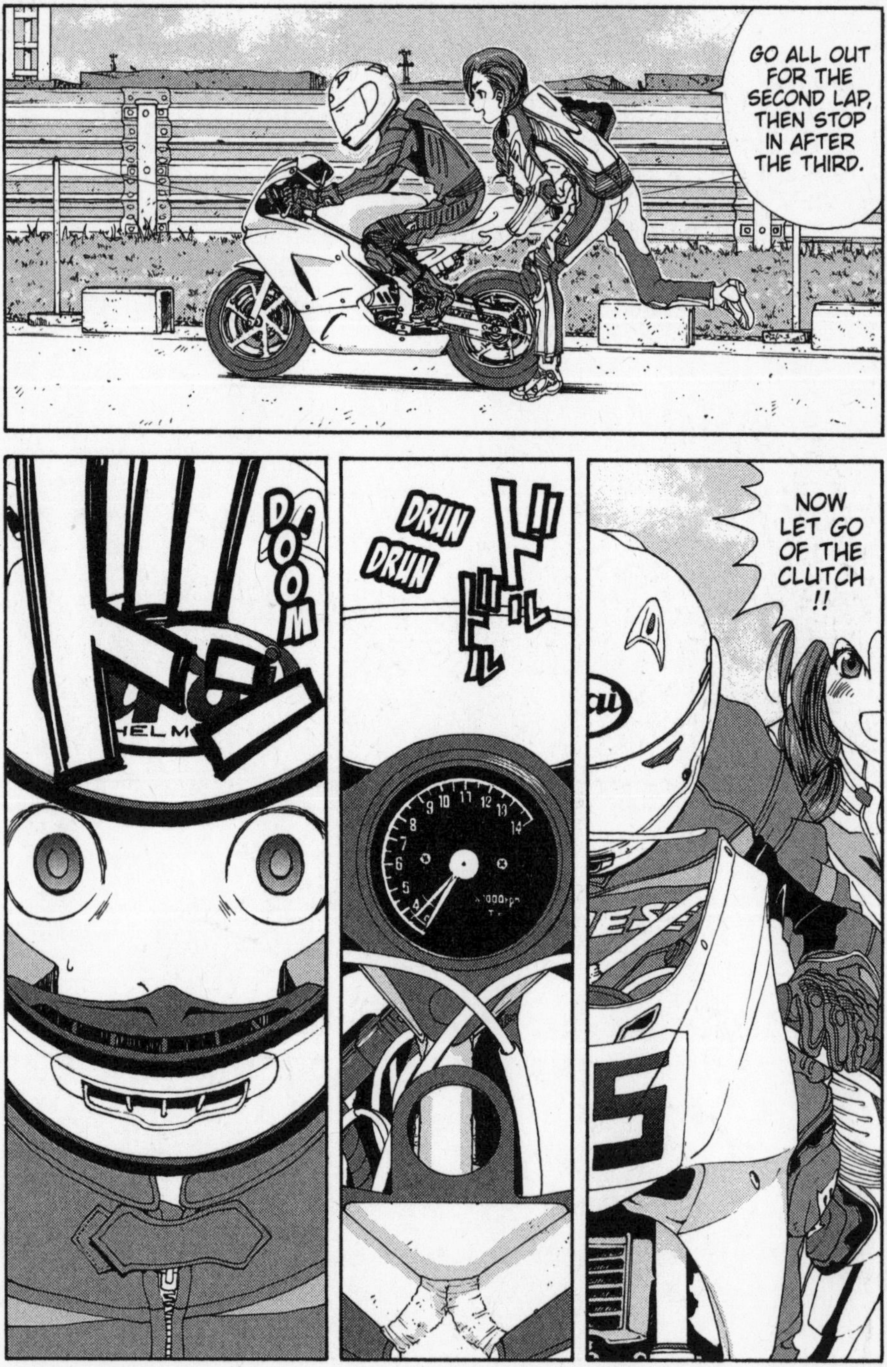
GO ALL OUT FOR THE SECOND LAP, THEN STOP IN AFTER THE THIRD.
NOW LET GO OF THE CLUTCH !!
DRUN DRUN
DOOM

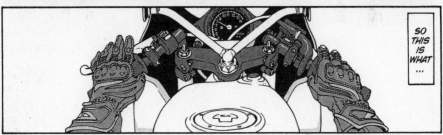

SO
THIS
IS
WHAT
...

...IT'S
LIKE.

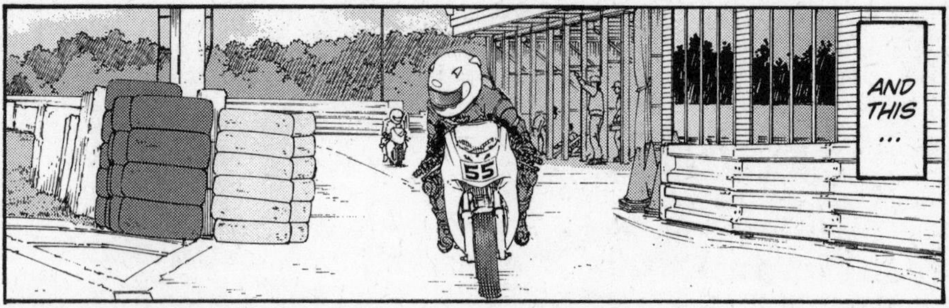
AND THIS ...
55

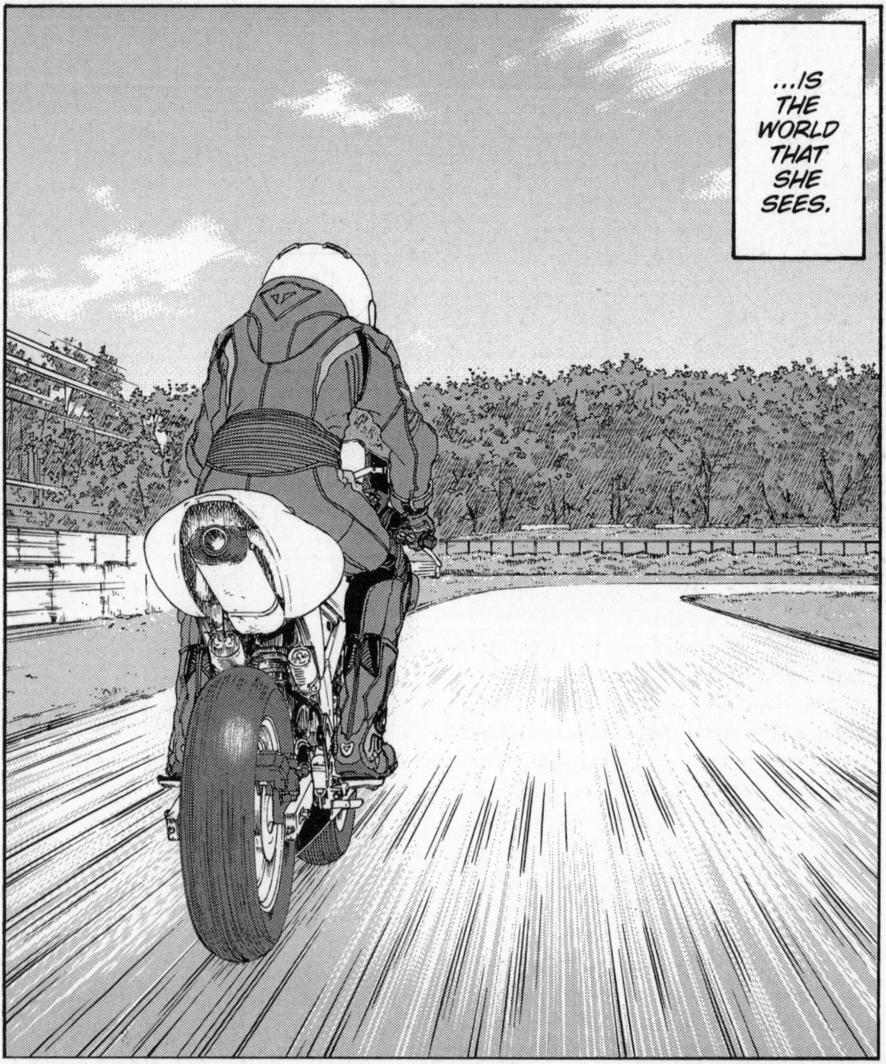
...IS THE WORLD THAT SHE SEES.

Lap 1: end

▶What is MotoGP?

MotoGP is the highest level of motorcycle road racing. Races are held at venues around the world—Spain, Italy, Malasia, and many more—with points being awarded to each rider based on their placement in the race. The total of these points decides the year's champion at the end of the racing season. The Japan round of the 2016 MotoGP season was held at the Twin Ring Motegi circuit from October 14–16.

The sport is especially popular in Europe, and the top riders are revered as heroes in their home nations. Champions like Valentino Rossi and Marc Márquez are beloved by fans worldwide.

TOPPU GP

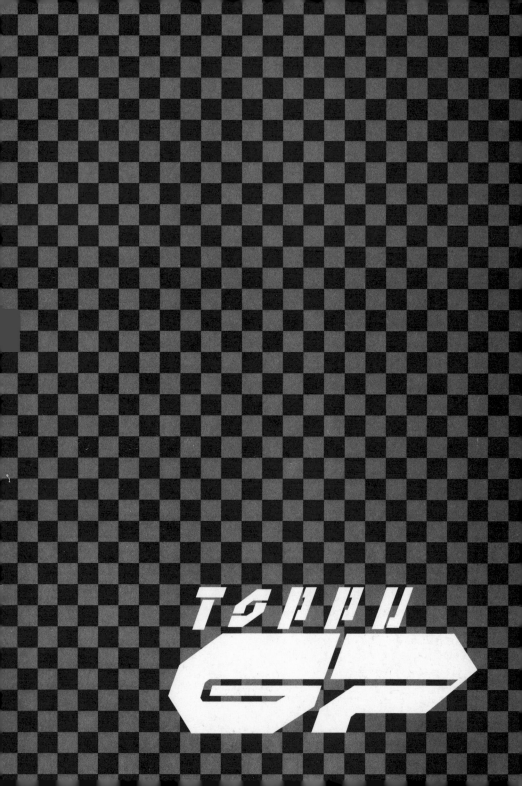

Lap 2:
FULL THROTTLE

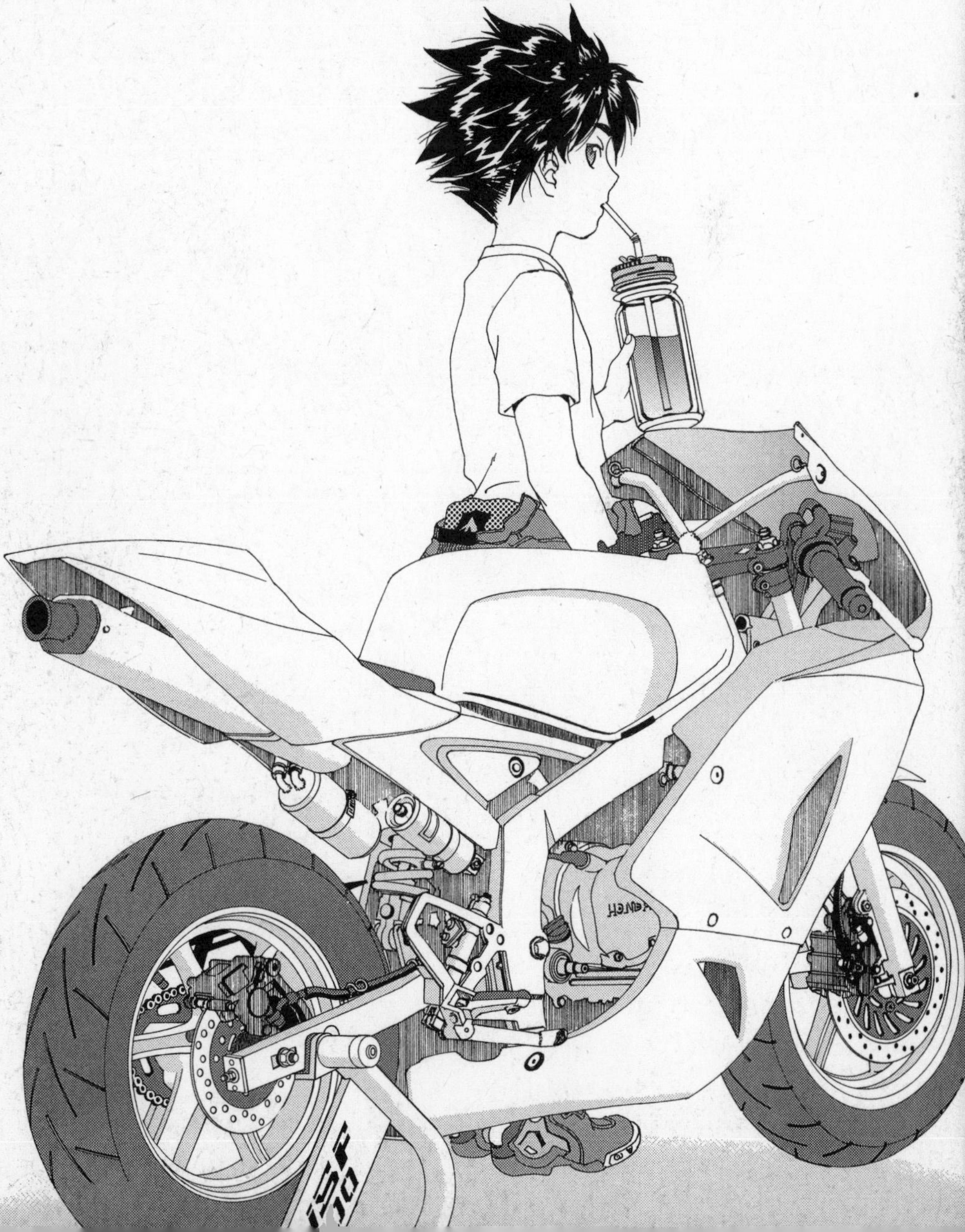

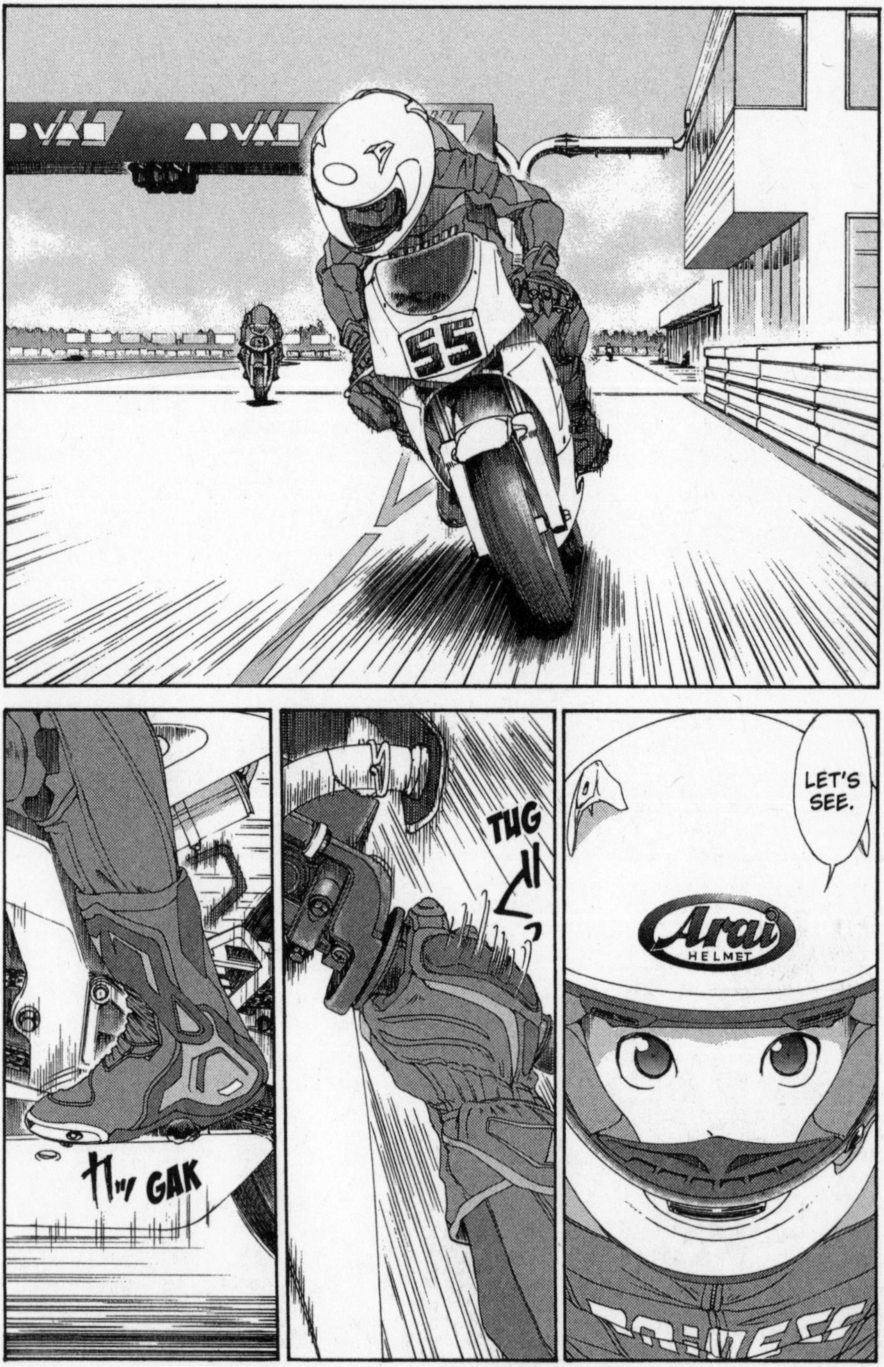
ADVAN
LET'S SEE.
Arai HELMET
TUG
GAK

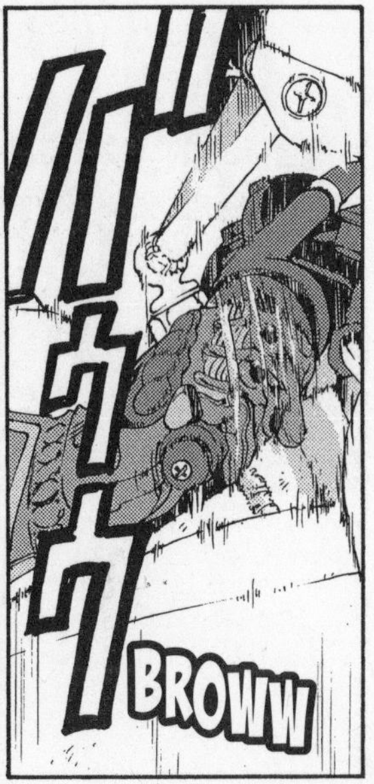
バウウウ
BROWW
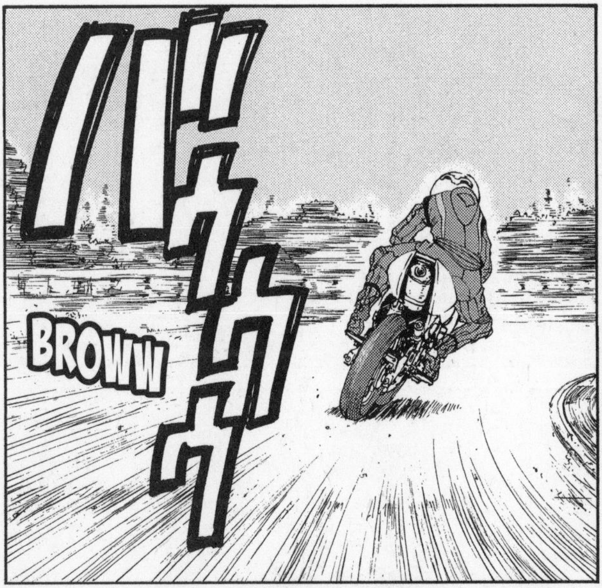
バウウウ
BROWW
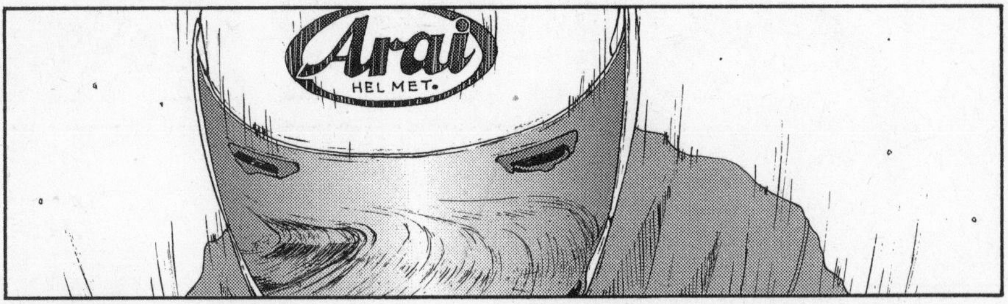
Arai
HELMET
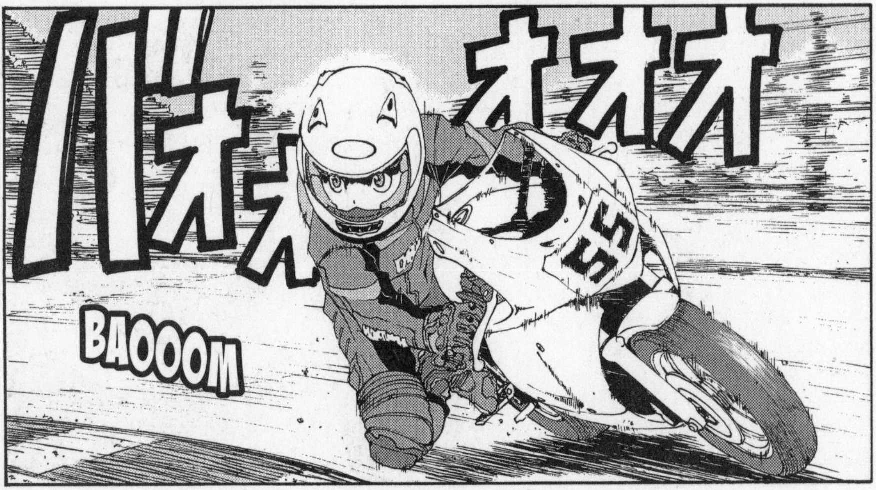
バオオオオオ
BAOOOM

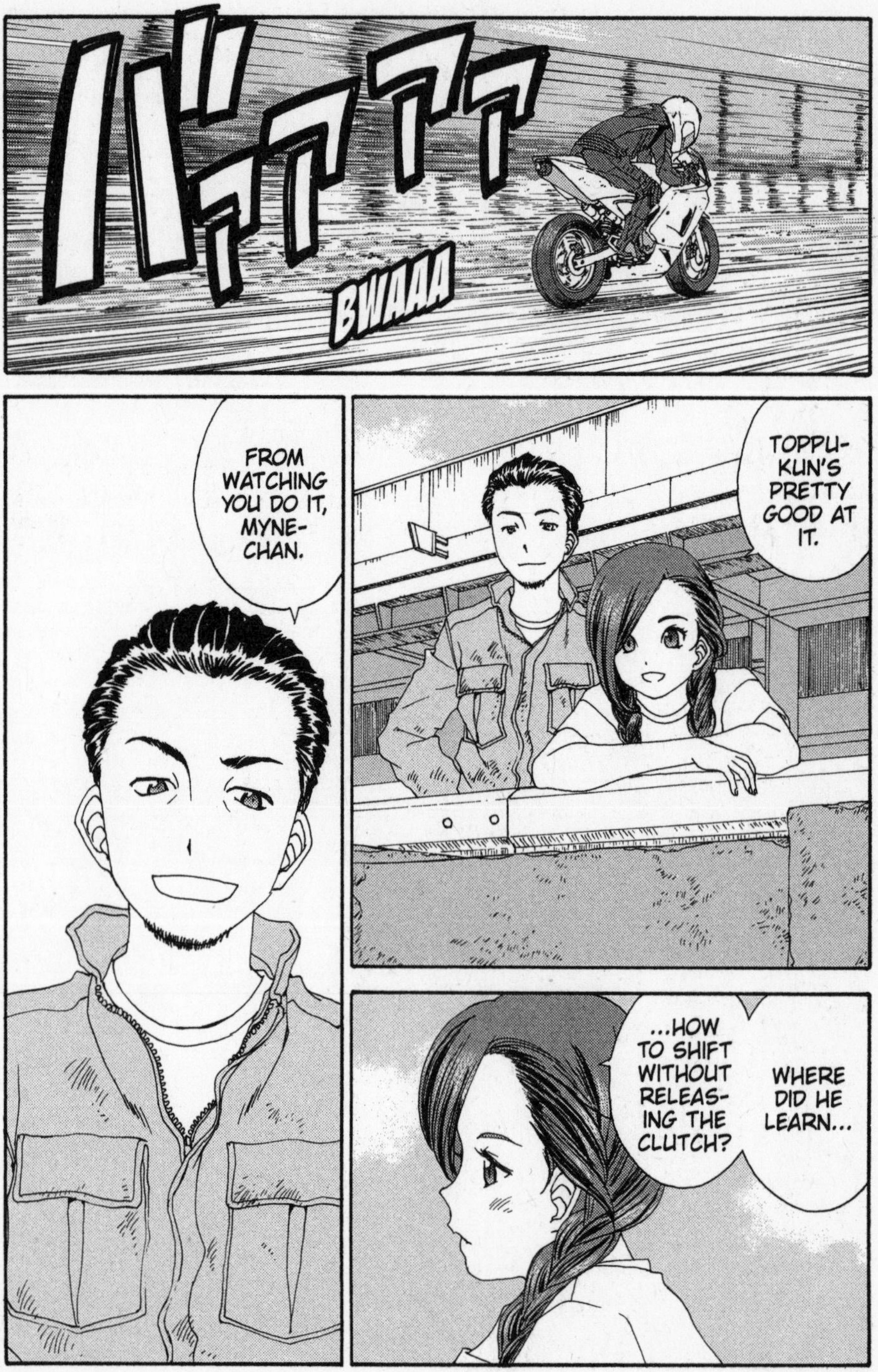
バァァァァ
BWAAA
TOPPU-KUN'S PRETTY GOOD AT IT.
WHERE DID HE LEARN...
...HOW TO SHIFT WITHOUT RELEASING THE CLUTCH?
FROM WATCHING YOU DO IT, MYNE-CHAN.

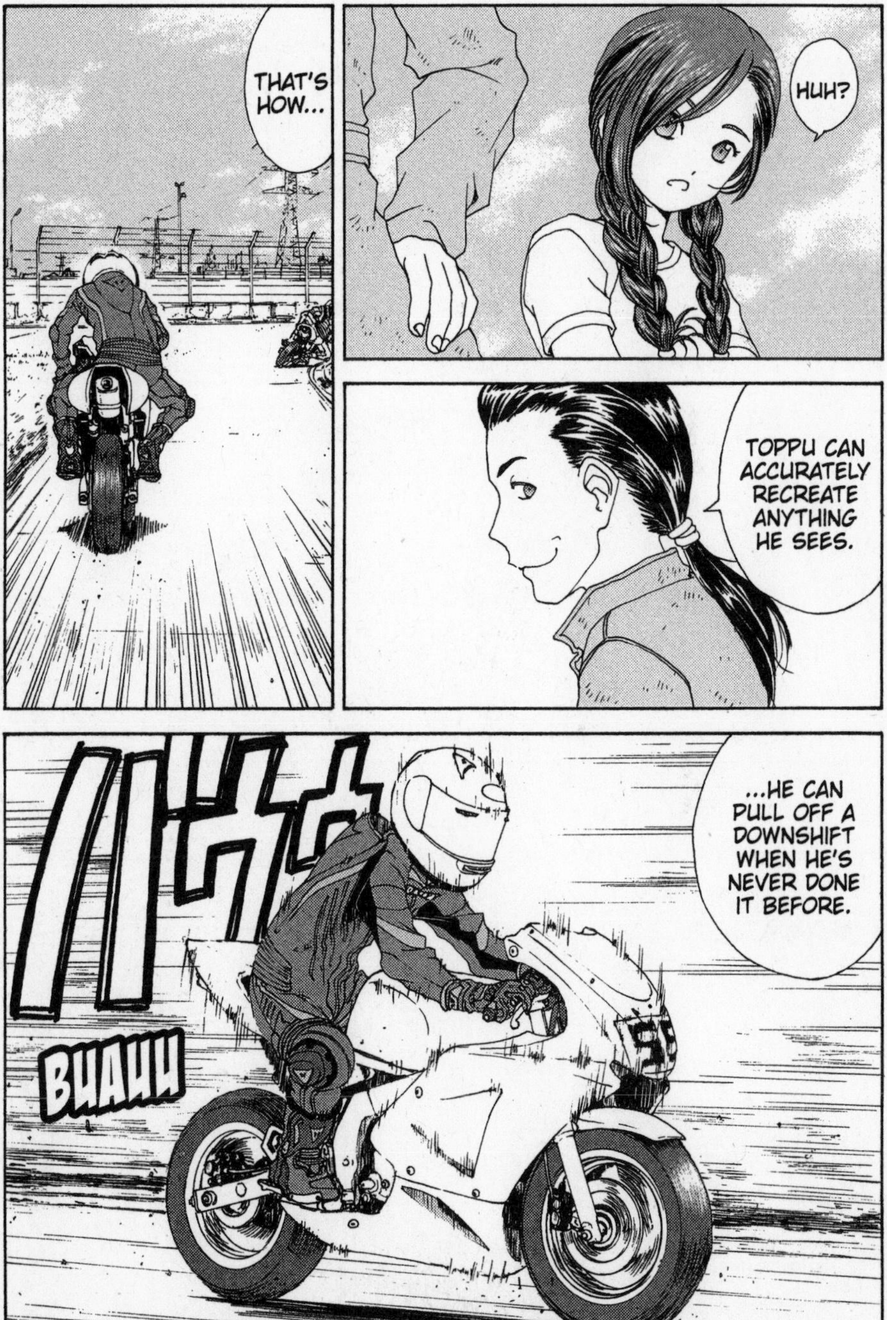
HUH?
TOPPU CAN ACCURATELY RECREATE ANYTHING HE SEES.
THAT'S HOW...
...HE CAN PULL OFF A DOWNSHIFT WHEN HE'S NEVER DONE IT BEFORE.
BUAUU

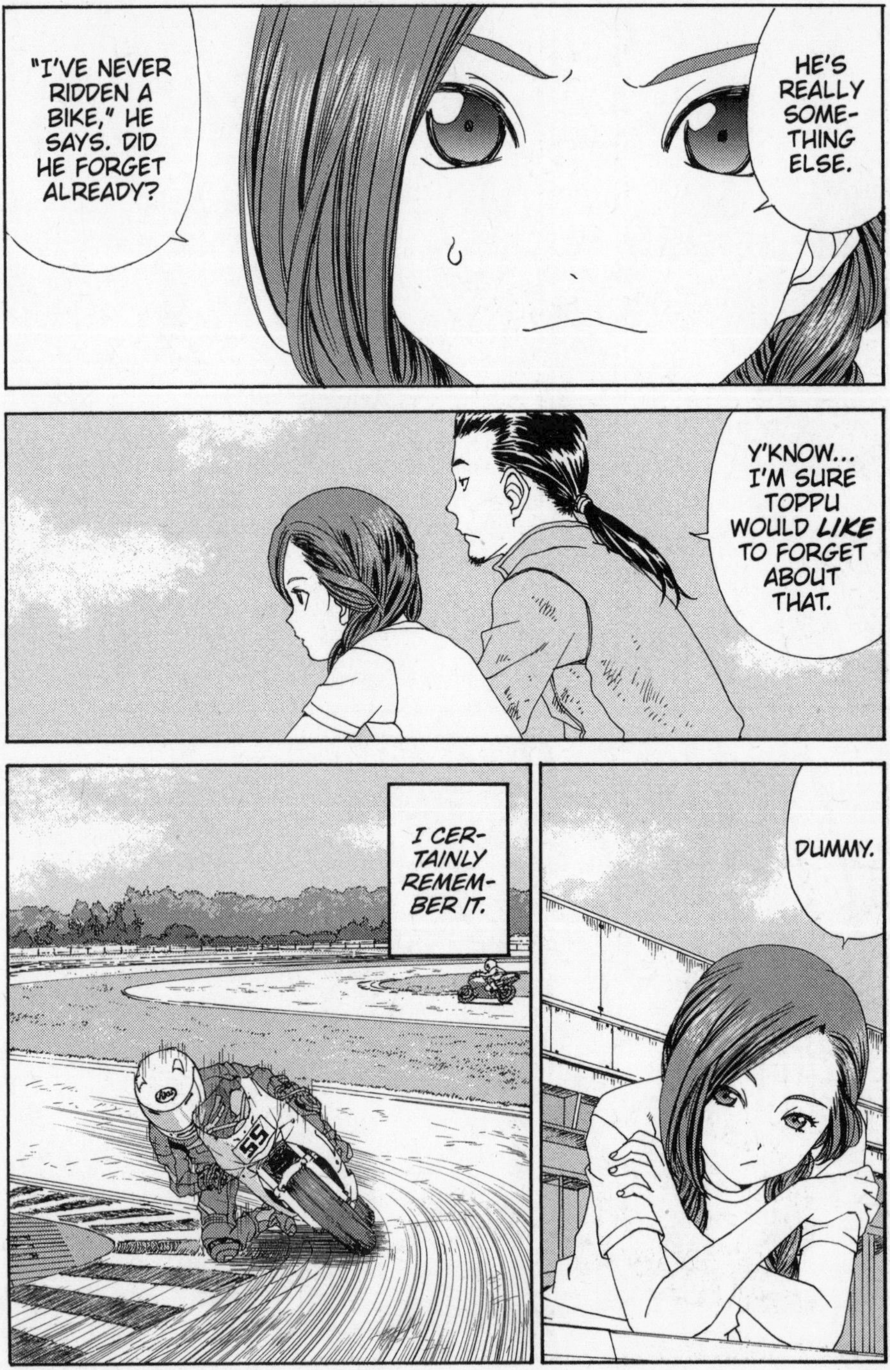
"I'VE NEVER RIDDEN A BIKE," HE SAYS. DID HE FORGET ALREADY?
HE'S REALLY SOME-THING ELSE.
Y'KNOW... I'M SURE TOPPU WOULD *LIKE* TO FORGET ABOUT THAT.
I CER-TAINLY REMEM-BER IT.
DUMMY.

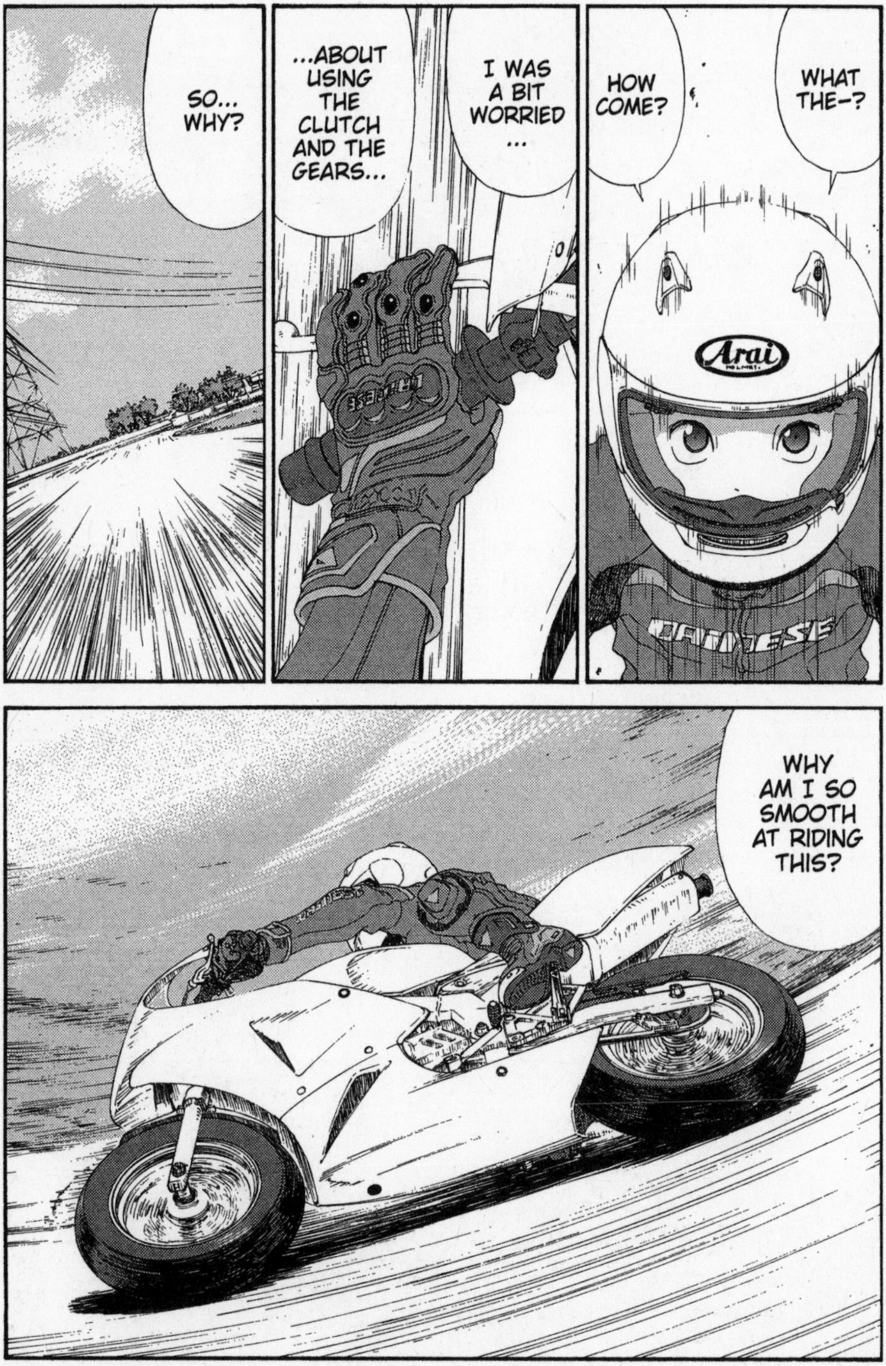
WHAT THE–?
HOW COME?
I WAS A BIT WORRIED ...
...ABOUT USING THE CLUTCH AND THE GEARS...
SO... WHY?
WHY AM I SO SMOOTH AT RIDING THIS?

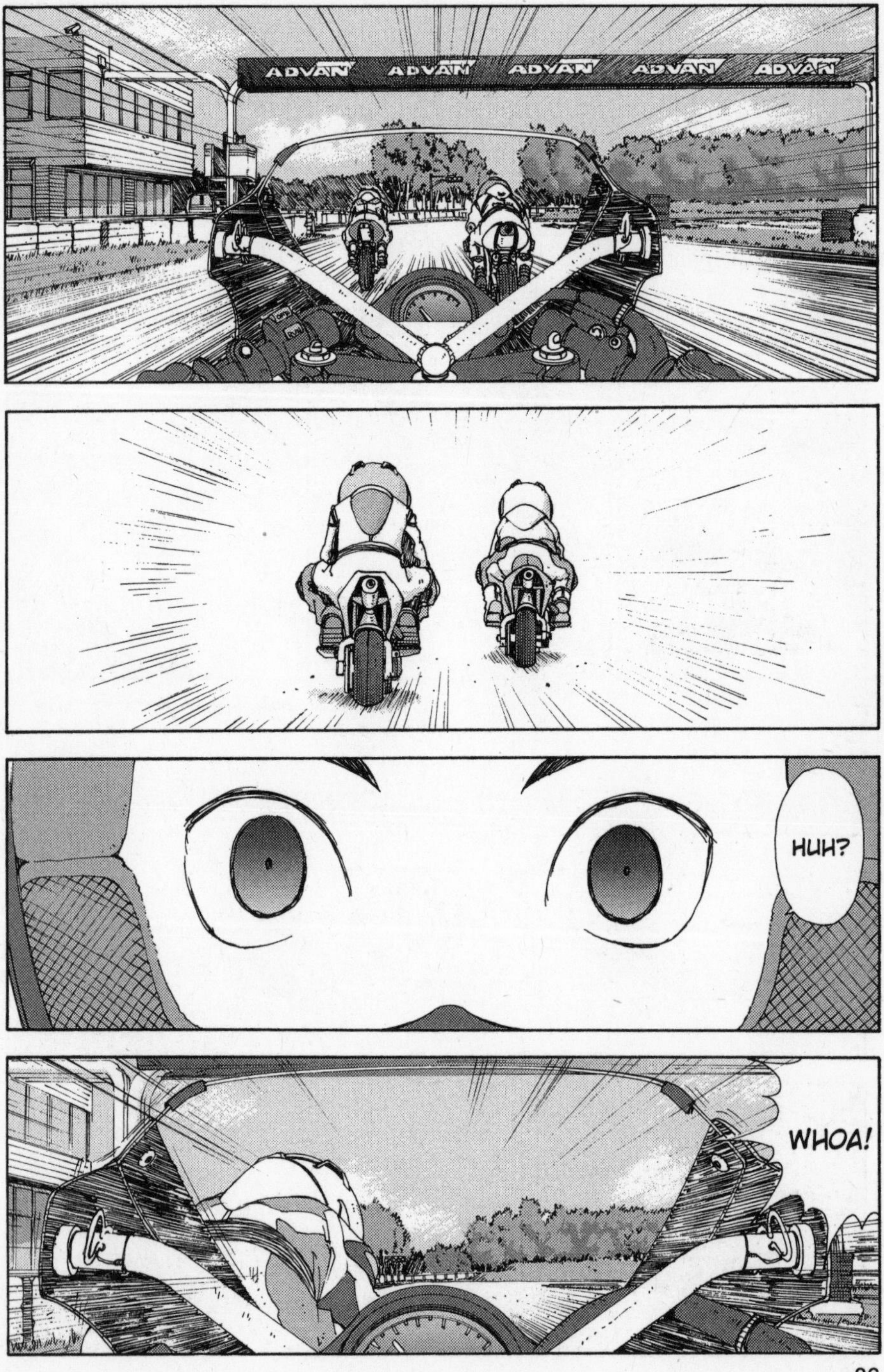
ADVAN ADVAN ADVAN ADVAN ADVAN
HUH?
WHOA!

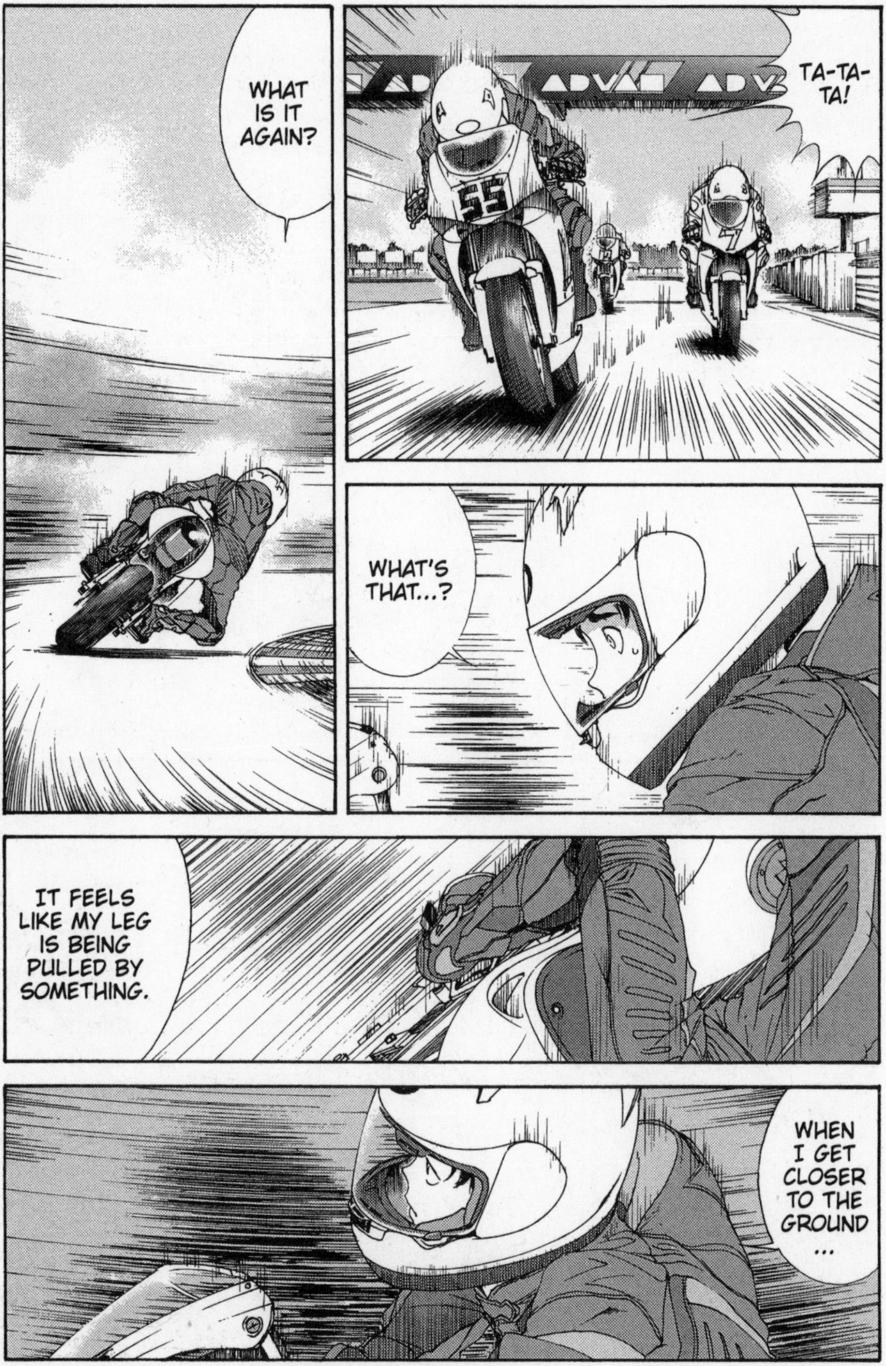
TA-TA-TA!
WHAT'S THAT...?
WHAT IS IT AGAIN?
IT FEELS LIKE MY LEG IS BEING PULLED BY SOMETHING.
WHEN I GET CLOSER TO THE GROUND ...

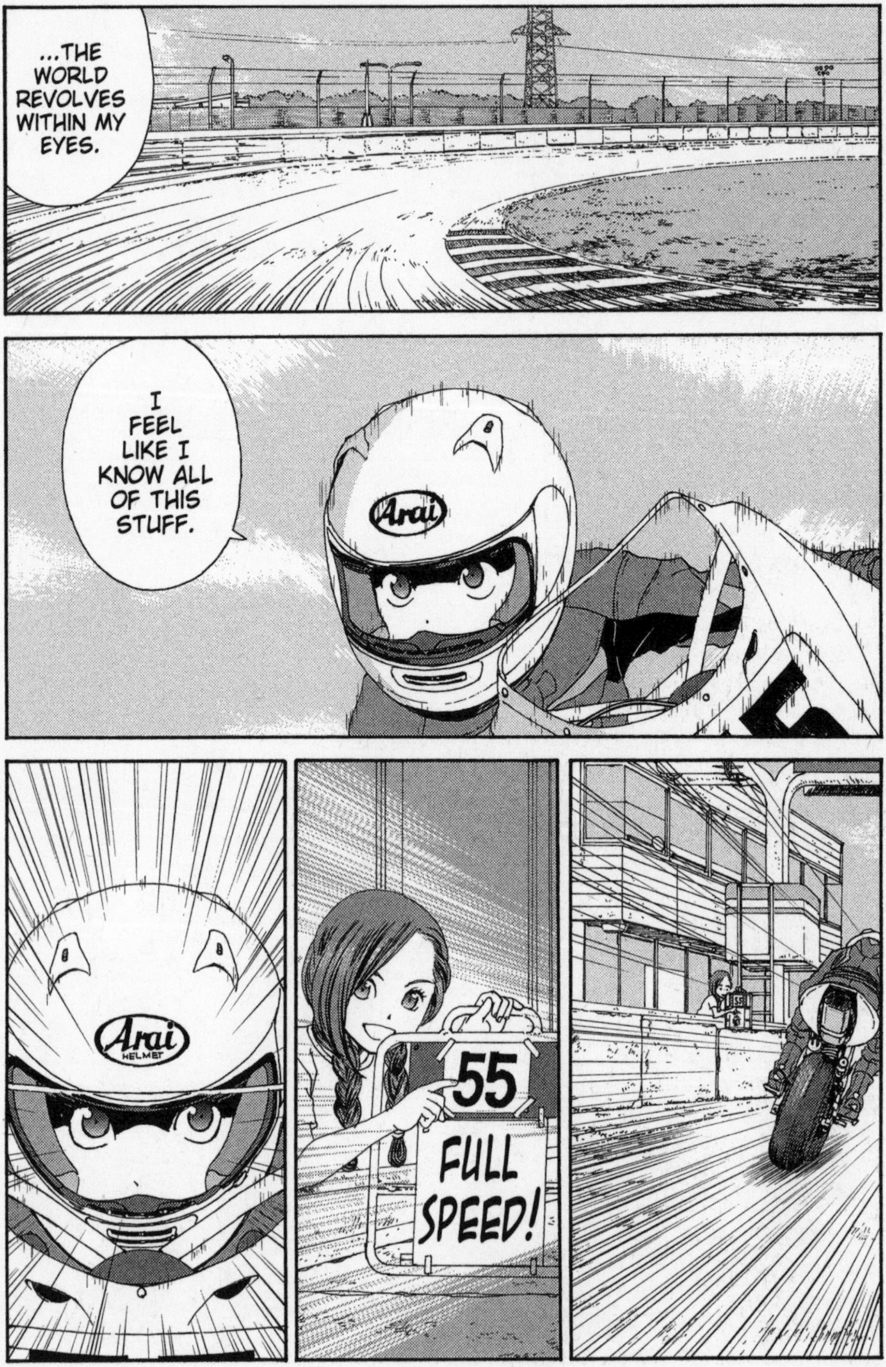
...THE WORLD REVOLVES WITHIN MY EYES.
I FEEL LIKE I KNOW ALL OF THIS STUFF.
Arai
55
FULL SPEED!
Arai HELMET

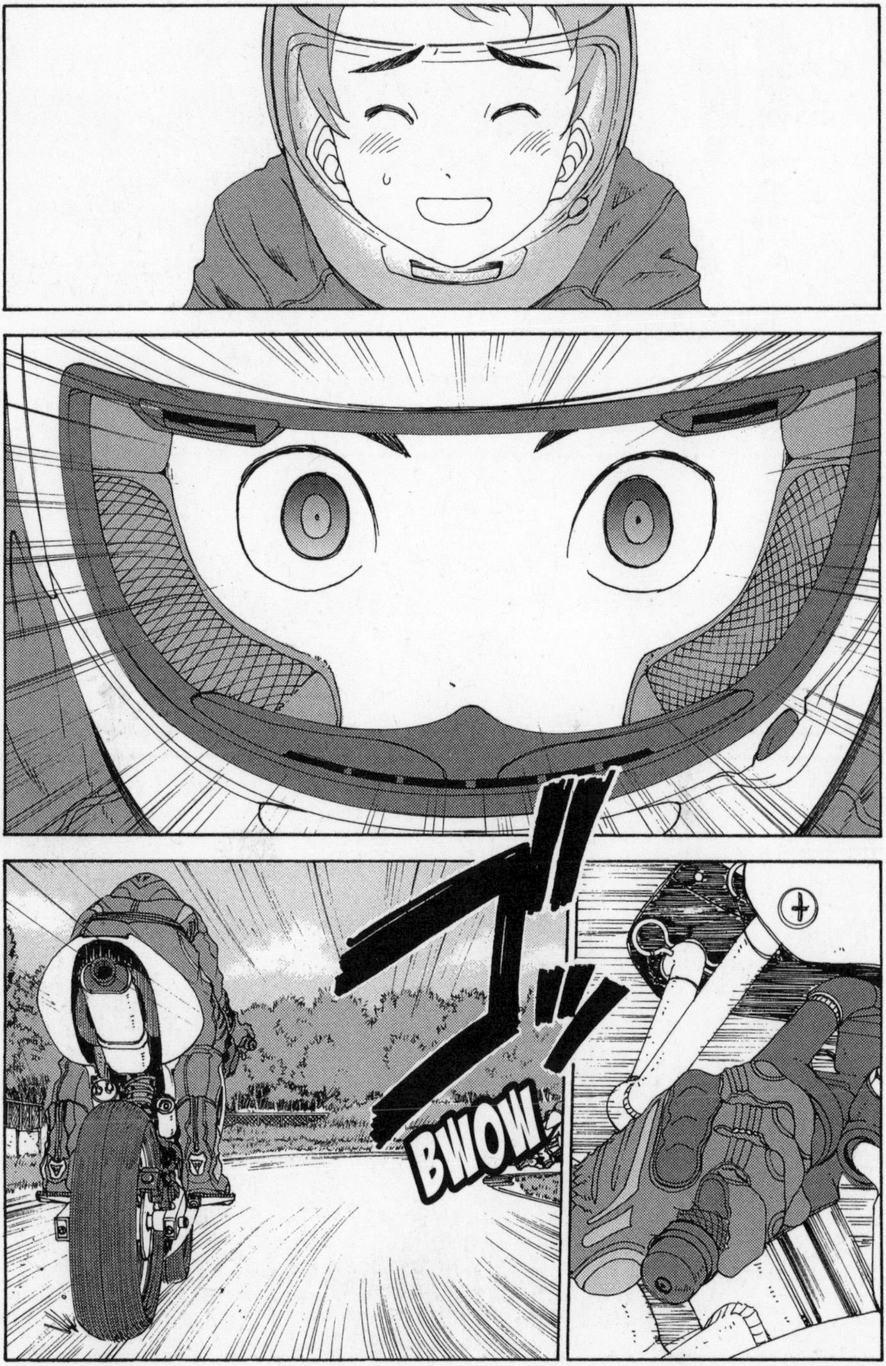
BWOW

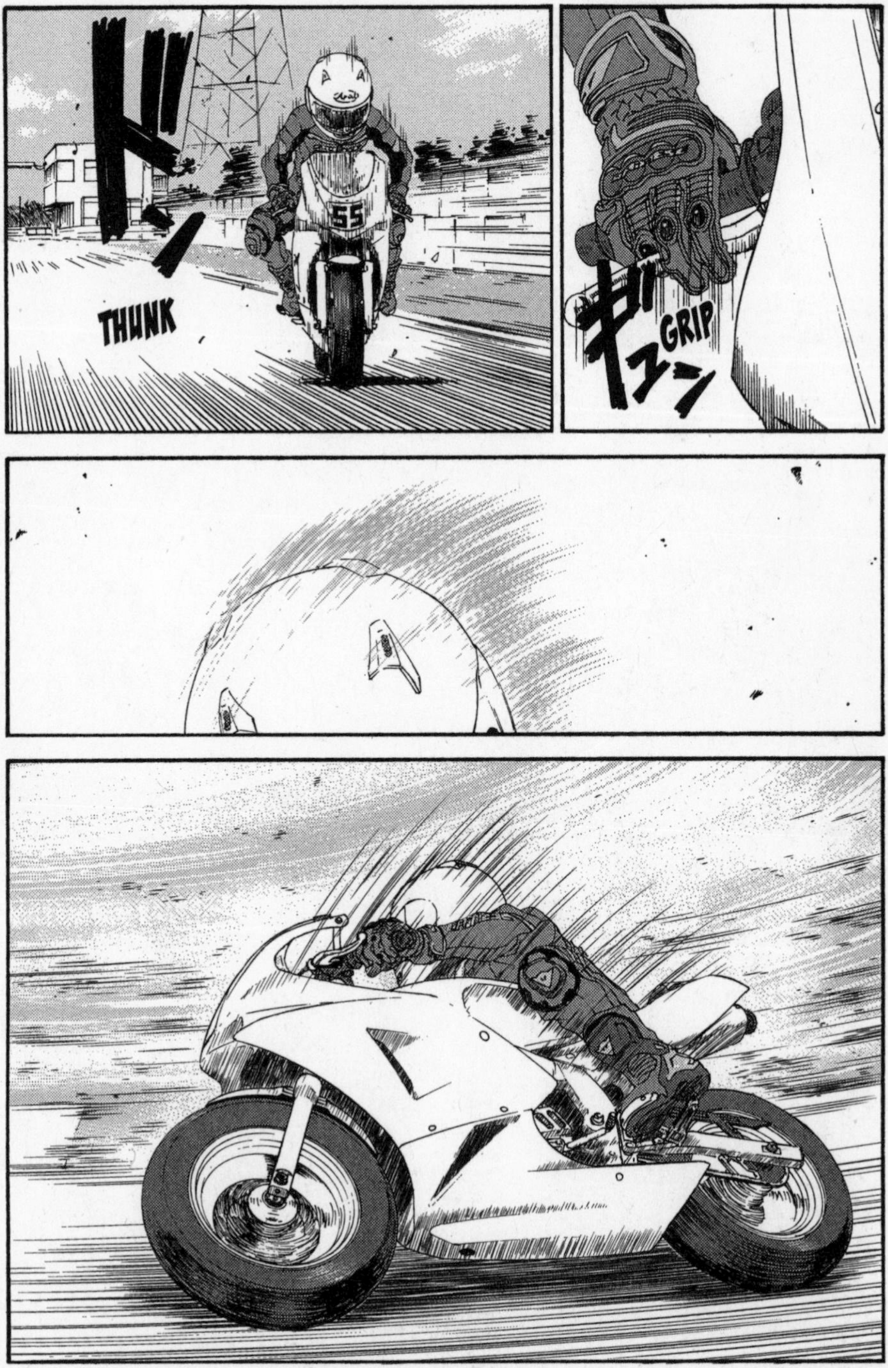
ギュン
GRIP
ドン
THUNK

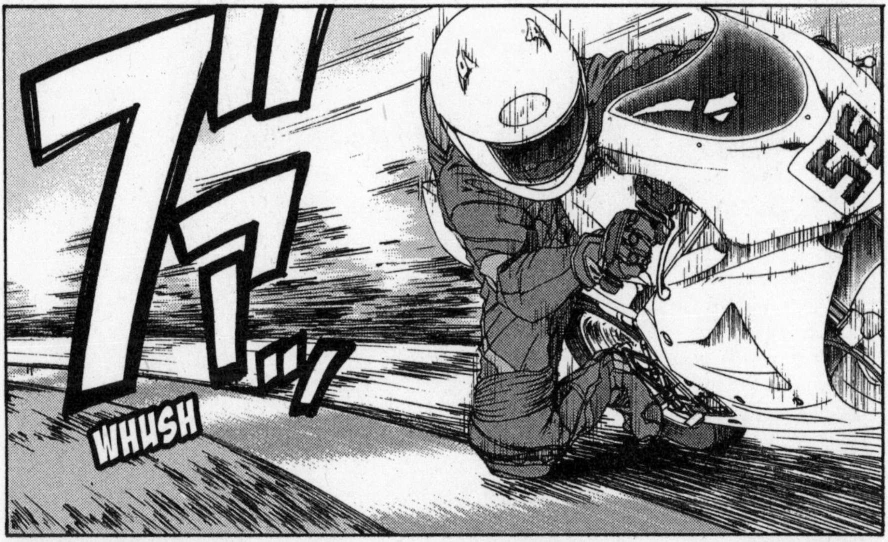
WHUSH
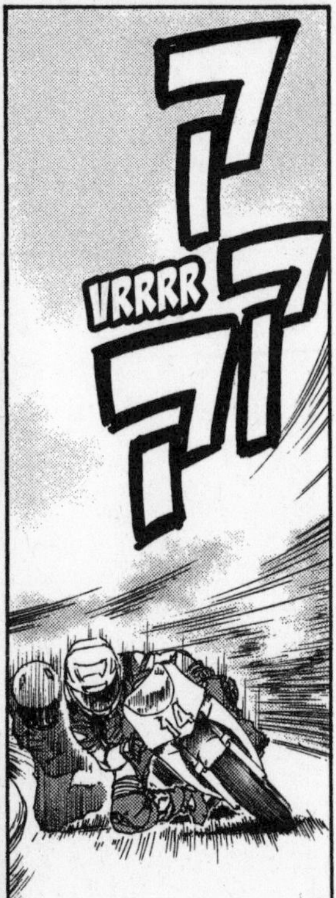
VRRRR
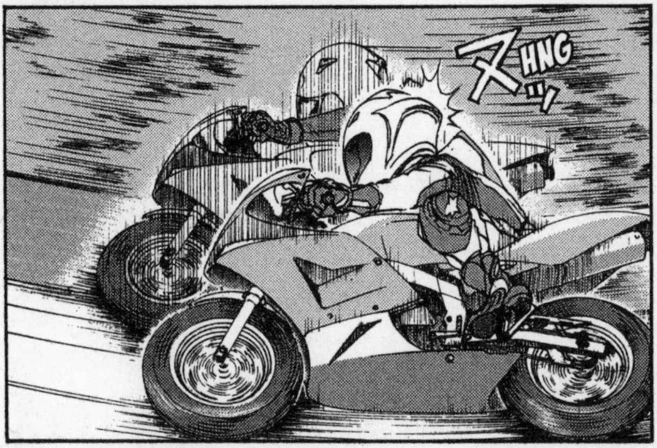
HNG
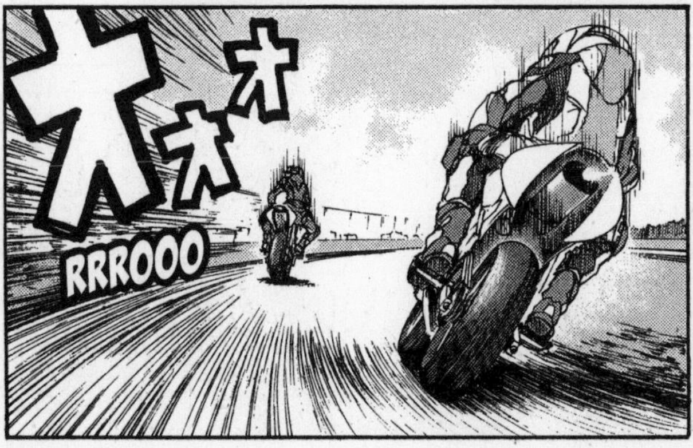
RRROOO

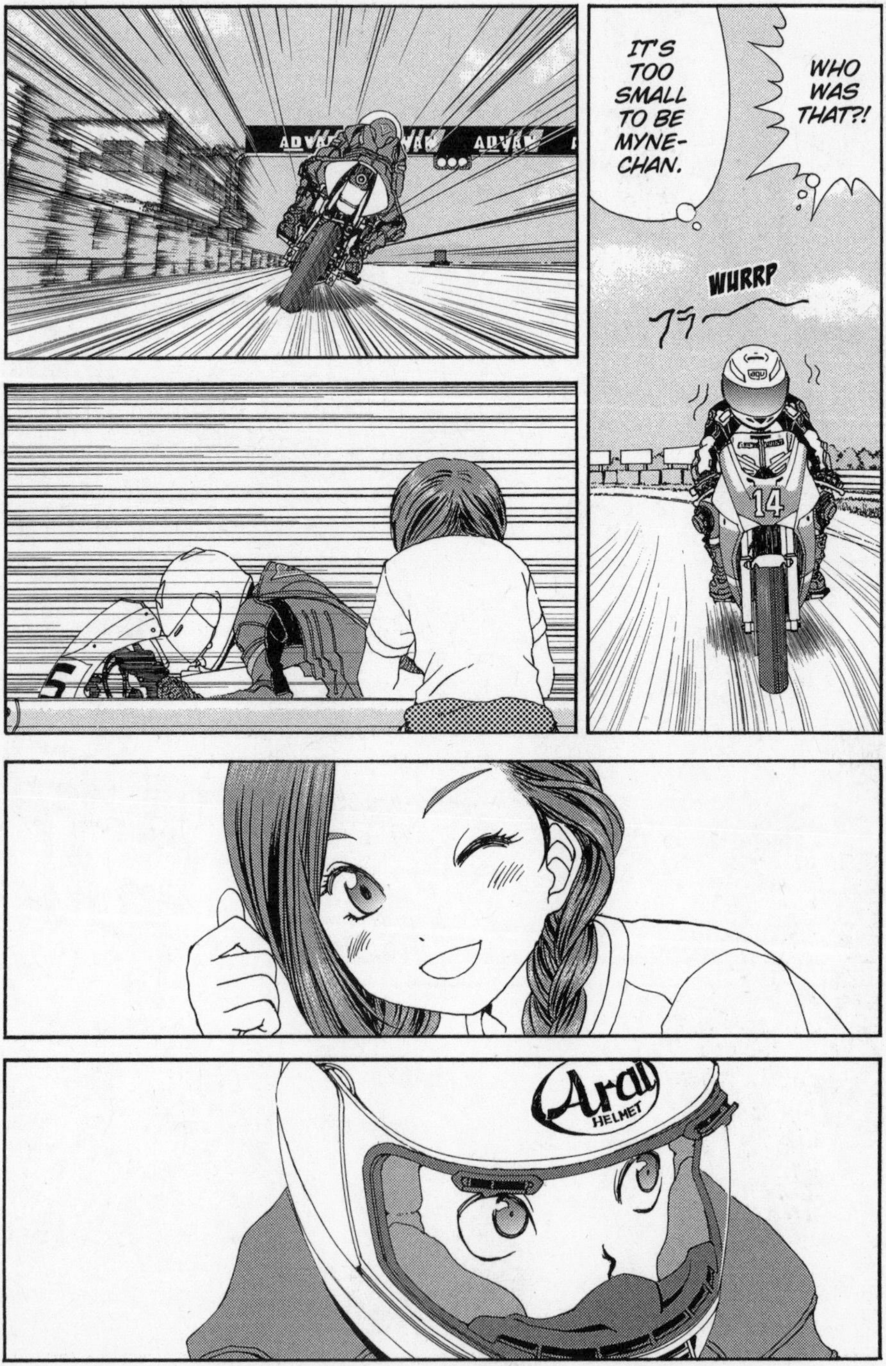
WHO WAS THAT?!
IT'S TOO SMALL TO BE MYNE-CHAN.
WURRP
14
ADVAN
Arai HELMET

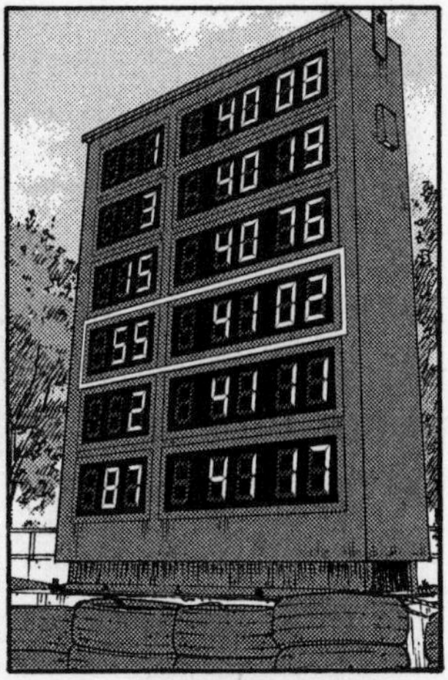
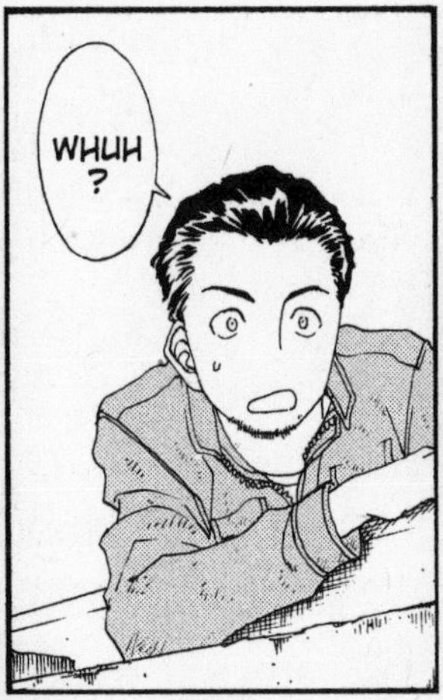
WHUH
?
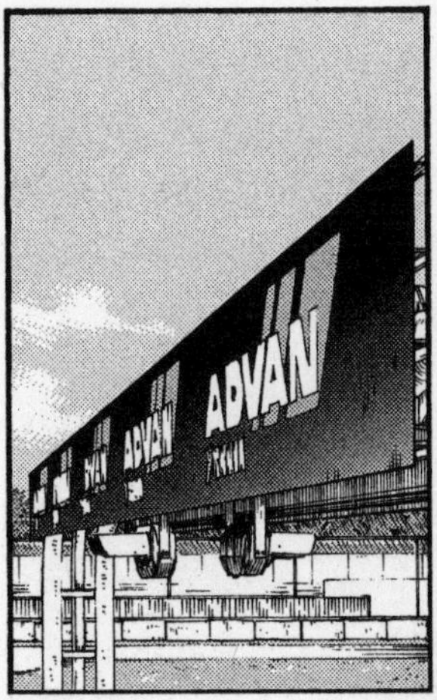
ADVAN
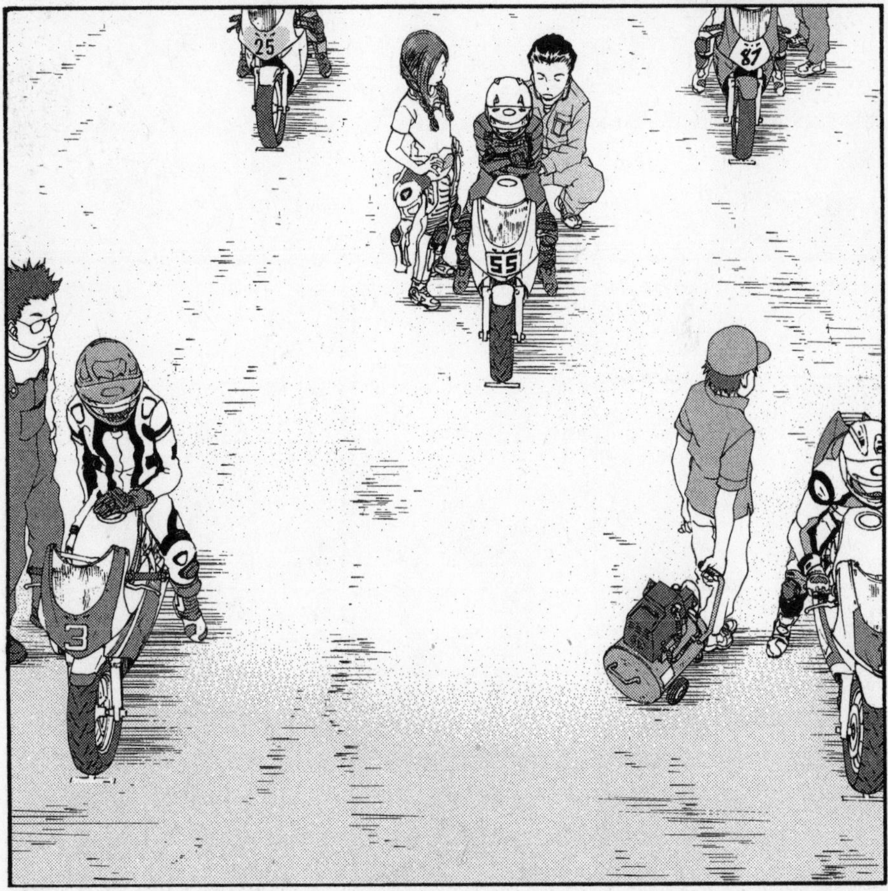

...
THIRD ON THE GRID! WELL DONE. ♡
I CAN'T REMEMBER ...
WHAT WAS IT, AGAIN?
TOPPU ...
TOPPU!

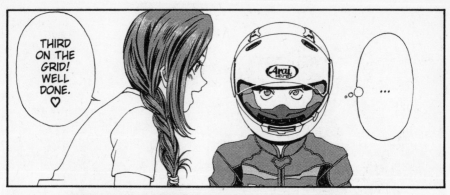

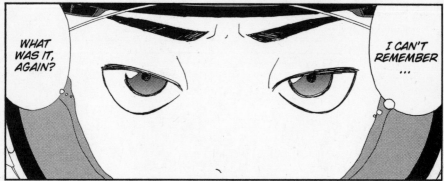

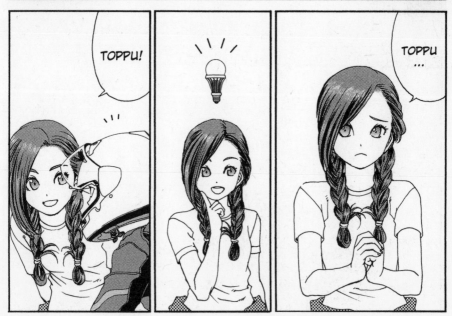

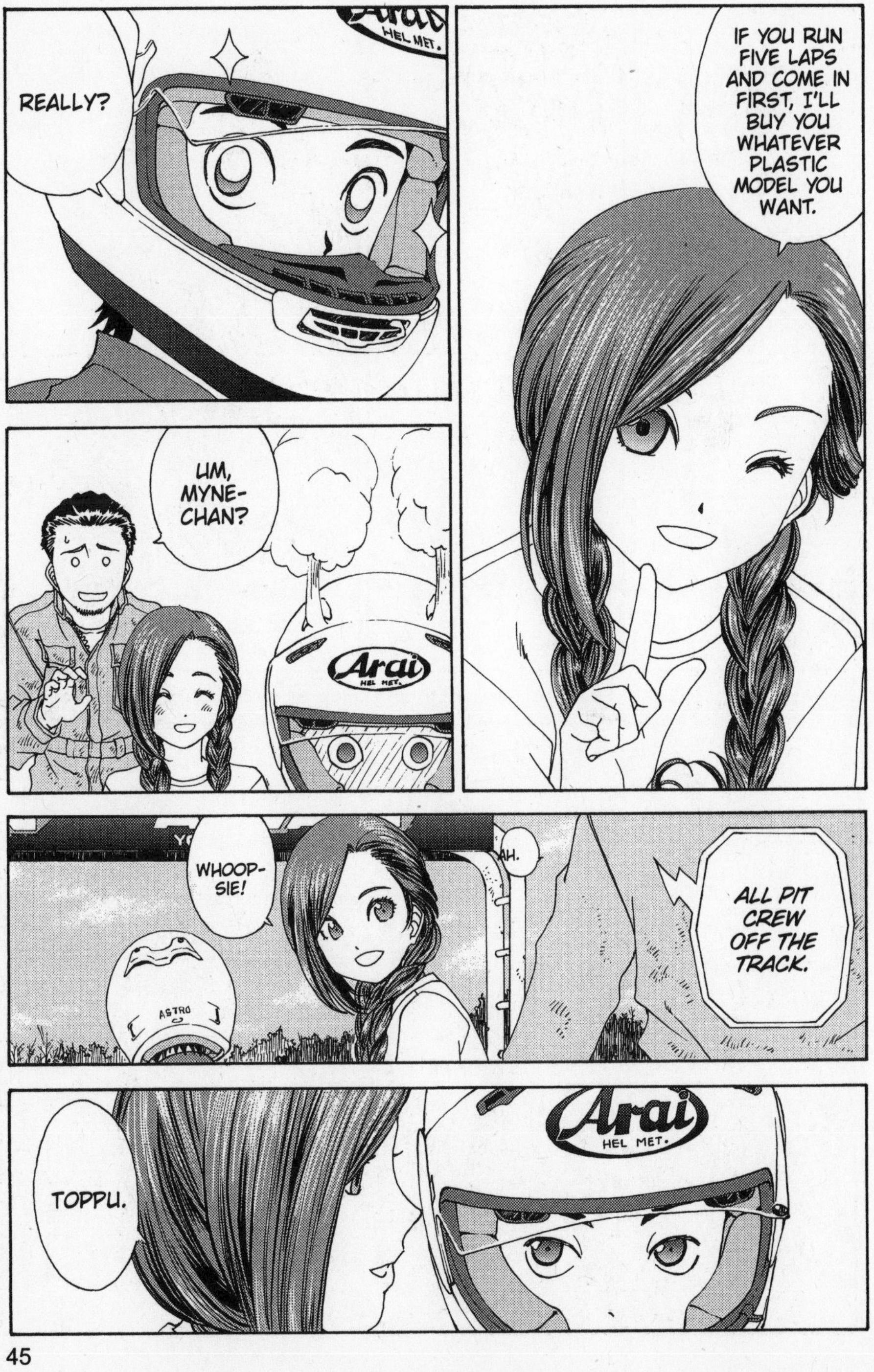
IF YOU RUN FIVE LAPS AND COME IN FIRST, I'LL BUY YOU WHATEVER PLASTIC MODEL YOU WANT.
REALLY?
UM, MYNE-CHAN?
ALL PIT CREW OFF THE TRACK.
AH.
WHOOPSIE!
TOPPU.

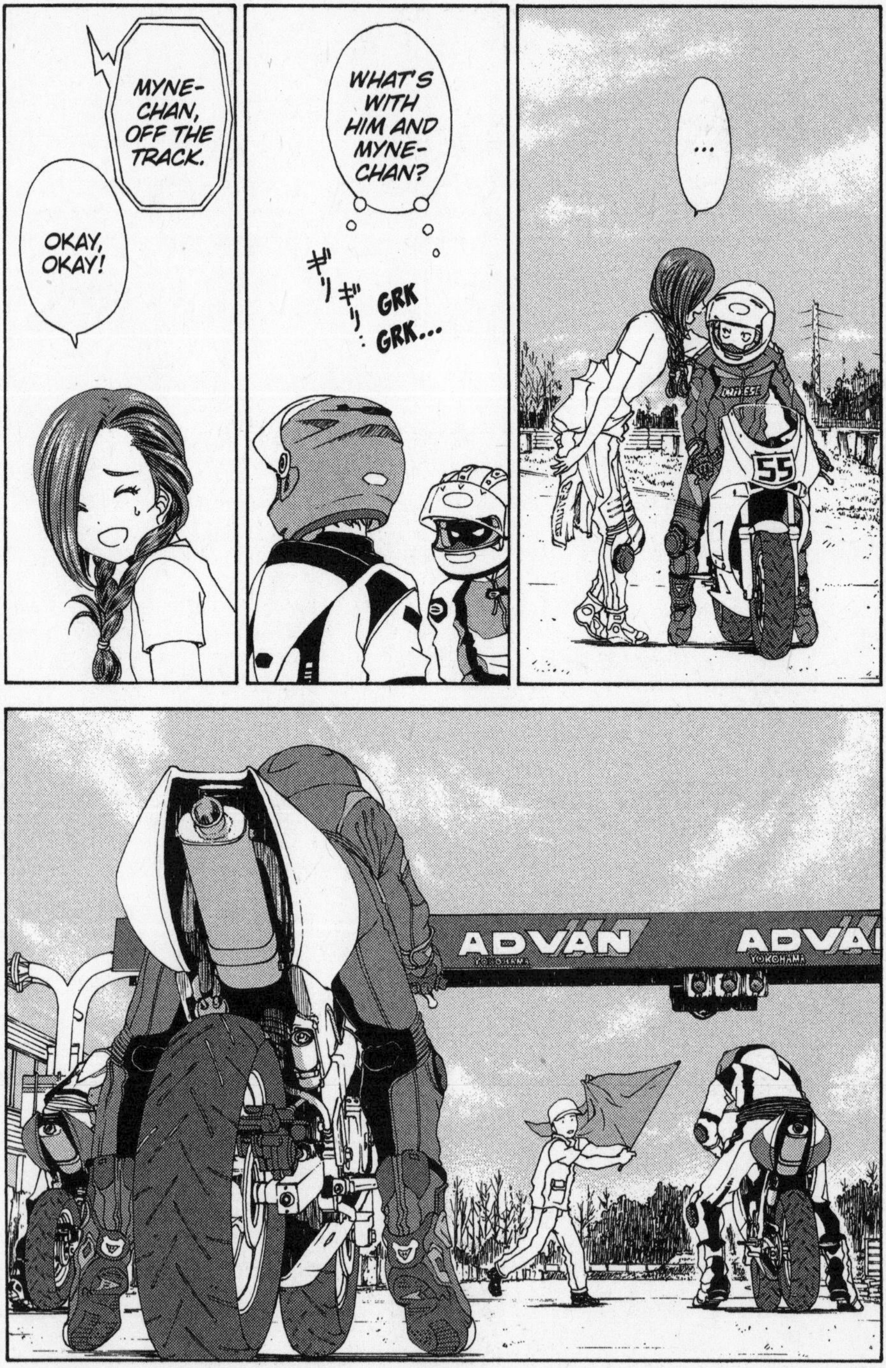
...
WHAT'S WITH HIM AND MYNE-CHAN?
ギリギリ
GRK GRK...
MYNE-CHAN, OFF THE TRACK.
OKAY, OKAY!
ADVAN
YOKOHAMA

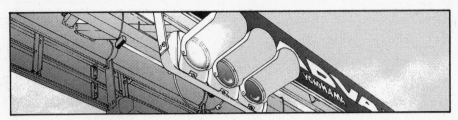

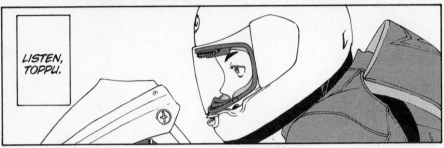

YOKOHAMA
LISTEN, TOPPU.
JUST USE YOUR GREATEST WEAPON.
BWOAA
YOU'RE VERY LIGHT...

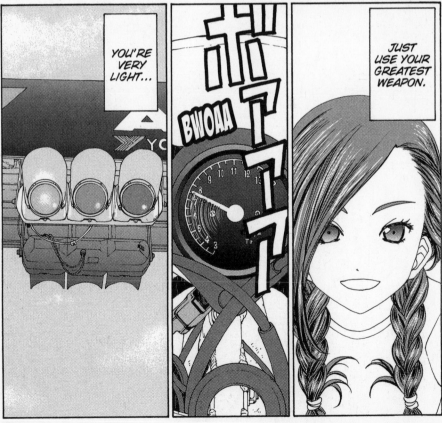

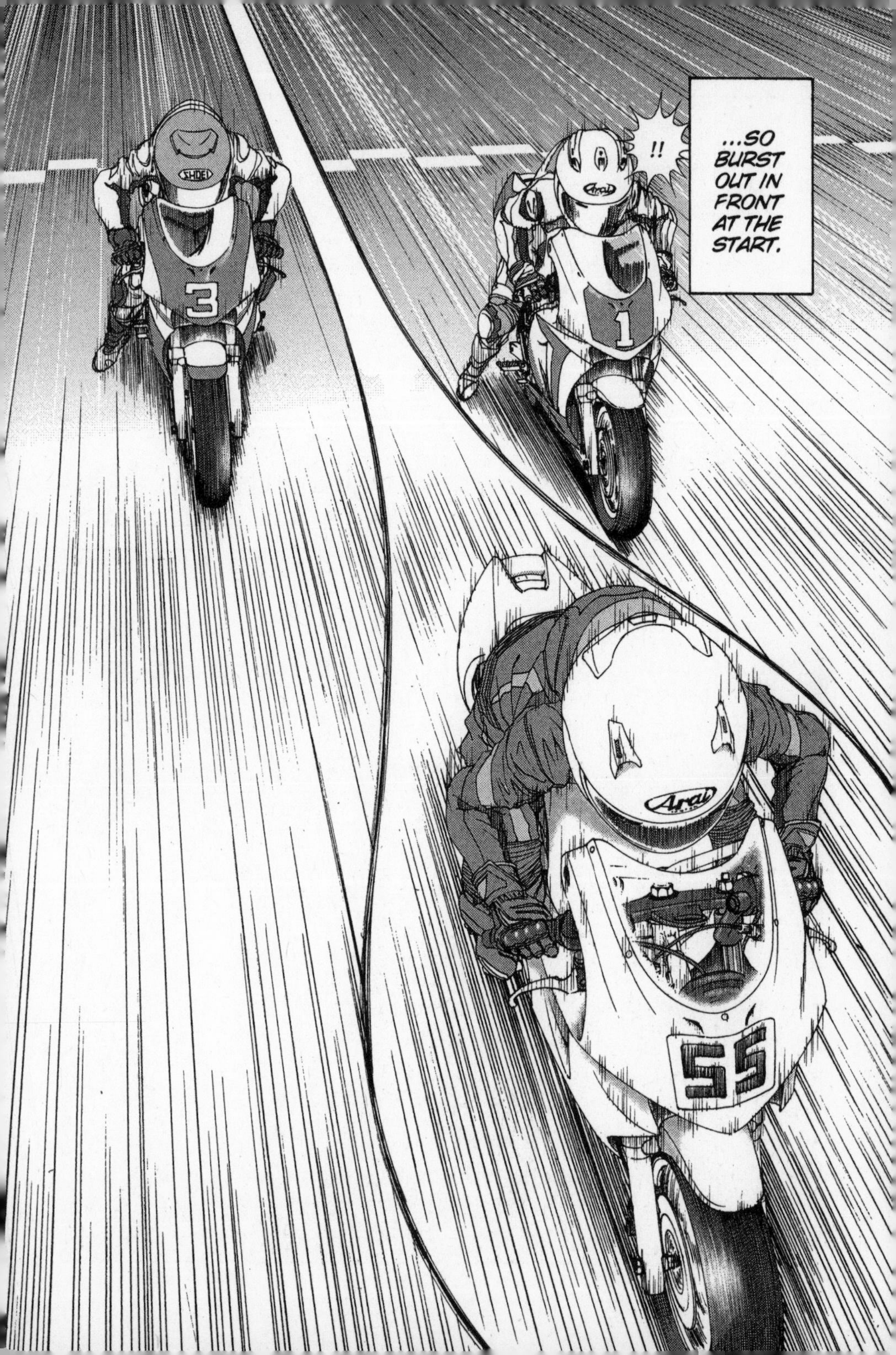
...SO BURST OUT IN FRONT AT THE START.
!!
SHOEI
Arai
3
1
Arai
55

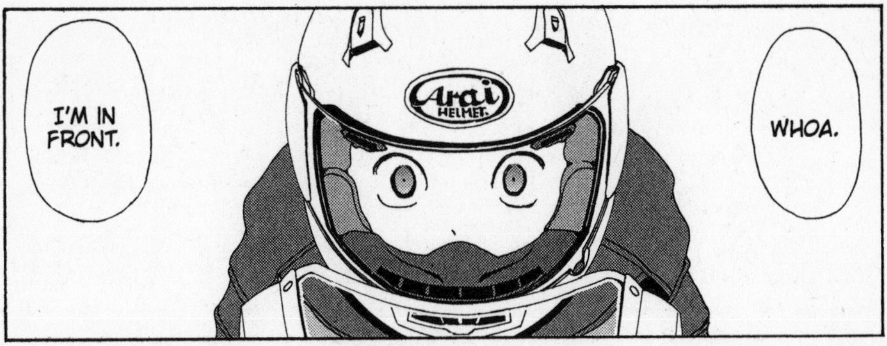
WHOA.
I'M IN FRONT.
Arai HELMET.

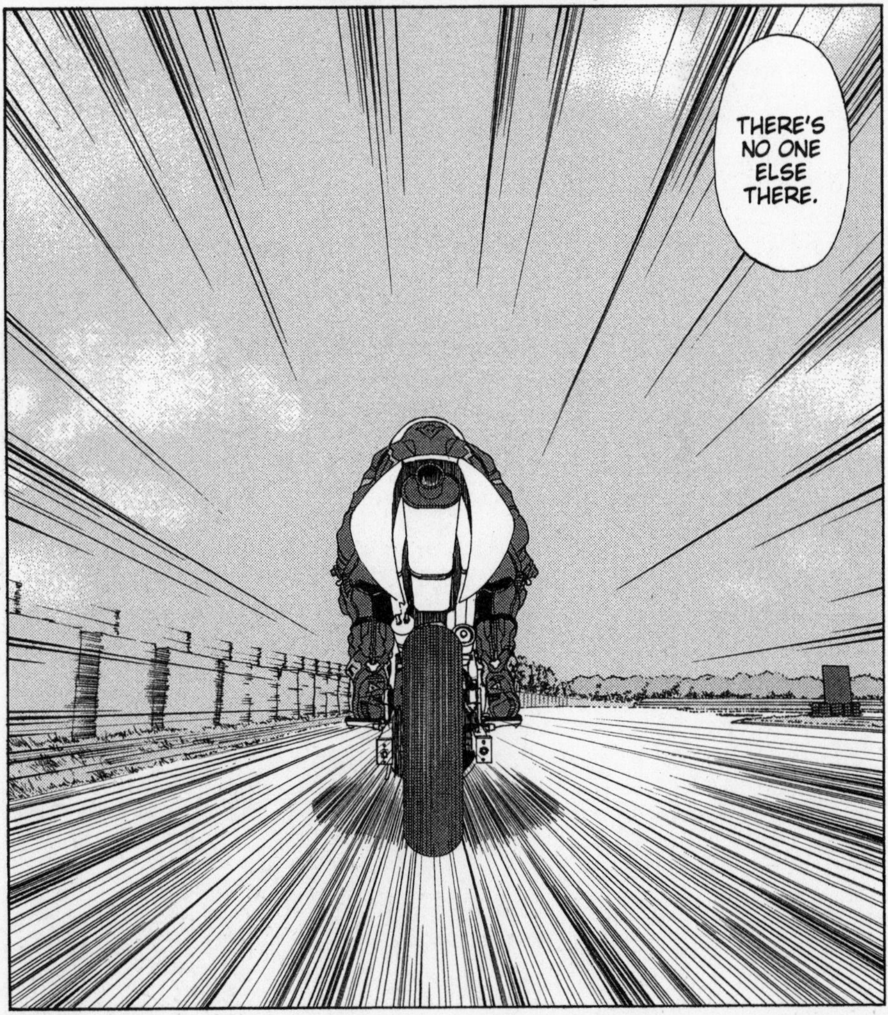
THERE'S NO ONE ELSE THERE.

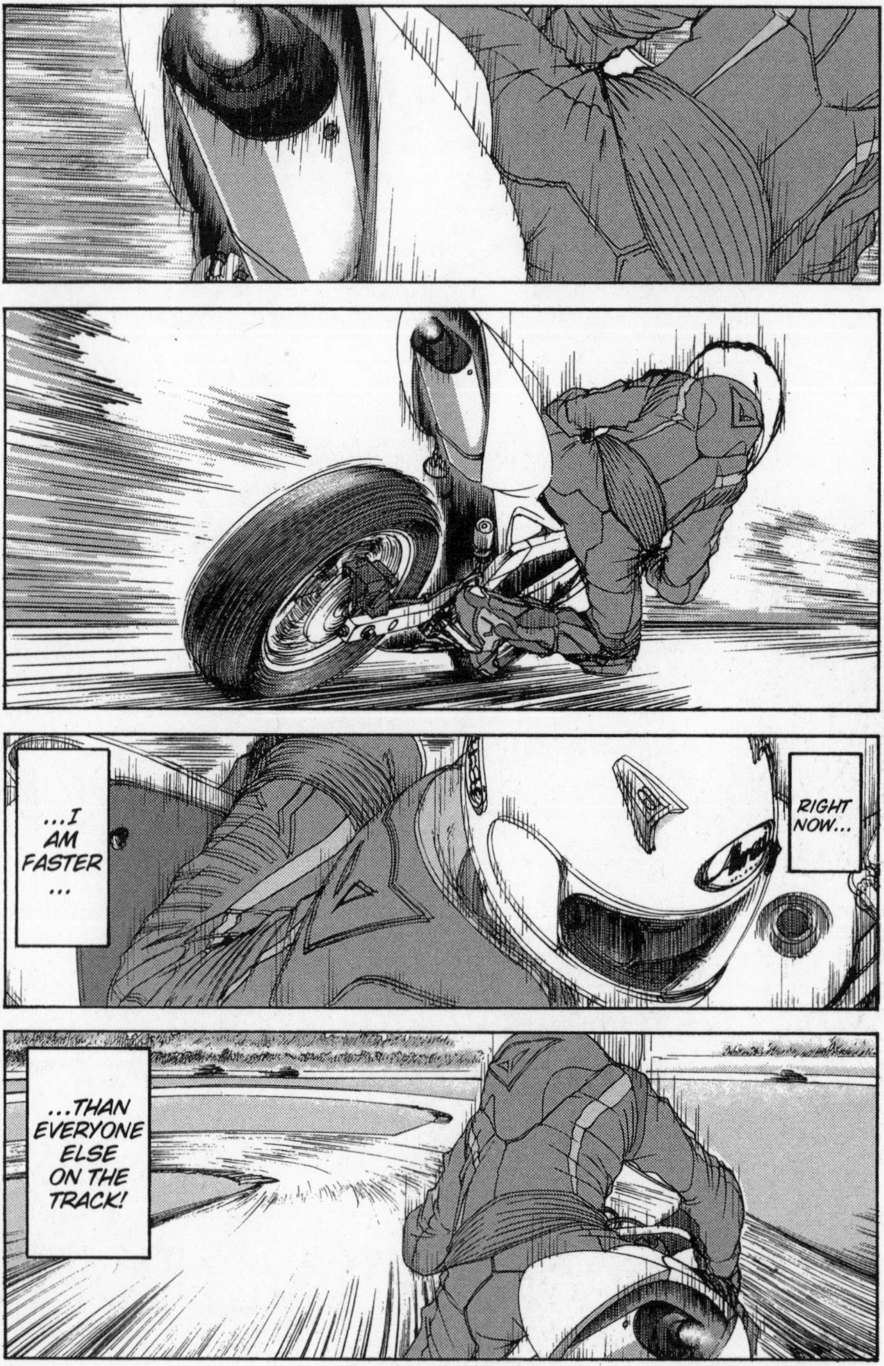
RIGHT NOW...
...I AM FASTER ...
...THAN EVERYONE ELSE ON THE TRACK!

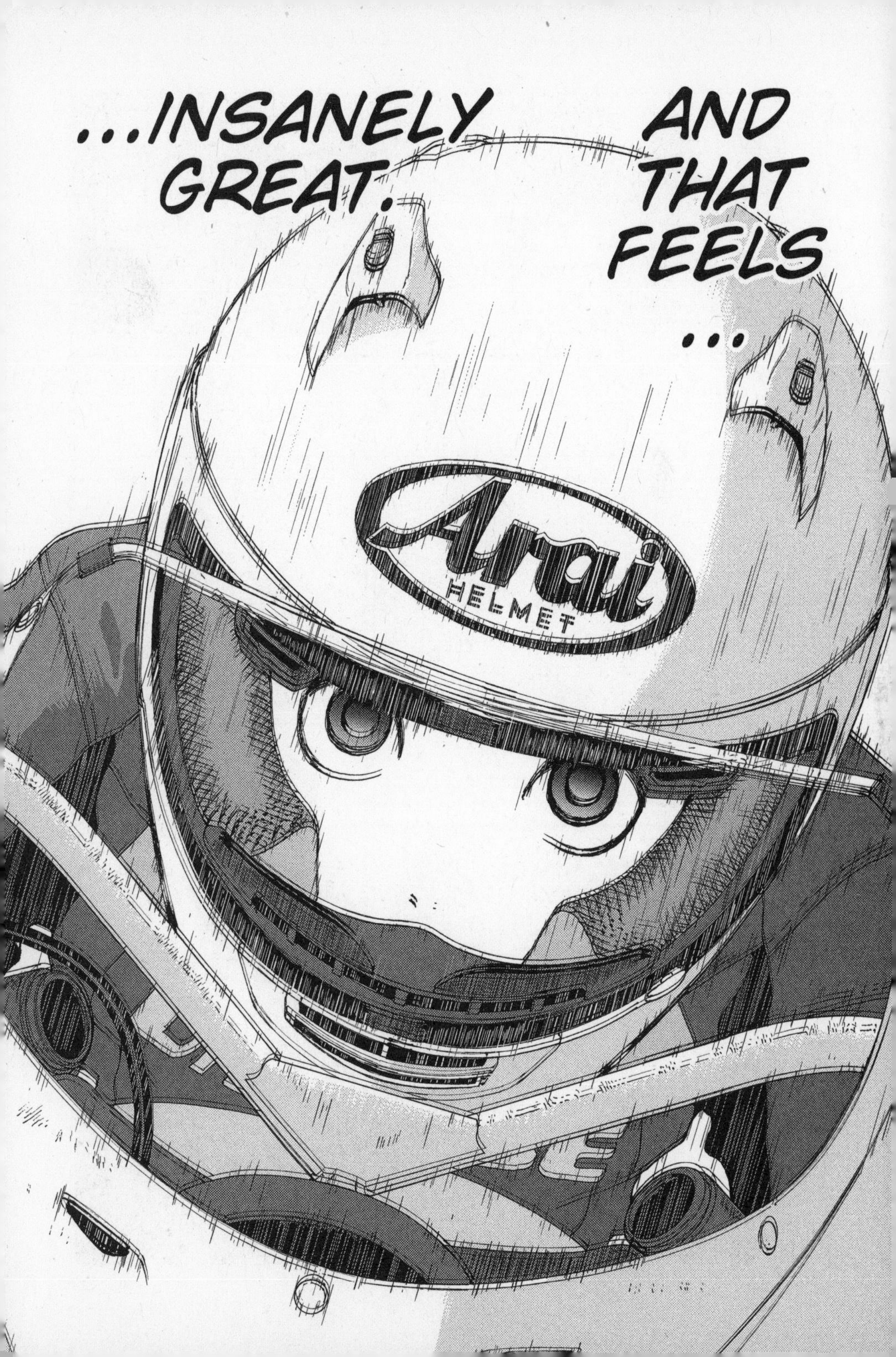
AND THAT FEELS ...
...INSANELY GREAT.
Arai
HELMET

BUT...
...WHY DO I FEEL KIND OF SAD, TOO?
55
P1
HEY, LET ME GO FIRST! HE'S PULLING AWAY!
I'M NOT GONNA LET YOU SHOW OFF IN FRONT OF MYNE-CHAN!
HA HA HA, HE'S GOT THEM FIGHTING EACH OTHER.
55

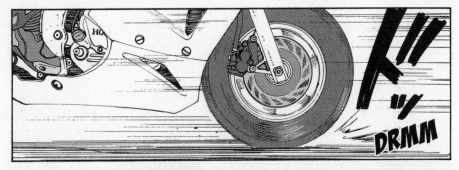

DRMM

GWAAH

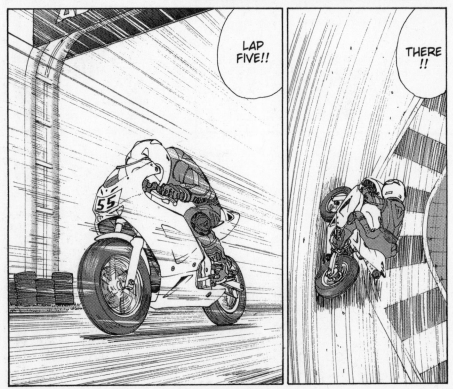

LAP FIVE!!

THERE!!

PWAAH!!
BWAAAH
HUH?
OH... WHOOPS.

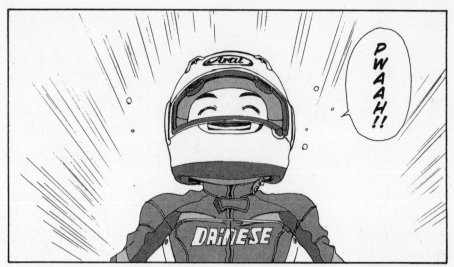

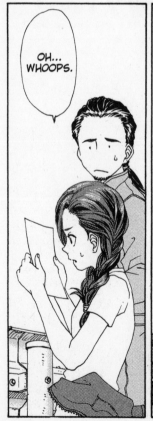

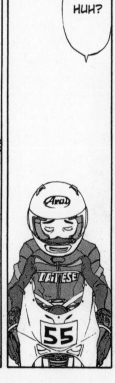

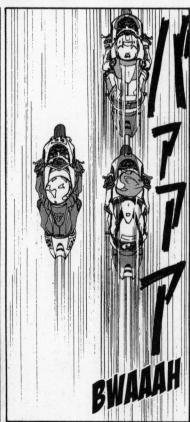

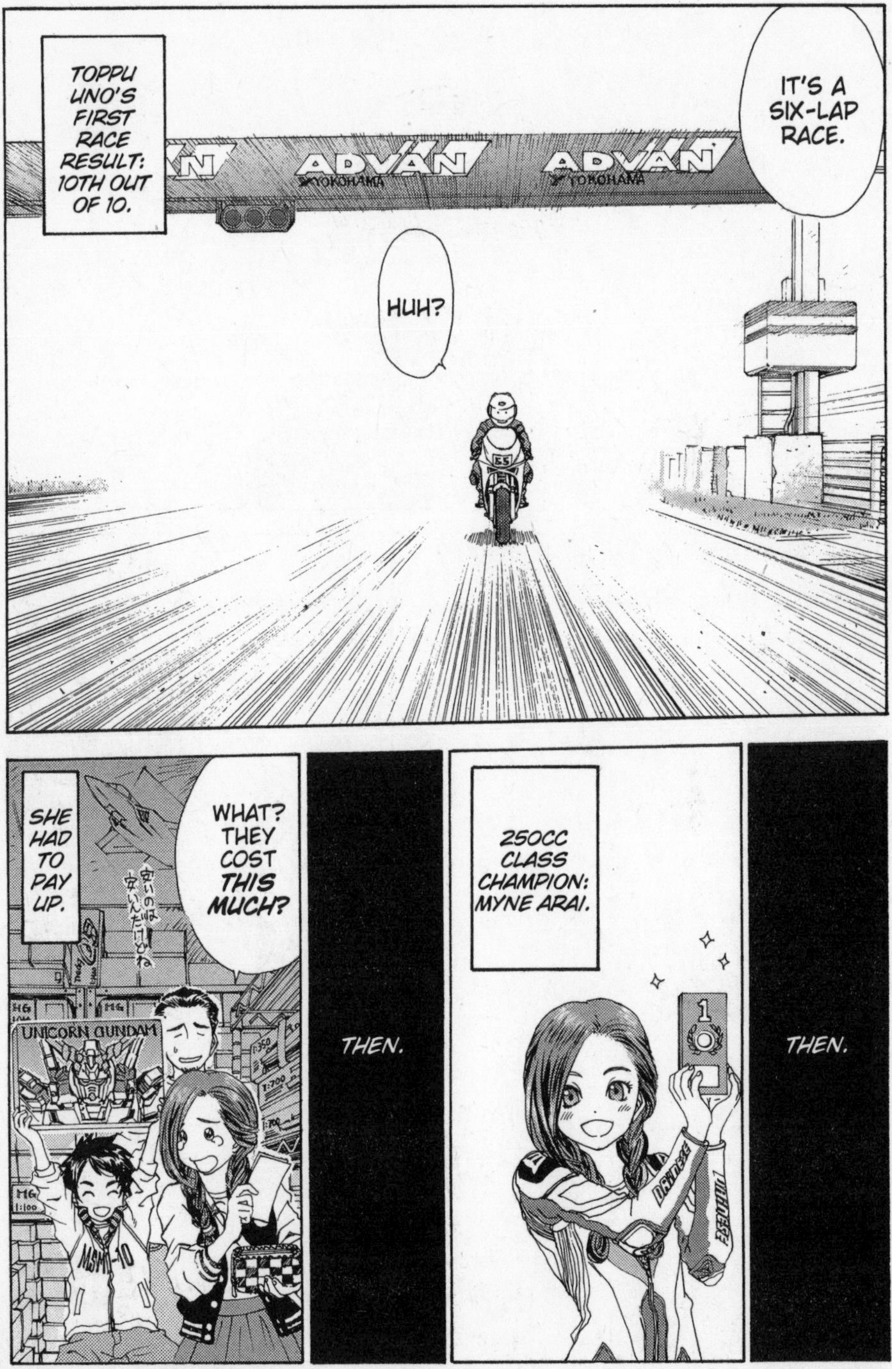
IT'S A SIX-LAP RACE.
TOPPU UNO'S FIRST RACE RESULT: 10TH OUT OF 10.
ADVAN
ADVAN
HUH?
THEN.
250CC CLASS CHAMPION: MYNE ARAI.
THEN.
WHAT? THEY COST *THIS MUCH?*
SHE HAD TO PAY UP.
安いのは安いんだけどね
UNICORN GUNDAM

Lap 2: end

TOPPU GP

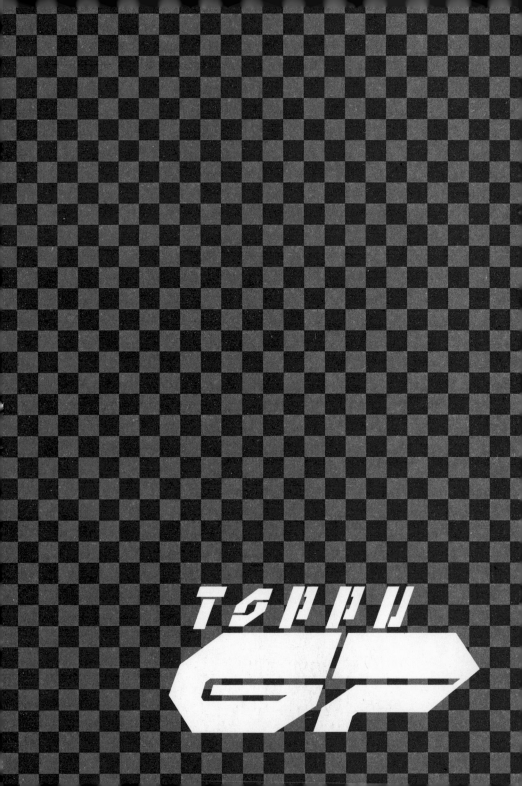

Lap 3:
TALKING WITH THE MACHINE

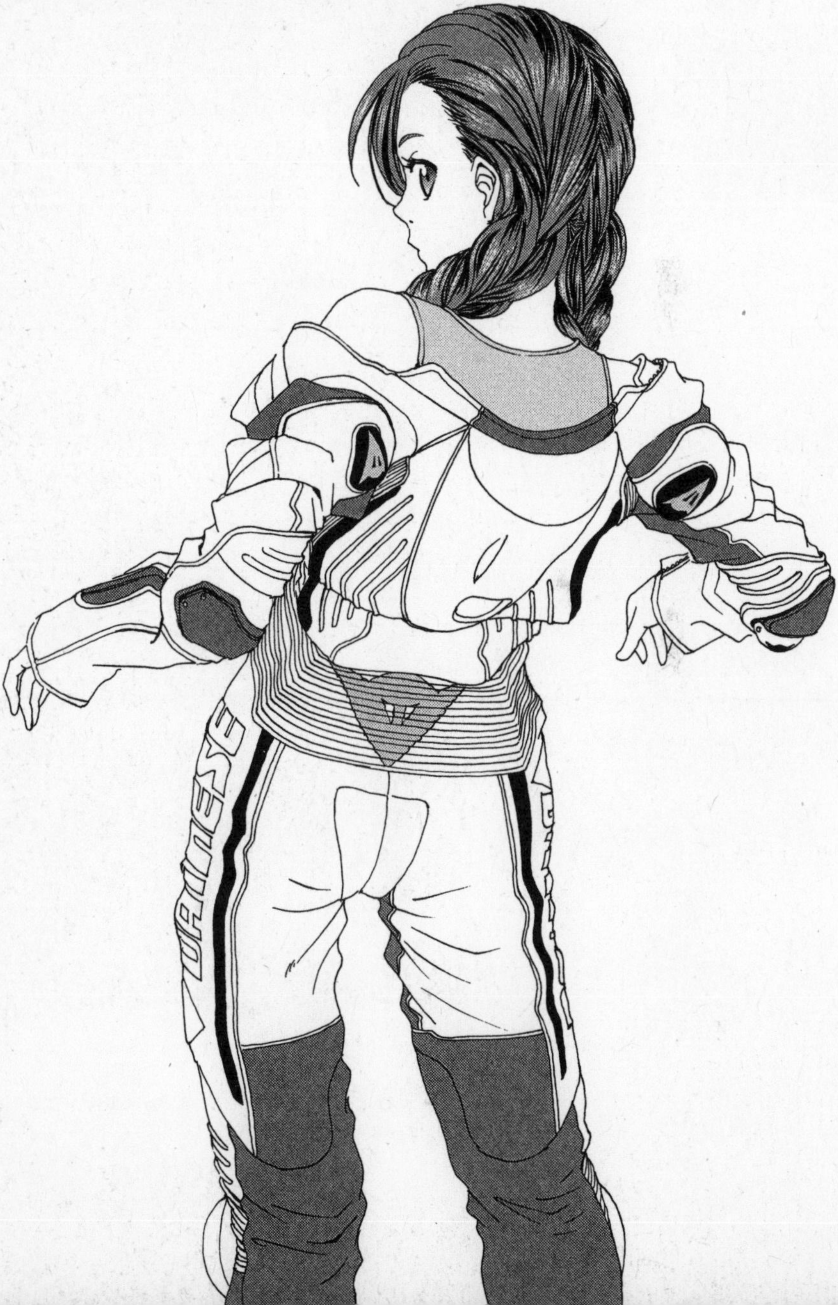

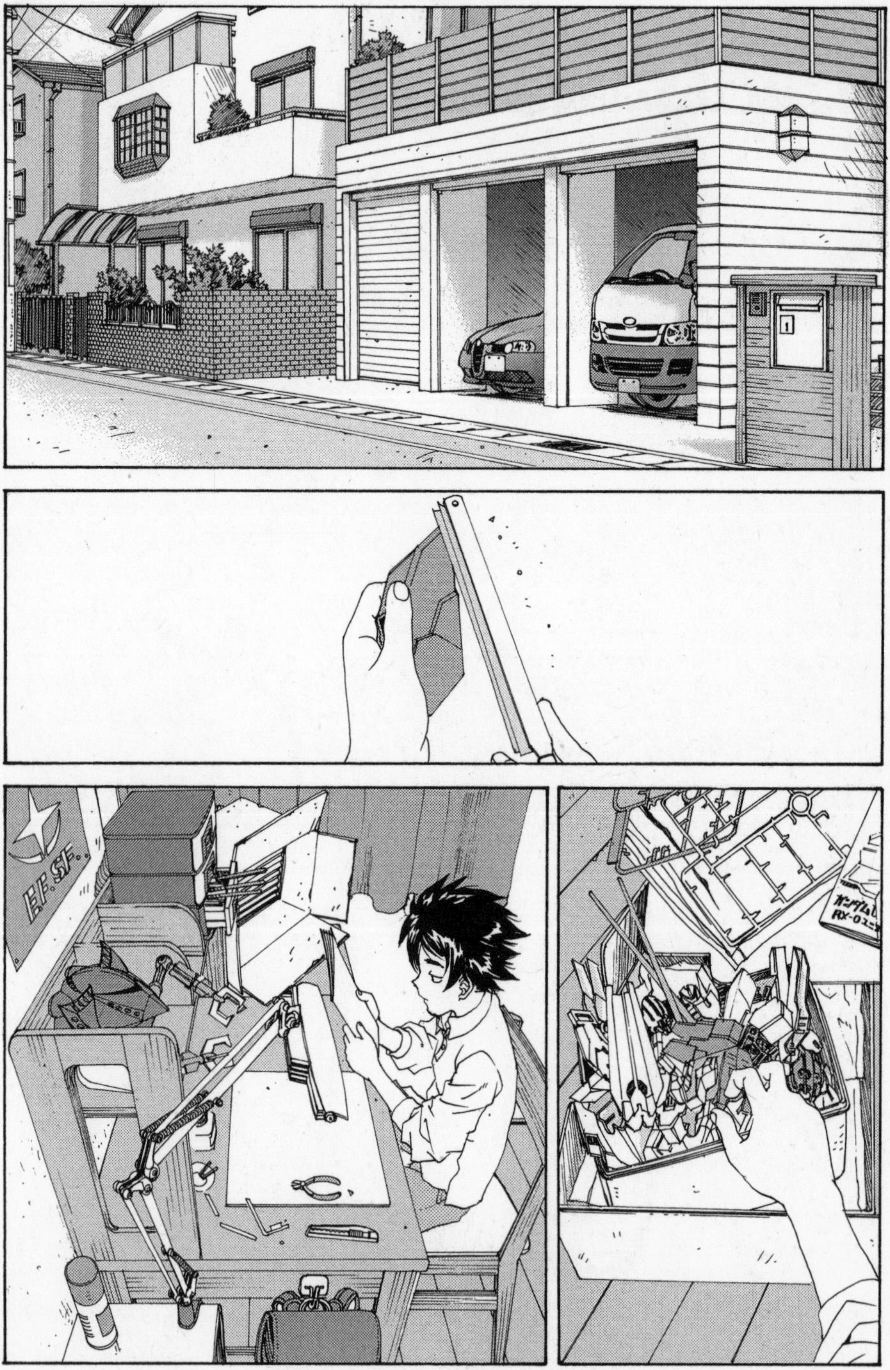
E.F.S.F.

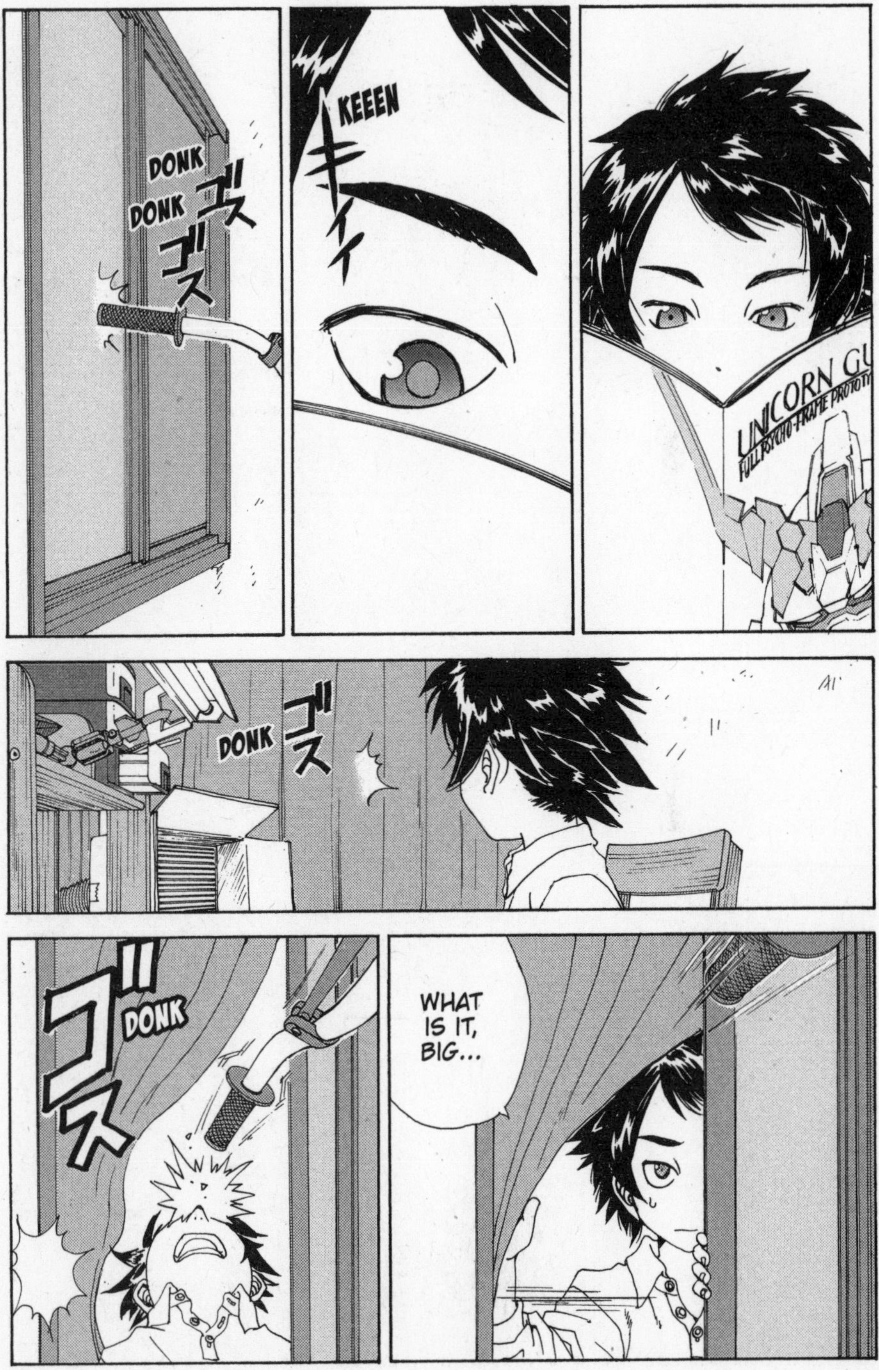
UNICORN GU
FULL PSYCHO-FRAME PROTOTY
KEEEN
キイイ
DONK
DONK
ゴス
ゴス
DONK
ゴス
WHAT IS IT, BIG...
DONK
ゴス

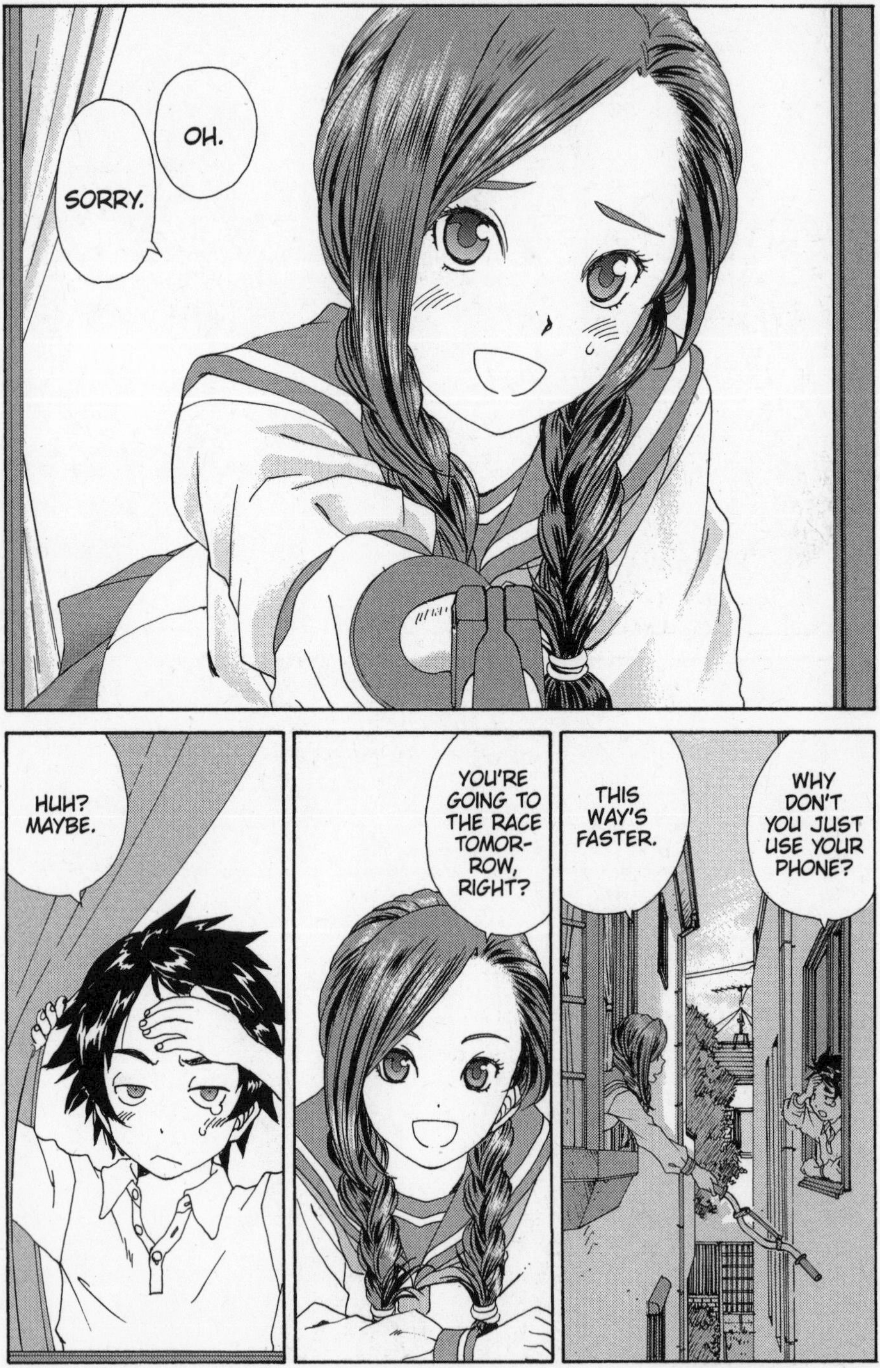
OH.
SORRY.
WHY DON'T YOU JUST USE YOUR PHONE?
THIS WAY'S FASTER.
YOU'RE GOING TO THE RACE TOMOR-ROW, RIGHT?
HUH? MAYBE.

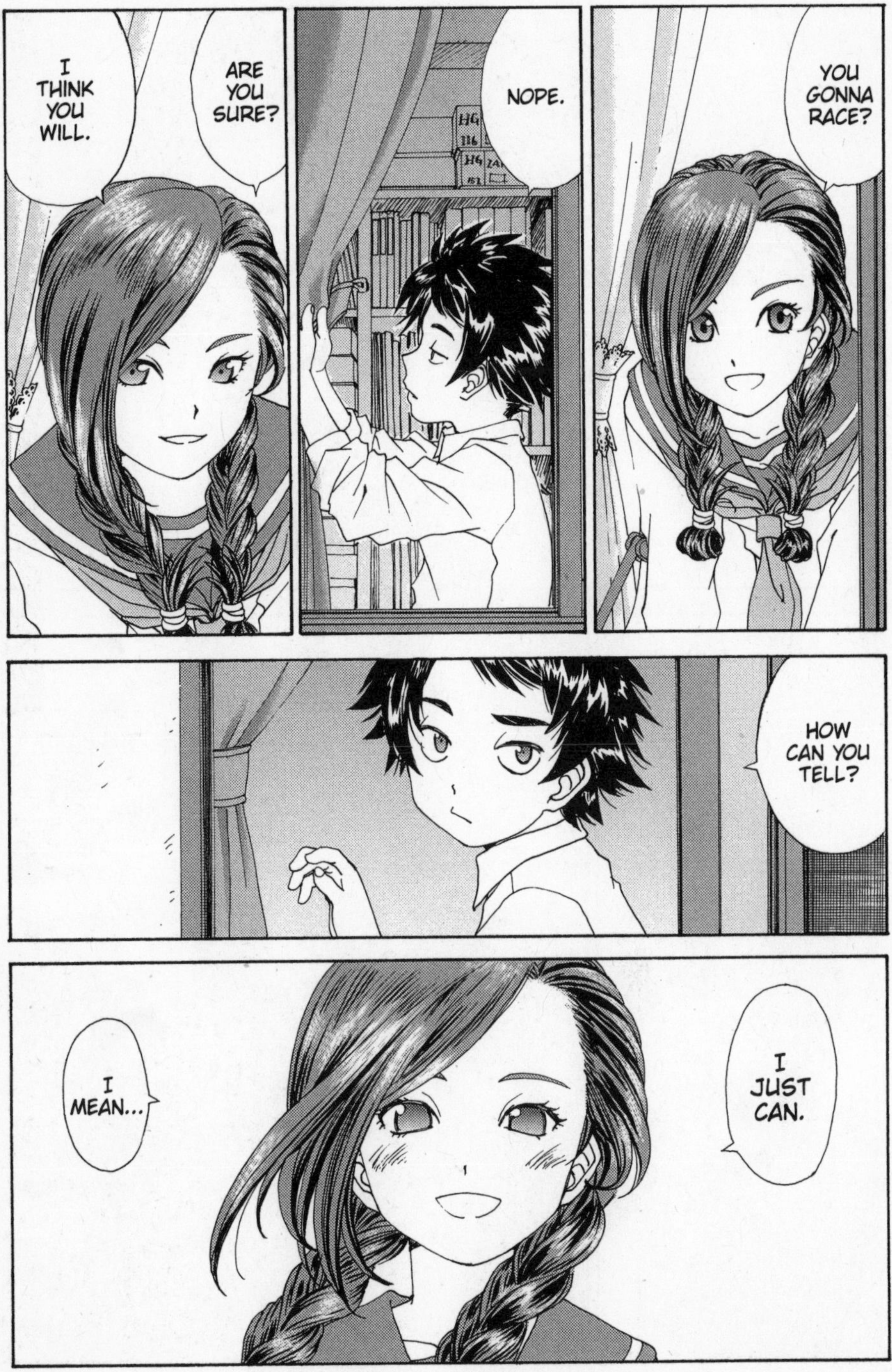
YOU GONNA RACE?
NOPE.
ARE YOU SURE?
I THINK YOU WILL.
HOW CAN YOU TELL?
I JUST CAN.
I MEAN...

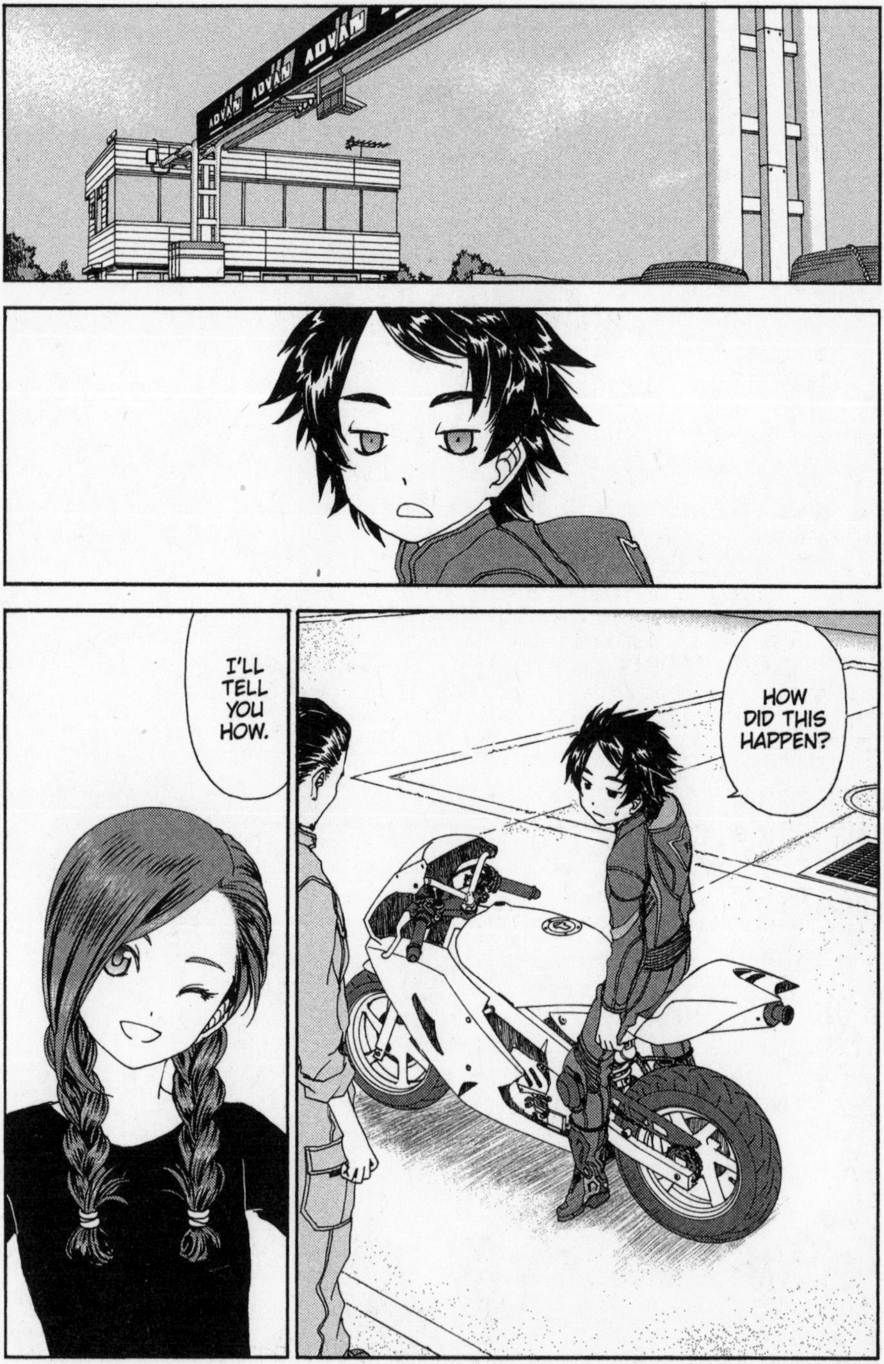
ADVAN
HOW DID THIS HAPPEN?
I'LL TELL YOU HOW.

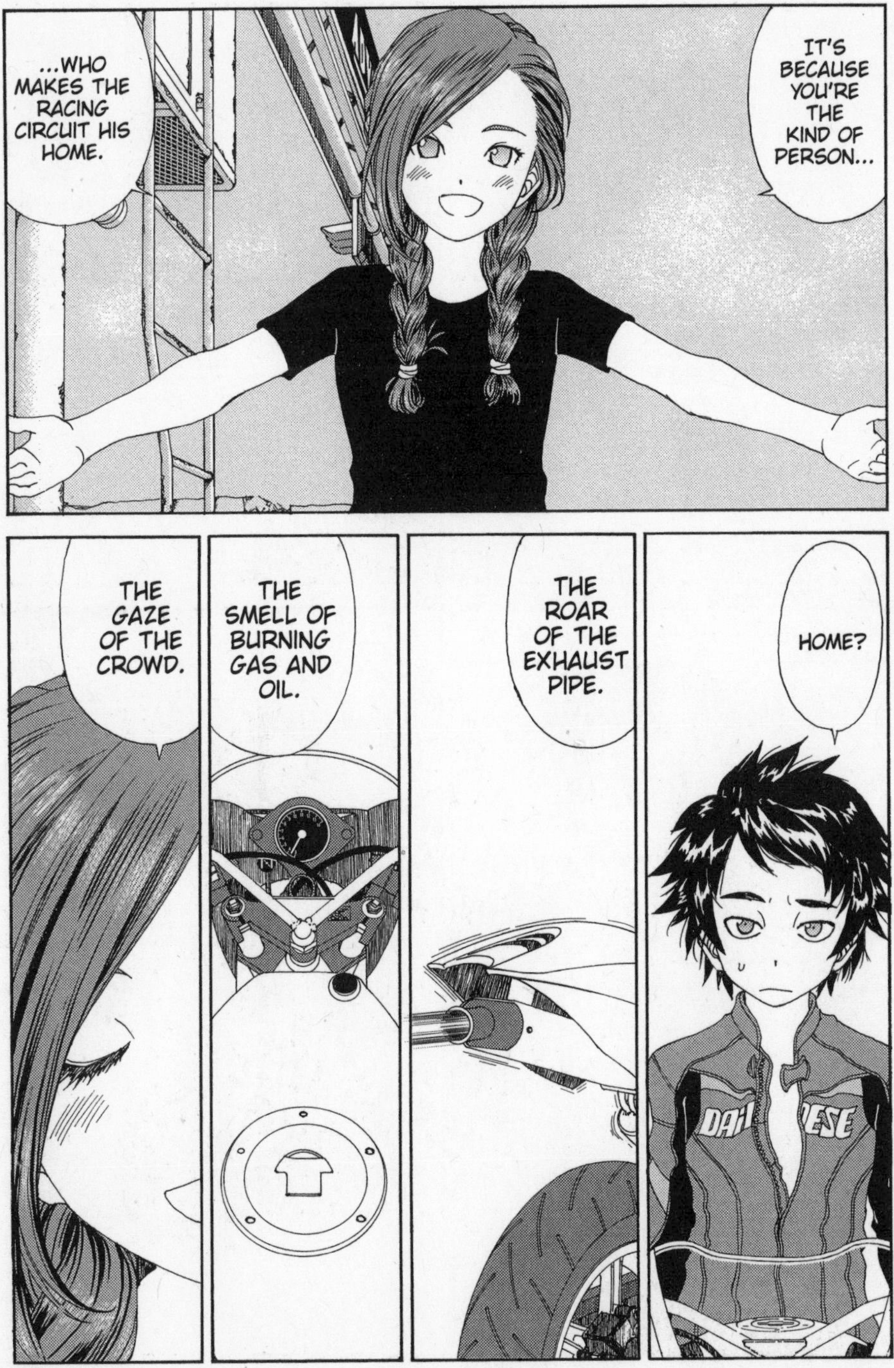
IT'S BECAUSE YOU'RE THE KIND OF PERSON...
...WHO MAKES THE RACING CIRCUIT HIS HOME.
HOME?
THE ROAR OF THE EXHAUST PIPE.
THE SMELL OF BURNING GAS AND OIL.
THE GAZE OF THE CROWD.

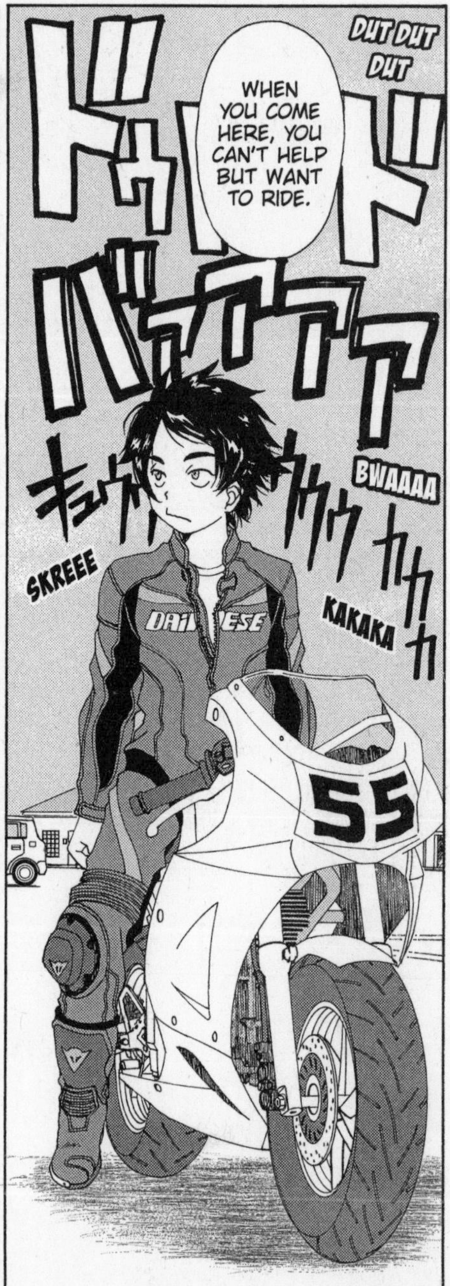
DUT DUT DUT
WHEN YOU COME HERE, YOU CAN'T HELP BUT WANT TO RIDE.
BWAAAA
KAKAKA
SKREEE

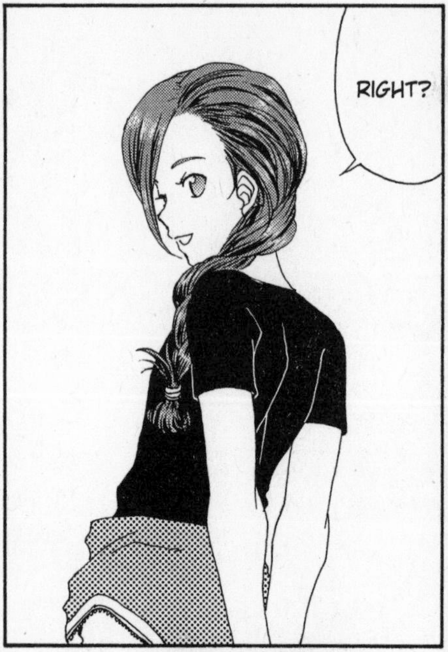
RIGHT?

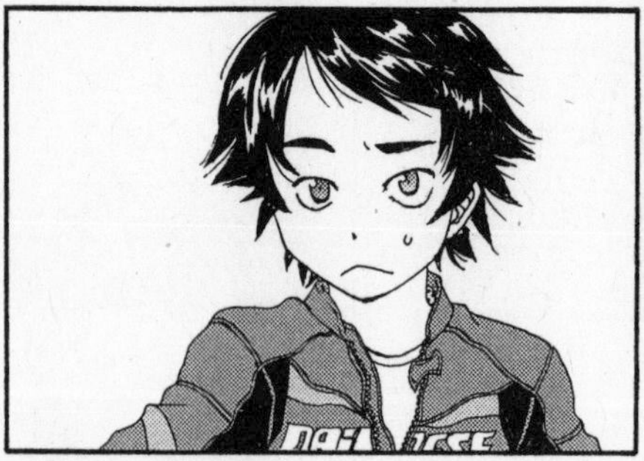

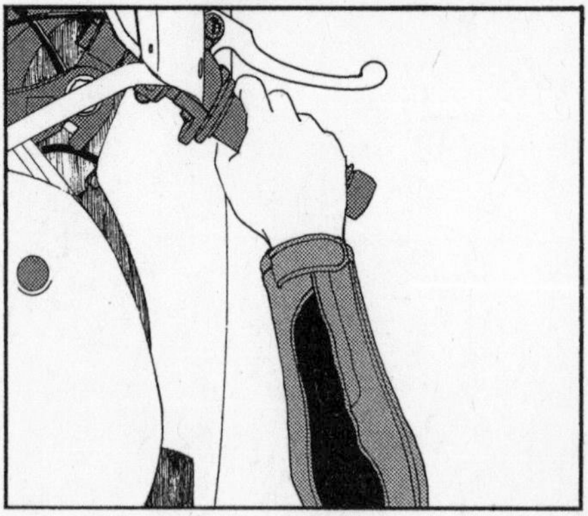

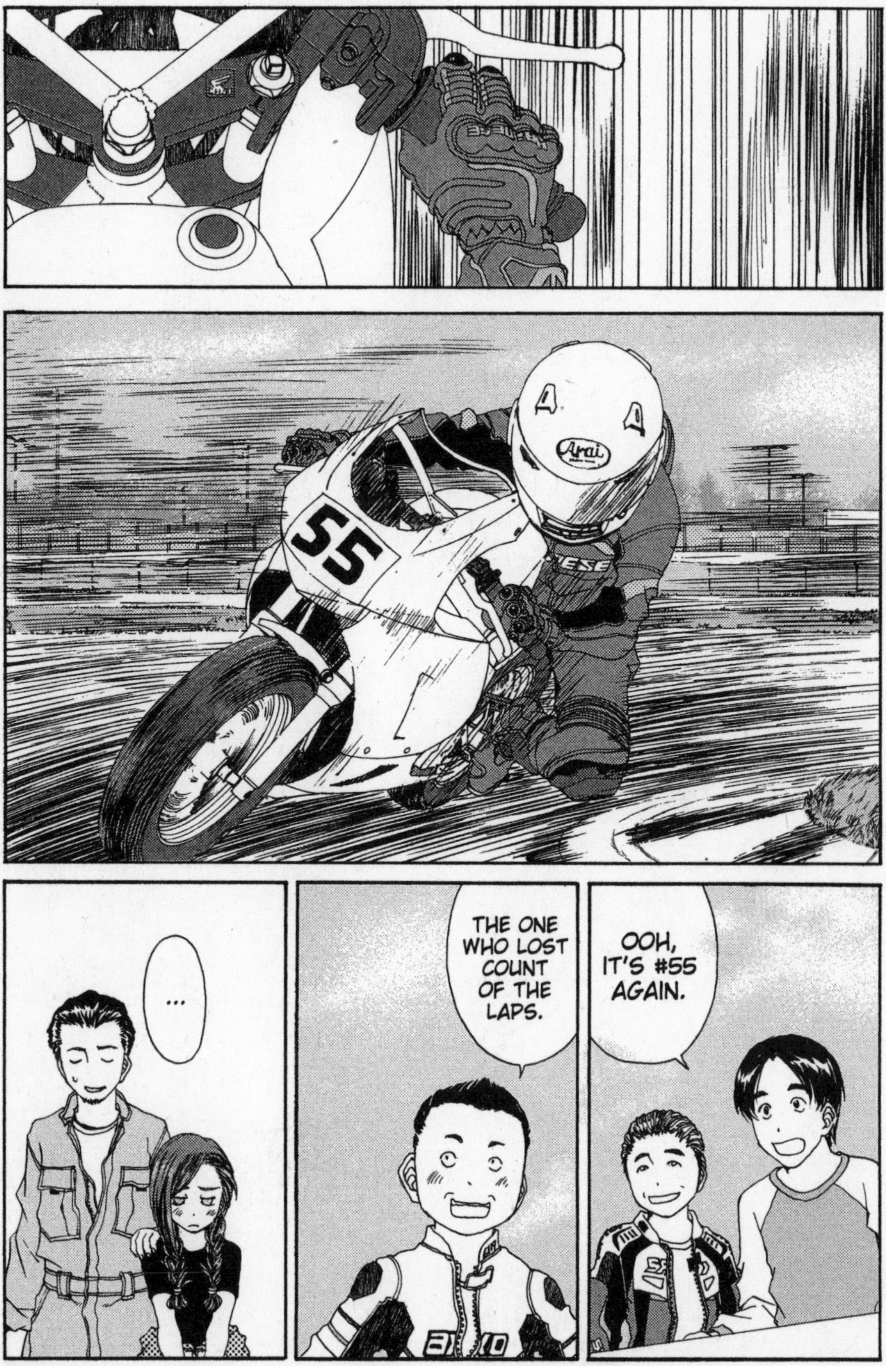
55
OOH, IT'S #55 AGAIN.
THE ONE WHO LOST COUNT OF THE LAPS.
...

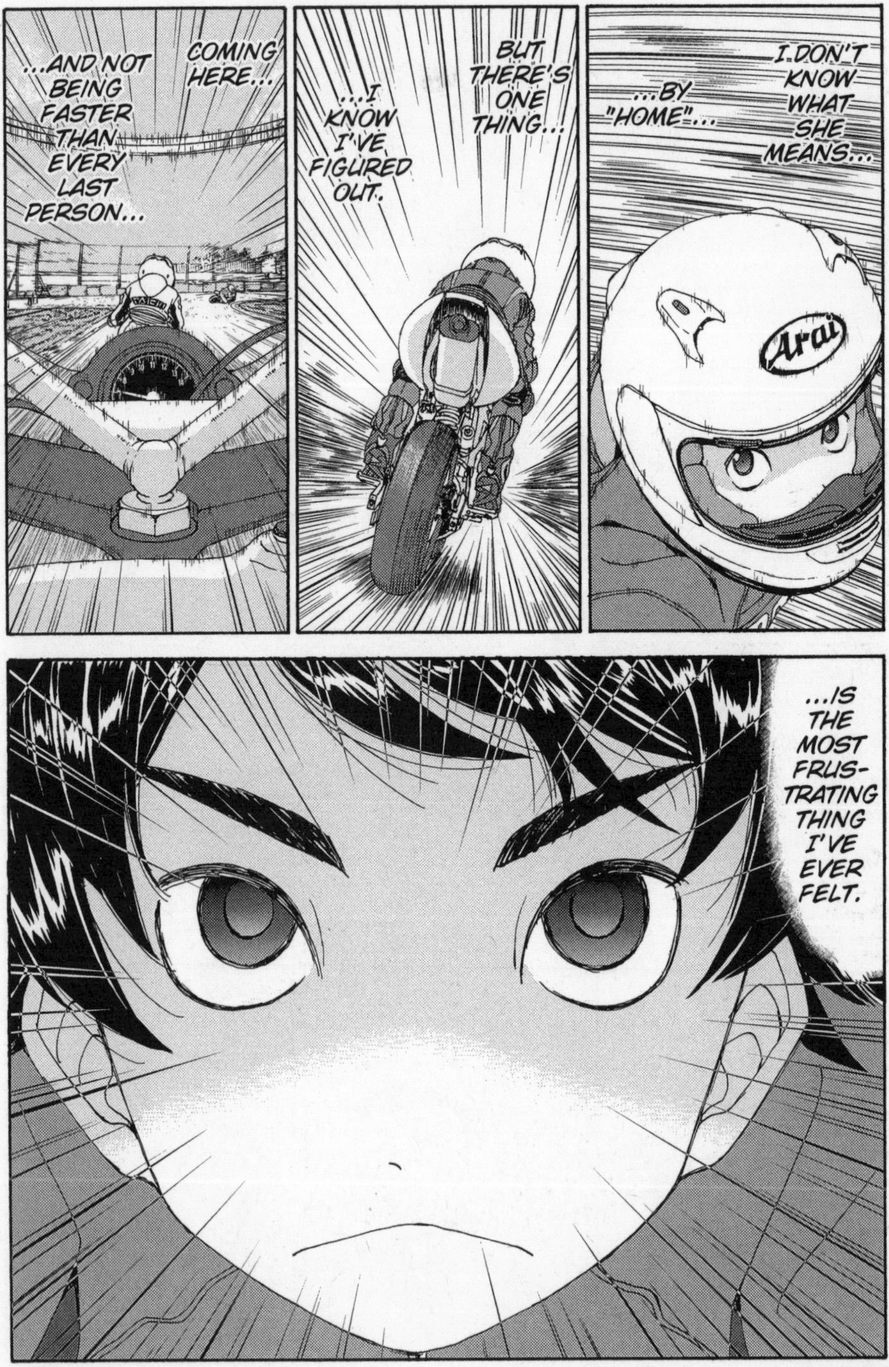
I DON'T KNOW WHAT SHE MEANS...
...BY "HOME"...
Arai
BUT THERE'S ONE THING...
...I KNOW I'VE FIGURED OUT.
COMING HERE...
...AND NOT BEING FASTER THAN EVERY LAST PERSON...
...IS THE MOST FRUS-TRATING THING I'VE EVER FELT.

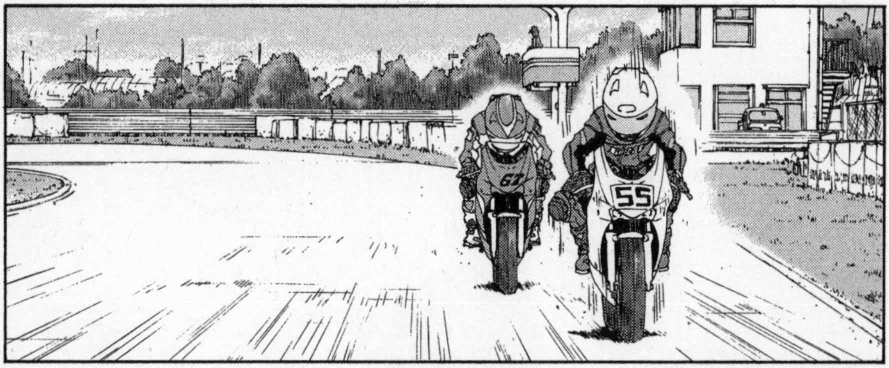

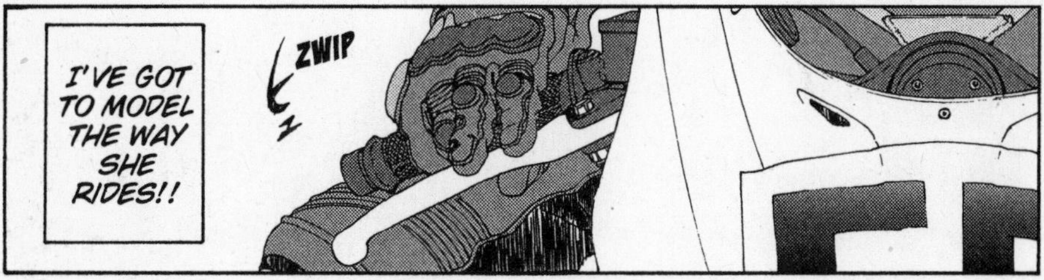
ZWIP
I'VE GOT TO MODEL THE WAY SHE RIDES!!

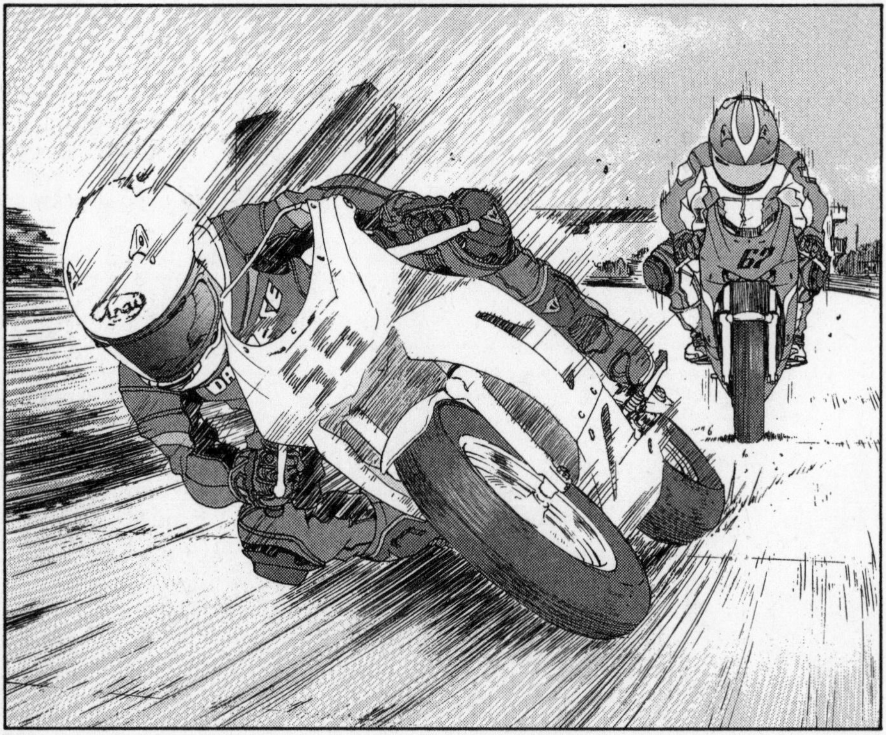

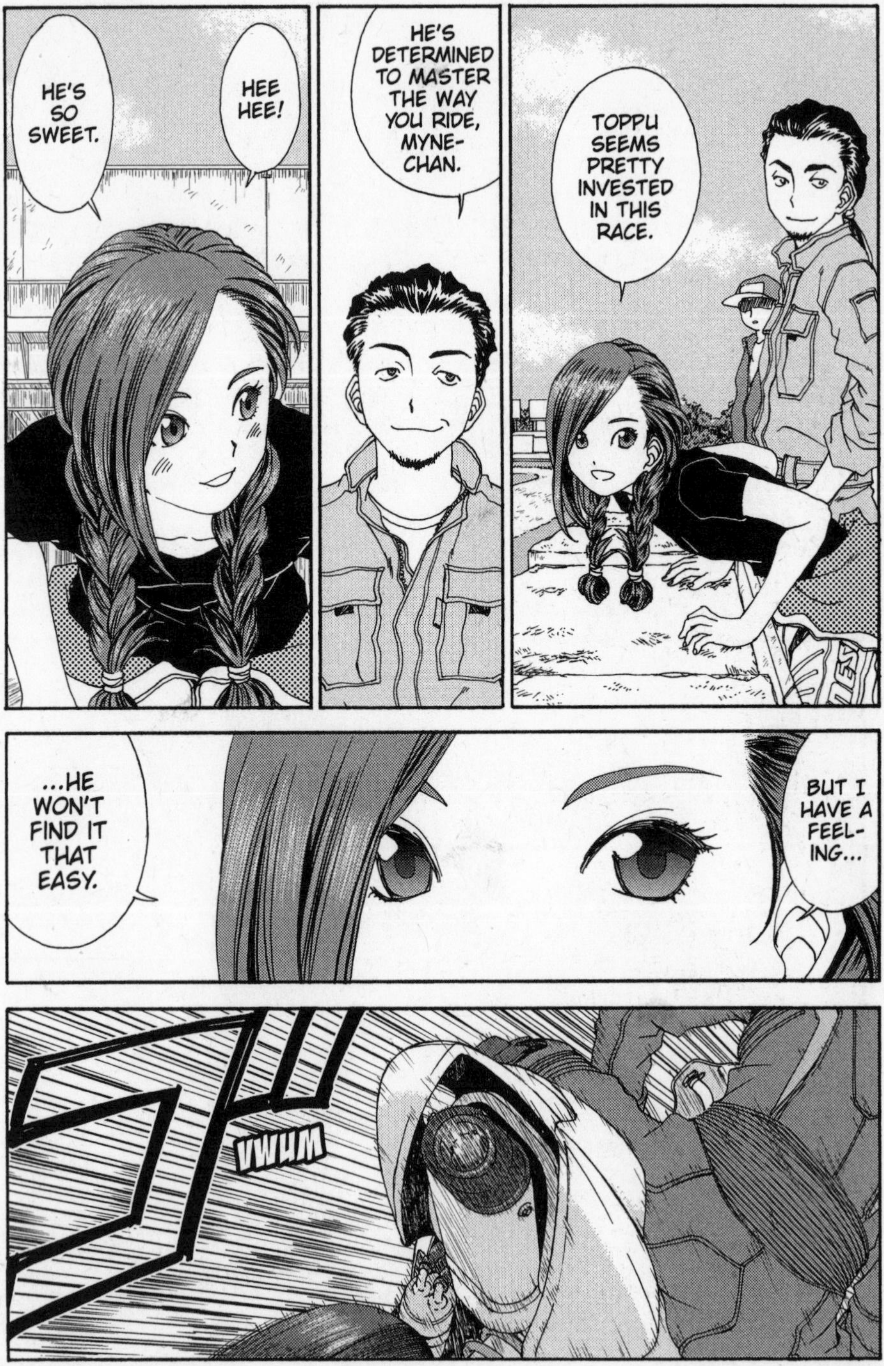
TOPPU SEEMS PRETTY INVESTED IN THIS RACE.
HE'S DETERMINED TO MASTER THE WAY YOU RIDE, MYNE-CHAN.
HEE HEE!
HE'S SO SWEET.
BUT I HAVE A FEEL-ING...
...HE WON'T FIND IT THAT EASY.
VWUM

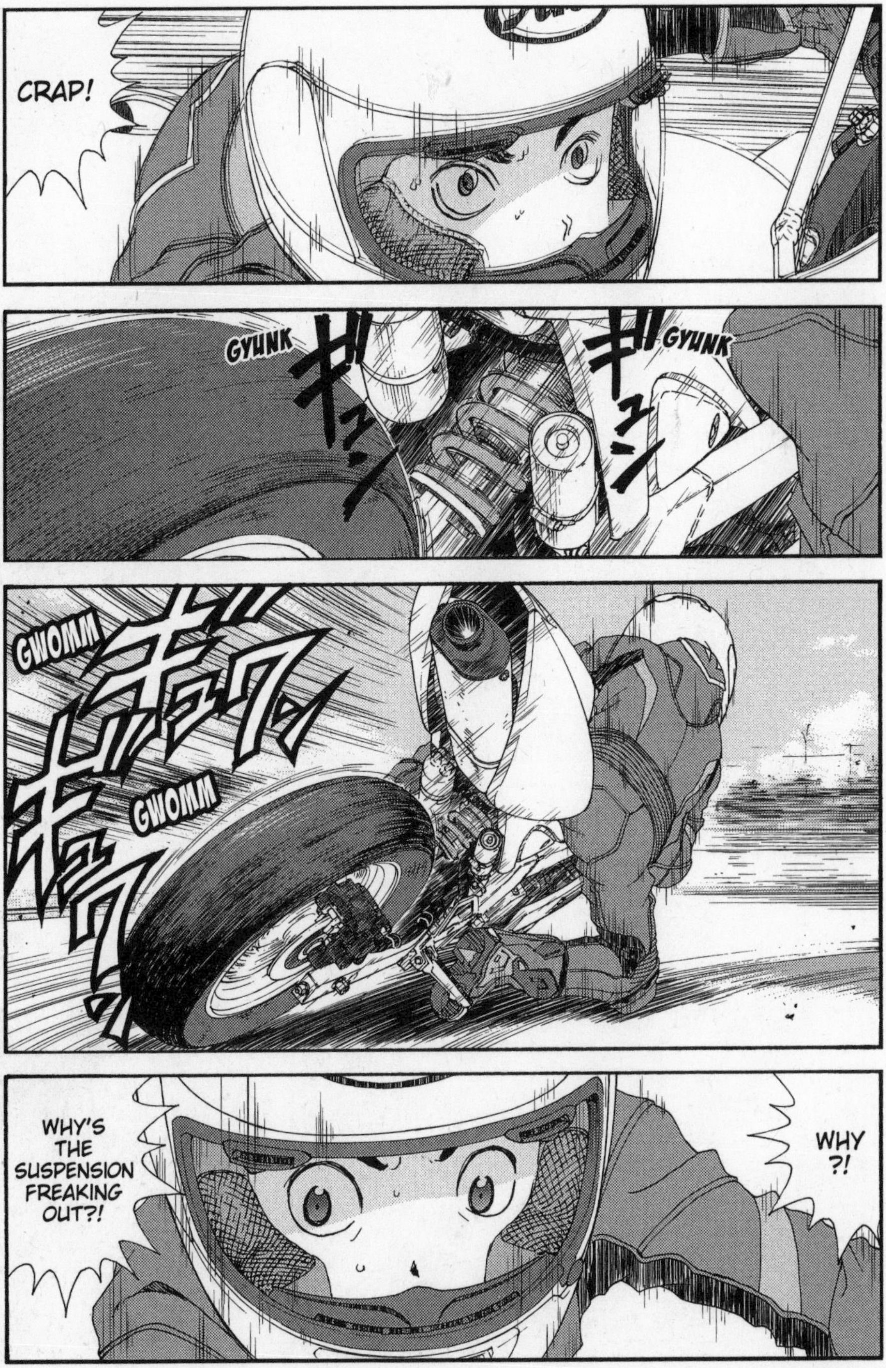
CRAP!
ギュン
GYUNK
ギュン
GYUNK
GWOMM
GWOMM
WHY ?!
WHY'S THE SUSPENSION FREAKING OUT?!

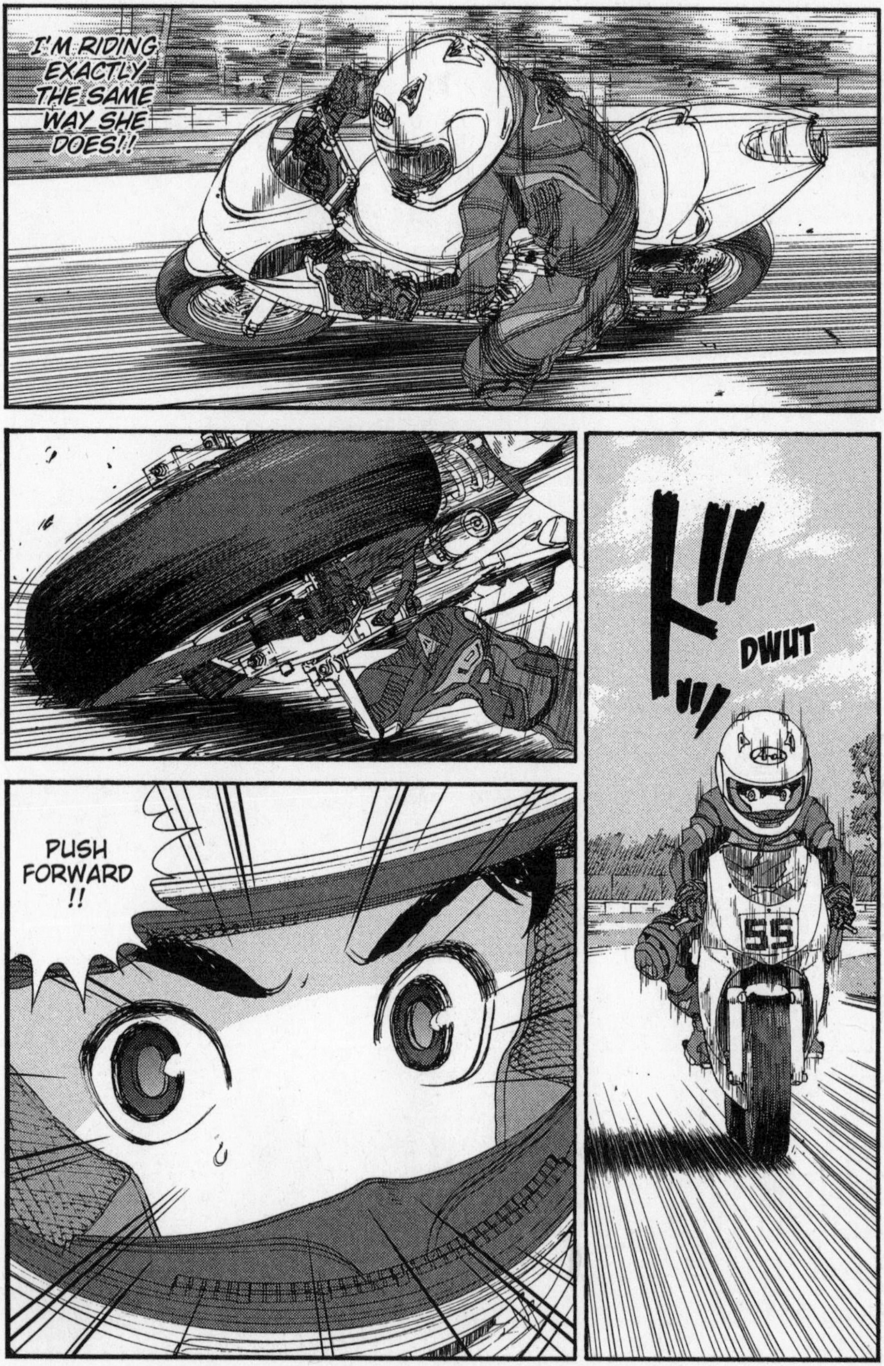
I'M RIDING EXACTLY THE SAME WAY SHE DOES!!
ドッ
DWHUT
PUSH FORWARD!!

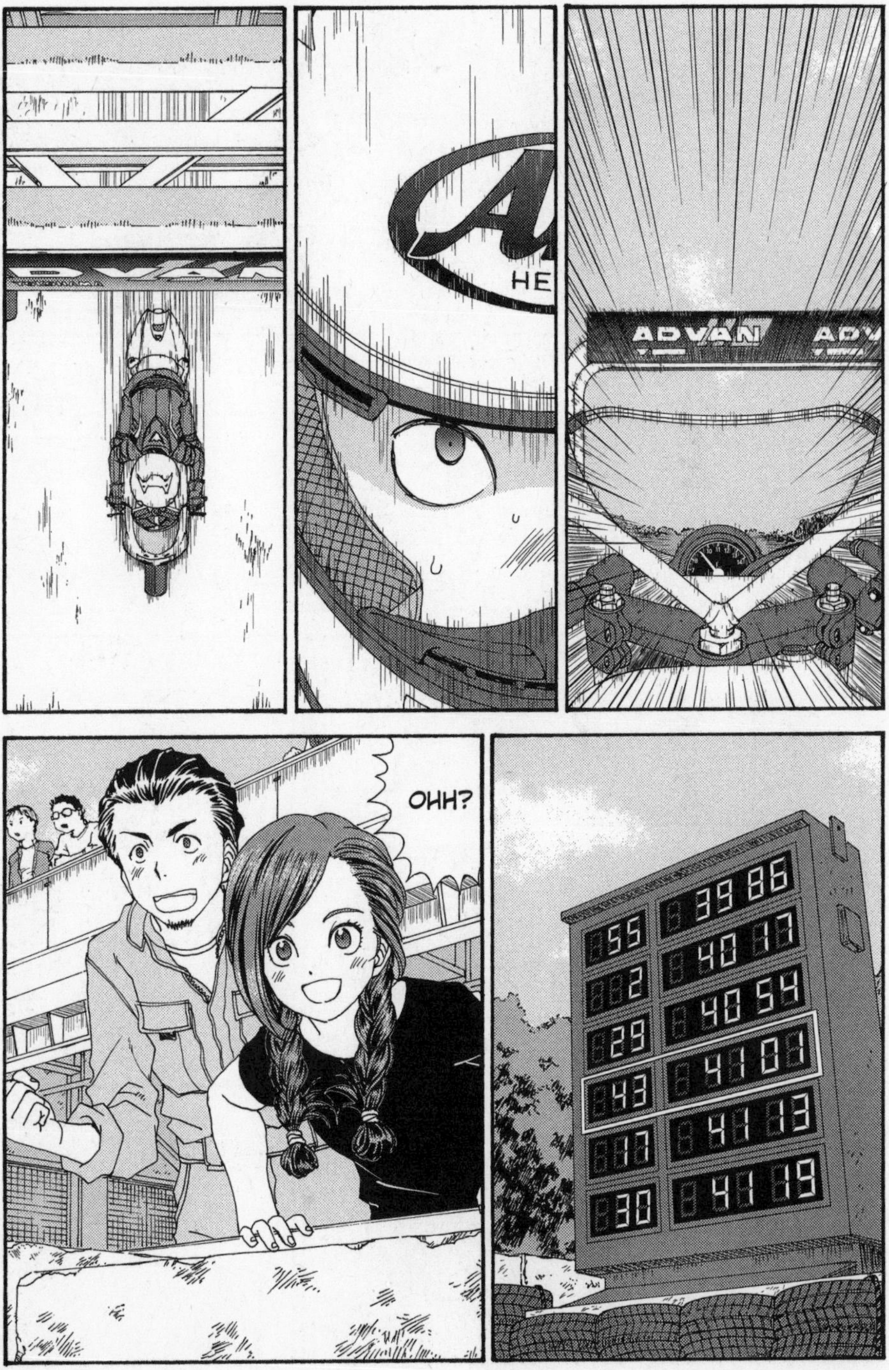
ADVAN
ADV
HE
OHH?

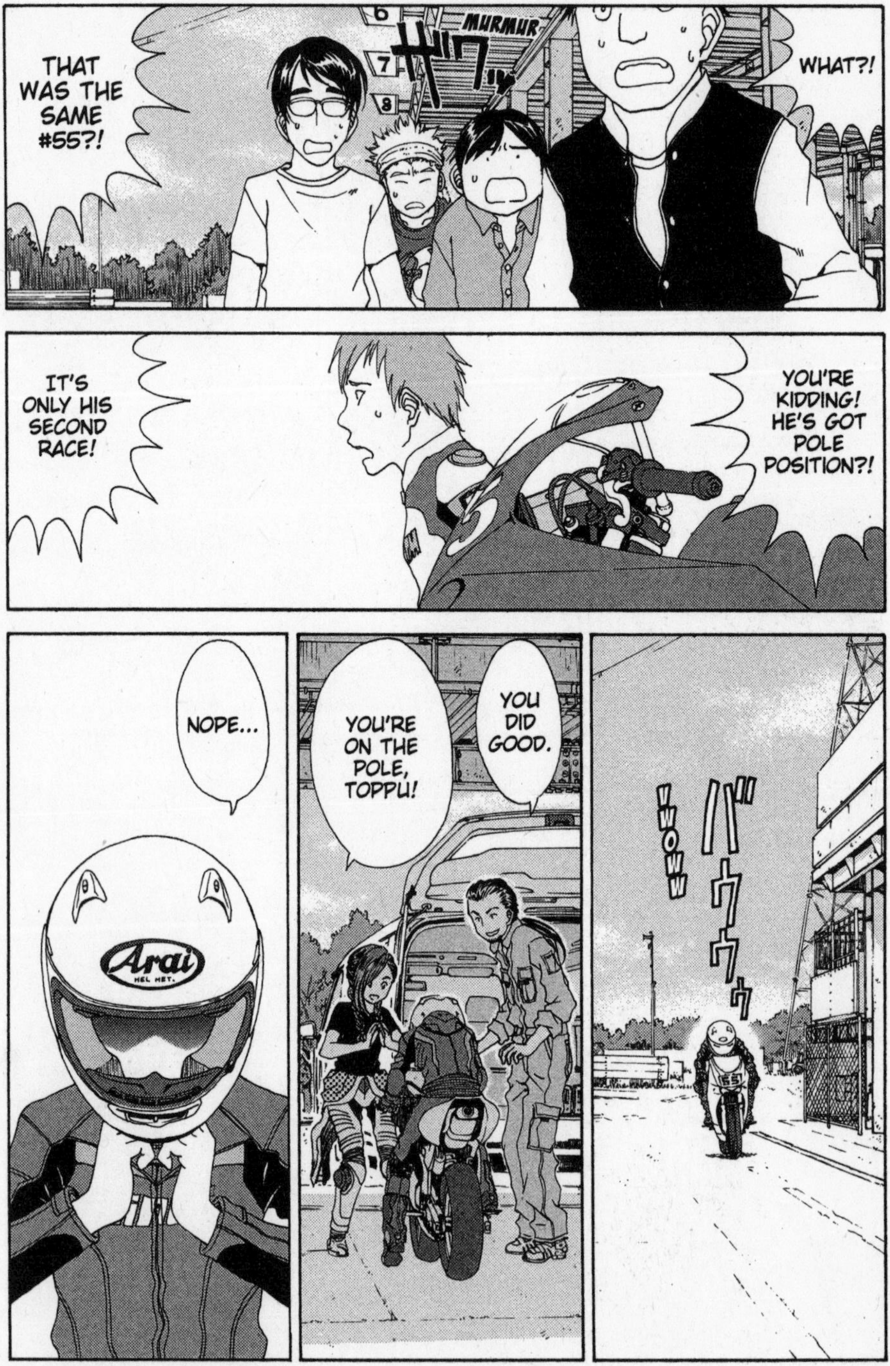
MURMUR
WHAT?!
THAT WAS THE SAME #55?!
YOU'RE KIDDING! HE'S GOT POLE POSITION?!
IT'S ONLY HIS SECOND RACE!
VWOWW
YOU DID GOOD.
YOU'RE ON THE POLE, TOPPU!
NOPE...

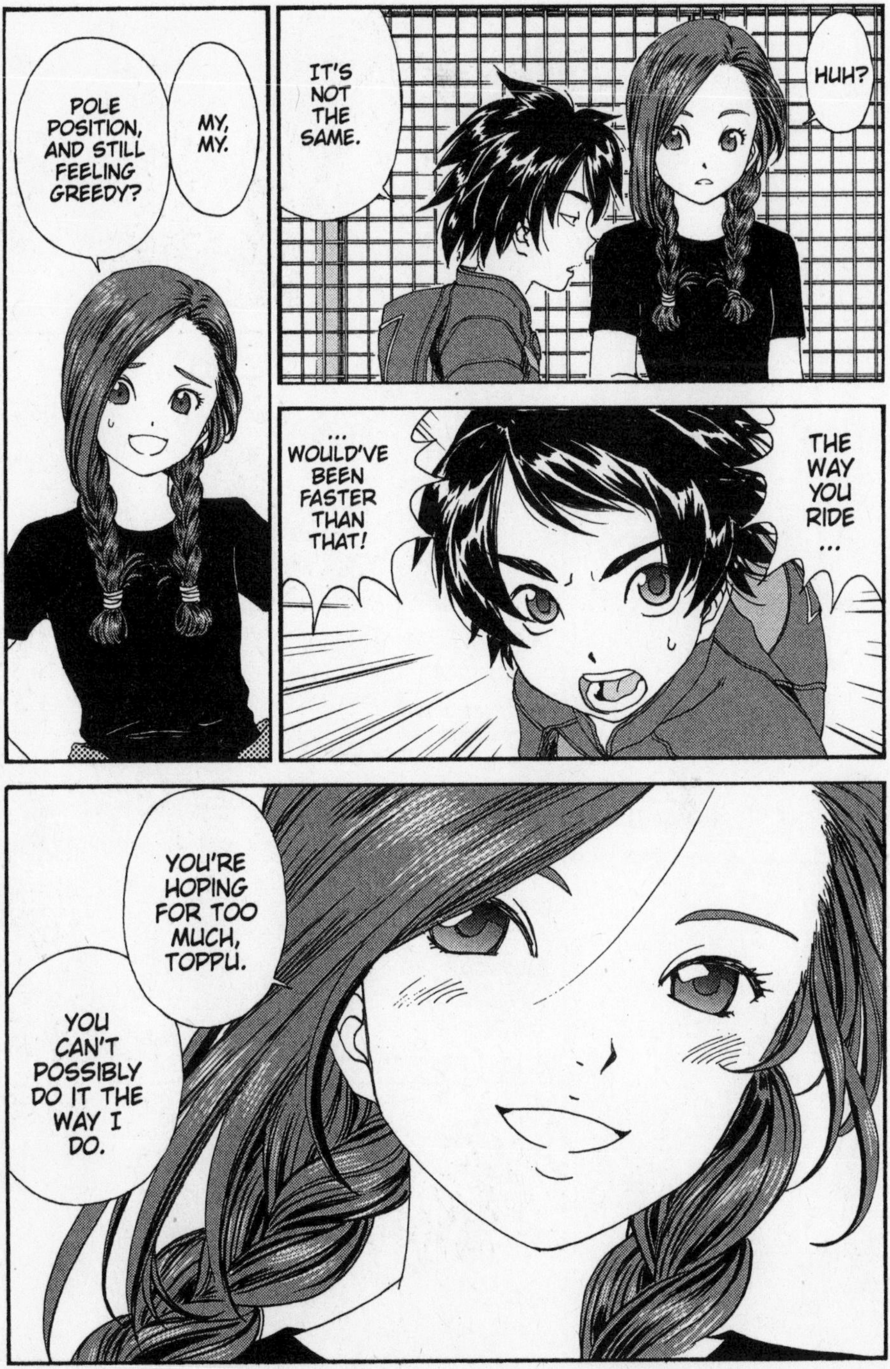
HUH?
IT'S NOT THE SAME.
THE WAY YOU RIDE ...
... WOULD'VE BEEN FASTER THAN THAT!
MY, MY.
POLE POSITION, AND STILL FEELING GREEDY?
YOU'RE HOPING FOR TOO MUCH, TOPPU.
YOU CAN'T POSSIBLY DO IT THE WAY I DO.

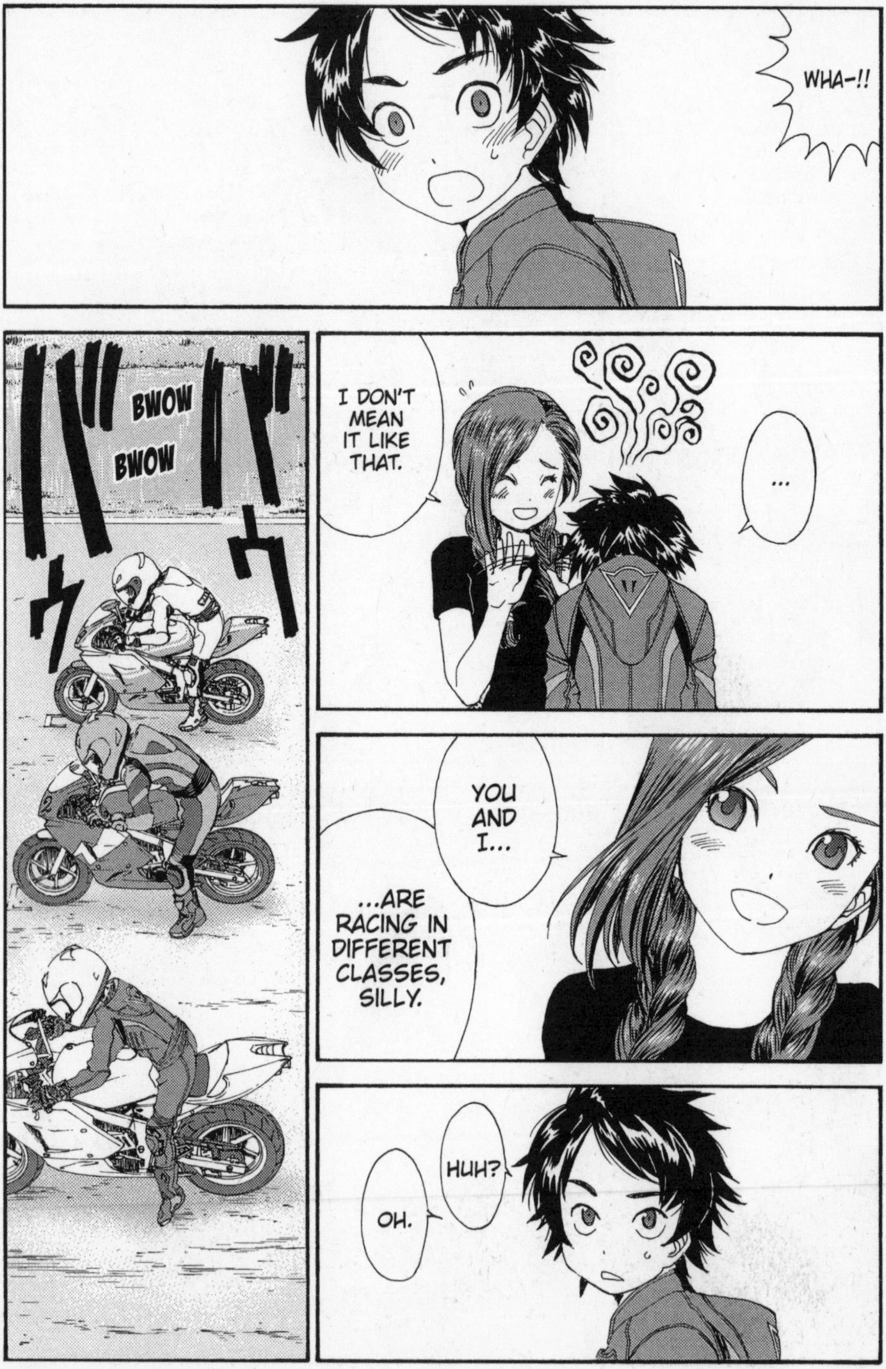
WHA-!!
...
I DON'T MEAN IT LIKE THAT.
YOU AND I...
...ARE RACING IN DIFFERENT CLASSES, SILLY.
HUH?
OH.
バウ
BWOW
BWOW
バウ

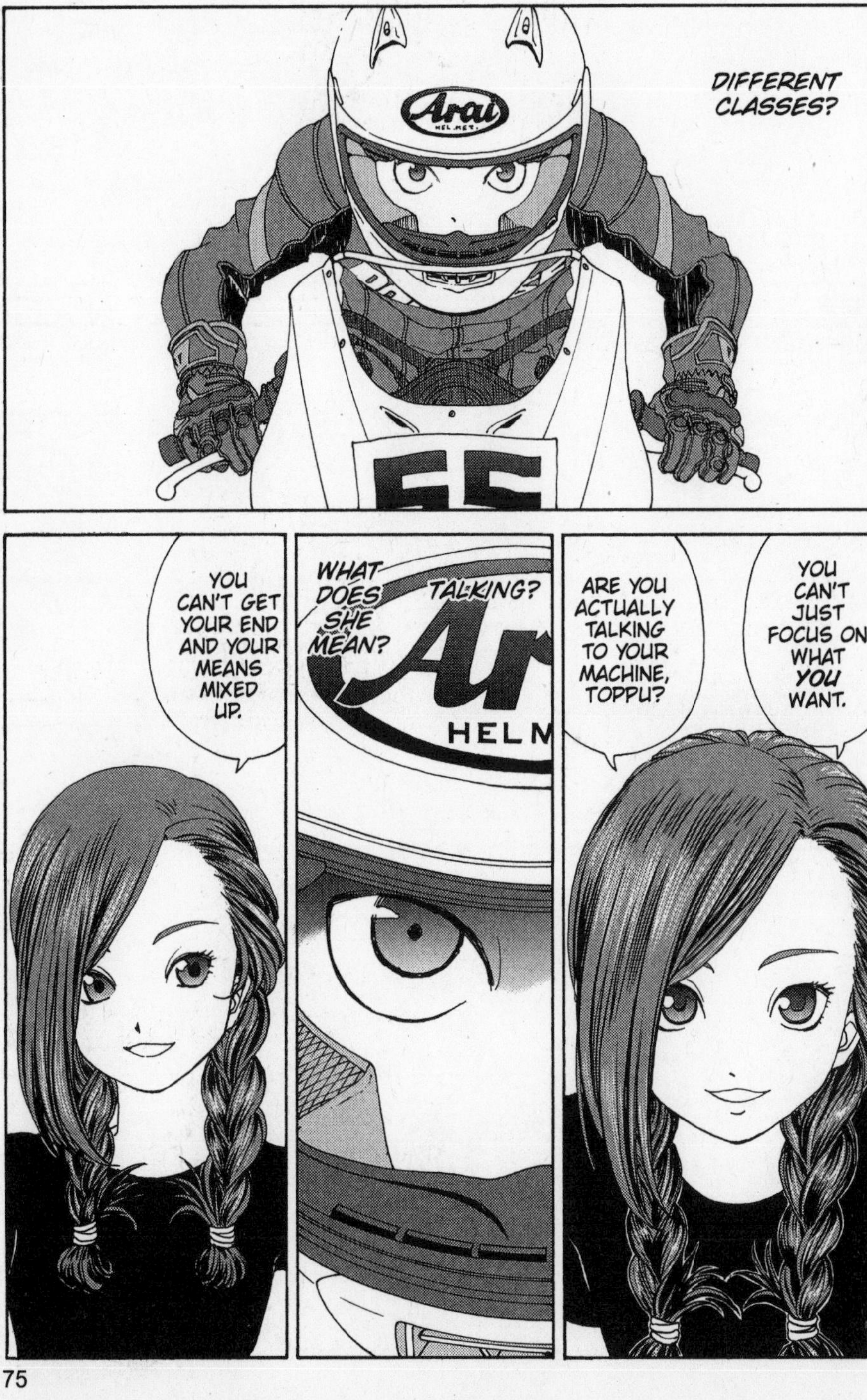
DIFFERENT CLASSES?
YOU CAN'T JUST FOCUS ON WHAT YOU WANT.
ARE YOU ACTUALLY TALKING TO YOUR MACHINE, TOPPU?
TALKING?
WHAT DOES SHE MEAN?
YOU CAN'T GET YOUR END AND YOUR MEANS MIXED UP.

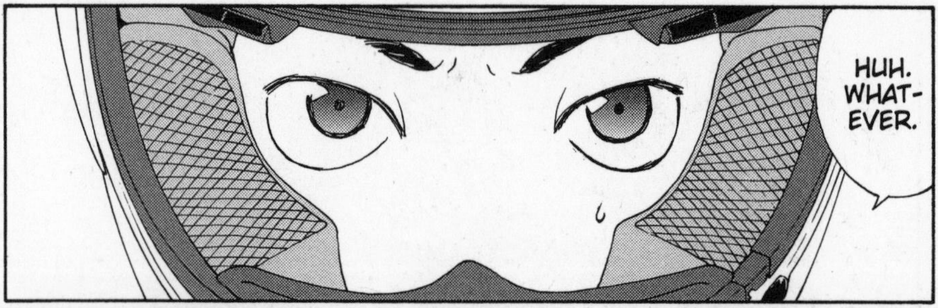
HUH. WHAT-EVER.
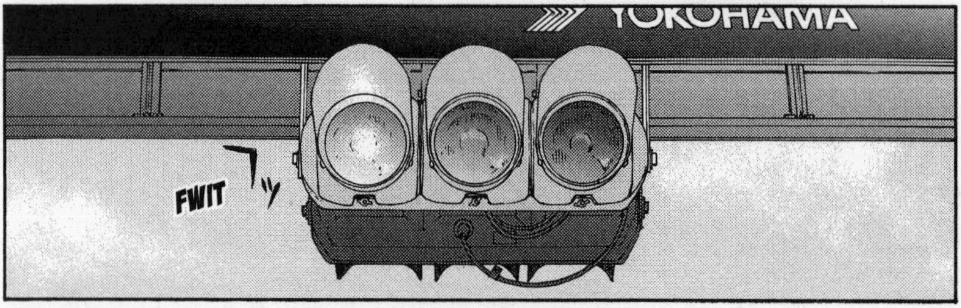
YOKOHAMA
FWIT
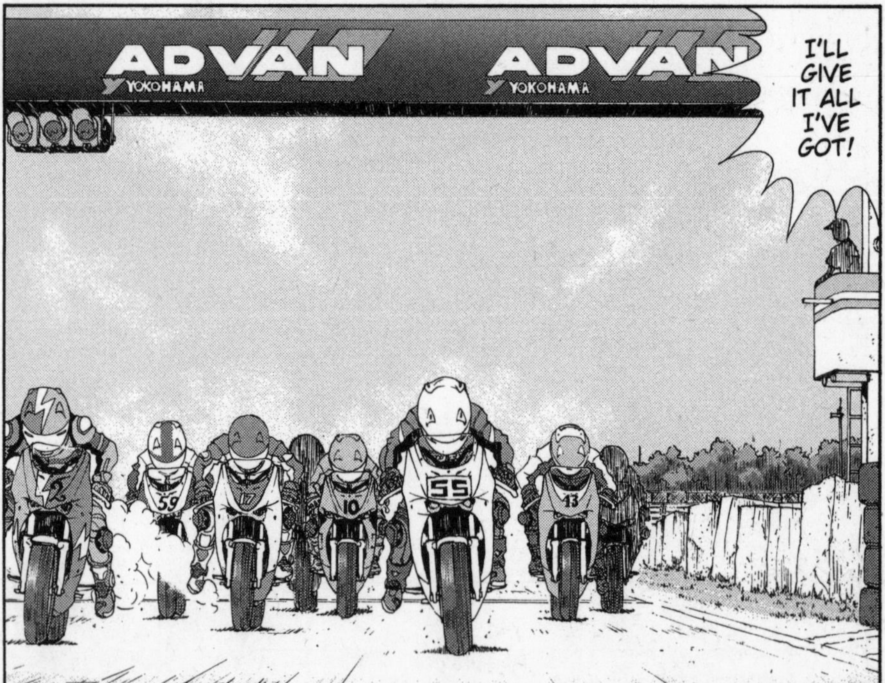
ADVAN
YOKOHAMA
ADVAN
YOKOHAMA
I'LL GIVE IT ALL I'VE GOT!

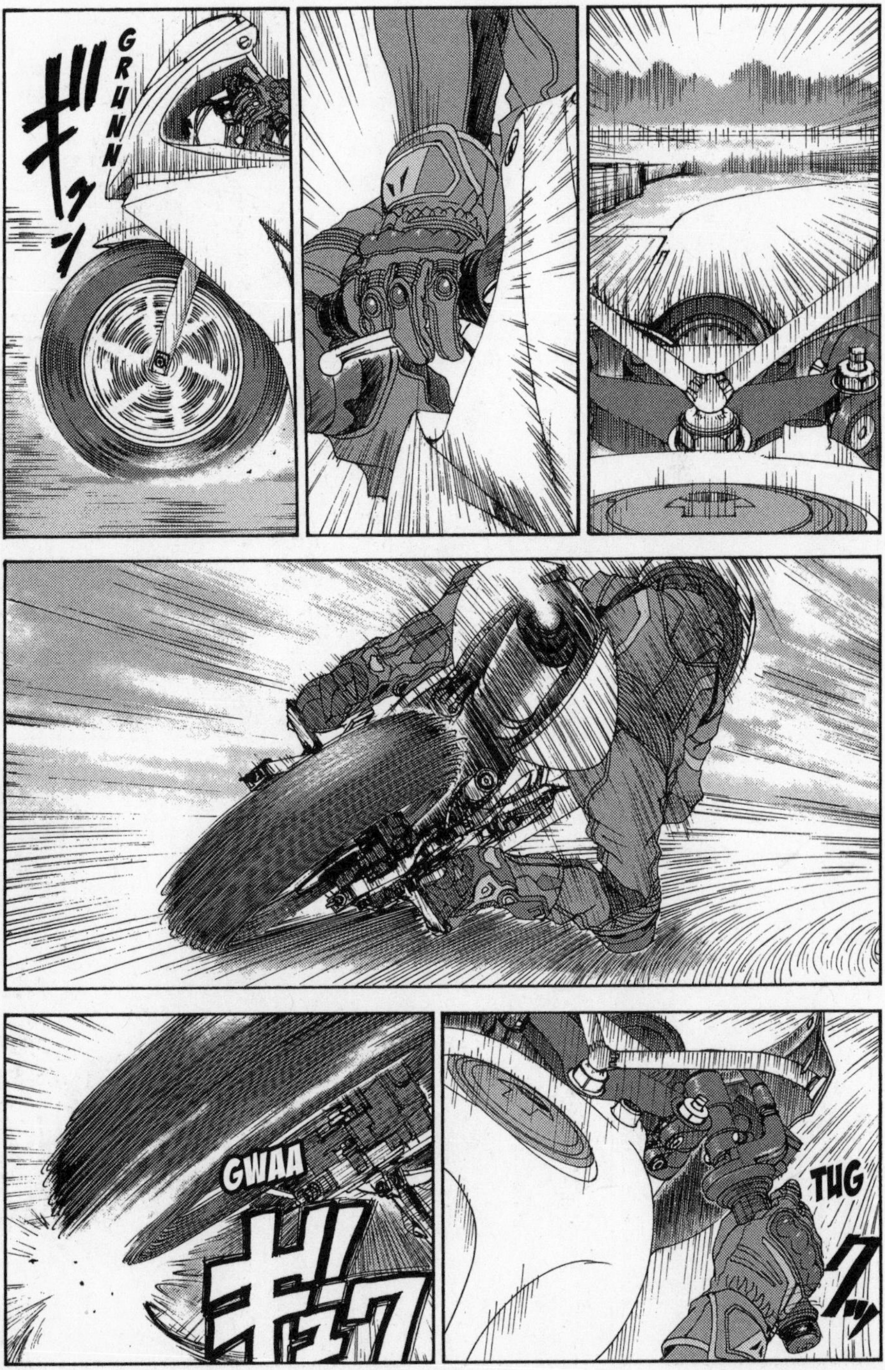
GRUNN
ギュン
TUG
クッ
GWAA

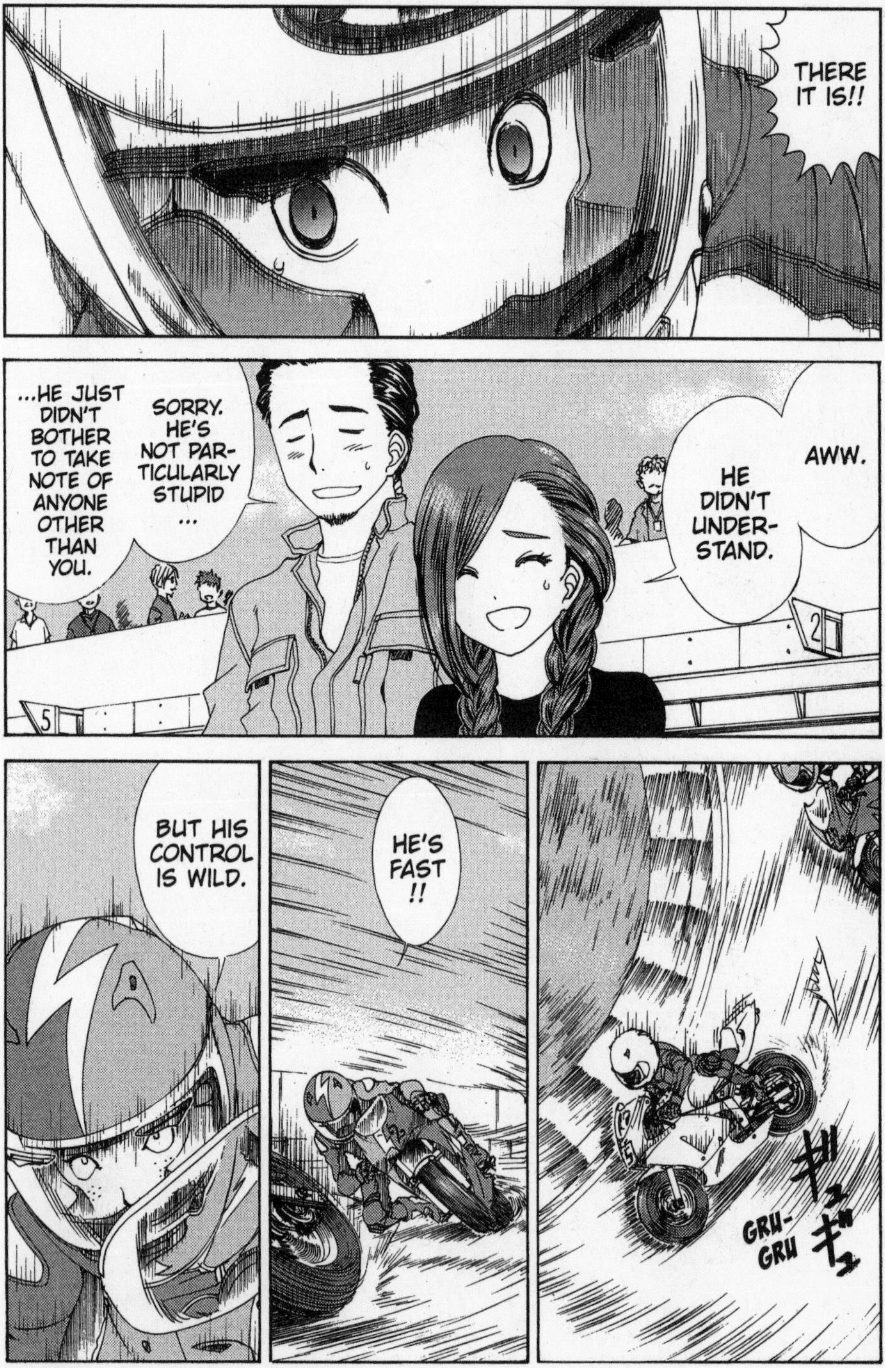
THERE IT IS!!
AWW.
HE DIDN'T UNDERSTAND.
SORRY. HE'S NOT PARTICULARLY STUPID ...
...HE JUST DIDN'T BOTHER TO TAKE NOTE OF ANYONE OTHER THAN YOU.
GRU-GRU
HE'S FAST !!
BUT HIS CONTROL IS WILD.

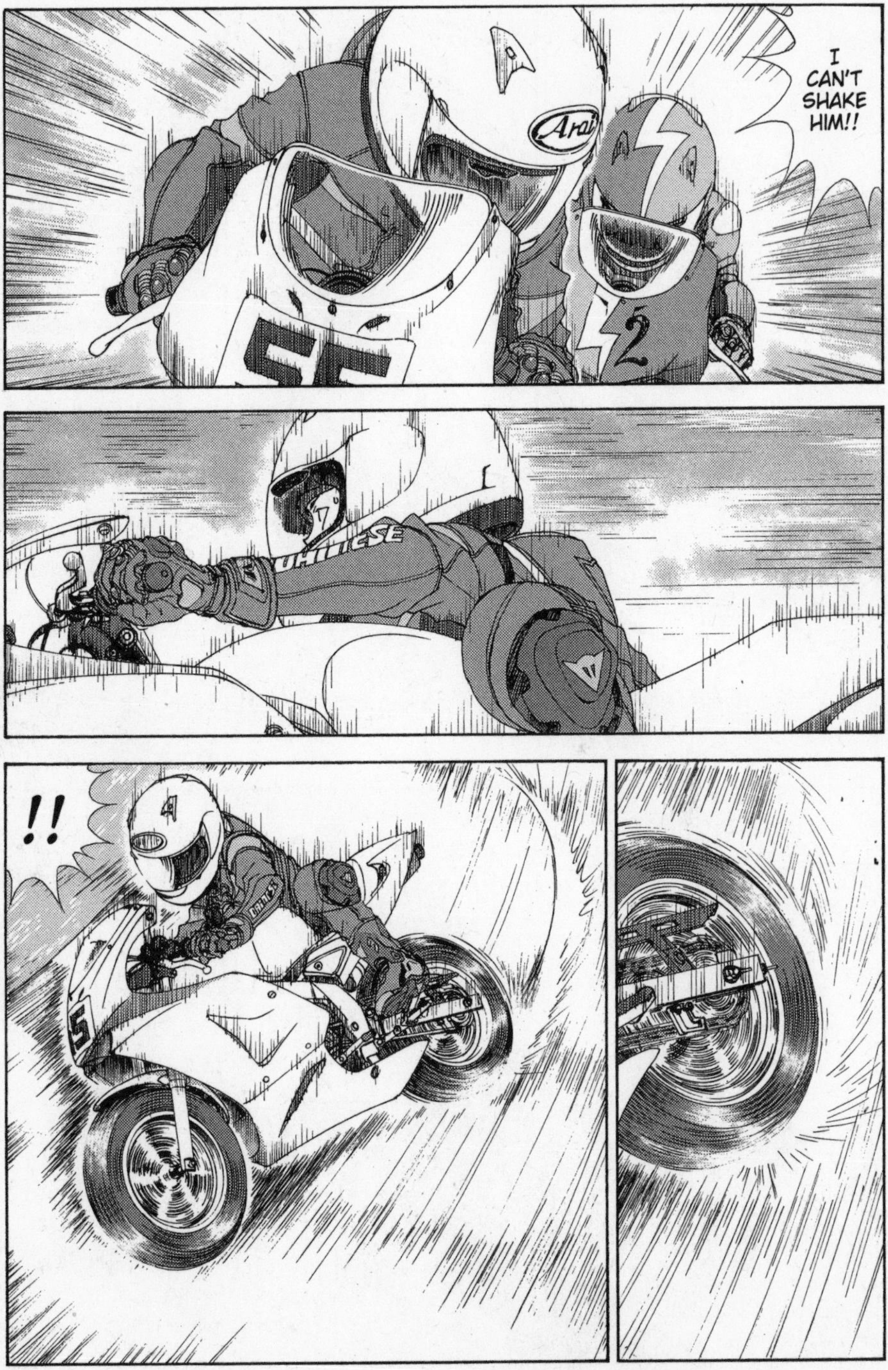
I CAN'T SHAKE HIM!!
!!

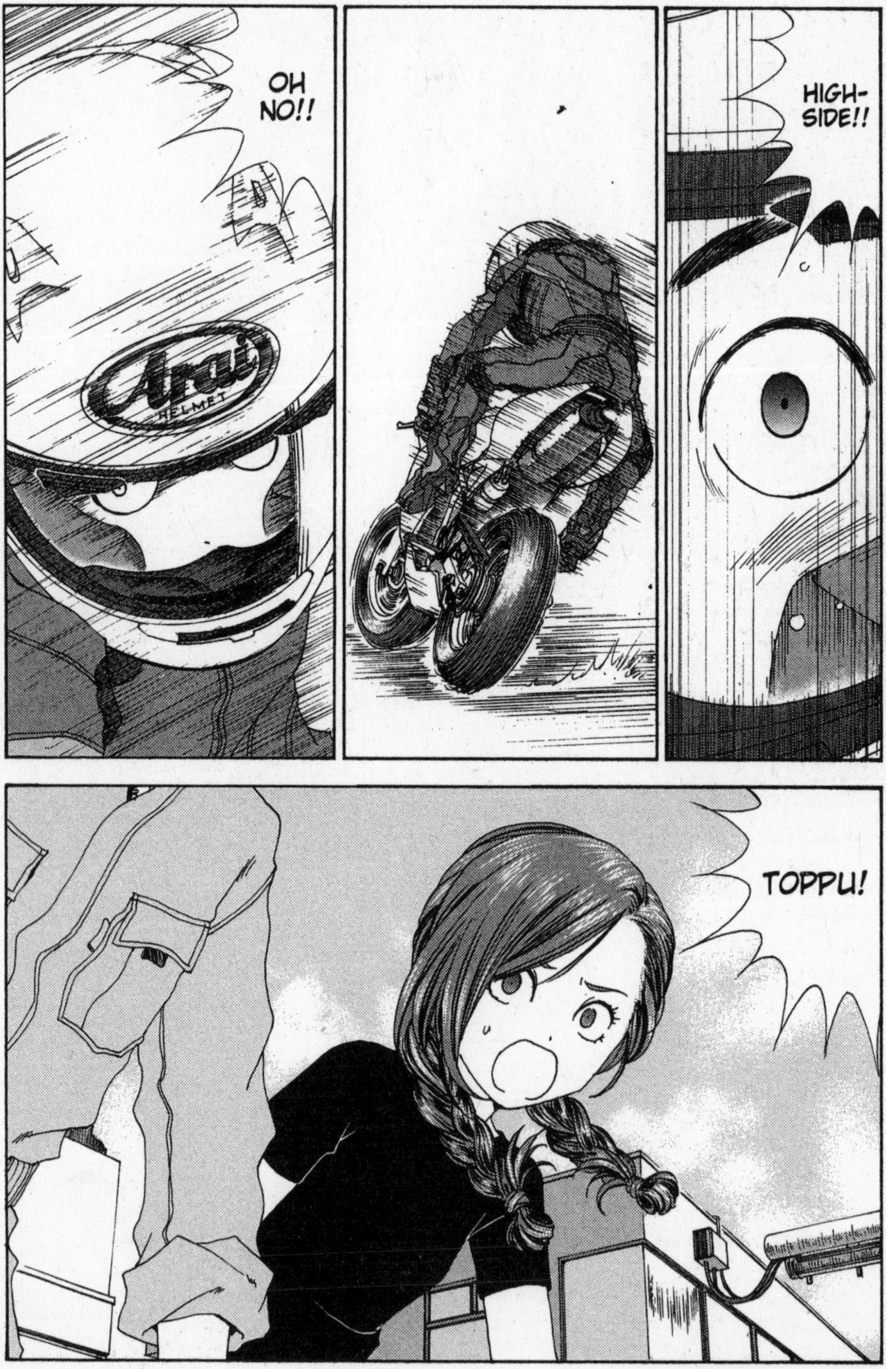
HIGH-SIDE!!
OH NO!!
Arai
HELMET
TOPPU!

Lap 3: end

▶ Glossary 1

Here are some of the motorcycle racing terms that appear in *Toppu GP*.

▶ **HAIRPIN**

A tight, sudden curve in a racetrack.

▶ **GRID**

The arrangement of riders before the start of the race.

▶ **BLIPPING**

Revving an engine by opening the throttle briefly.

▶ **POLE POSITION**

The first position on the grid, given to the racer with the best qualifying time. The rider with this position is said to be "on the pole."

▶ **HIGHSIDE**

With the extreme lean angles involved in cornering, loss of traction is always a risk. Laying the bike down—skidding out and falling all the way over—is known as a "lowside." A highside is the opposite, and occurs when the rear wheel loses, then suddenly regains, traction. This causes the bike to straighten violently towards the outside of the corner. In extreme cases, a highside can throw the rider completely off the motorcycle.

Toppu GP

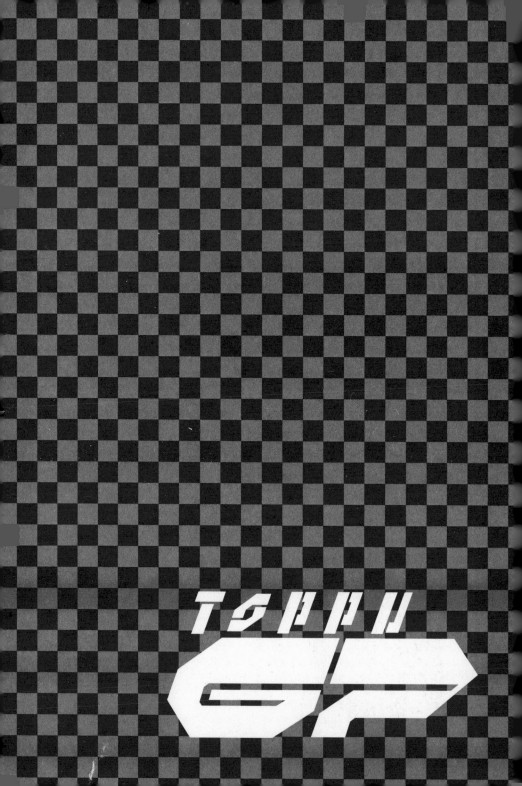

Lap 4:
MEANS AND OBJECTIVES

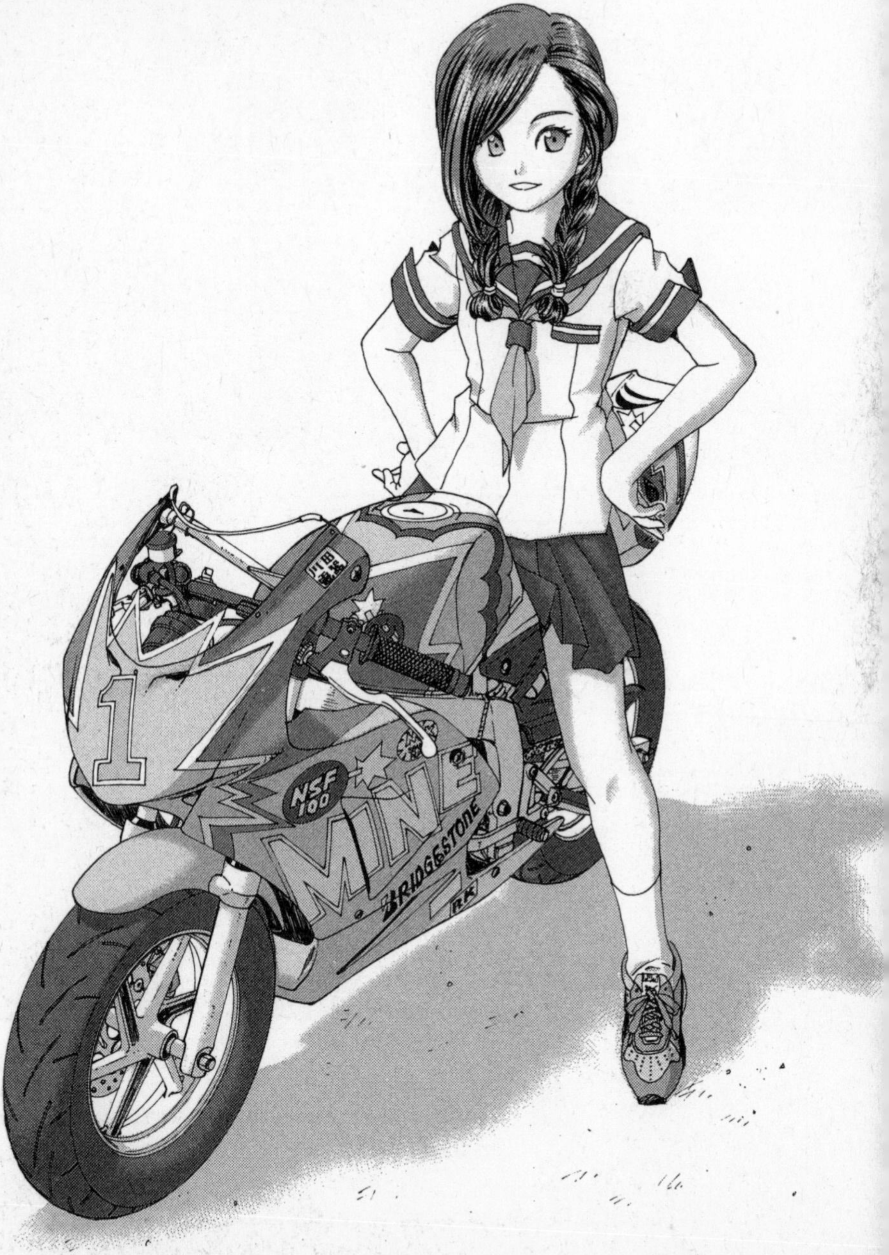
1
NSF 100
MINE
BRIDGESTONE

TOPPU!!

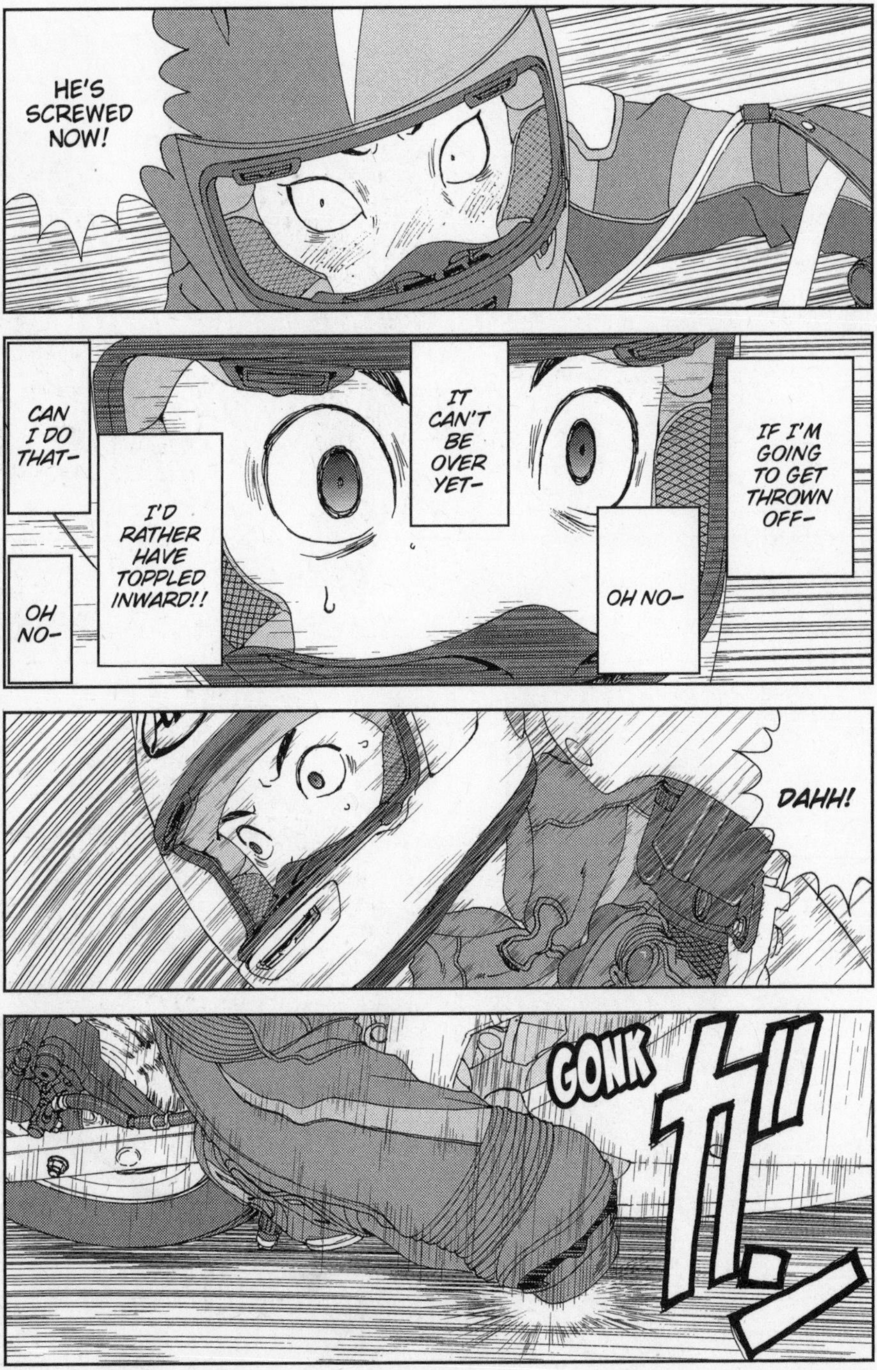
HE'S SCREWED NOW!
IF I'M GOING TO GET THROWN OFF-
OH NO-
IT CAN'T BE OVER YET-
I'D RATHER HAVE TOPPLED INWARD!!
CAN I DO THAT-
OH NO-
DAHH!
GONK

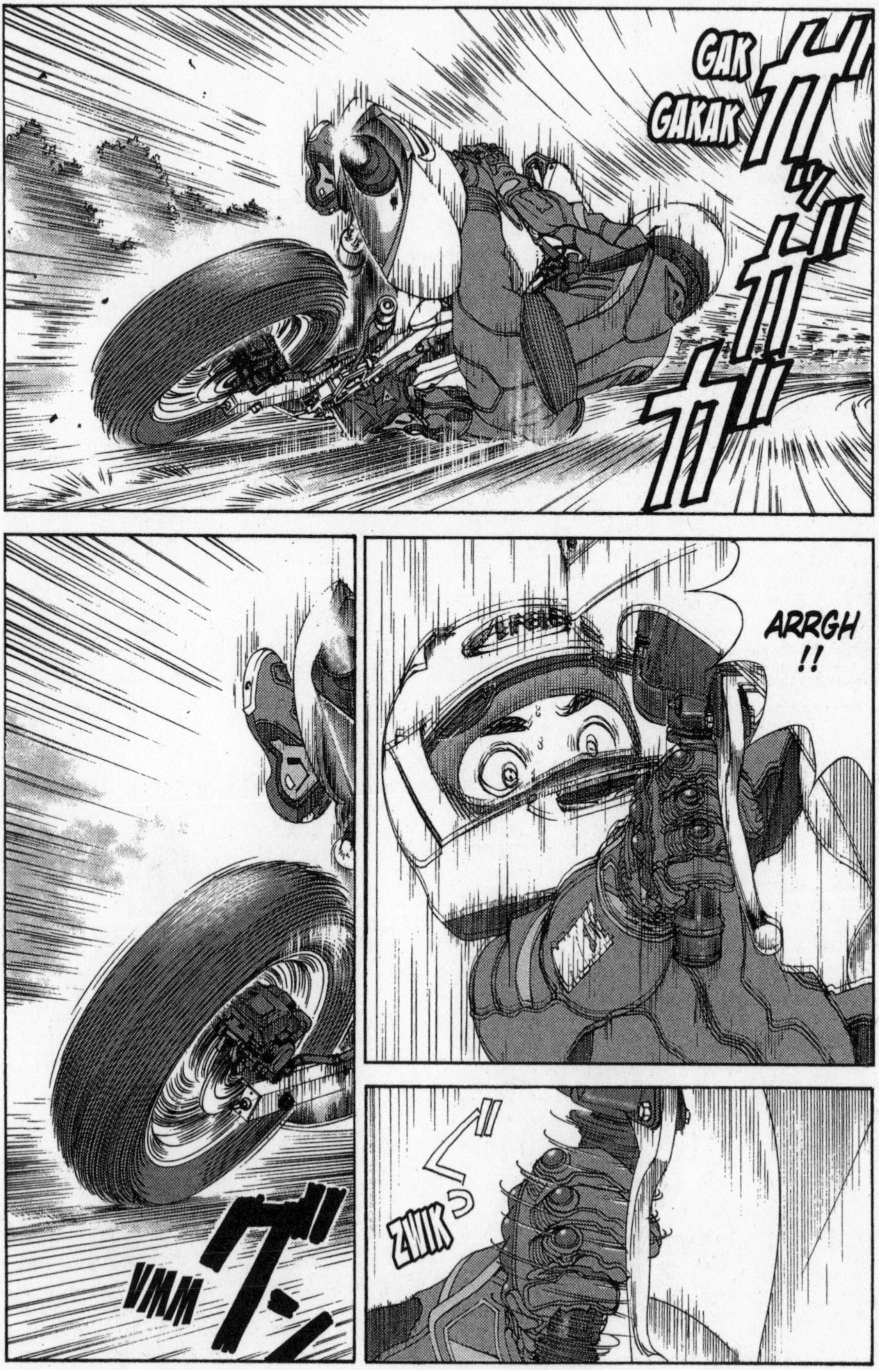
GAK
GAKAK
ARRGH
!!
ZWIK
VMM

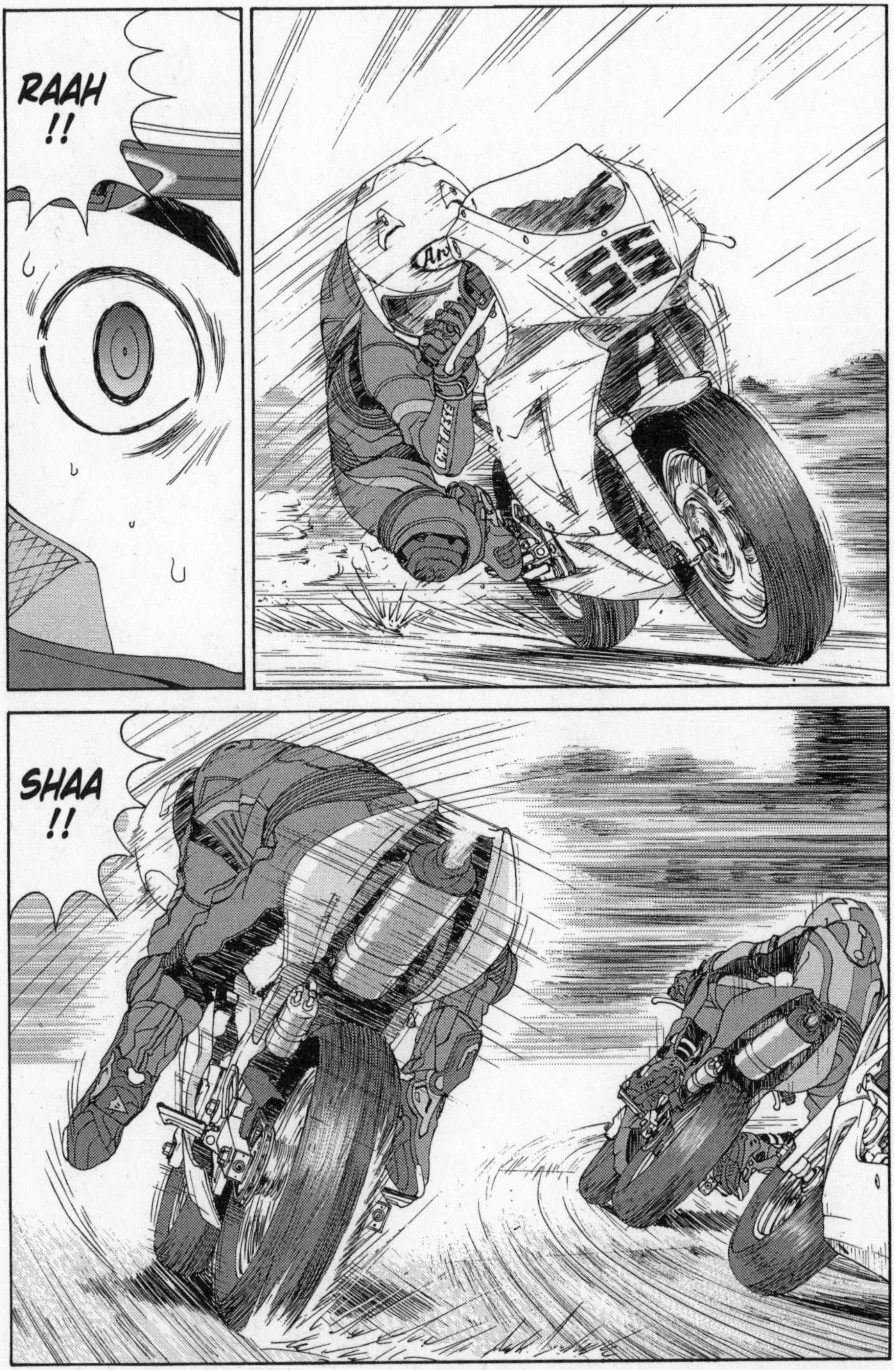
RAAH !!
SHAA !!

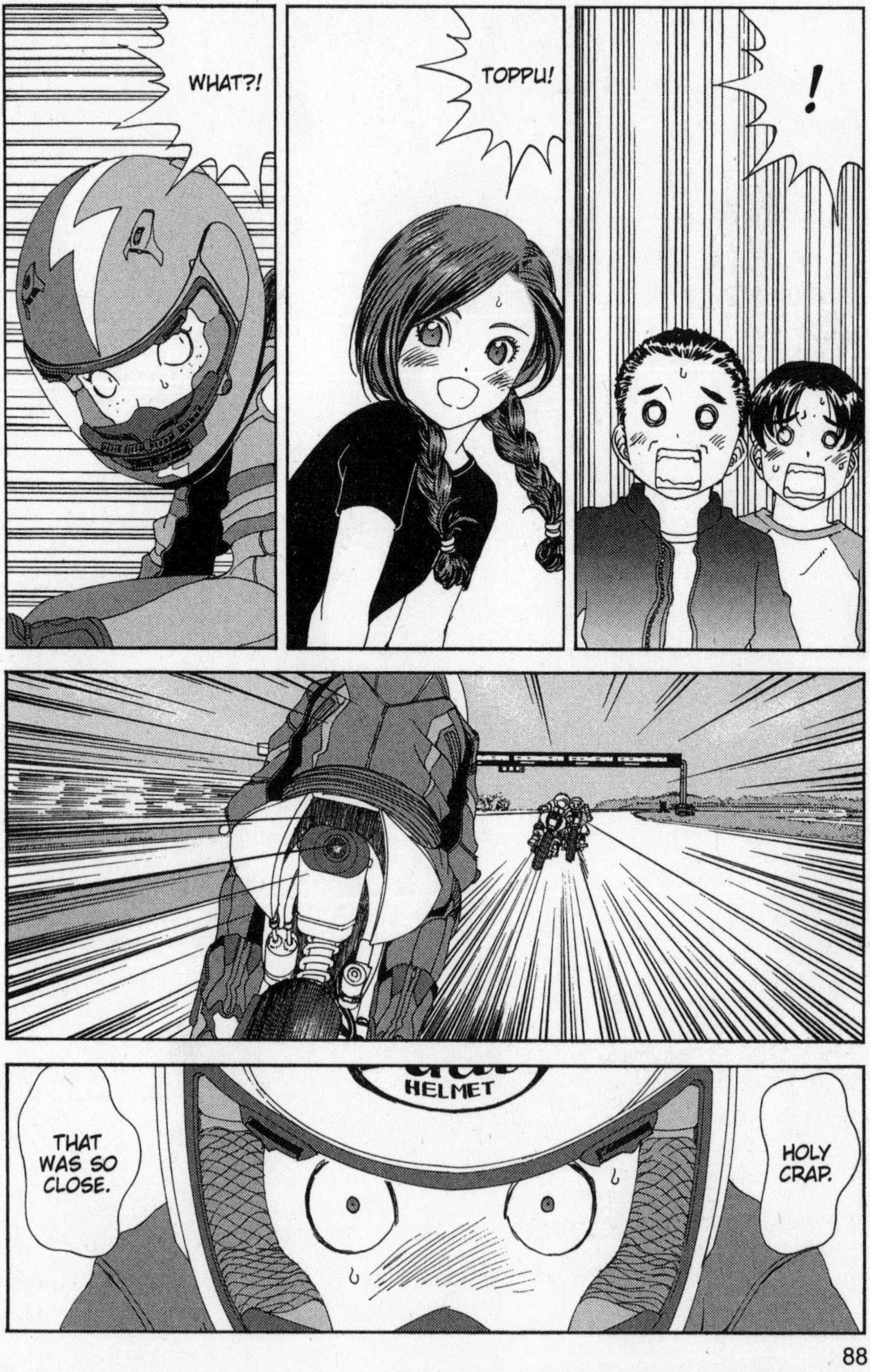
!
TOPPU!
WHAT?!
HOLY CRAP.
HELMET
THAT WAS SO CLOSE.

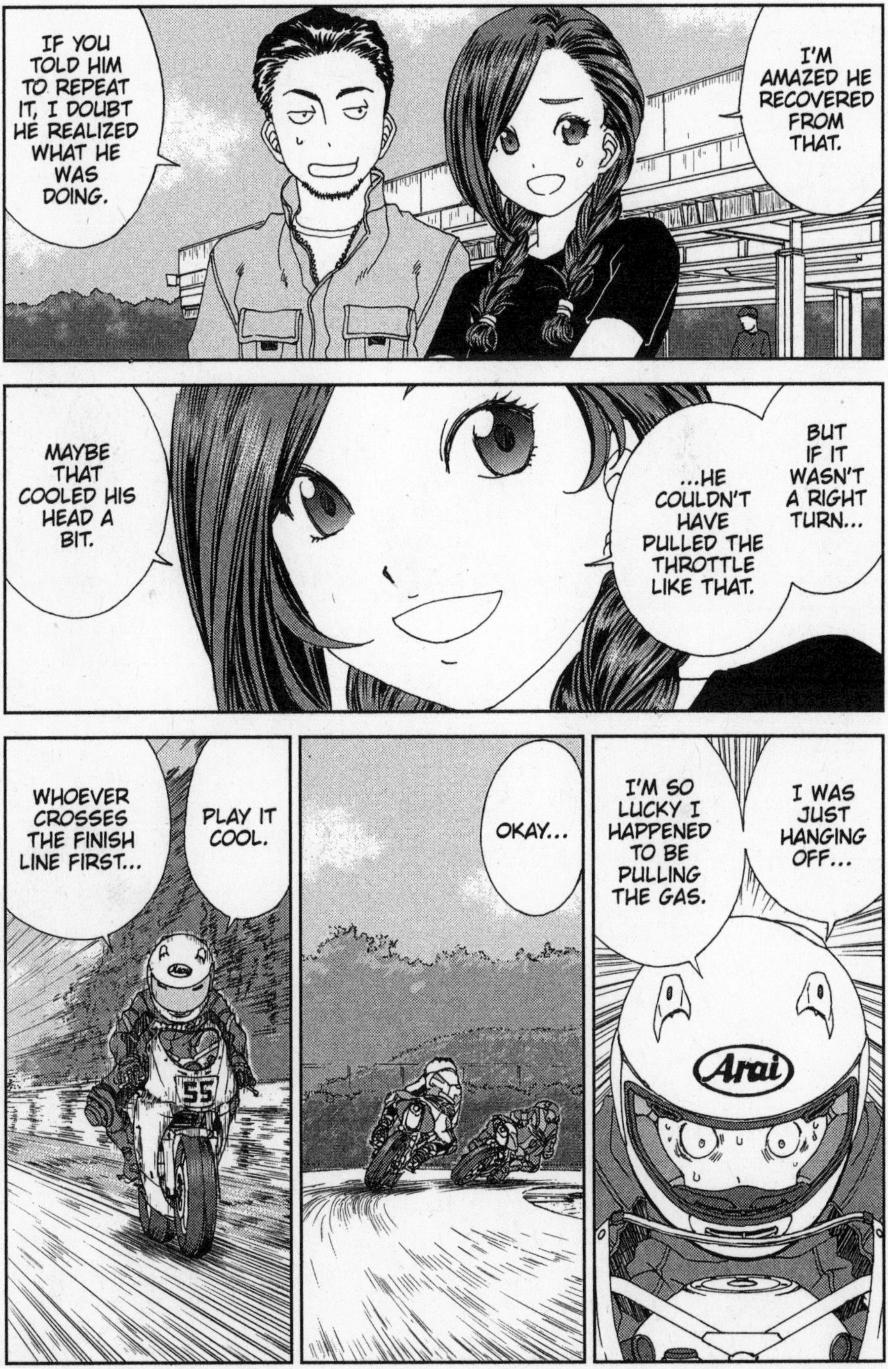
I'M AMAZED HE RECOVERED FROM THAT.
IF YOU TOLD HIM TO REPEAT IT, I DOUBT HE REALIZED WHAT HE WAS DOING.
BUT IF IT WASN'T A RIGHT TURN...
...HE COULDN'T HAVE PULLED THE THROTTLE LIKE THAT.
MAYBE THAT COOLED HIS HEAD A BIT.
I WAS JUST HANGING OFF...
I'M SO LUCKY I HAPPENED TO BE PULLING THE GAS.
Arai
OKAY...
PLAY IT COOL.
WHOEVER CROSSES THE FINISH LINE FIRST...
55

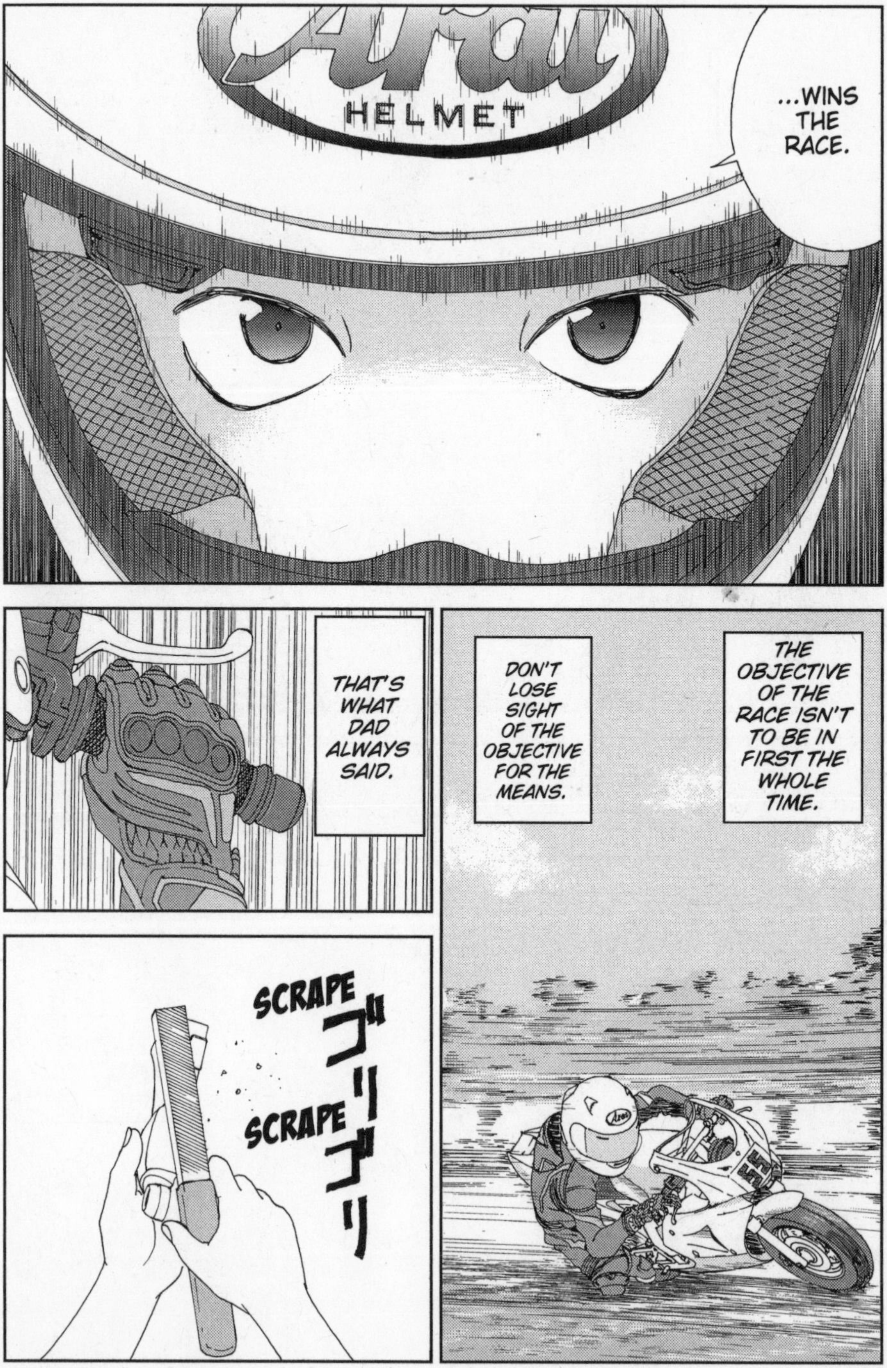
Arai
HELMET
...WINS THE RACE.
THE OBJECTIVE OF THE RACE ISN'T TO BE IN FIRST THE WHOLE TIME.
DON'T LOSE SIGHT OF THE OBJECTIVE FOR THE MEANS.
THAT'S WHAT DAD ALWAYS SAID.
SCRAPE
ゴリ
SCRAPE
ゴリ

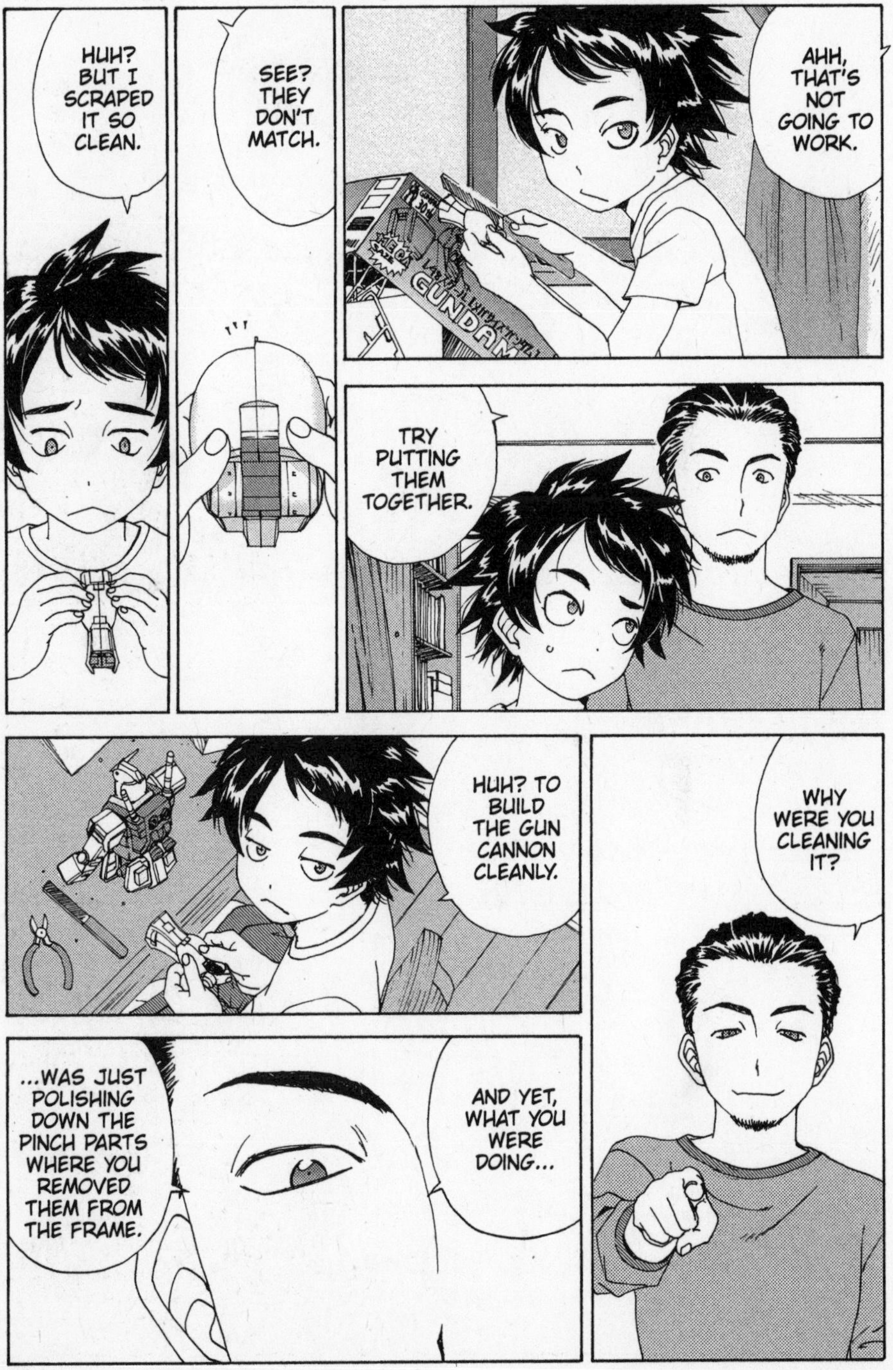
AHH, THAT'S NOT GOING TO WORK.
GUNDAM
TRY PUTTING THEM TOGETHER.
SEE? THEY DON'T MATCH.
HUH? BUT I SCRAPED IT SO CLEAN.
WHY WERE YOU CLEANING IT?
HUH? TO BUILD THE GUN CANNON CLEANLY.
AND YET, WHAT YOU WERE DOING...
...WAS JUST POLISHING DOWN THE PINCH PARTS WHERE YOU REMOVED THEM FROM THE FRAME.

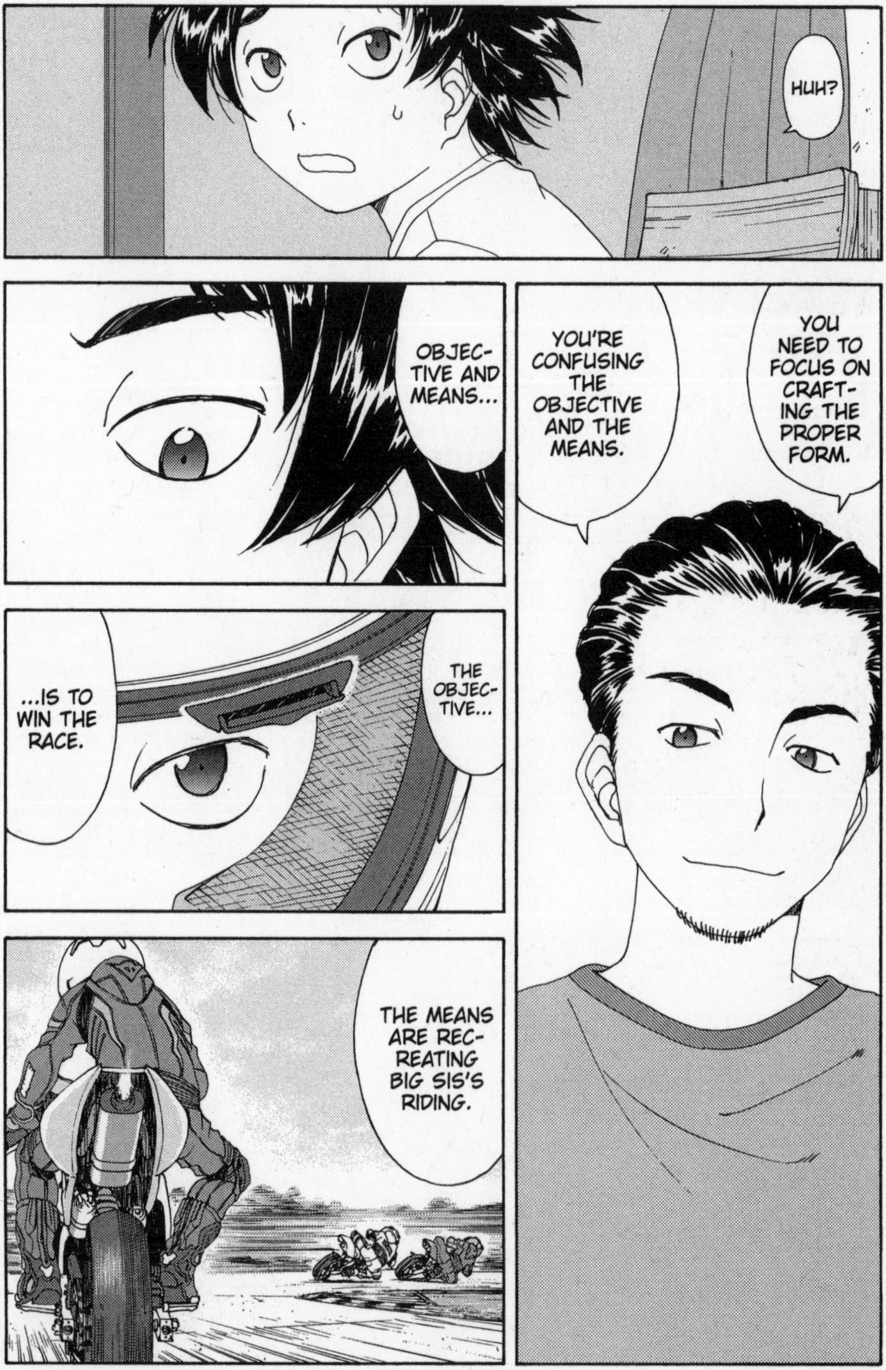
HUH?
YOU NEED TO FOCUS ON CRAFTING THE PROPER FORM.
YOU'RE CONFUSING THE OBJECTIVE AND THE MEANS.
OBJECTIVE AND MEANS...
THE OBJECTIVE...
...IS TO WIN THE RACE.
THE MEANS ARE RECREATING BIG SIS'S RIDING.

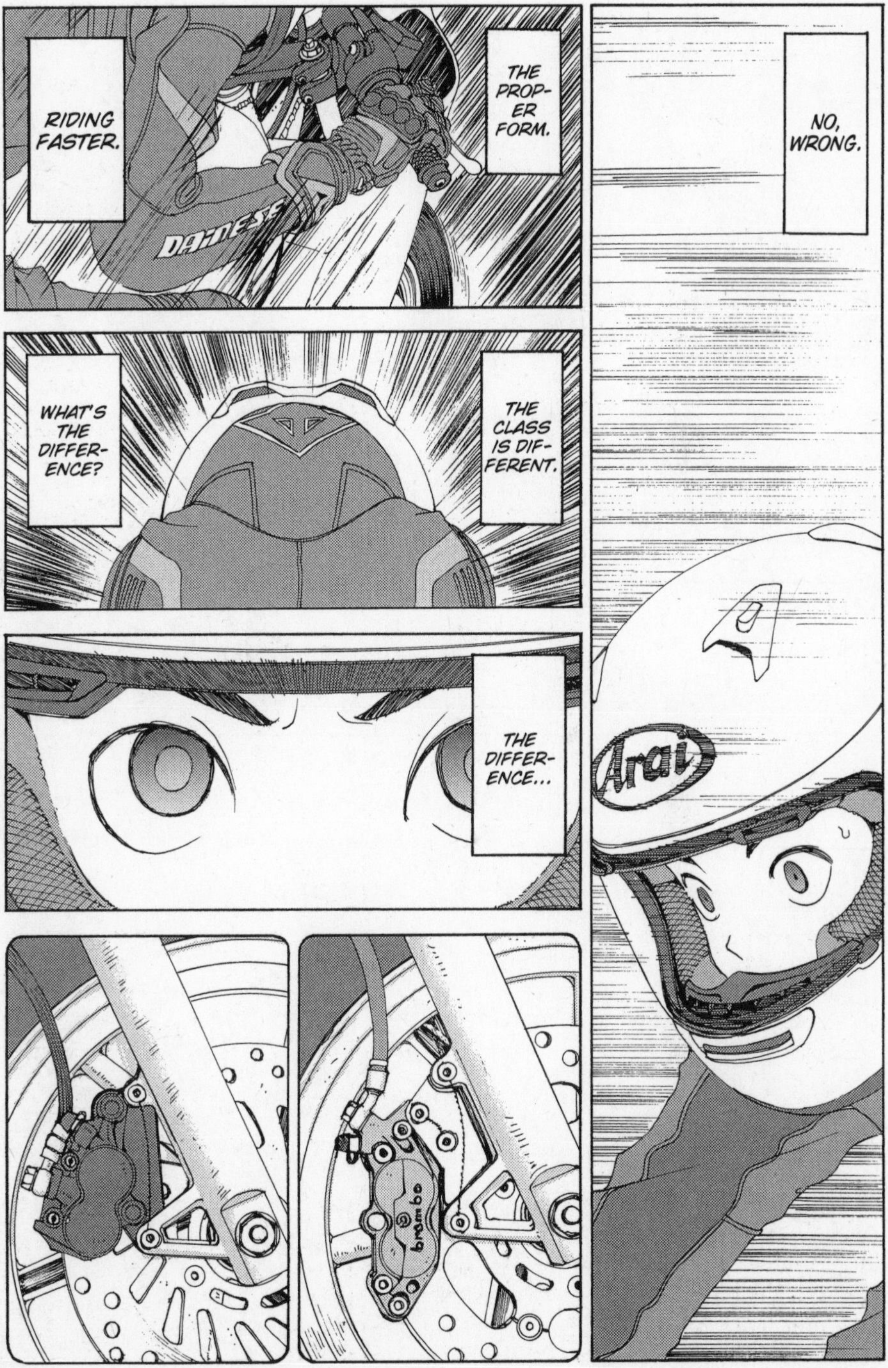
NO, WRONG.
THE PROPER-ER FORM.
RIDING FASTER.
THE CLASS IS DIF-FERENT.
WHAT'S THE DIFFER-ENCE?
THE DIFFER-ENCE...
Arai
Dainese
brembo

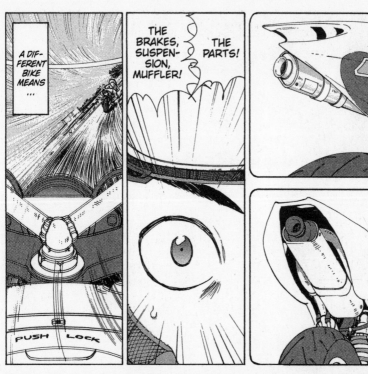

THE PARTS!
THE BRAKES, SUSPENSION, MUFFLER!
A DIFFERENT BIKE MEANS ...
PUSH LOCK
...I CAN'T RIDE IT THE SAME WAY!!

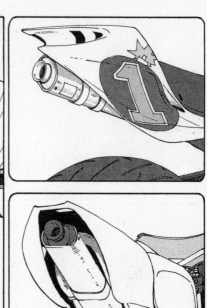

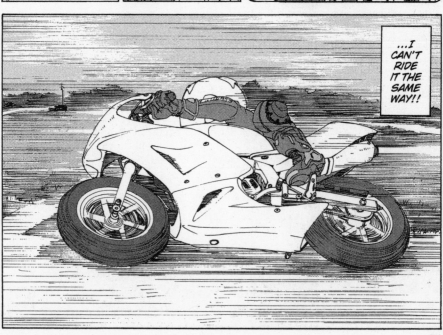

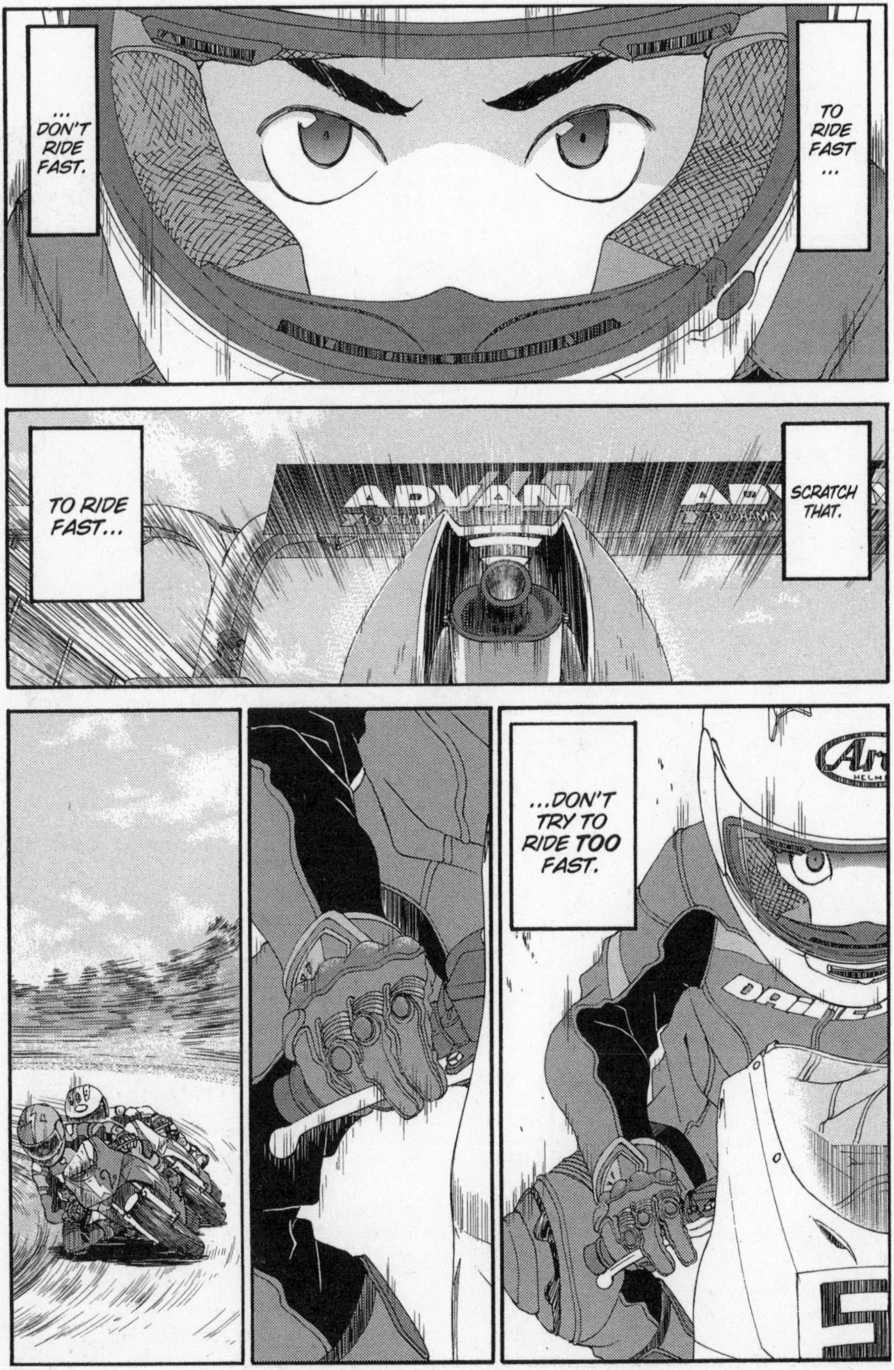
TO RIDE FAST ...
... DON'T RIDE FAST.
SCRATCH THAT.
ADVAN
TO RIDE FAST...
...DON'T TRY TO RIDE **TOO** FAST.

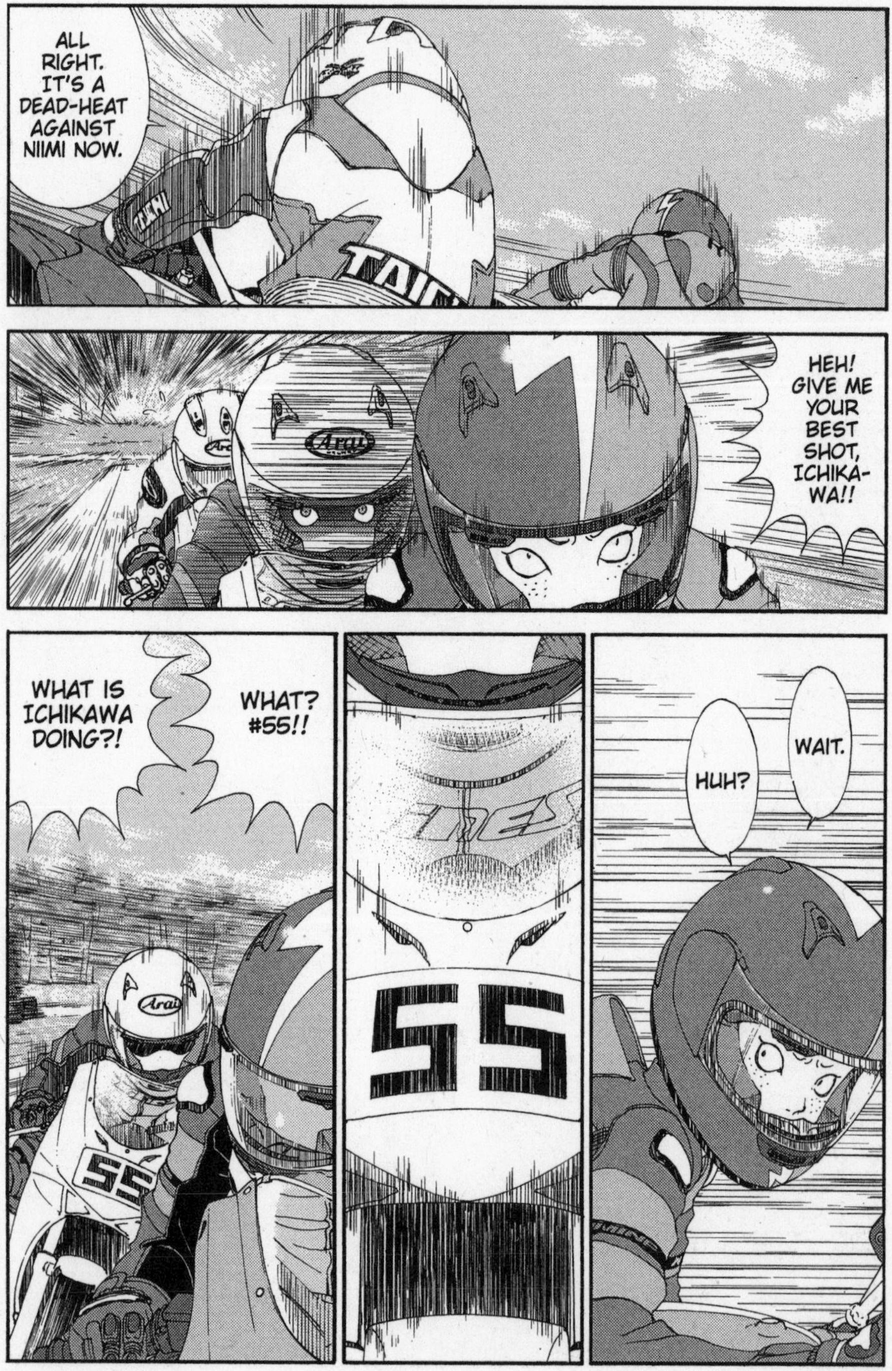
ALL RIGHT. IT'S A DEAD-HEAT AGAINST NIIMI NOW.
HEH! GIVE ME YOUR BEST SHOT, ICHIKA-WA!!
WAIT.
HUH?
WHAT? #55!!
WHAT IS ICHIKAWA DOING?!

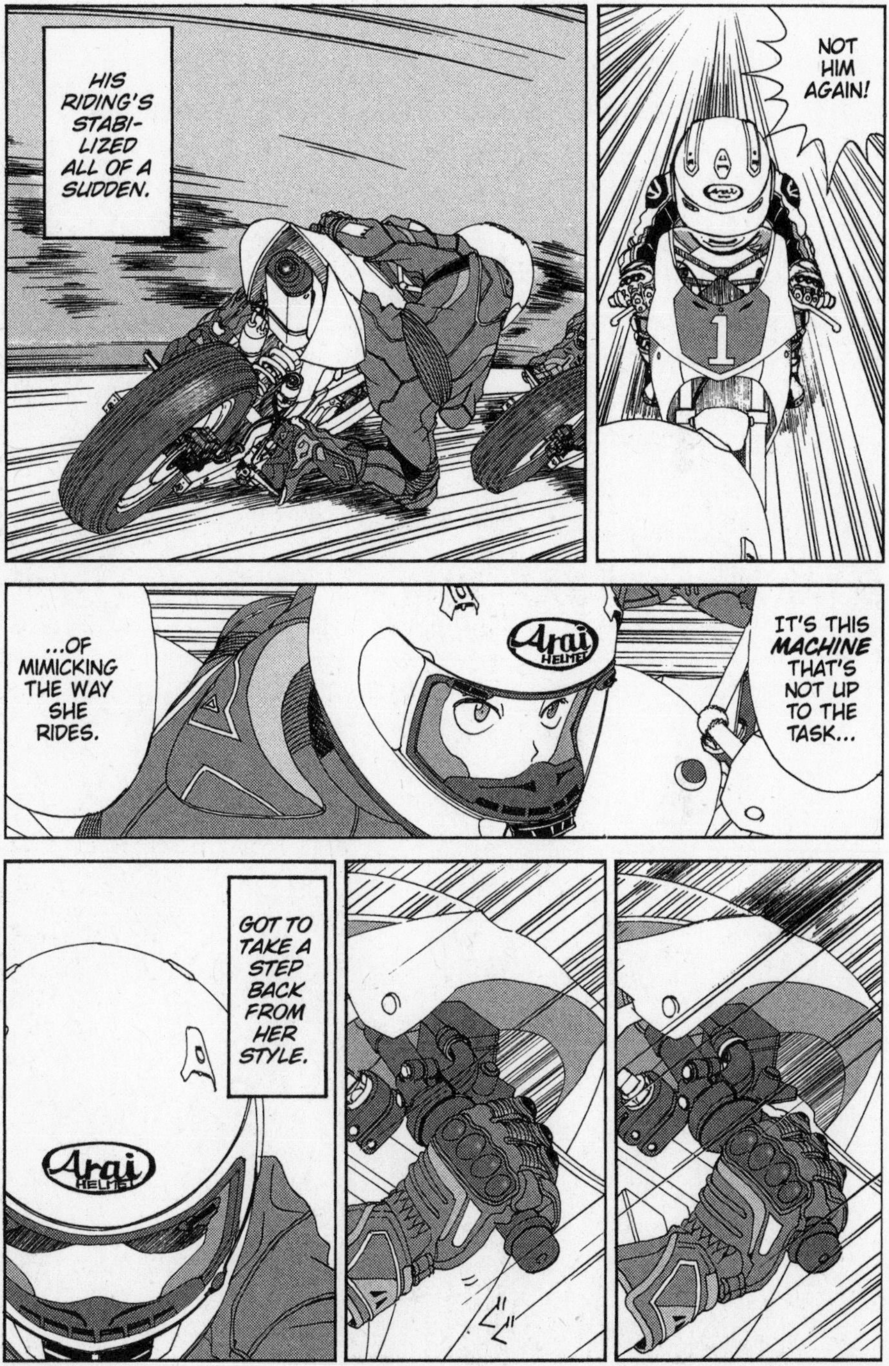
NOT HIM AGAIN!
HIS RIDING'S STABI-LIZED ALL OF A SUDDEN.
Arai HELMET
IT'S THIS MACHINE THAT'S NOT UP TO THE TASK...
...OF MIMICKING THE WAY SHE RIDES.
GOT TO TAKE A STEP BACK FROM HER STYLE.
Arai HELMET

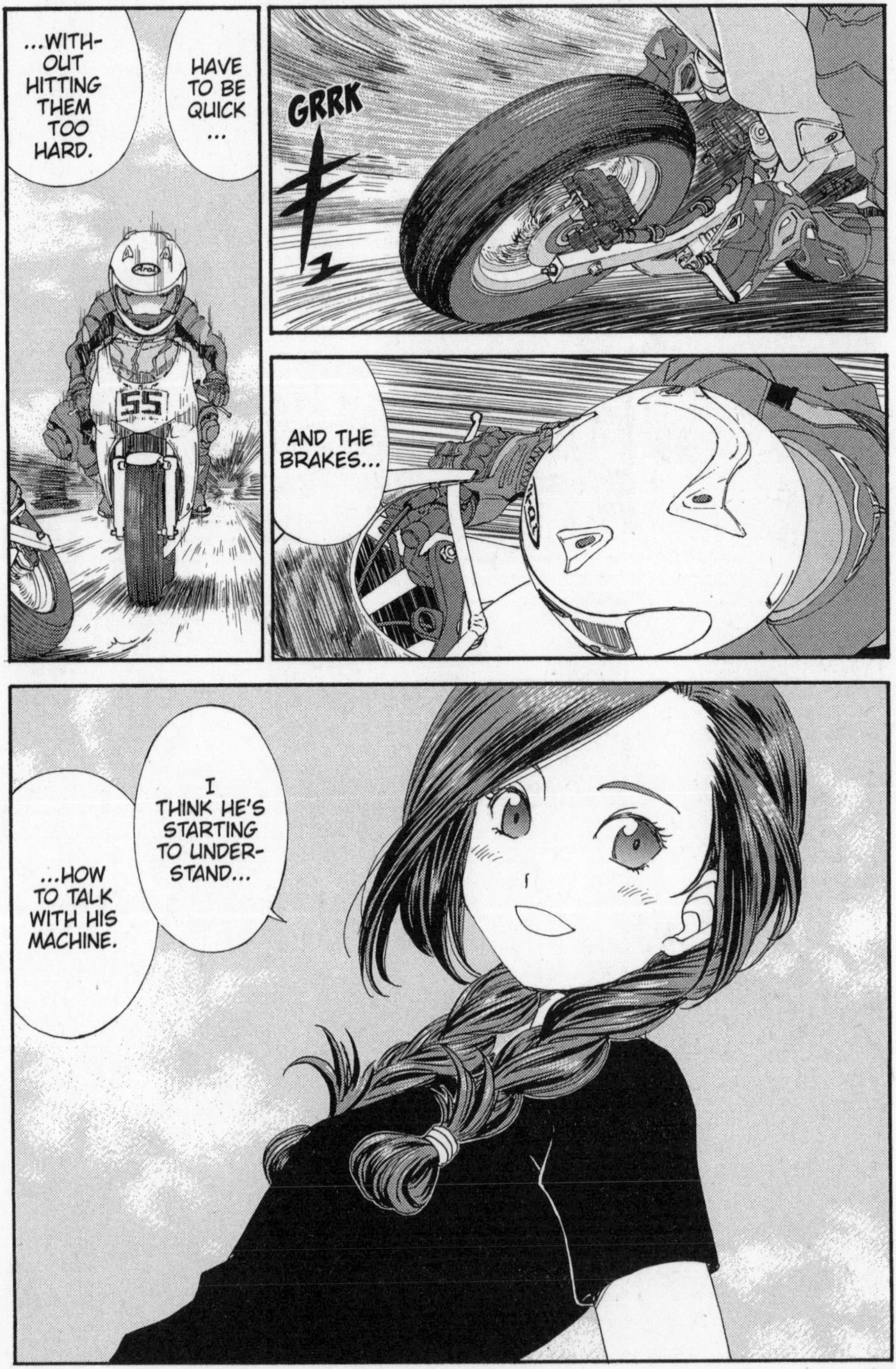
GRRK
AND THE BRAKES...
HAVE TO BE QUICK ...
...WITH-OUT HITTING THEM TOO HARD.
I THINK HE'S STARTING TO UNDER-STAND...
...HOW TO TALK WITH HIS MACHINE.

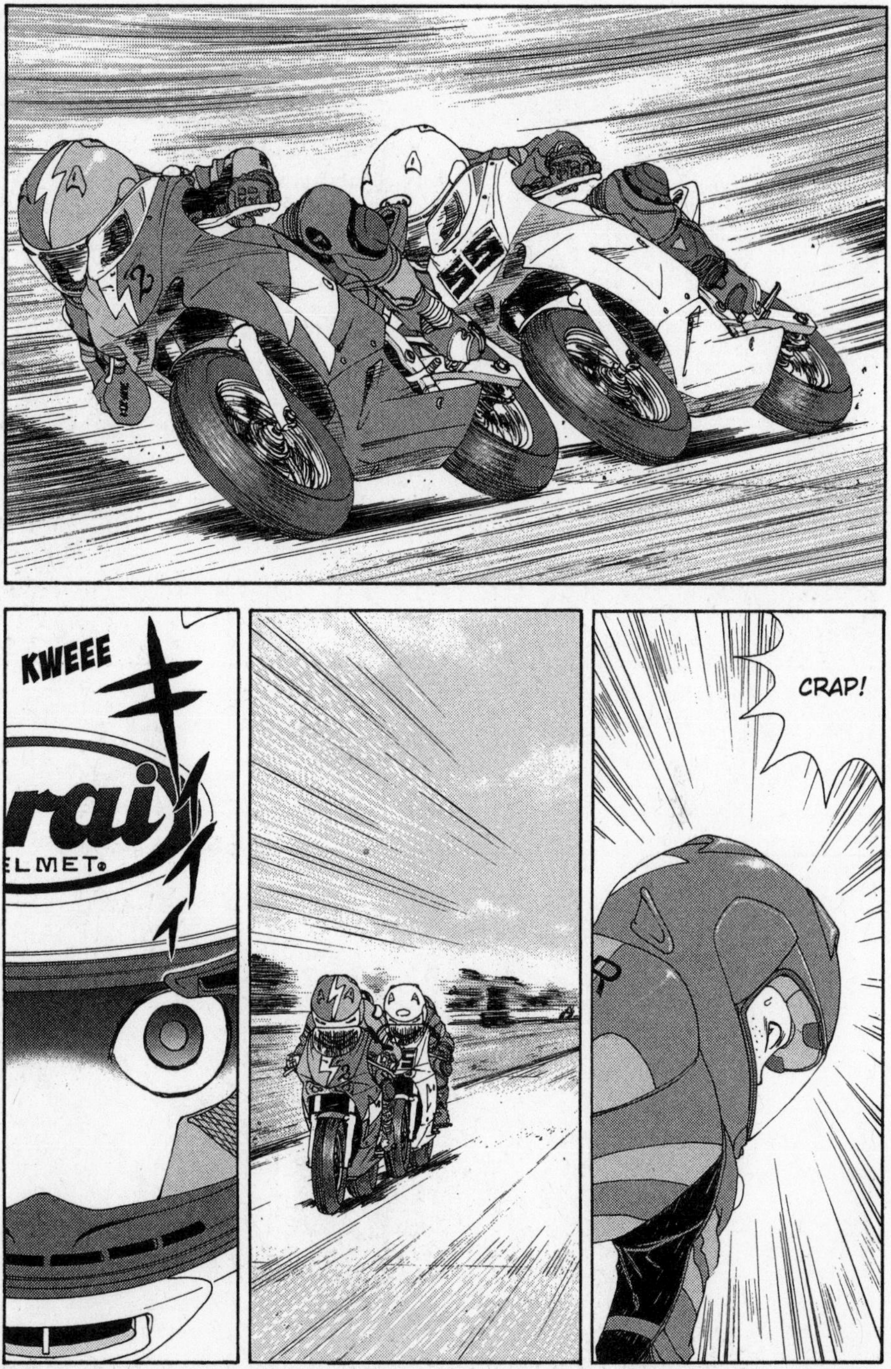
CRAP!
KWEEE

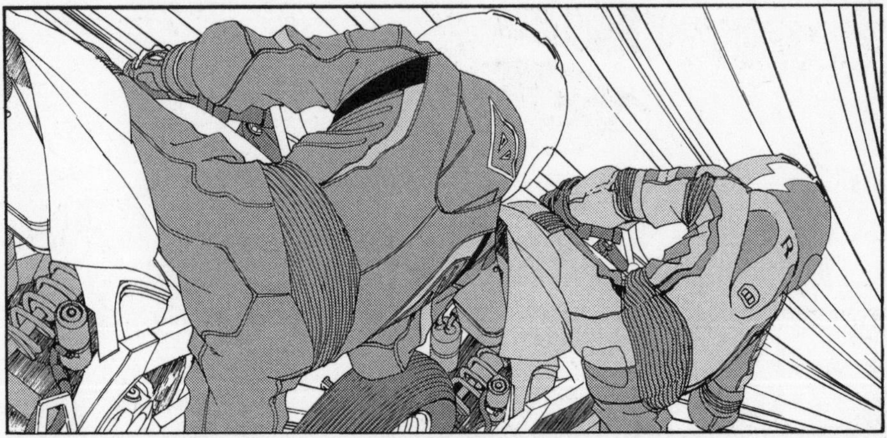
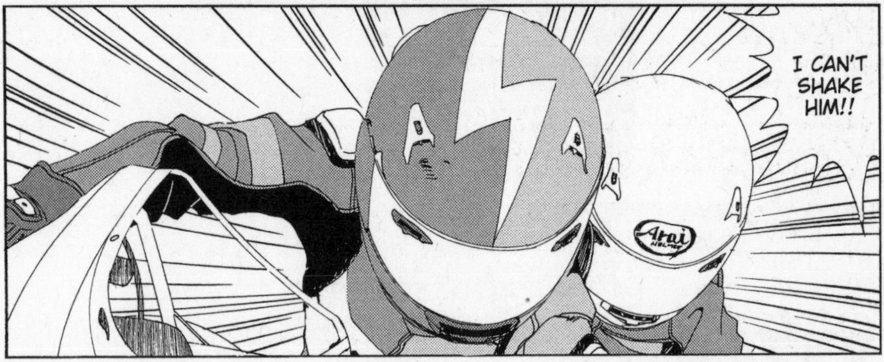
I CAN'T SHAKE HIM!!
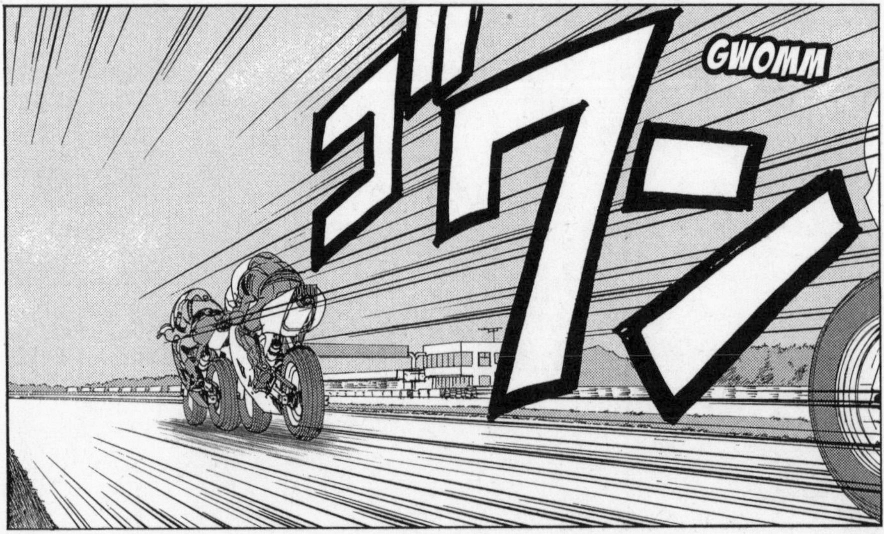
GWOMM

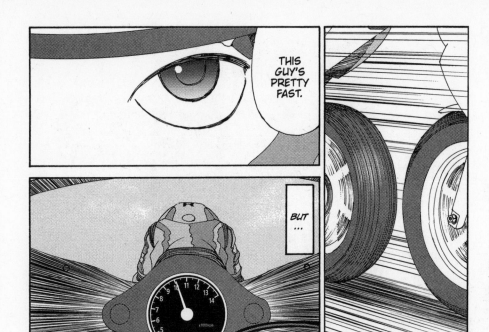

THIS GUY'S PRETTY FAST.

BUT ...

I KNOW I'M FASTER!!

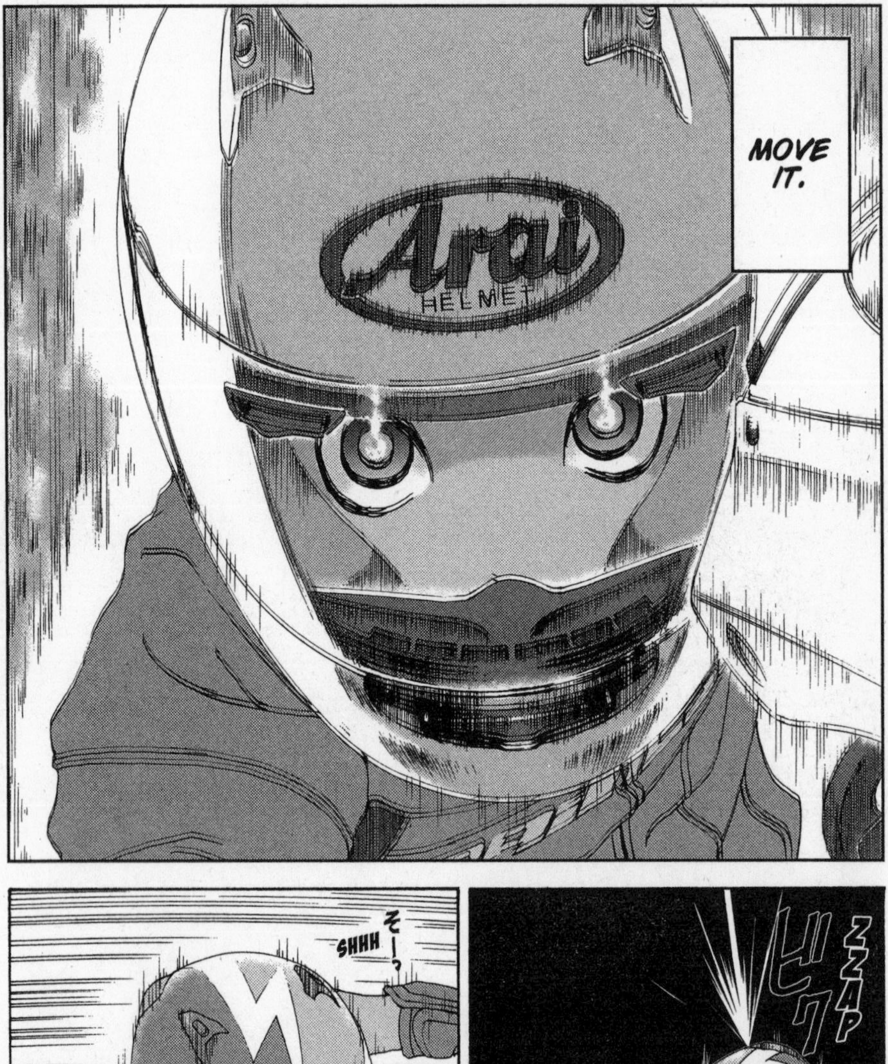
MOVE IT.
Arai
HELMET

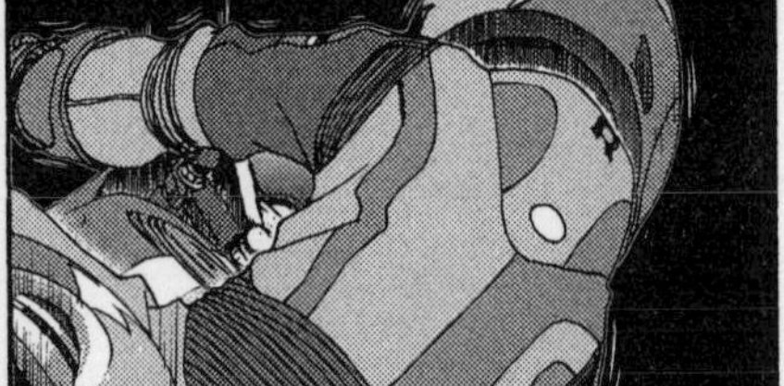
ビク
ZZAP

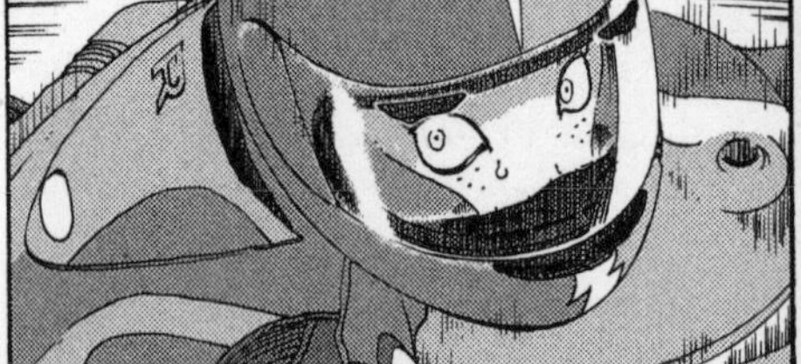
そーっ
SHHH

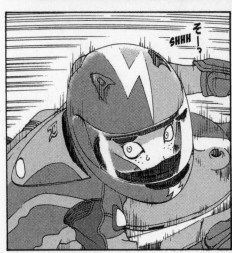

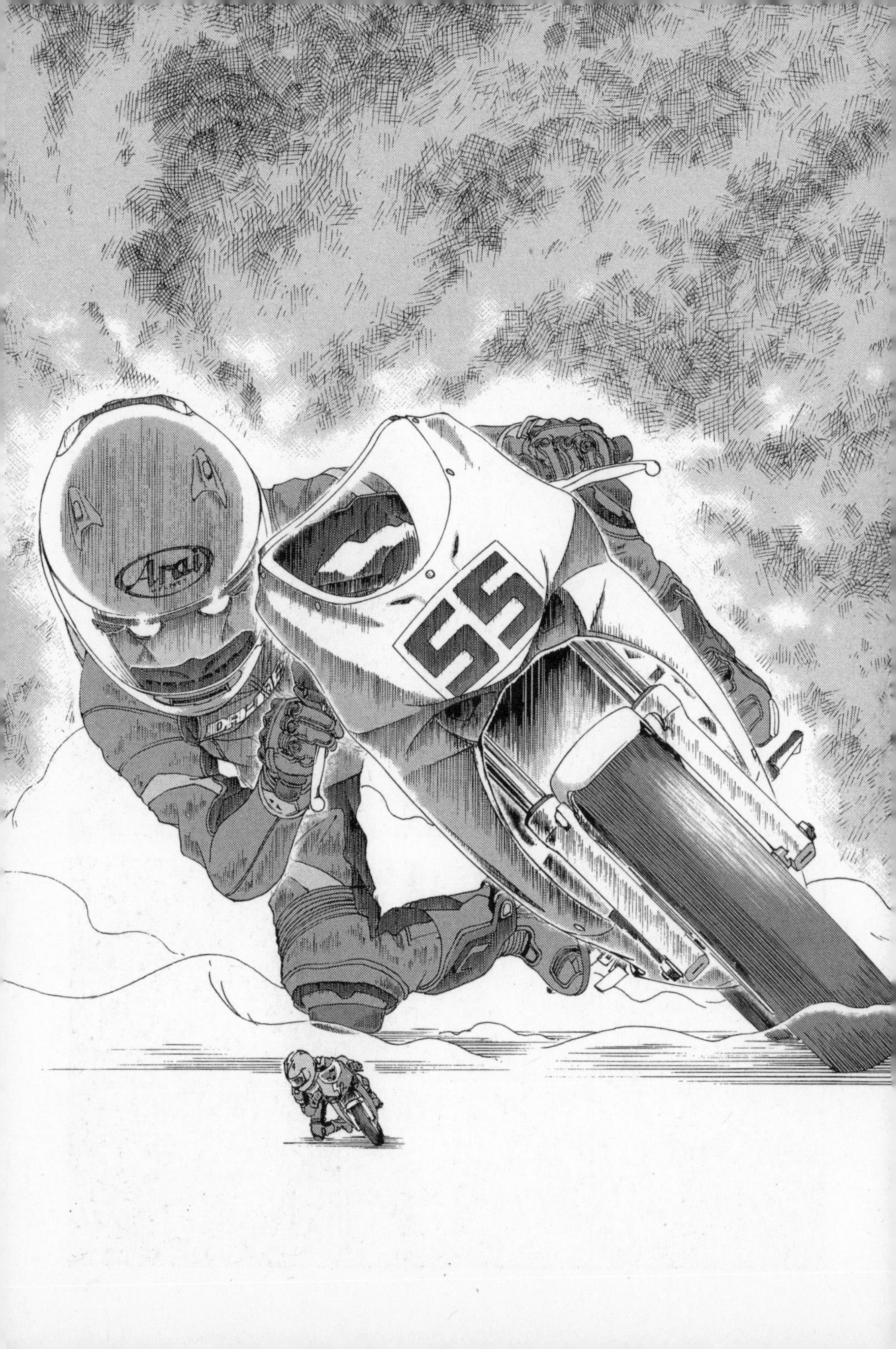
Arai
55

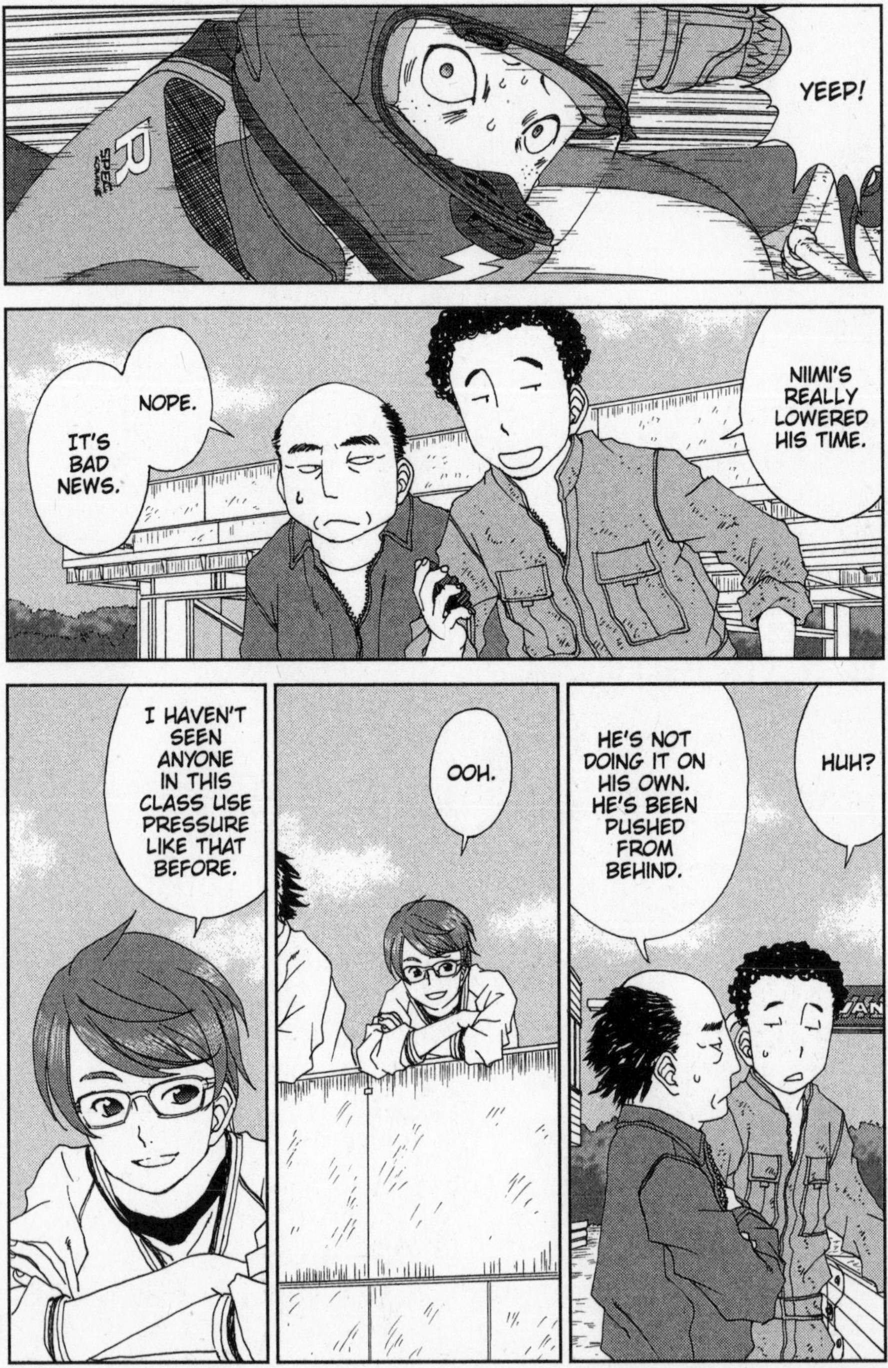
YEEP!
NIIMI'S REALLY LOWERED HIS TIME.
NOPE. IT'S BAD NEWS.
HUH?
HE'S NOT DOING IT ON HIS OWN. HE'S BEEN PUSHED FROM BEHIND.
OOH.
I HAVEN'T SEEN ANYONE IN THIS CLASS USE PRESSURE LIKE THAT BEFORE.

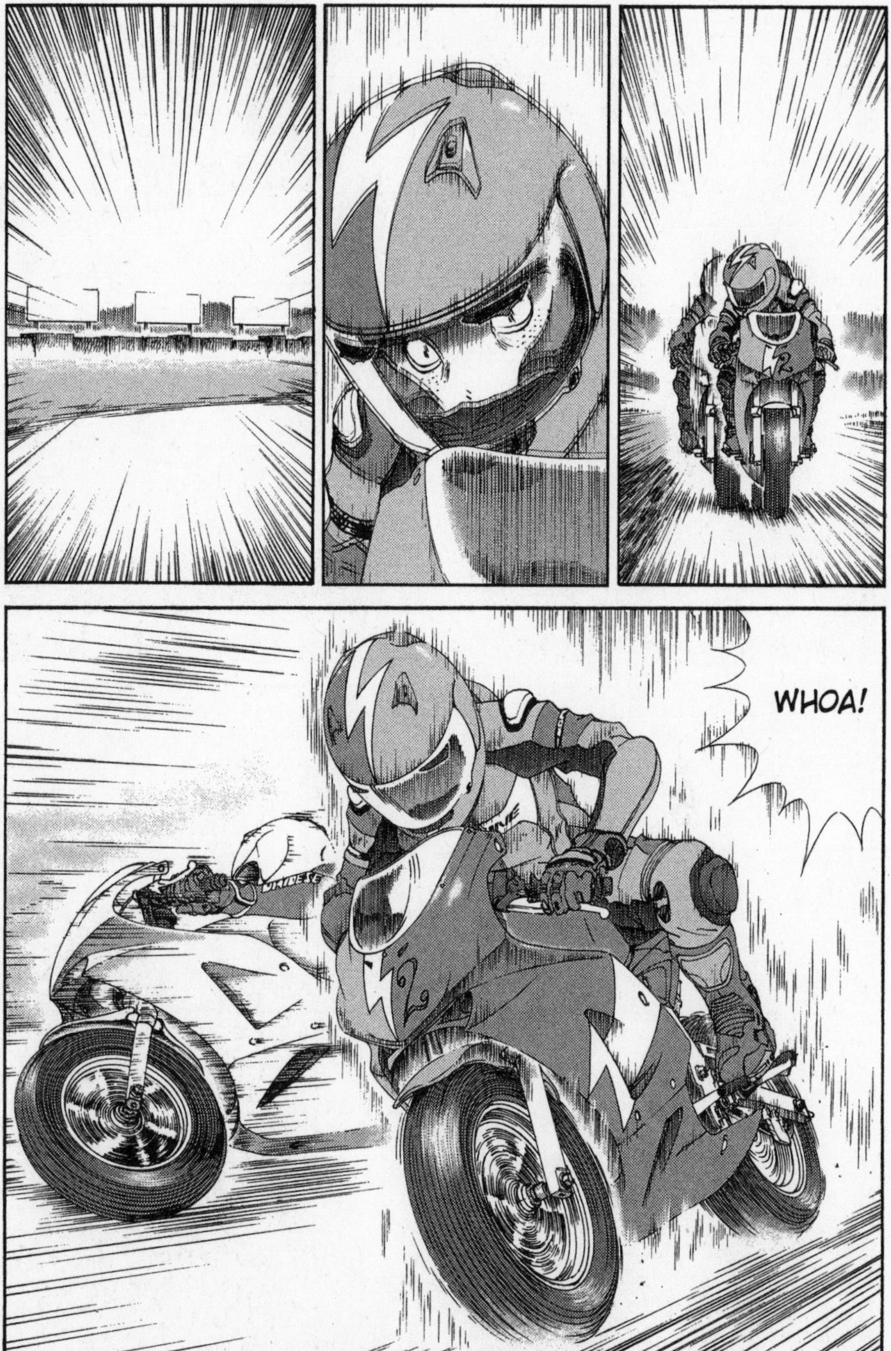
WHOA!

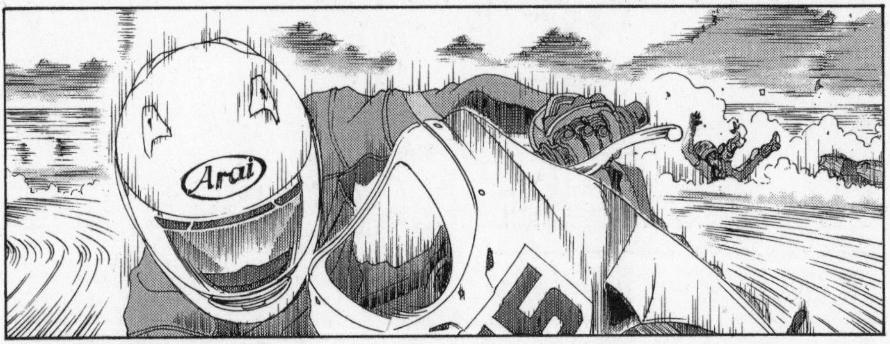

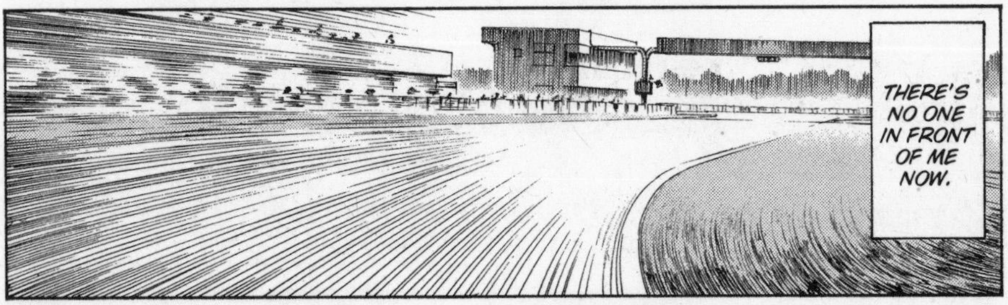
THERE'S NO ONE IN FRONT OF ME NOW.

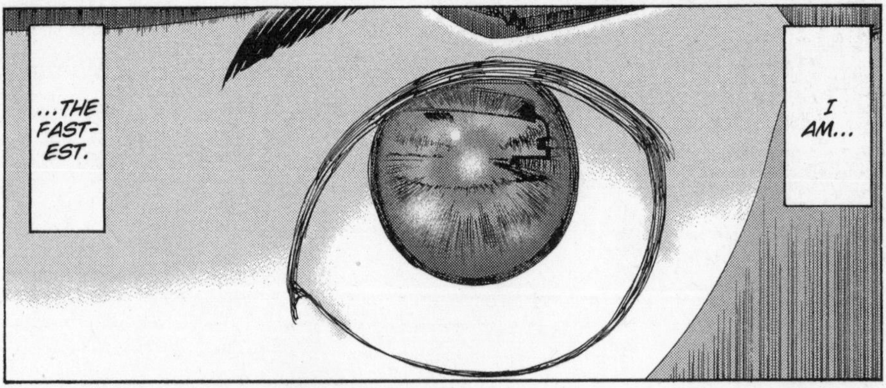
I AM...
...THE FAST-EST.

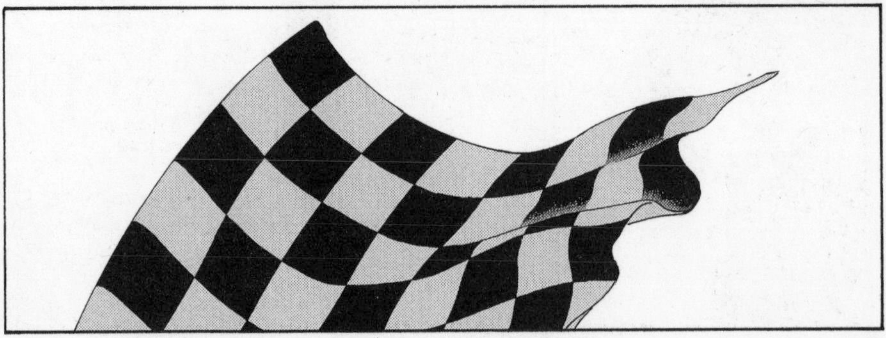

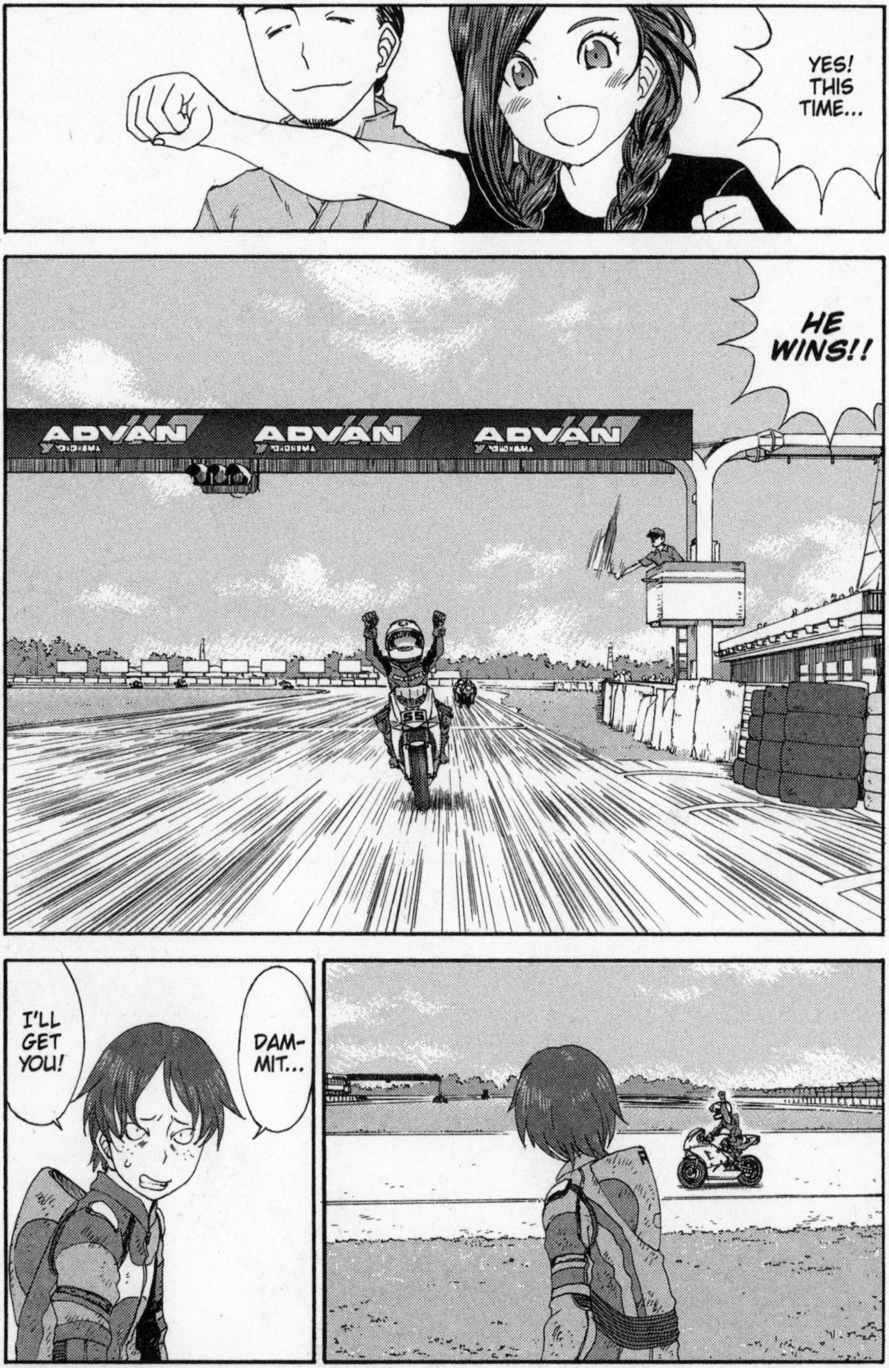
YES! THIS TIME...
HE WINS!!
DAM-MIT...
I'LL GET YOU!

Lap 4: end

TOPPU
GP

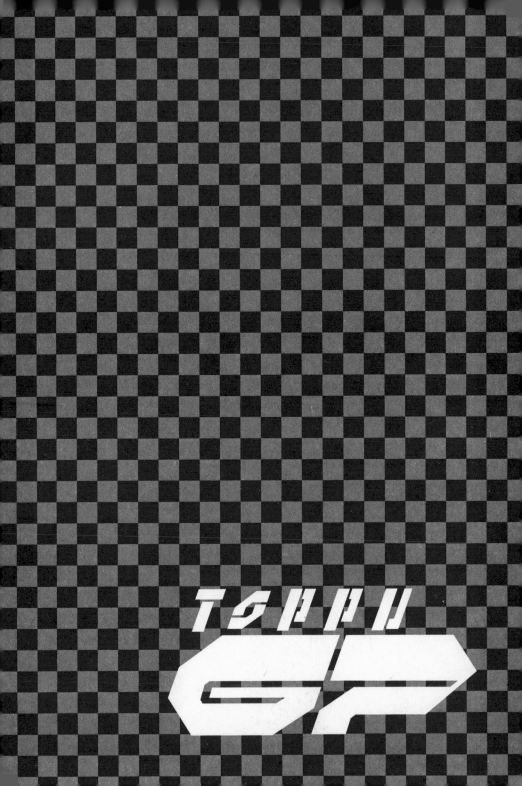

Lap 5:
WEIGHTED

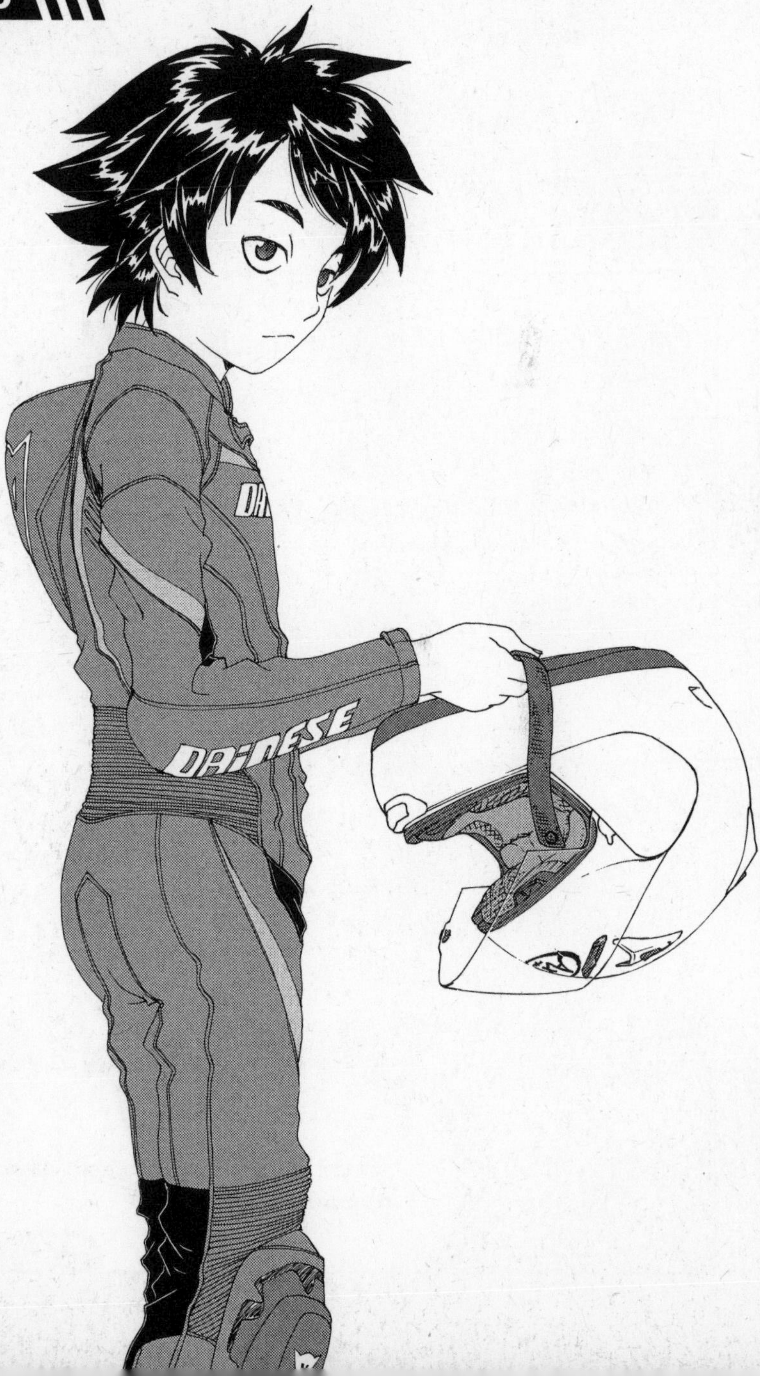

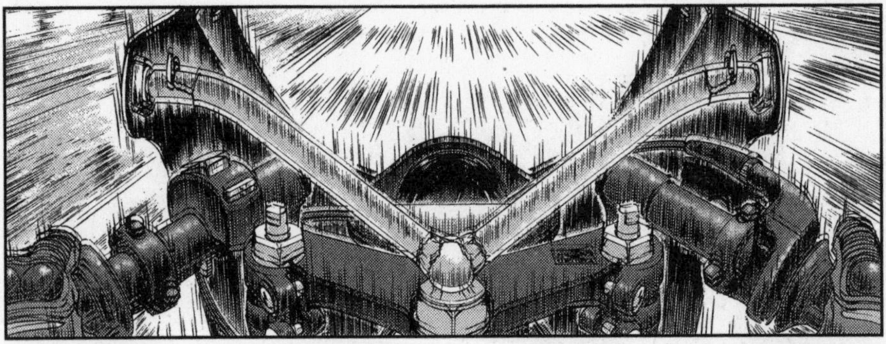

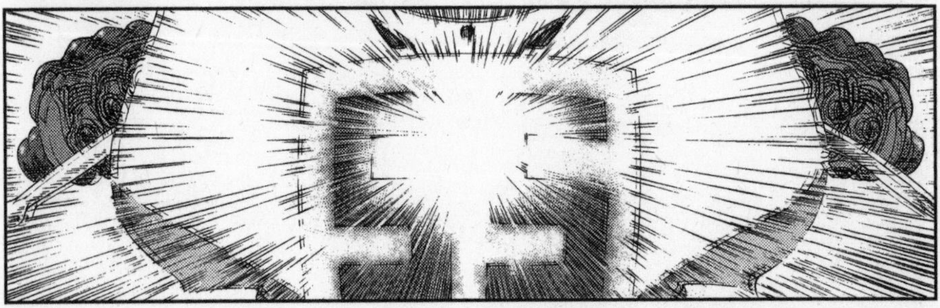
55

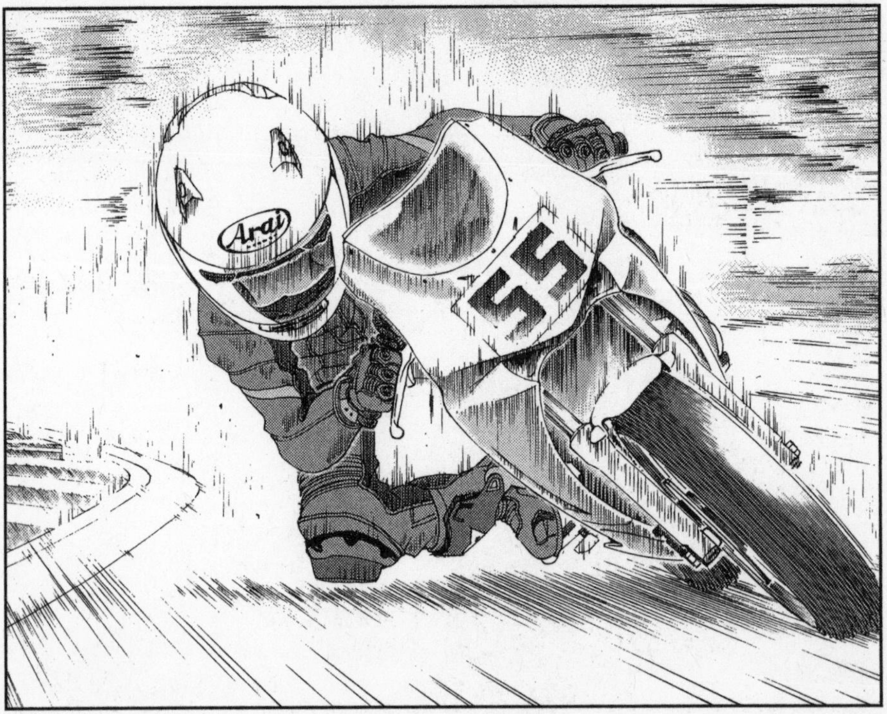
Arai
55

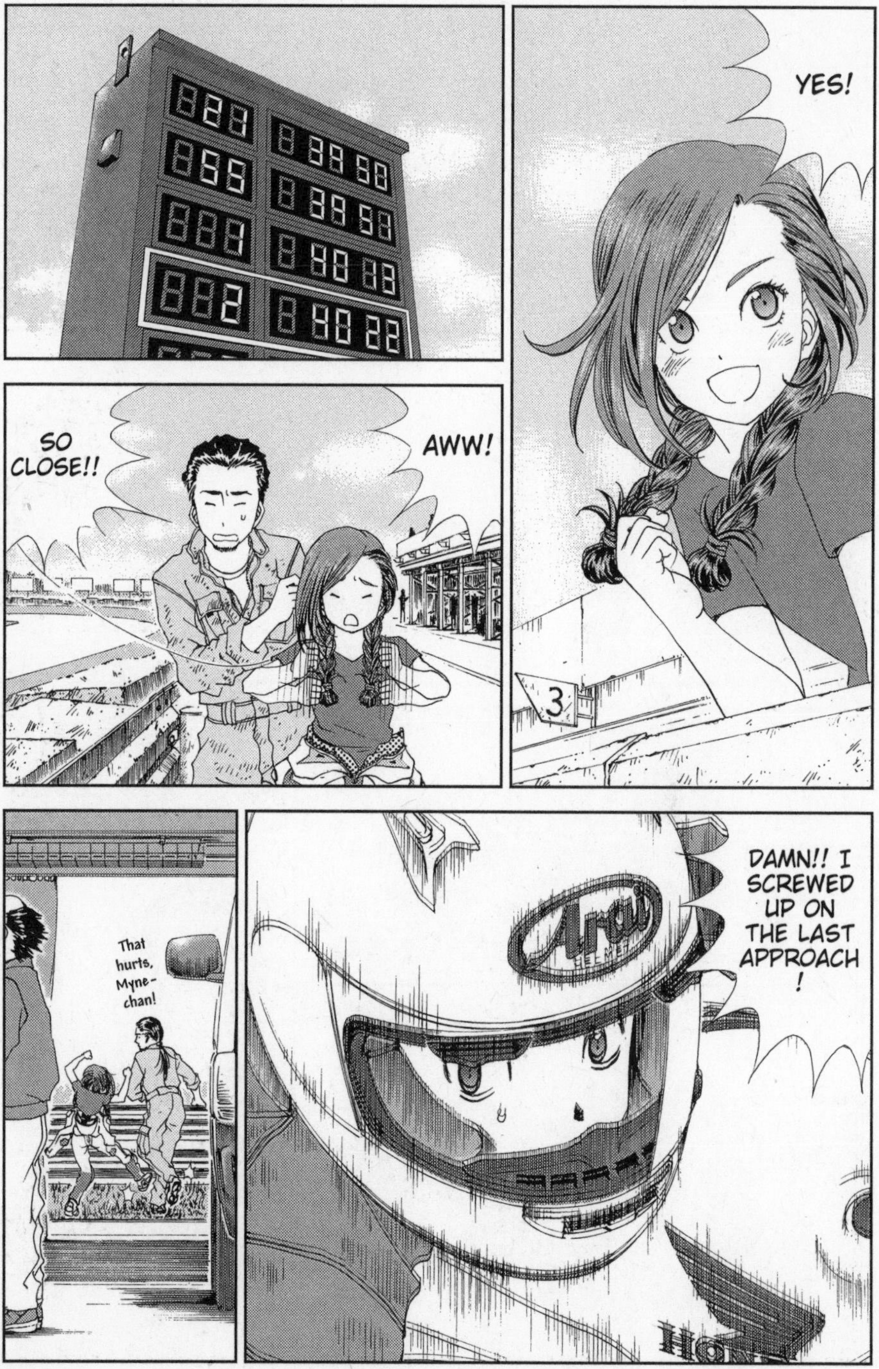
YES!
AWW!
SO CLOSE!!
DAMN!! I SCREWED UP ON THE LAST APPROACH!
That hurts, Myne-chan!

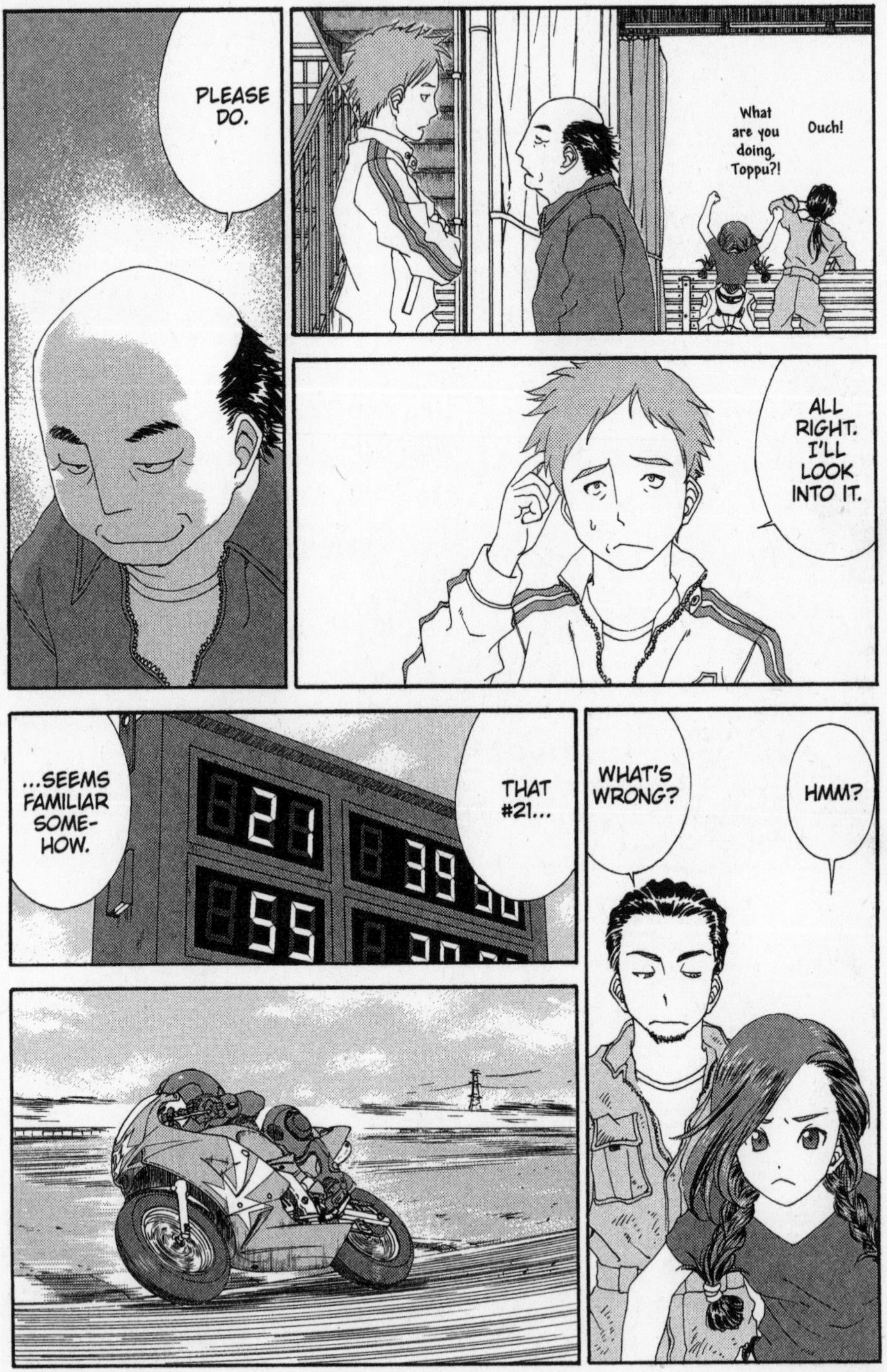
Ouch!
What are you doing, Toppu?!
ALL RIGHT. I'LL LOOK INTO IT.
PLEASE DO.
HMM?
WHAT'S WRONG?
THAT #21...
...SEEMS FAMILIAR SOME-HOW.

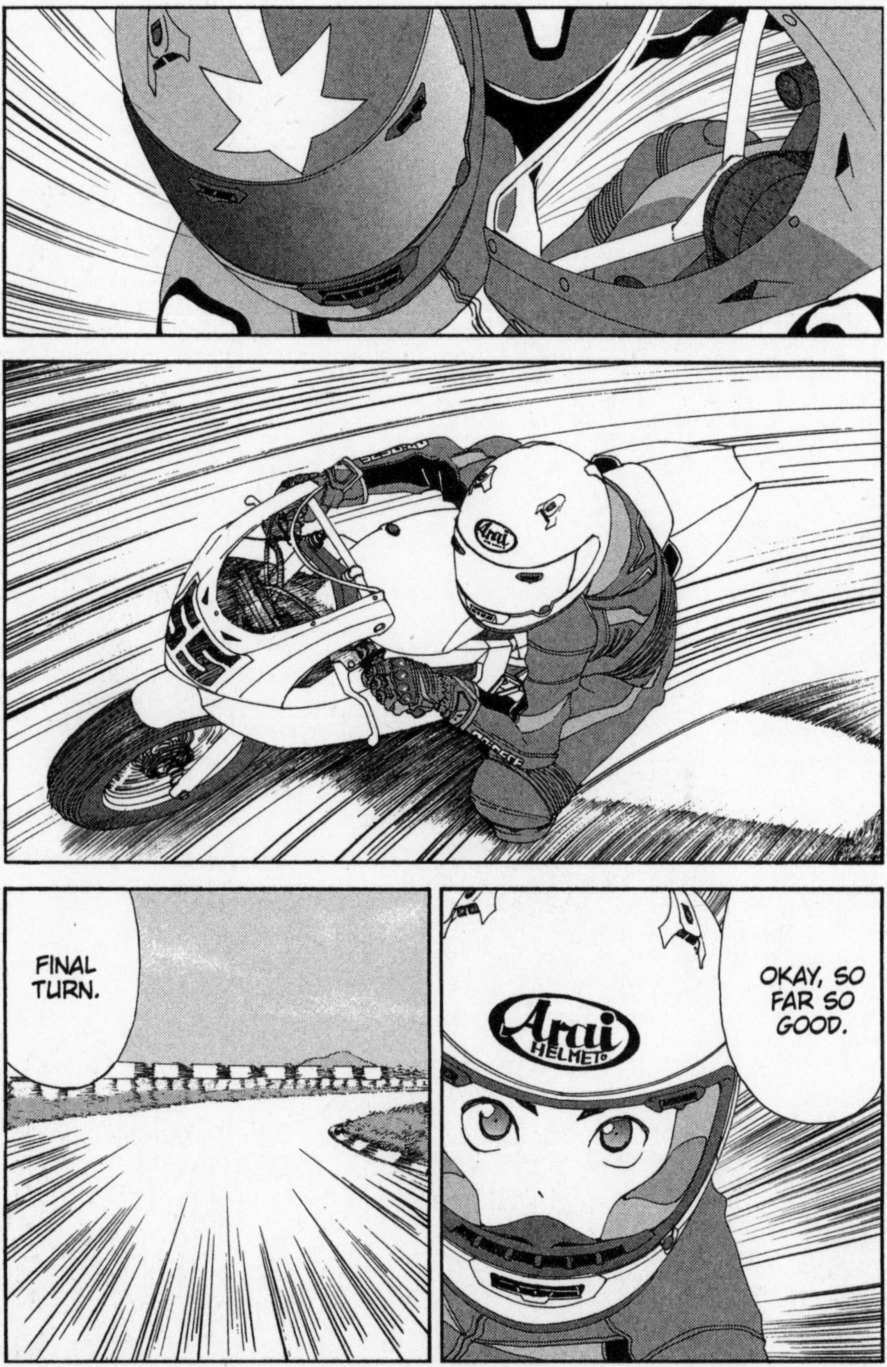
Arai
HELMET
OKAY, SO FAR SO GOOD.
FINAL TURN.

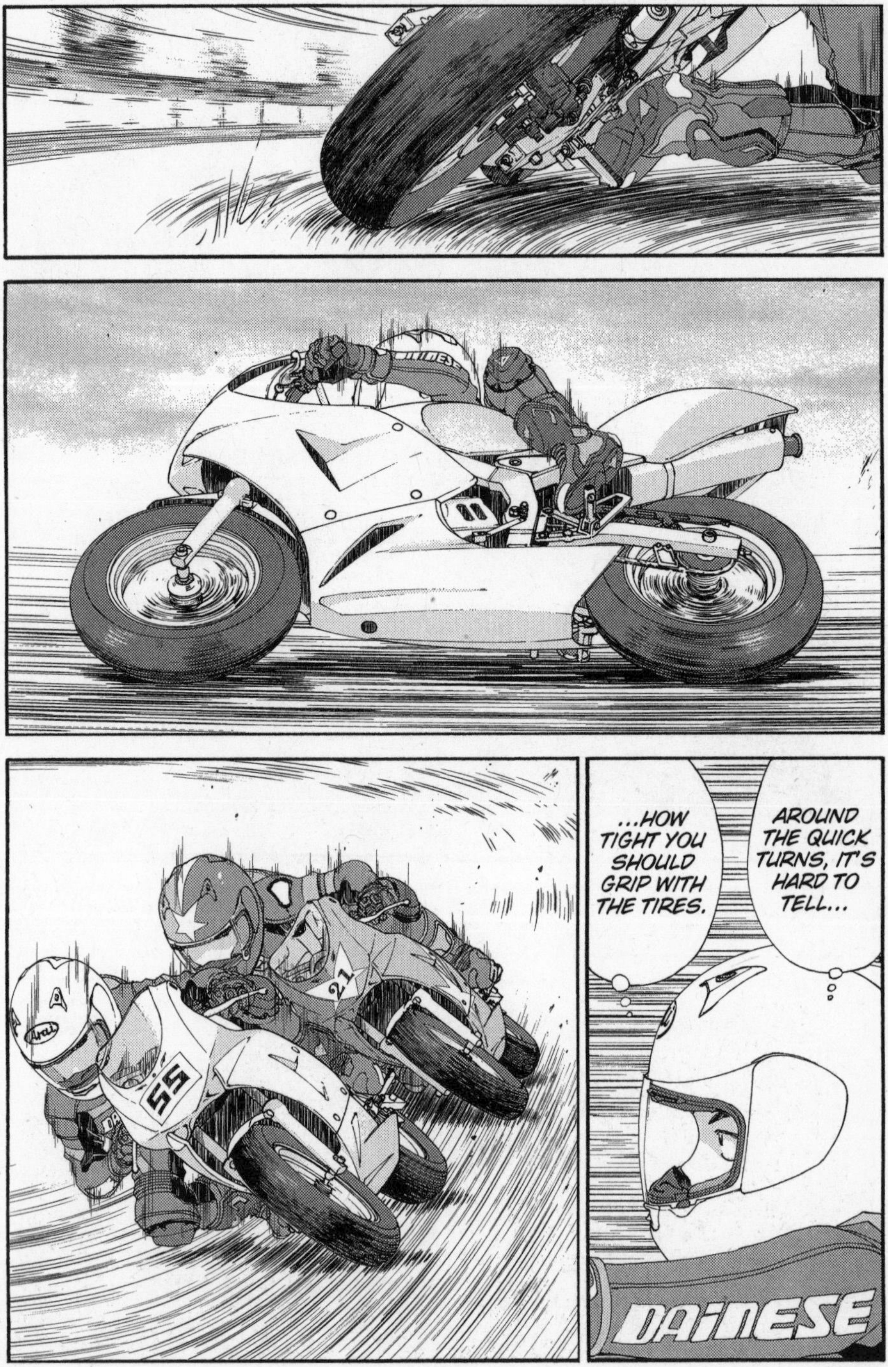
AROUND THE QUICK TURNS, IT'S HARD TO TELL...
...HOW TIGHT YOU SHOULD GRIP WITH THE TIRES.
DAINESE

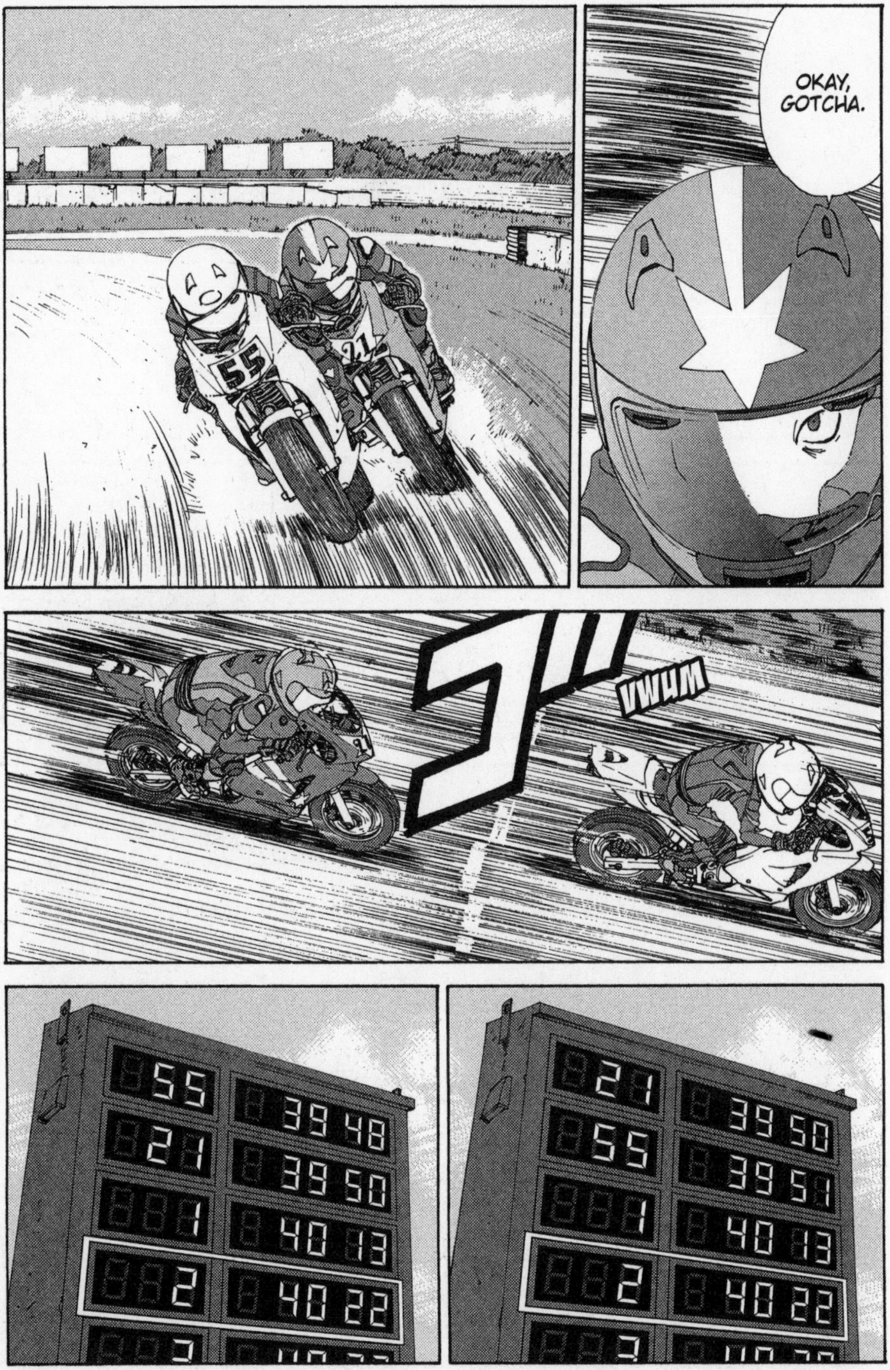
OKAY, GOTCHA.
VWUM
55 39 48
21 39 50
1 40 13
2 40 22
21 39 50
55 39 51
1 40 13
2 40 22

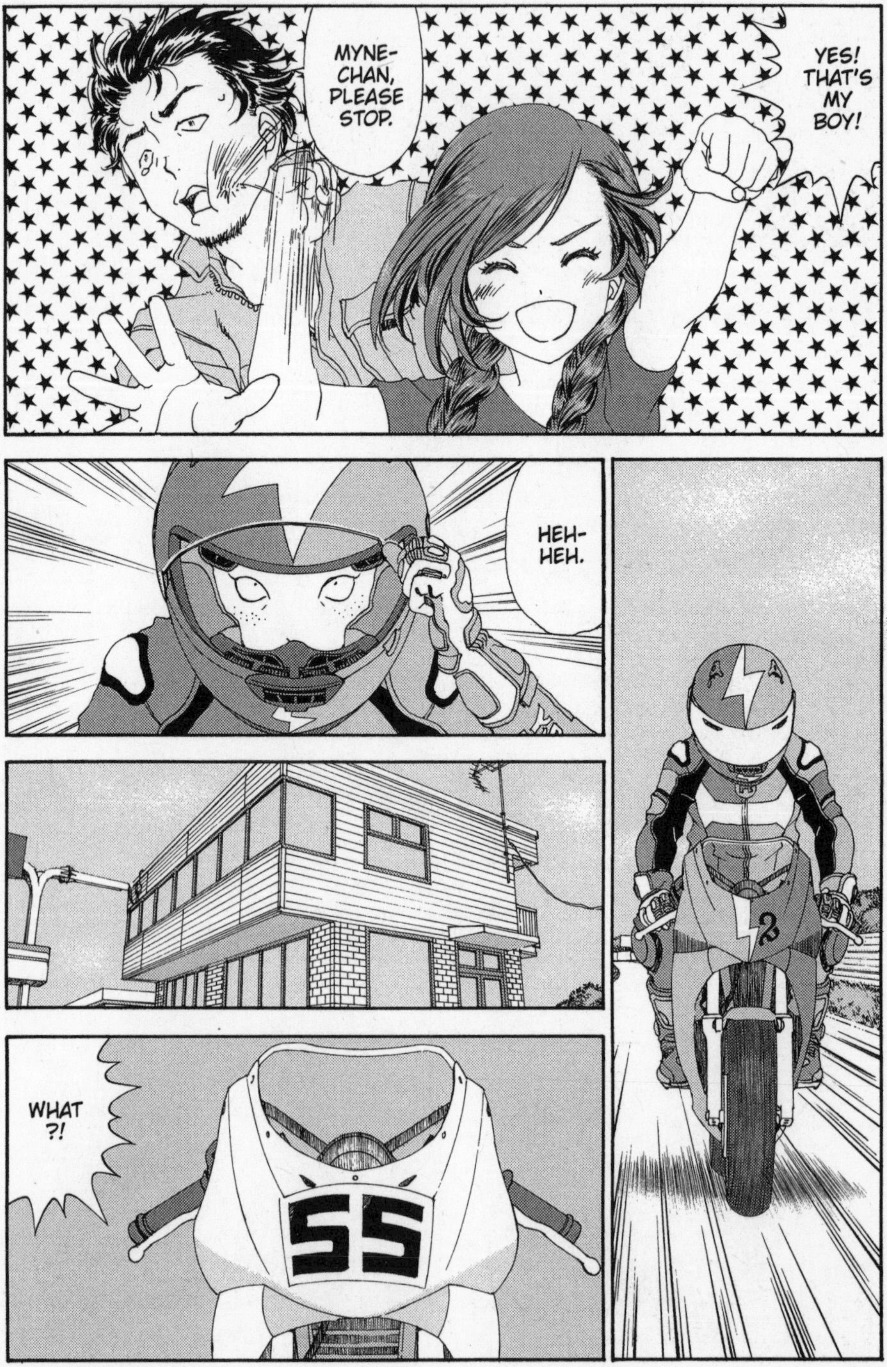
YES! THAT'S MY BOY!
MYNE-CHAN, PLEASE STOP.
HEH-HEH.
WHAT ?!

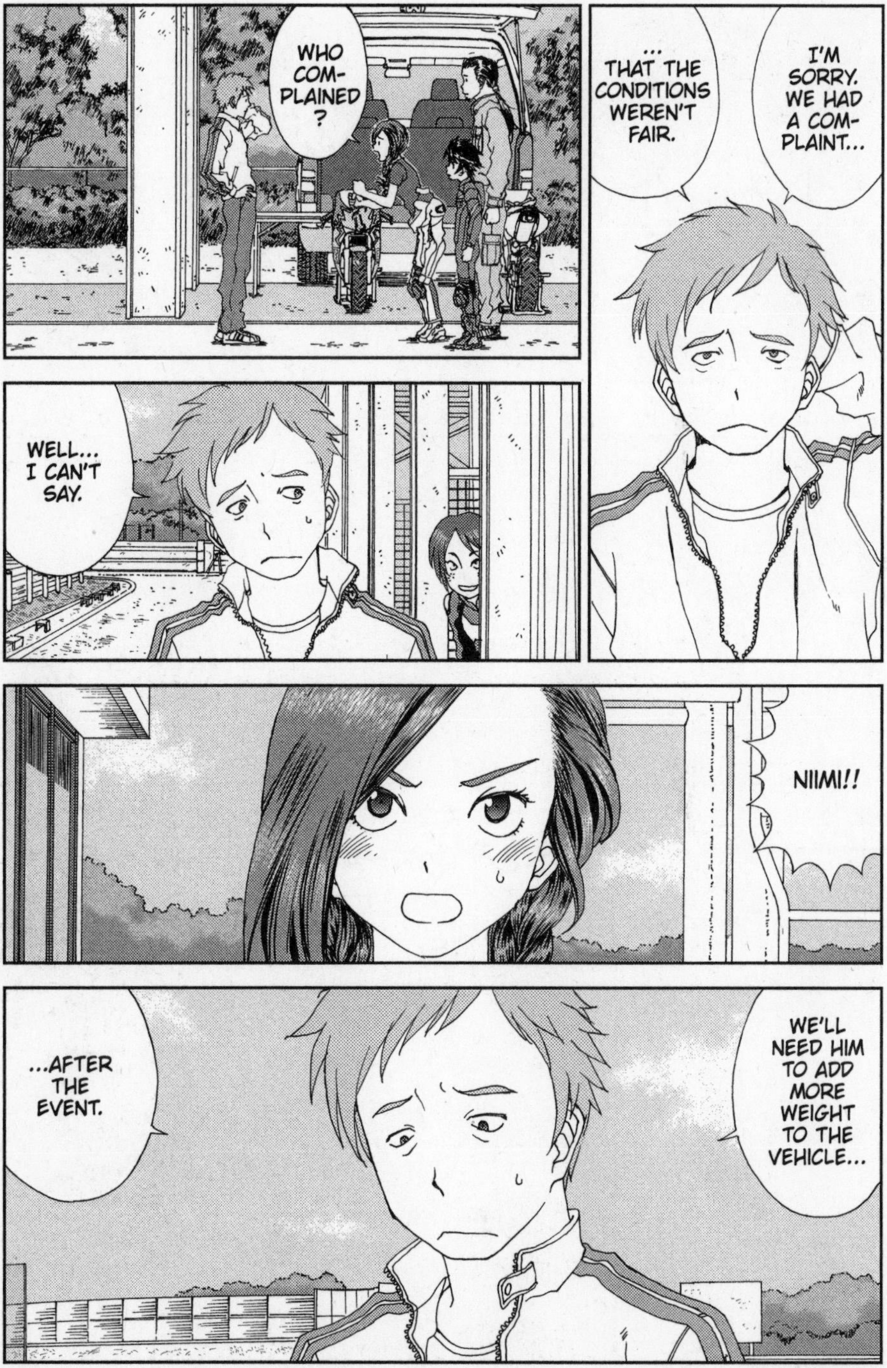
I'M SORRY. WE HAD A COMPLAINT...
... THAT THE CONDITIONS WEREN'T FAIR.
WHO COMPLAINED?
WELL... I CAN'T SAY.
NIIMI!!
WE'LL NEED HIM TO ADD MORE WEIGHT TO THE VEHICLE...
...AFTER THE EVENT.

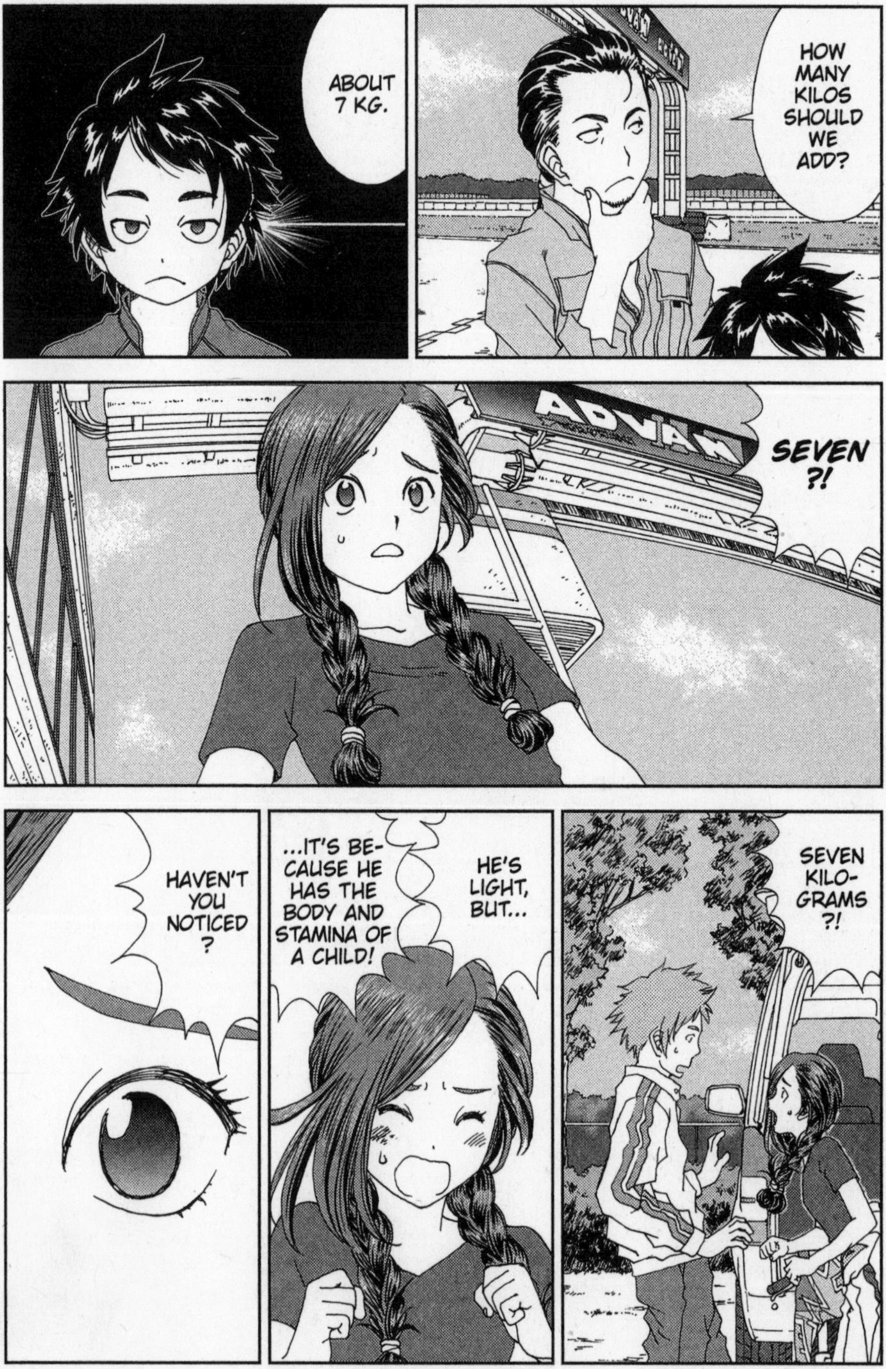
HOW MANY KILOS SHOULD WE ADD?
ABOUT 7 KG.
SEVEN ?!
SEVEN KILO-GRAMS ?!
HE'S LIGHT, BUT...
...IT'S BE-CAUSE HE HAS THE BODY AND STAMINA OF A CHILD!
HAVEN'T YOU NOTICED ?

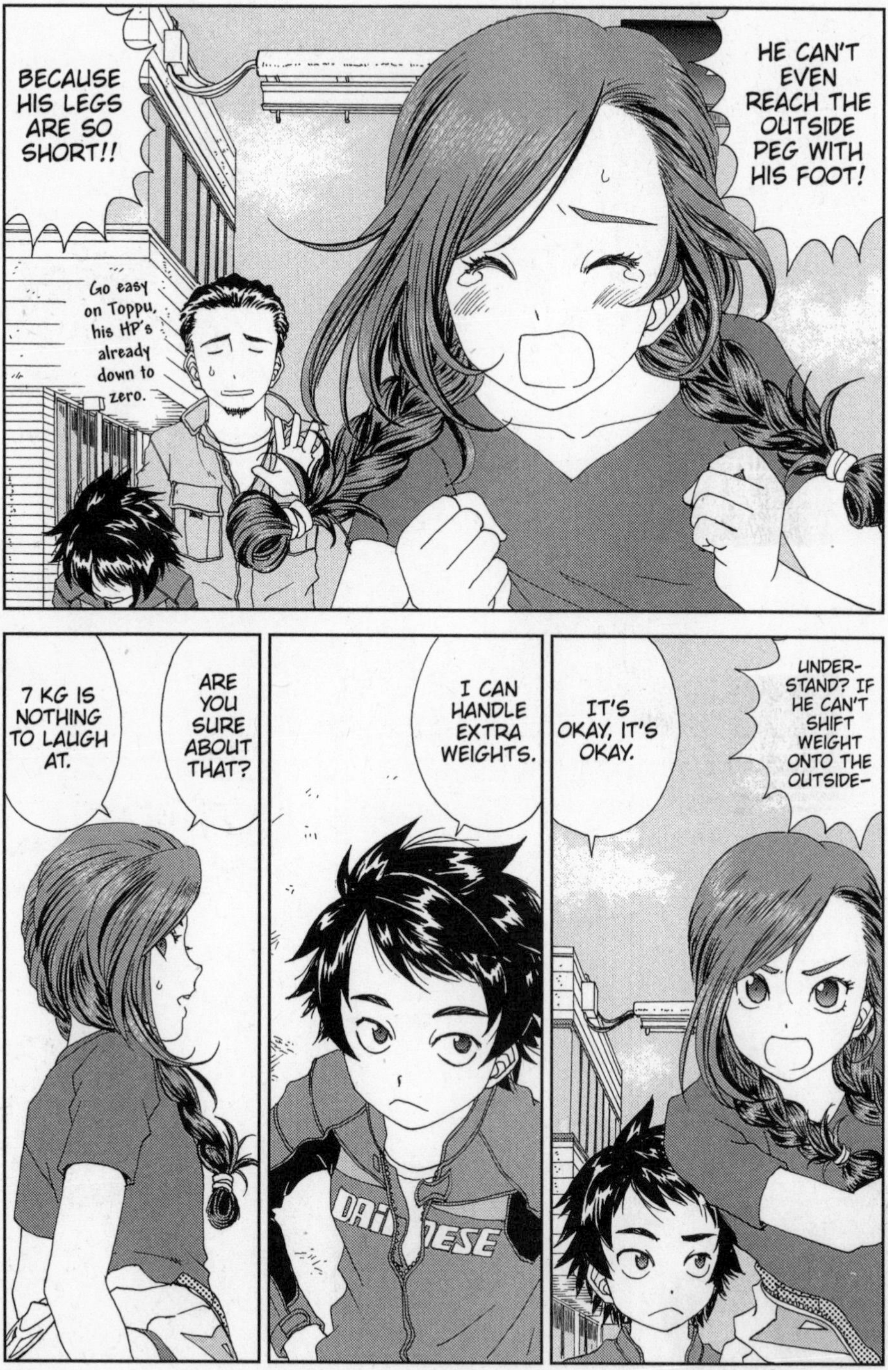
HE CAN'T EVEN REACH THE OUTSIDE PEG WITH HIS FOOT!
BECAUSE HIS LEGS ARE SO SHORT!!
Go easy on Toppu, his HP's already down to zero.
UNDER-STAND? IF HE CAN'T SHIFT WEIGHT ONTO THE OUTSIDE-
IT'S OKAY, IT'S OKAY.
I CAN HANDLE EXTRA WEIGHTS.
ARE YOU SURE ABOUT THAT?
7 KG IS NOTHING TO LAUGH AT.
DAINESE

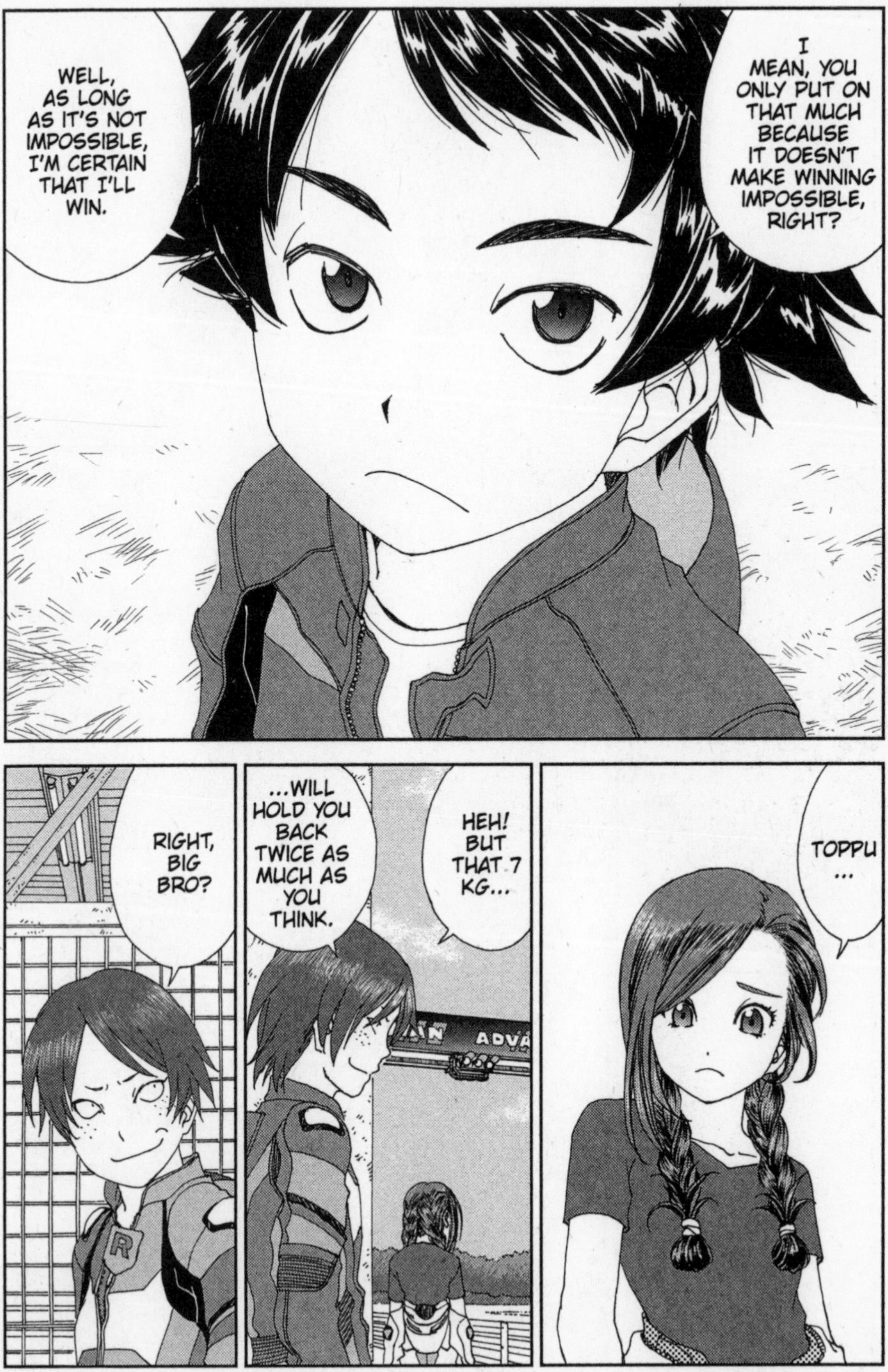
I MEAN, YOU ONLY PUT ON THAT MUCH BECAUSE IT DOESN'T MAKE WINNING IMPOSSIBLE, RIGHT?
WELL, AS LONG AS IT'S NOT IMPOSSIBLE, I'M CERTAIN THAT I'LL WIN.
TOPPU ...
HEH! BUT THAT 7 KG...
...WILL HOLD YOU BACK TWICE AS MUCH AS YOU THINK.
RIGHT, BIG BRO?

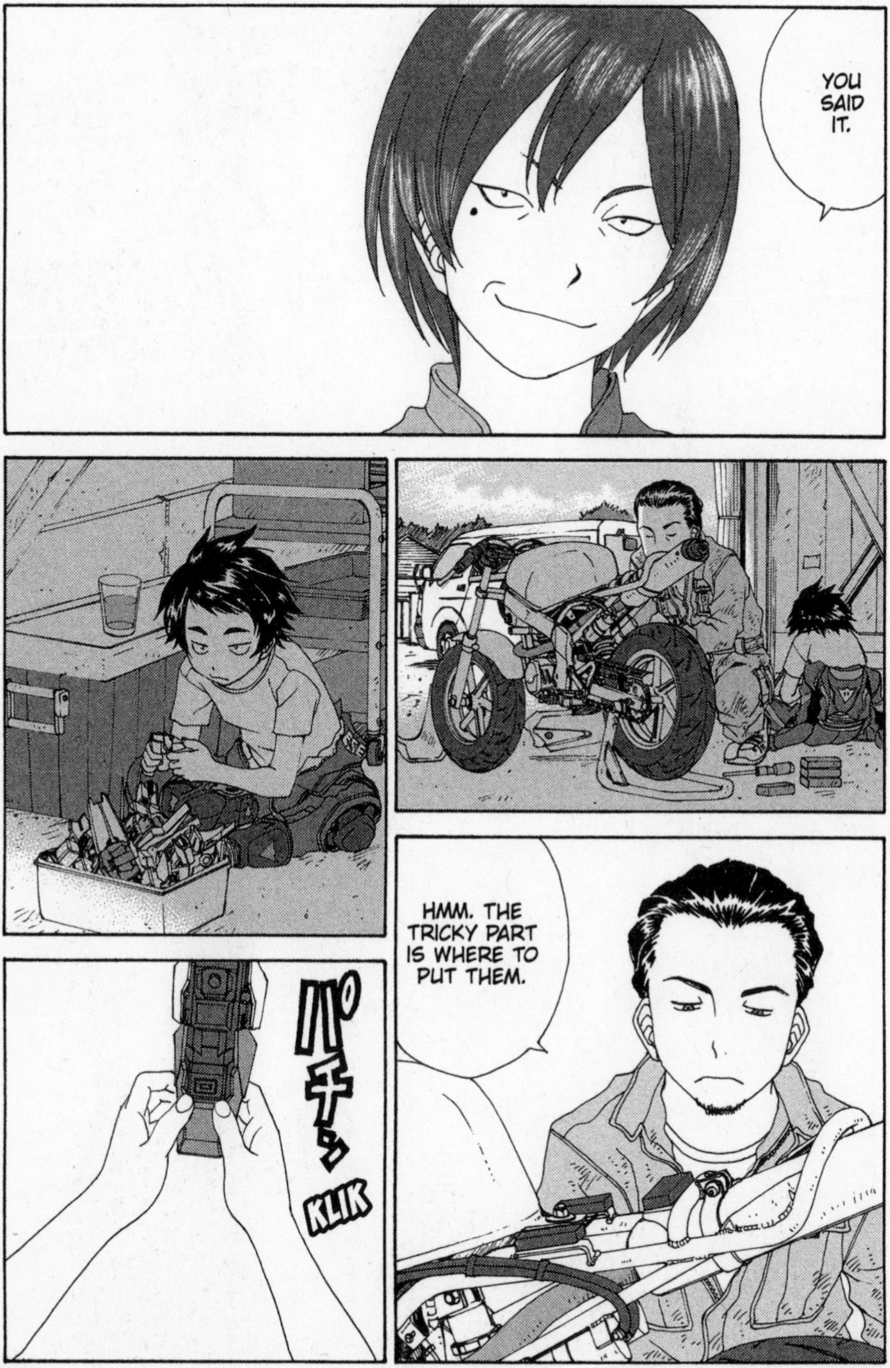
YOU SAID IT.
HMM. THE TRICKY PART IS WHERE TO PUT THEM.
パチッ
KLIK

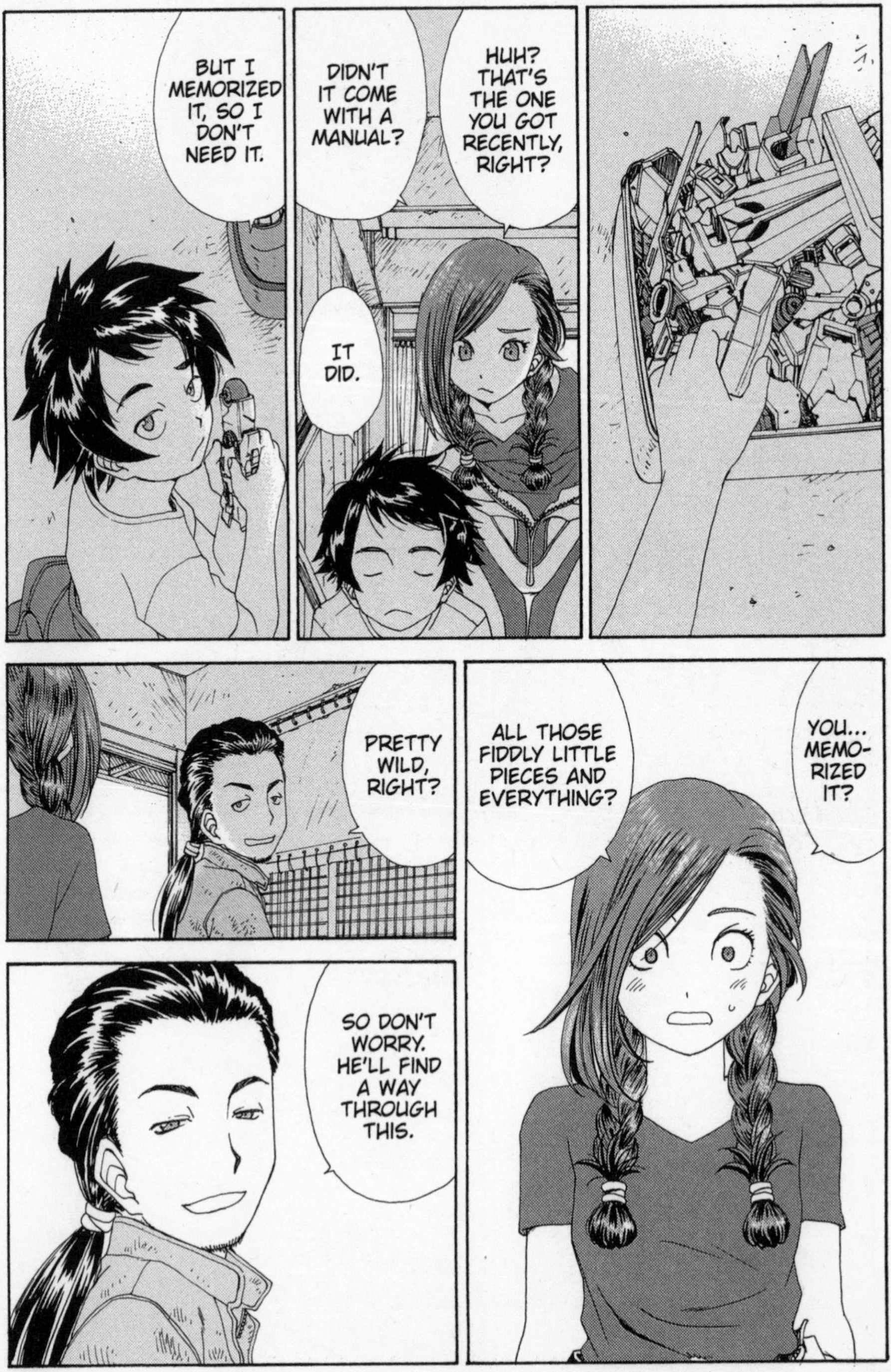
HUH? THAT'S THE ONE YOU GOT RECENTLY, RIGHT?
DIDN'T IT COME WITH A MANUAL?
IT DID.
BUT I MEMORIZED IT, SO I DON'T NEED IT.
YOU... MEMO-RIZED IT?
ALL THOSE FIDDLY LITTLE PIECES AND EVERYTHING?
PRETTY WILD, RIGHT?
SO DON'T WORRY. HE'LL FIND A WAY THROUGH THIS.

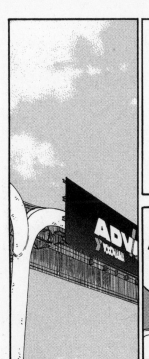

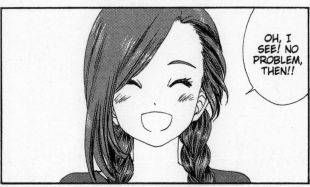

OH, I SEE! NO PROBLEM, THEN!!
BUT HOW IS THAT GOING TO HELP?
THAT'S A GOOD QUES-TION.
ADVI
YOKOHAMA

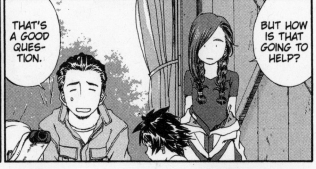

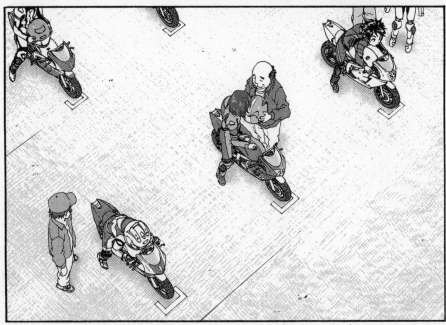

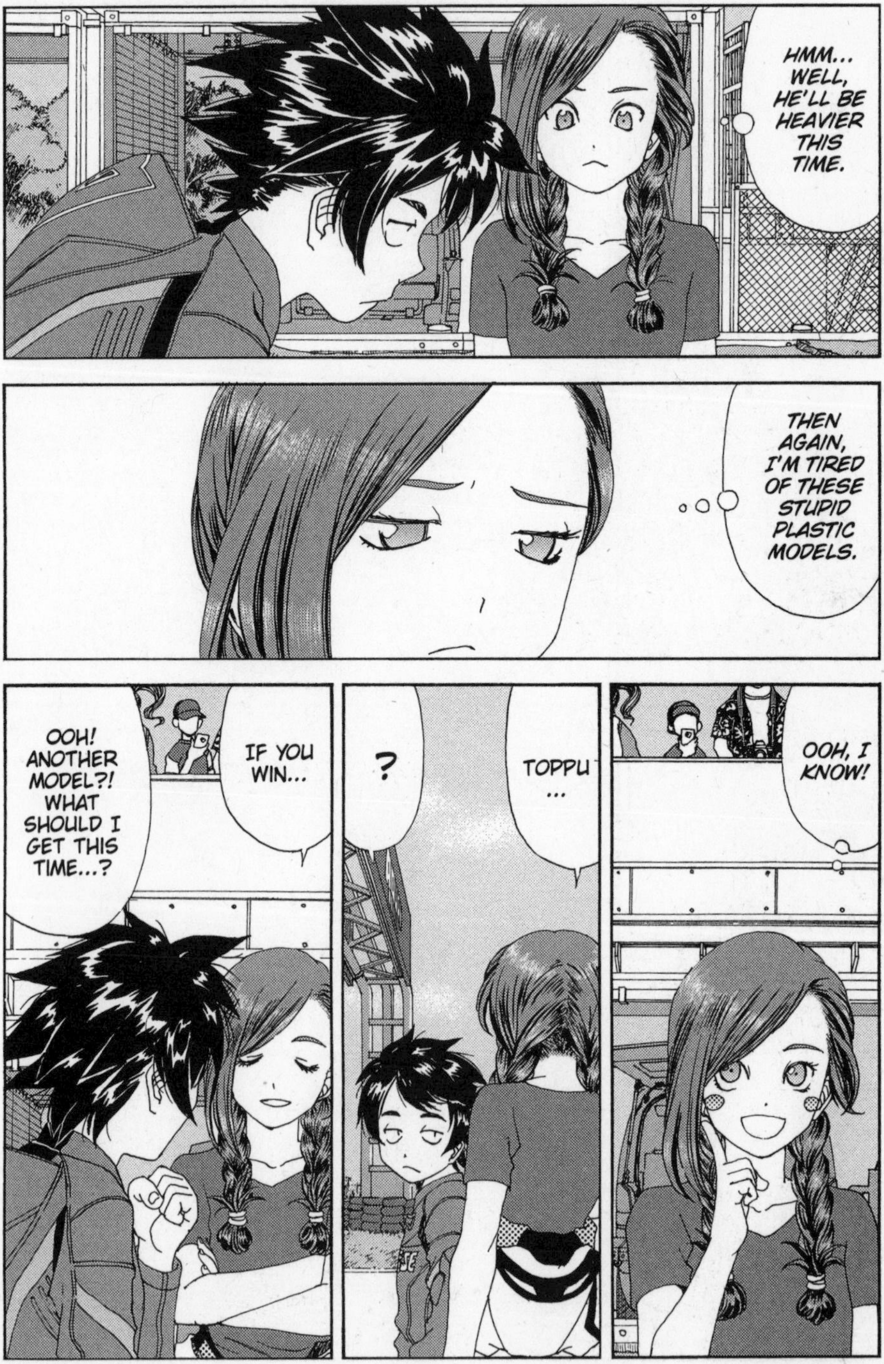
HMM... WELL, HE'LL BE HEAVIER THIS TIME.
THEN AGAIN, I'M TIRED OF THESE STUPID PLASTIC MODELS.
OOH, I KNOW!
TOPPU ...
?
IF YOU WIN...
OOH! ANOTHER MODEL?! WHAT SHOULD I GET THIS TIME...?

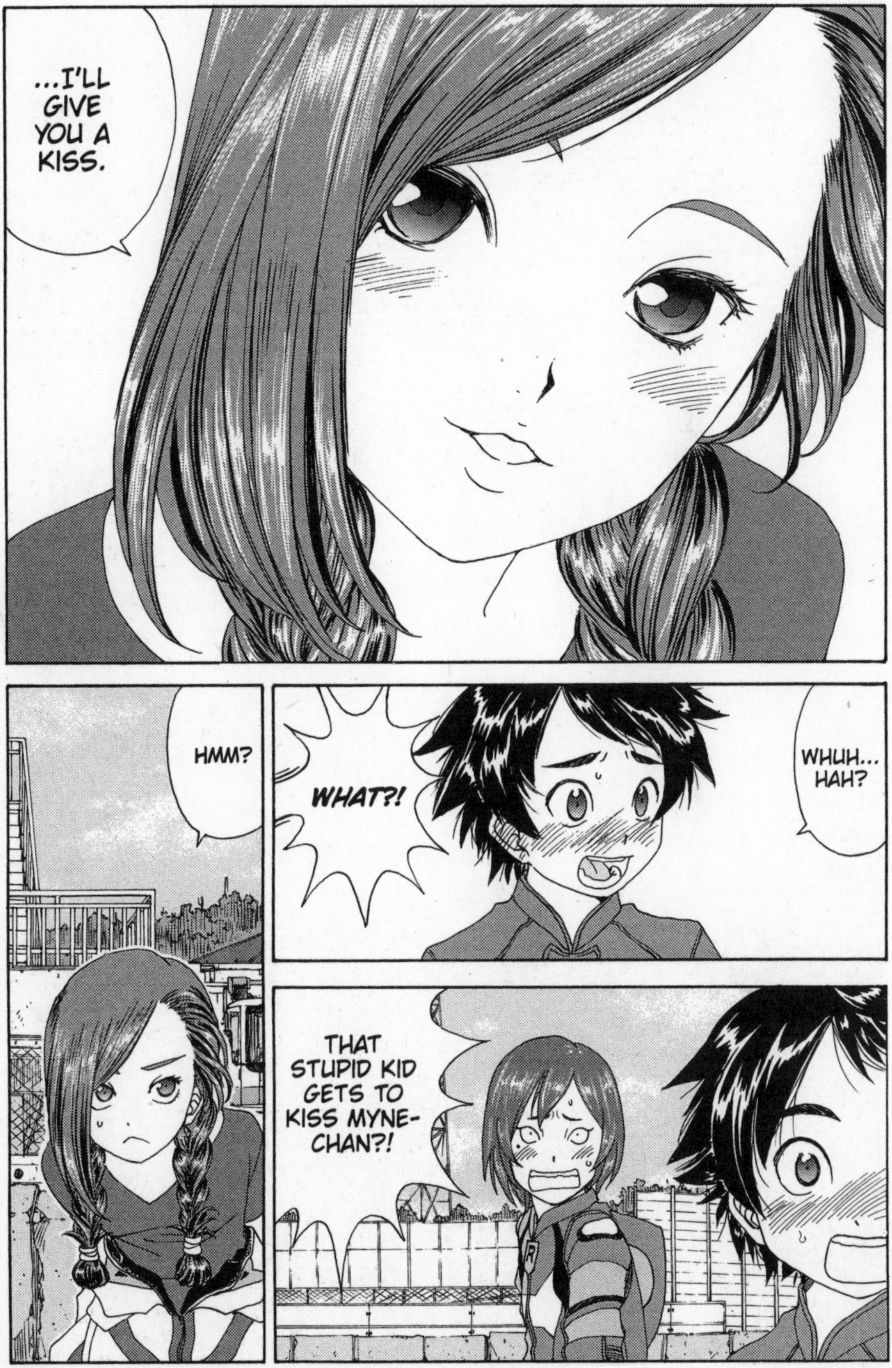
...I'LL GIVE YOU A KISS.
WHUH... HAH?
WHAT?!
THAT STUPID KID GETS TO KISS MYNE-CHAN?!
HMM?

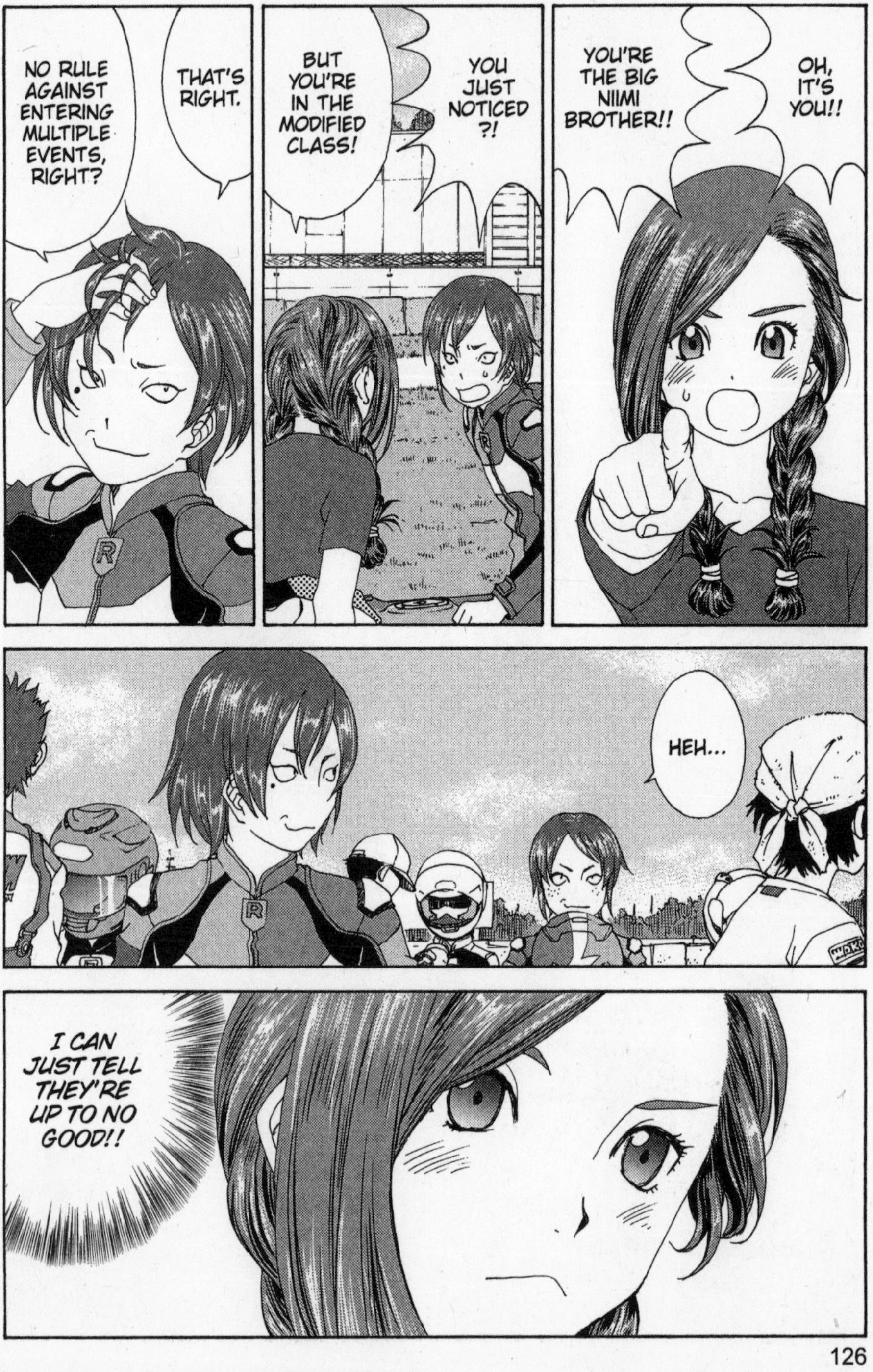
OH, IT'S YOU!!
YOU'RE THE BIG NIIMI BROTHER!!
YOU JUST NOTICED ?!
BUT YOU'RE IN THE MODIFIED CLASS!
THAT'S RIGHT.
NO RULE AGAINST ENTERING MULTIPLE EVENTS, RIGHT?
HEH...
I CAN JUST TELL THEY'RE UP TO NO GOOD!!

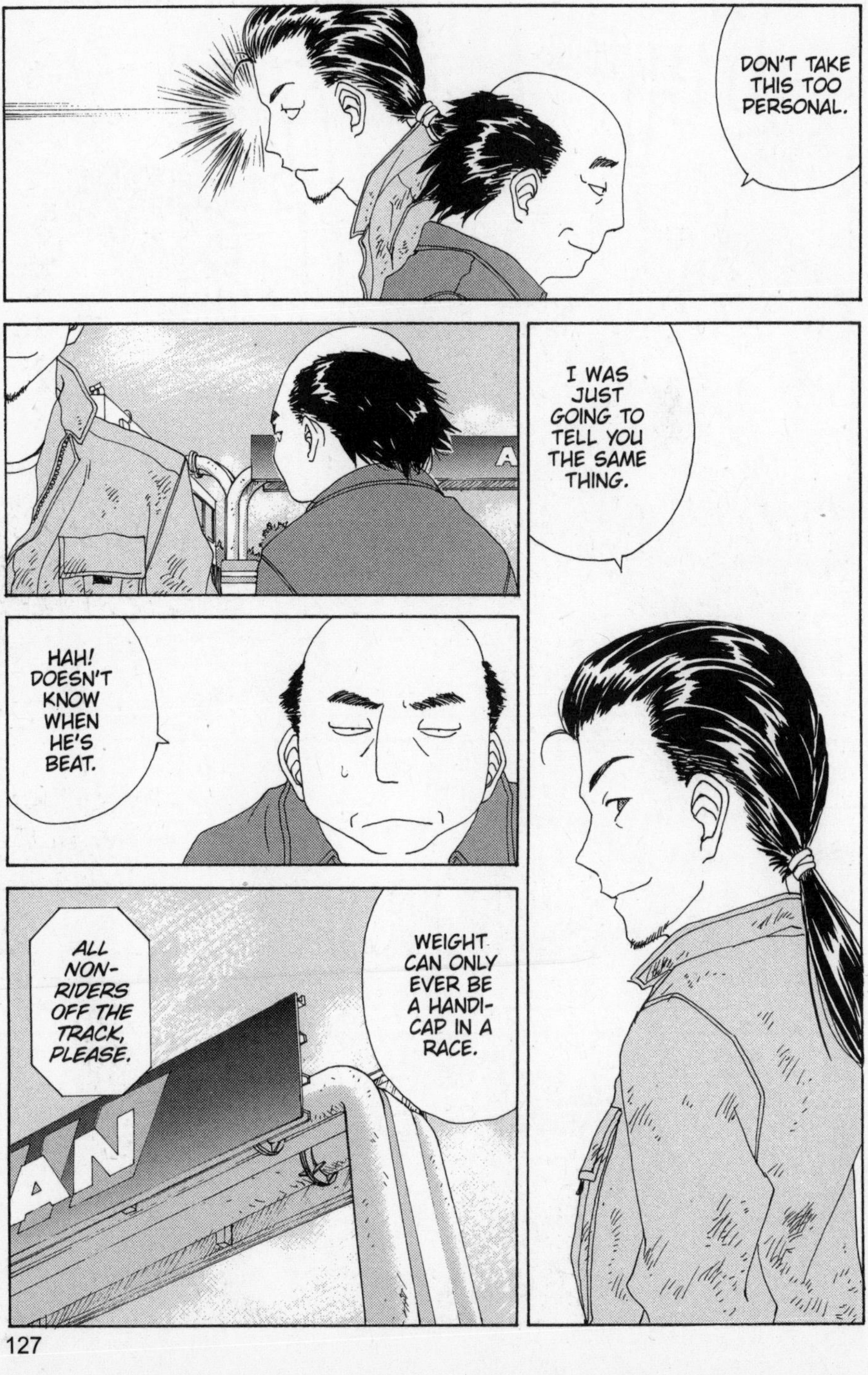
DON'T TAKE THIS TOO PERSONAL.
I WAS JUST GOING TO TELL YOU THE SAME THING.
HAH! DOESN'T KNOW WHEN HE'S BEAT.
WEIGHT CAN ONLY EVER BE A HANDI-CAP IN A RACE.
ALL NON-RIDERS OFF THE TRACK, PLEASE.

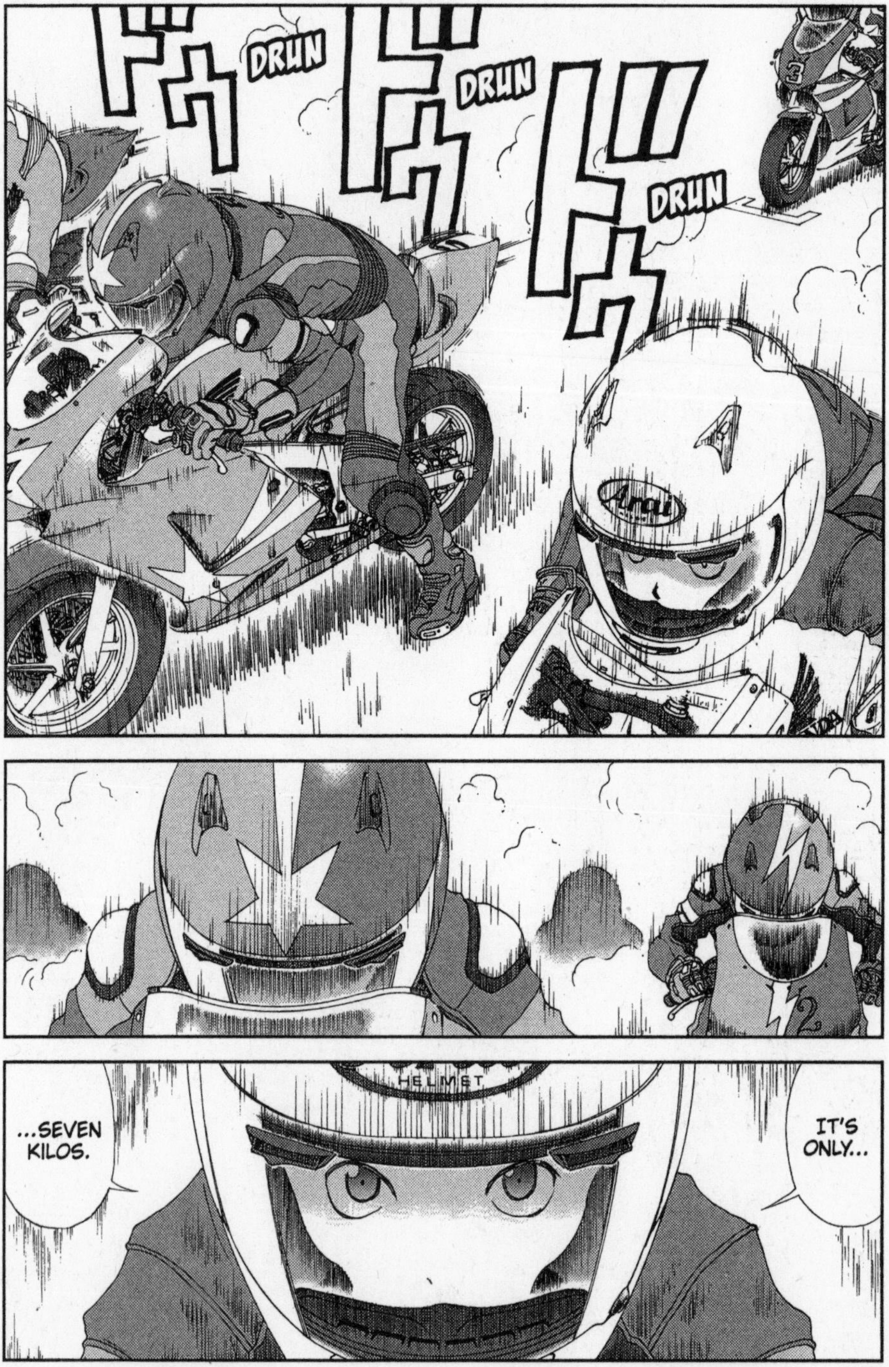
ドゥ
DRUN
ドゥ
DRUN
ドゥ
DRUN
Arai
IT'S ONLY...
HELMET
...SEVEN KILOS.

YOKOHAMA
DAINESE
HRGH!
VMM
DAINESE

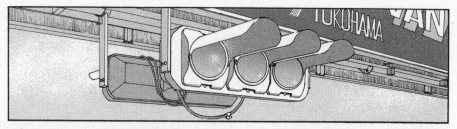

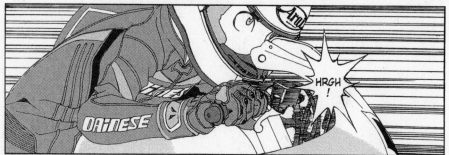

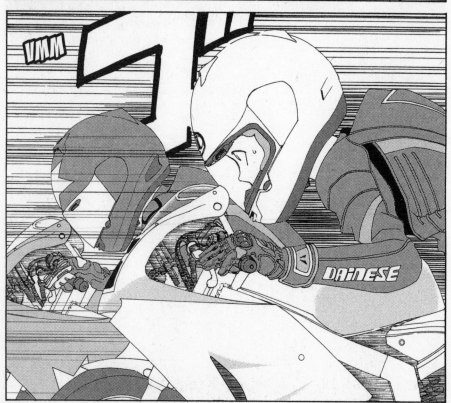

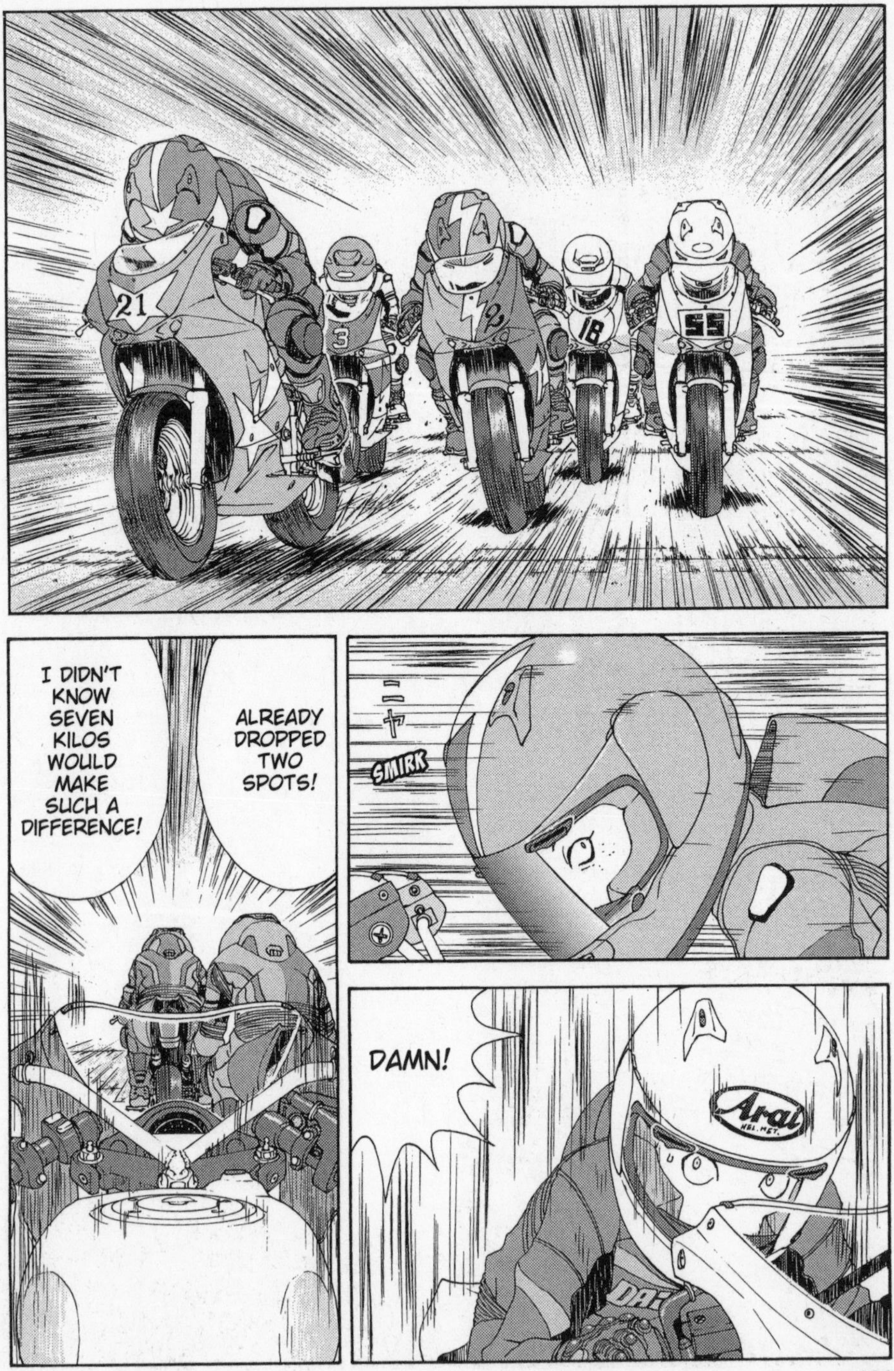
ニヤ
SMIRK
DAMN!
ALREADY DROPPED TWO SPOTS!
I DIDN'T KNOW SEVEN KILOS WOULD MAKE SUCH A DIFFERENCE!

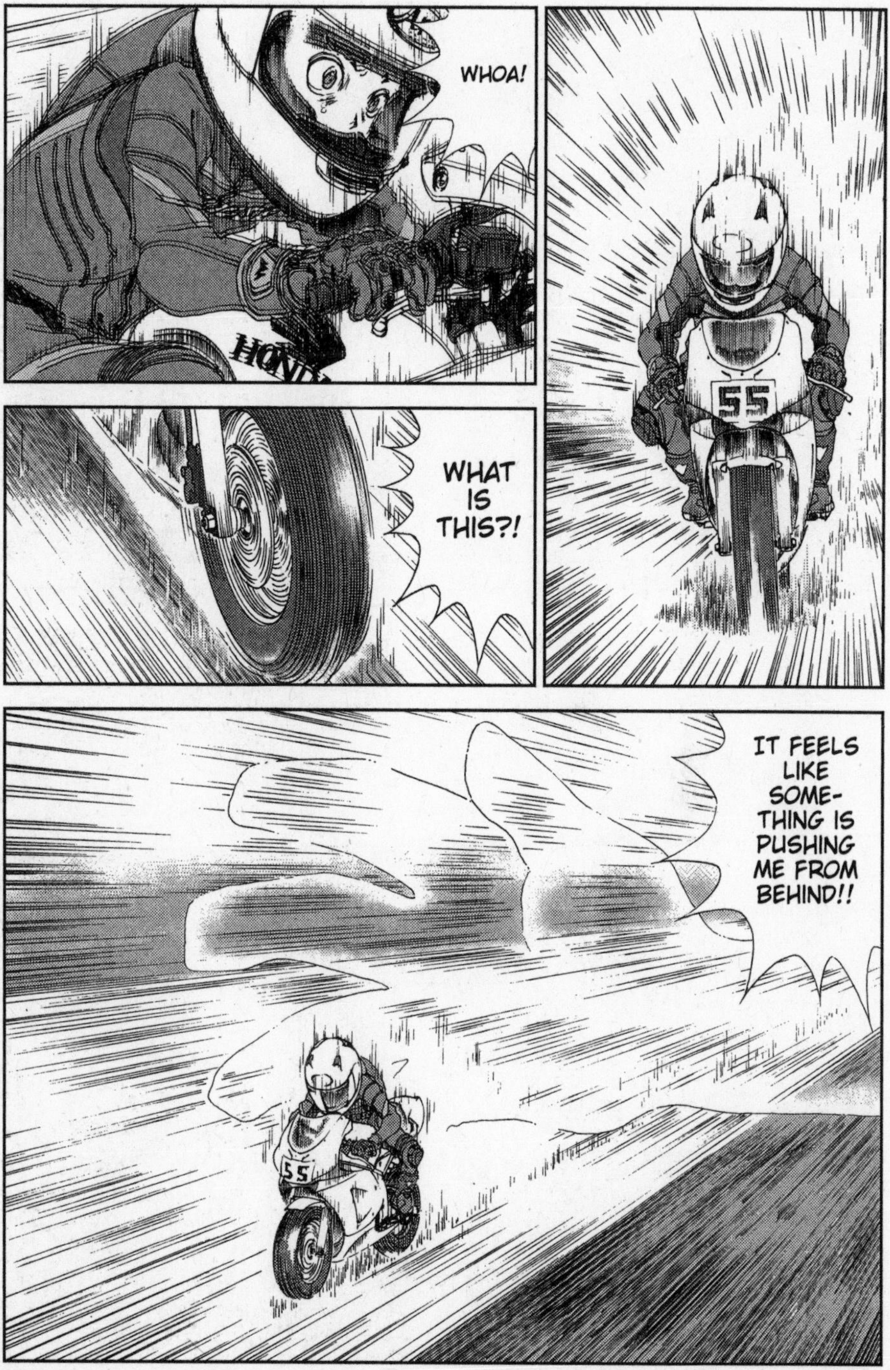
WHOA!
WHAT IS THIS?!
IT FEELS LIKE SOME-THING IS PUSHING ME FROM BEHIND!!

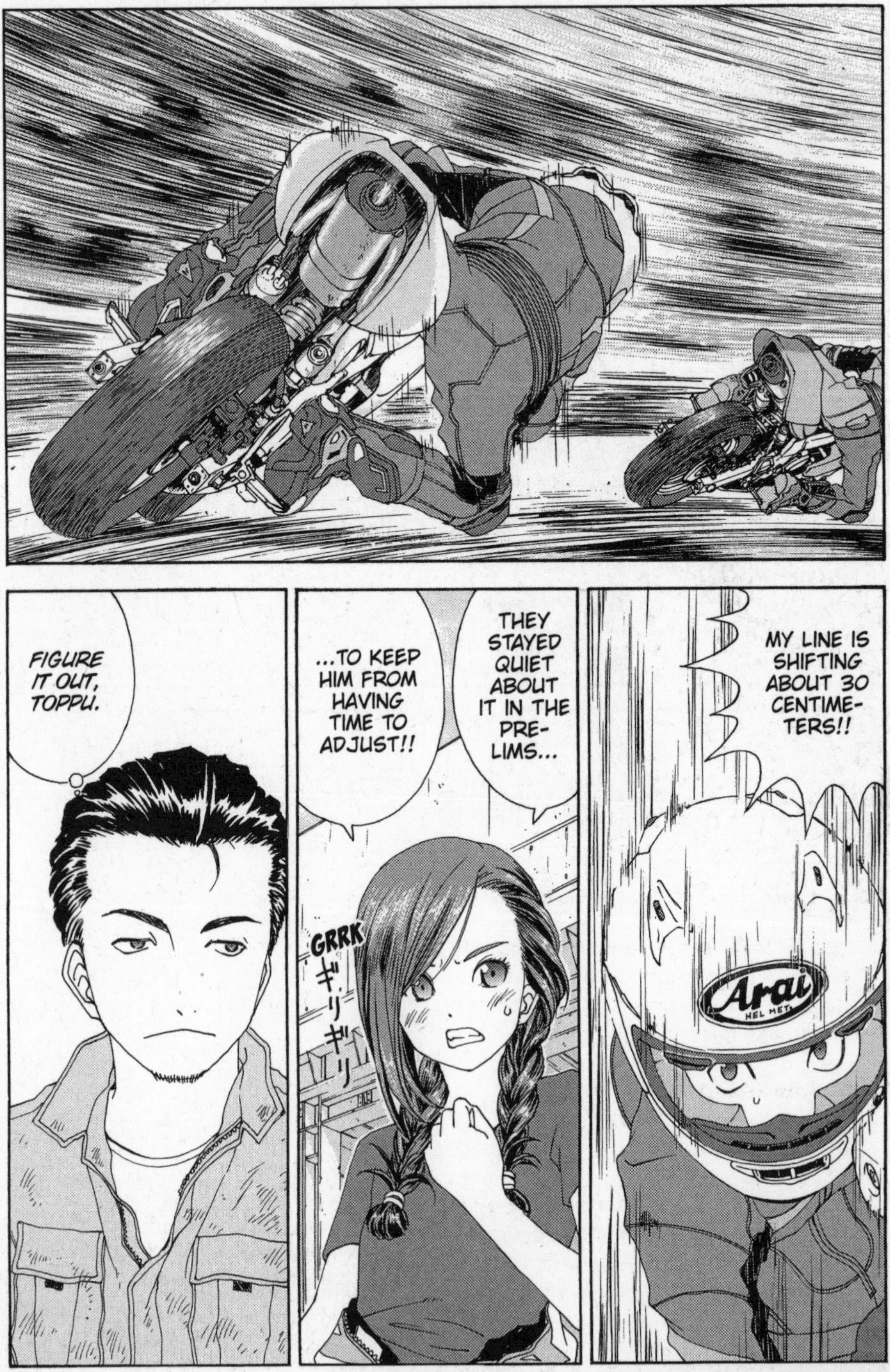
MY LINE IS SHIFTING ABOUT 30 CENTIMETERS!!
THEY STAYED QUIET ABOUT IT IN THE PRE-LIMS...
...TO KEEP HIM FROM HAVING TIME TO ADJUST!!
GRRK
ギリギリ
FIGURE IT OUT, TOPPU.

Lap 5: end

▶ The Road to MotoGP

The MotoGP series has three separate engine displacement classes, each of which has its own qualifying sessions, races, and championship.

▶ **MotoGP Class: 1000cc**
▶ **Moto2 Class: 600cc**
▶ **Moto3 Class: 250cc**

Japanese racers aspiring to compete in MotoGP must first prove themselves in youth racing series in Japan or abroad before they qualify to compete in the Moto3 class.

TOPPU GP

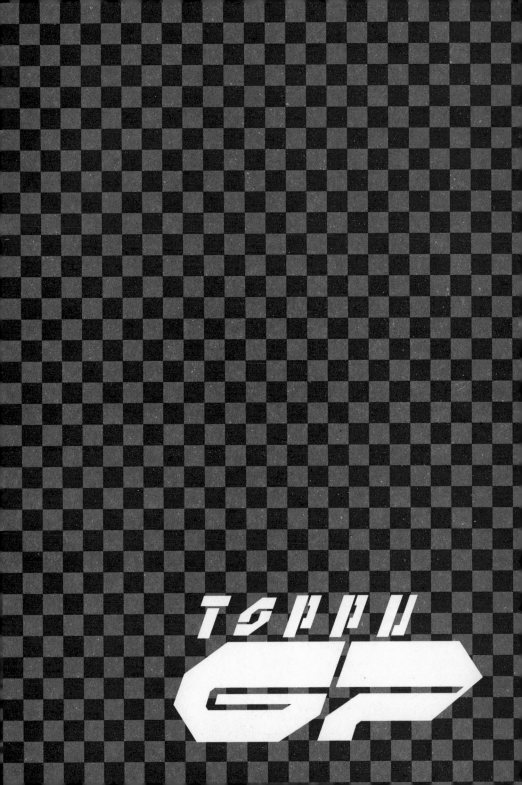

Lap 6:
YESTERDAY'S ENEMY IS...

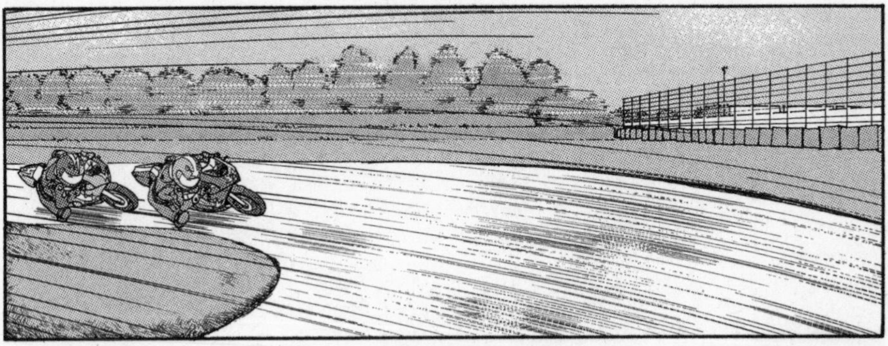
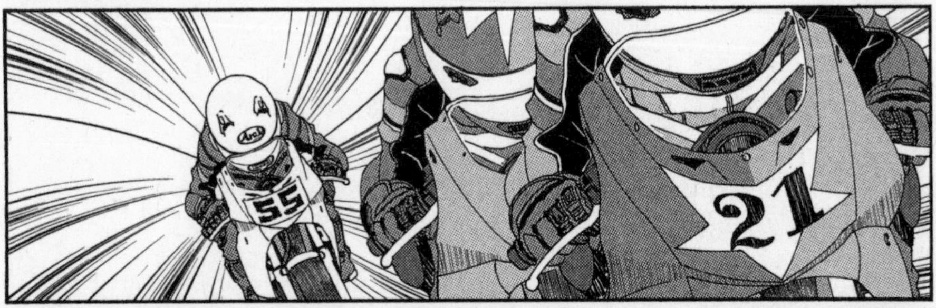
55
21
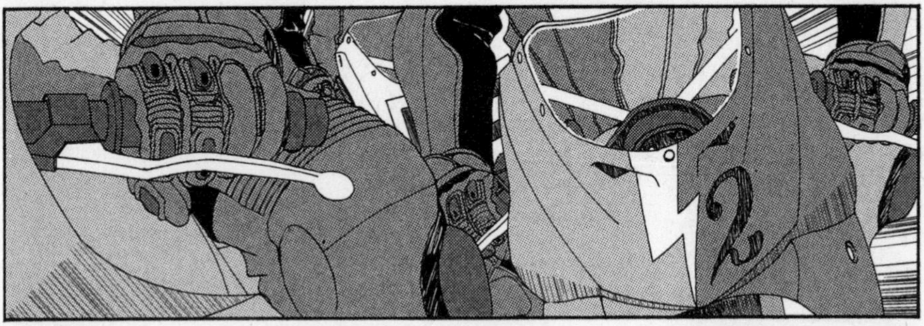
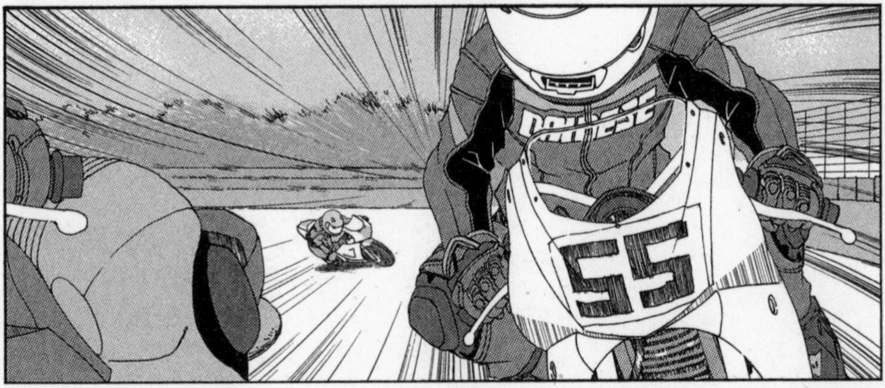
55

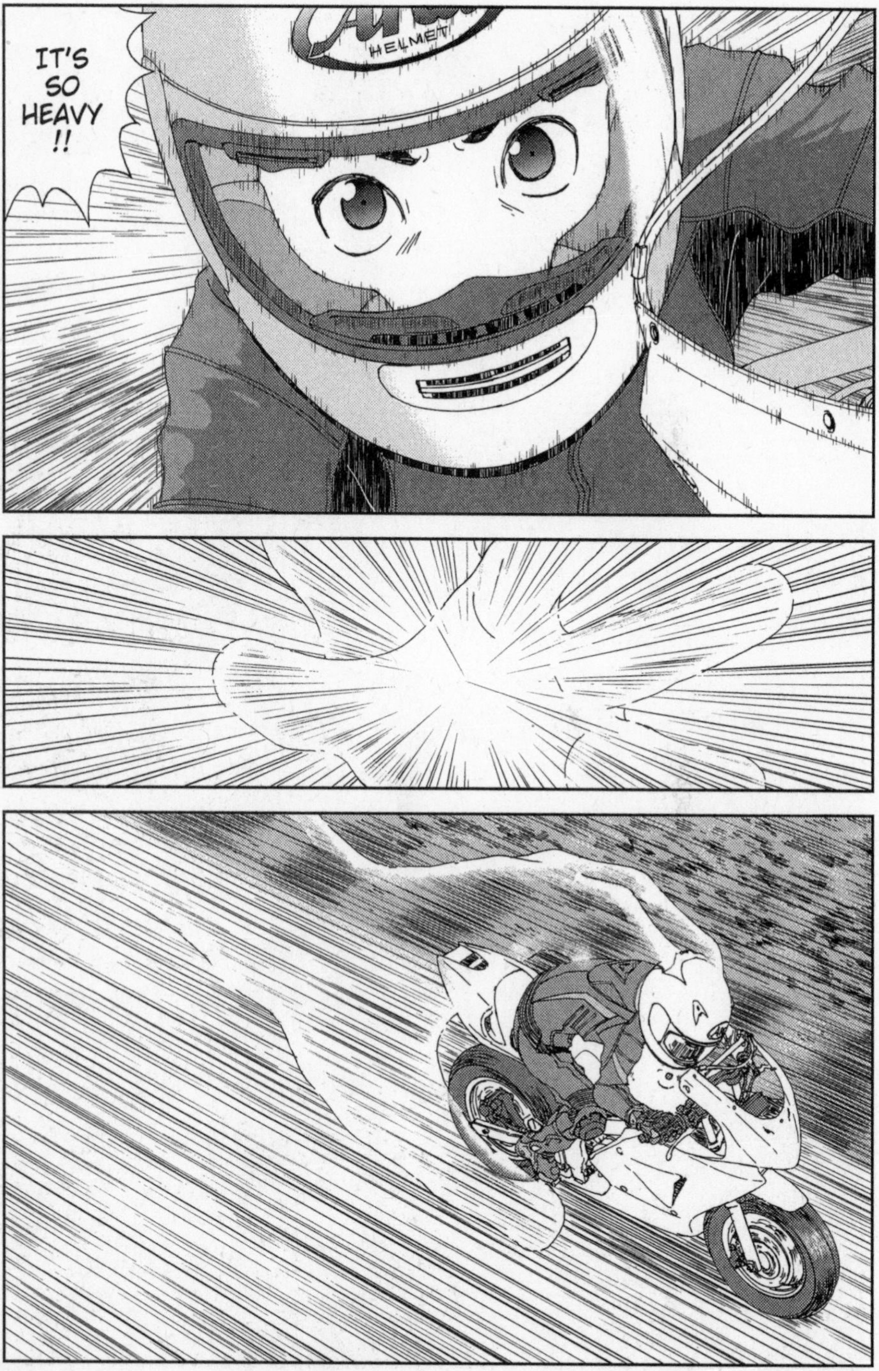
IT'S SO HEAVY !!
HELMET

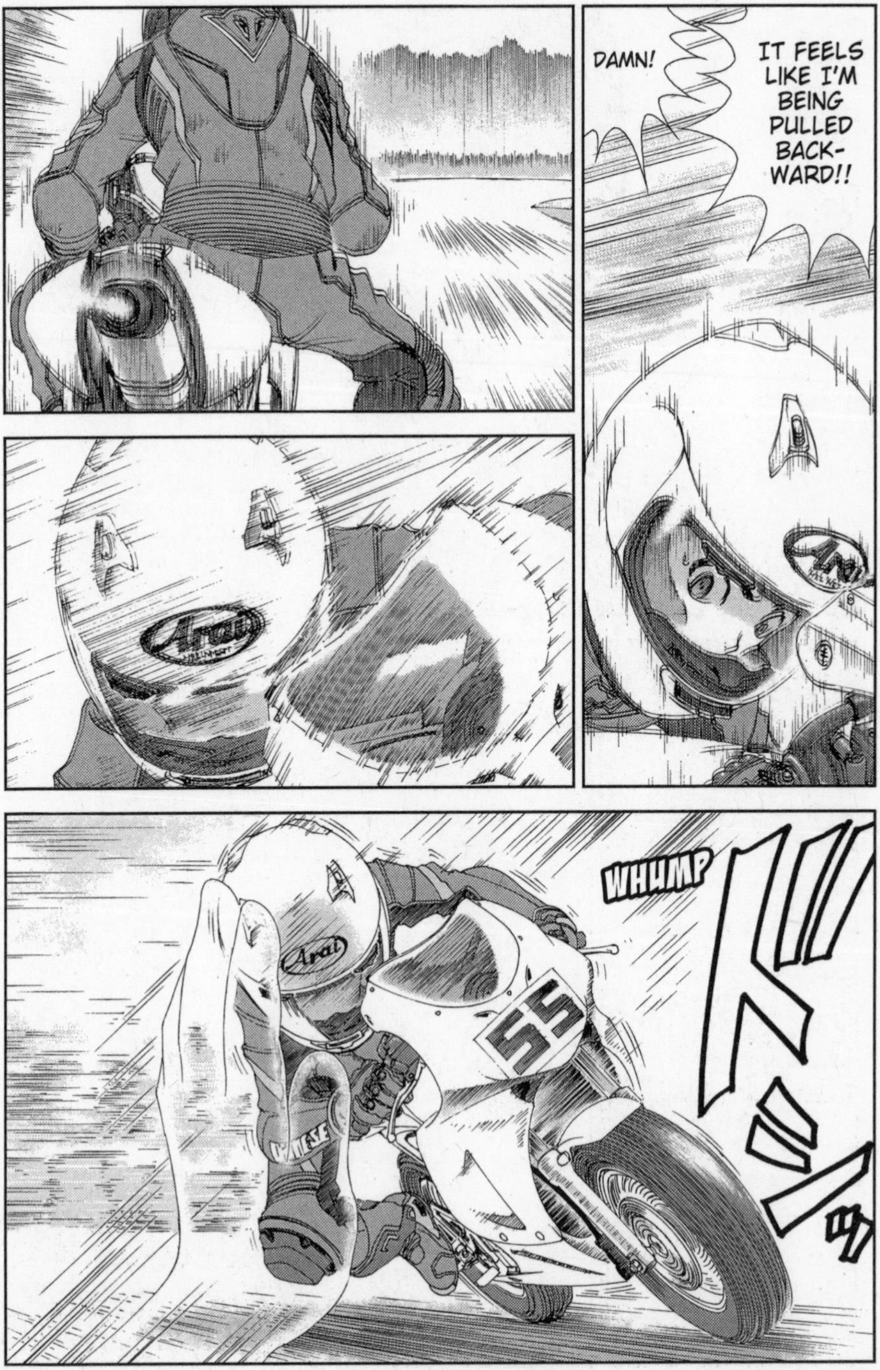
IT FEELS LIKE I'M BEING PULLED BACK-WARD!!
DAMN!
WHUMP

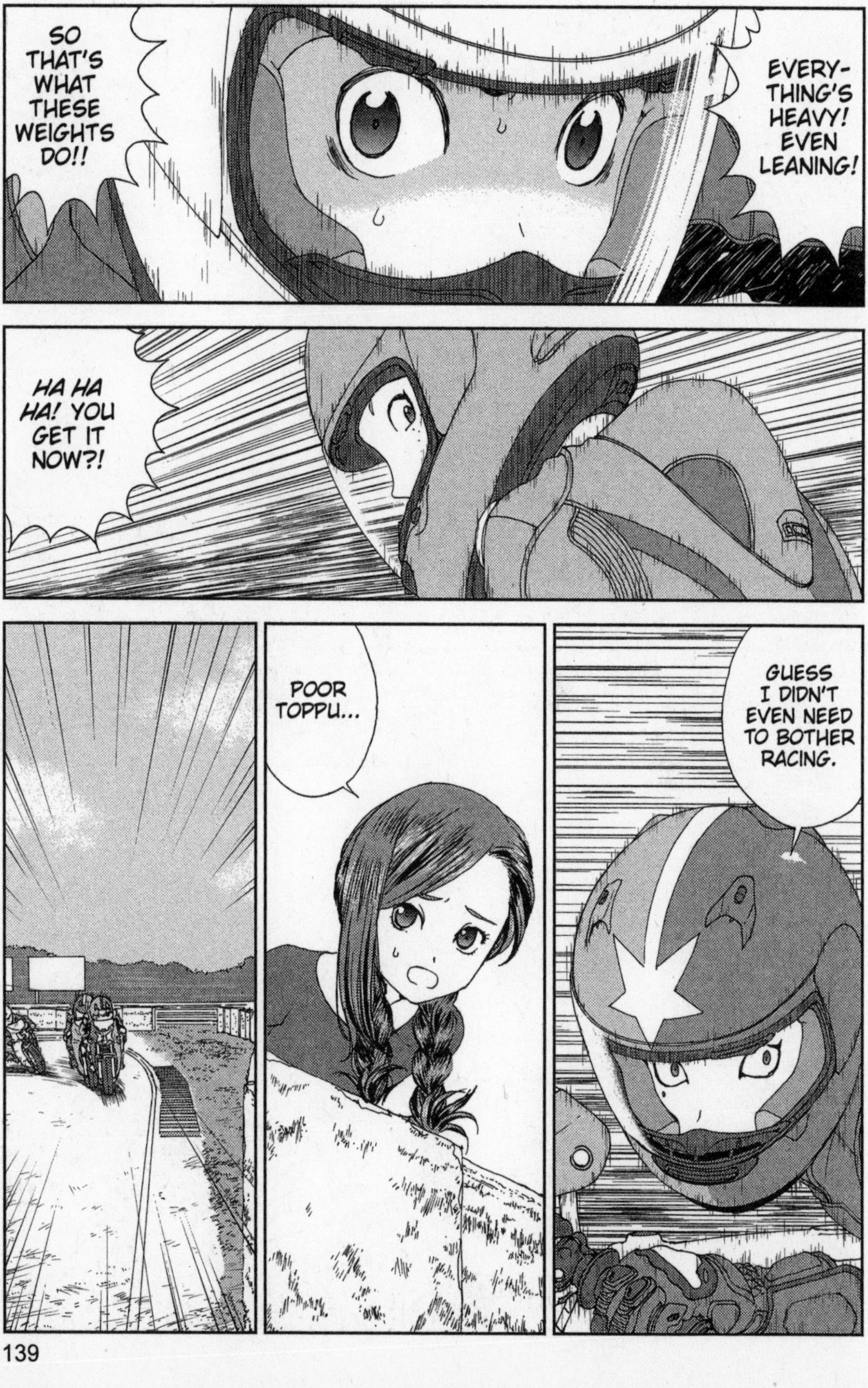
EVERY-THING'S HEAVY! EVEN LEANING!
SO THAT'S WHAT THESE WEIGHTS DO!!
HA HA HA! YOU GET IT NOW?!
GUESS I DIDN'T EVEN NEED TO BOTHER RACING.
POOR TOPPU...

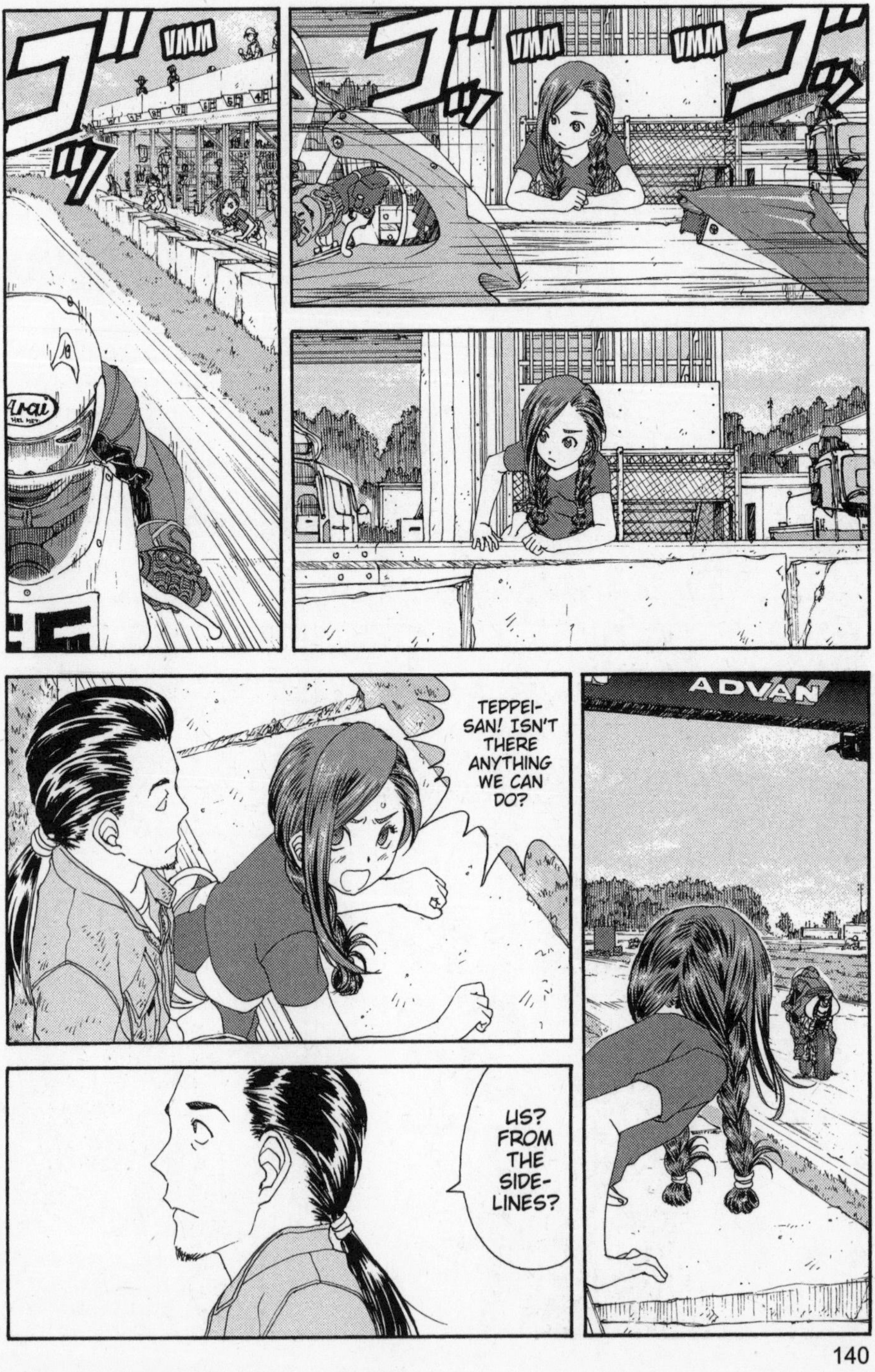
VMM
VMM
VMM
Arai
ADVAN
TEPPEI-SAN! ISN'T THERE ANYTHING WE CAN DO?
US? FROM THE SIDELINES?

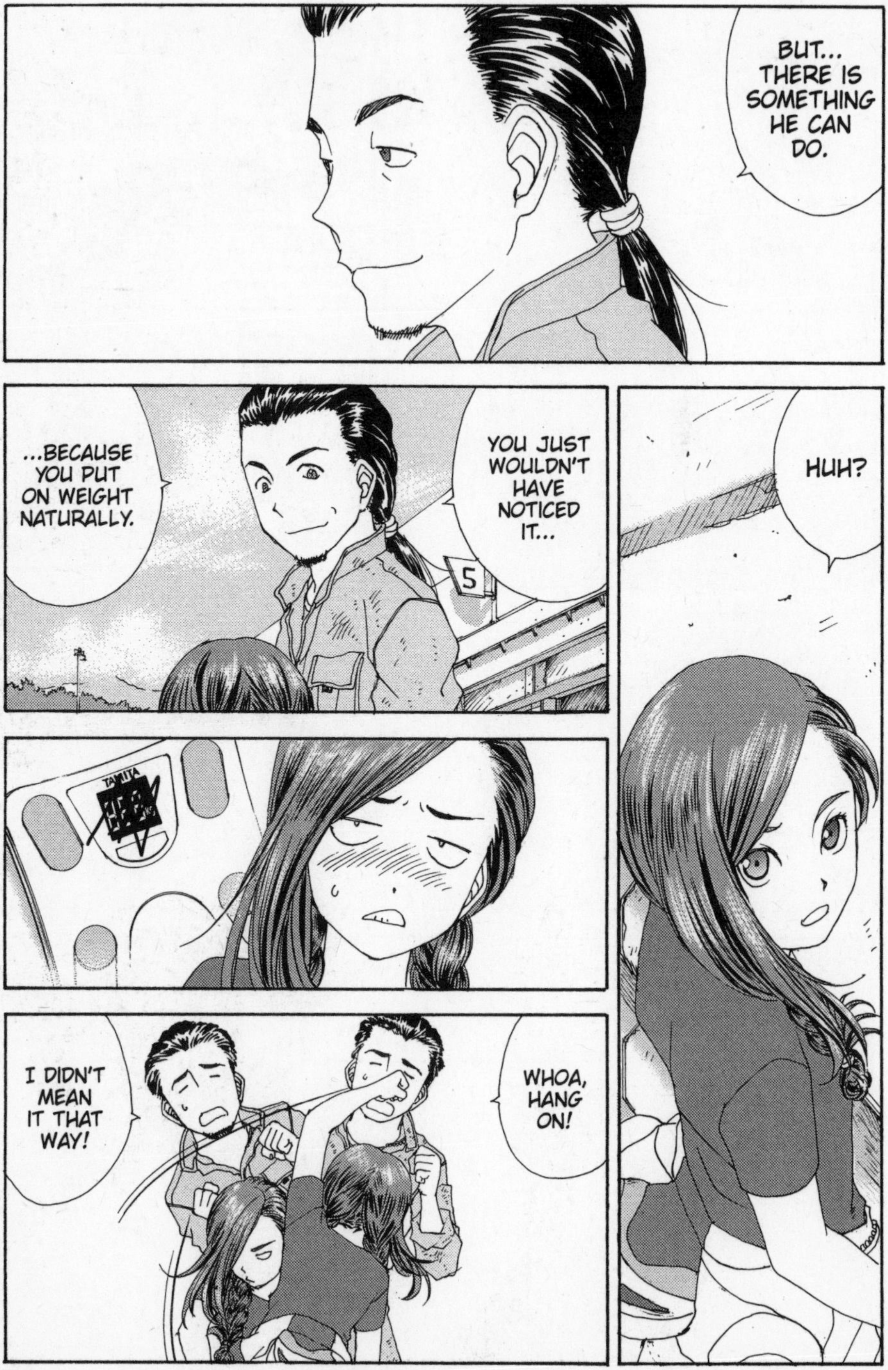
BUT... THERE IS SOMETHING HE CAN DO.
HUH?
YOU JUST WOULDN'T HAVE NOTICED IT...
...BECAUSE YOU PUT ON WEIGHT NATURALLY.
WHOA, HANG ON!
I DIDN'T MEAN IT THAT WAY!

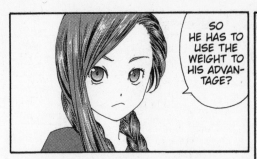

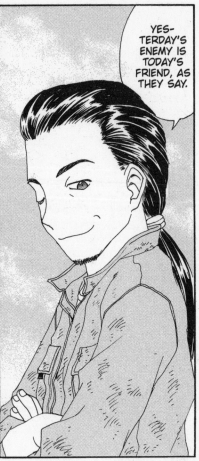

YES-TERDAY'S ENEMY IS TODAY'S FRIEND, AS THEY SAY.
SO HE HAS TO USE THE WEIGHT TO HIS ADVAN-TAGE?
OH! SO THAT'S WHAT YOU MEAN.
I'VE GOT TO GO TELL HIM.
HANG ON!!
TOPPU WILL FIGURE IT OUT.
BESIDES, IF HE CAN'T REALIZE THIS ON HIS OWN...

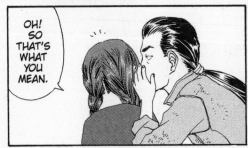

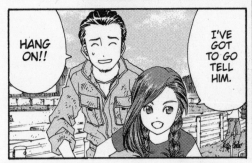

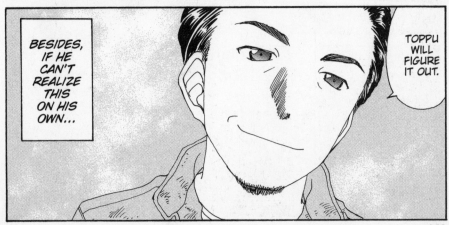

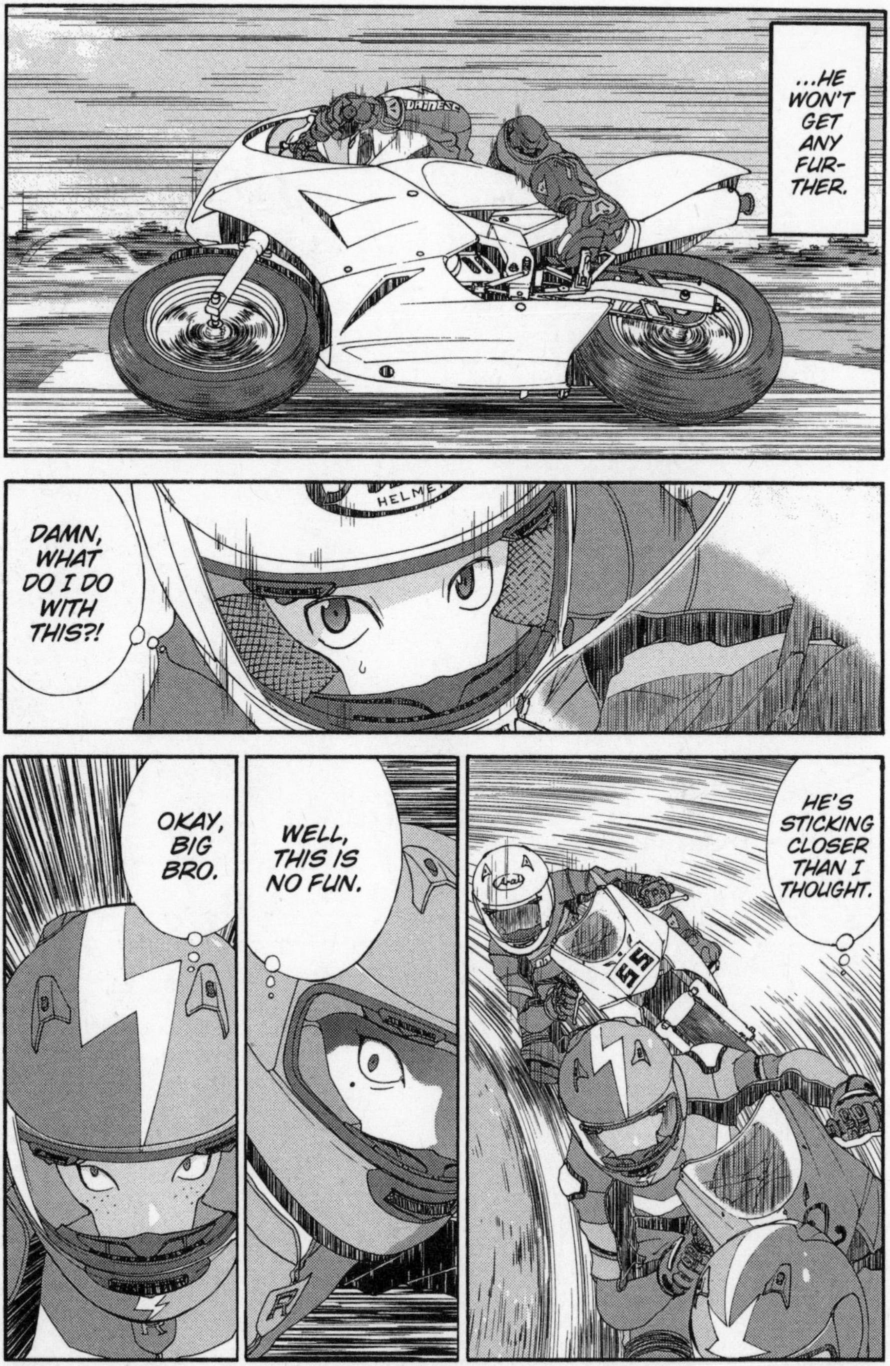
...HE WON'T GET ANY FUR-THER.
DAMN, WHAT DO I DO WITH THIS?!
HE'S STICKING CLOSER THAN I THOUGHT.
WELL, THIS IS NO FUN.
OKAY, BIG BRO.

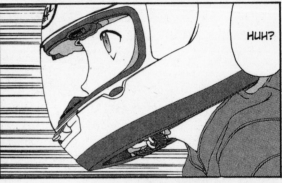

HUH?

HE'S KEEPING THE GAP CLOSE!

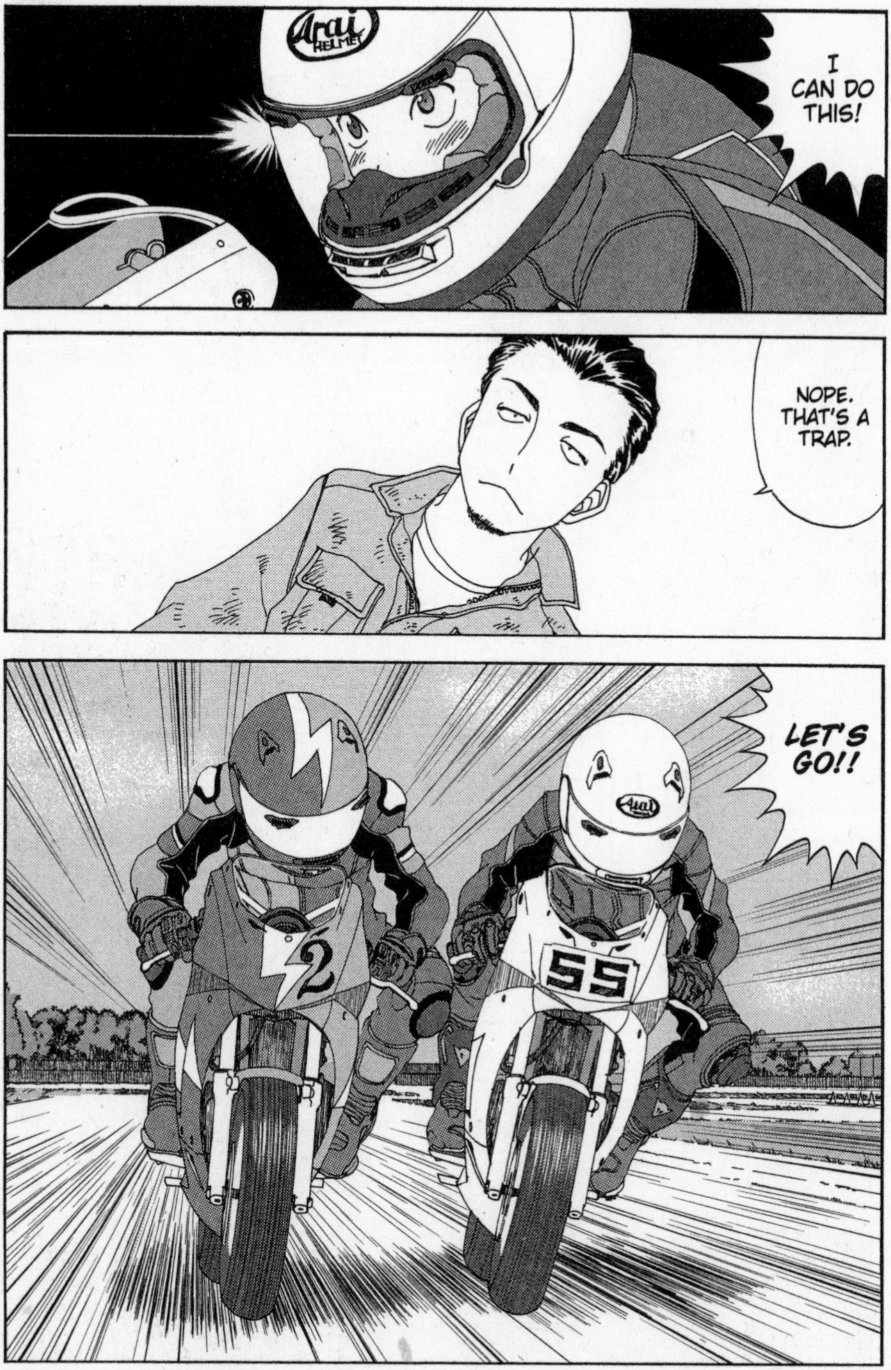
I CAN DO THIS!
NOPE. THAT'S A TRAP.
LET'S GO!!

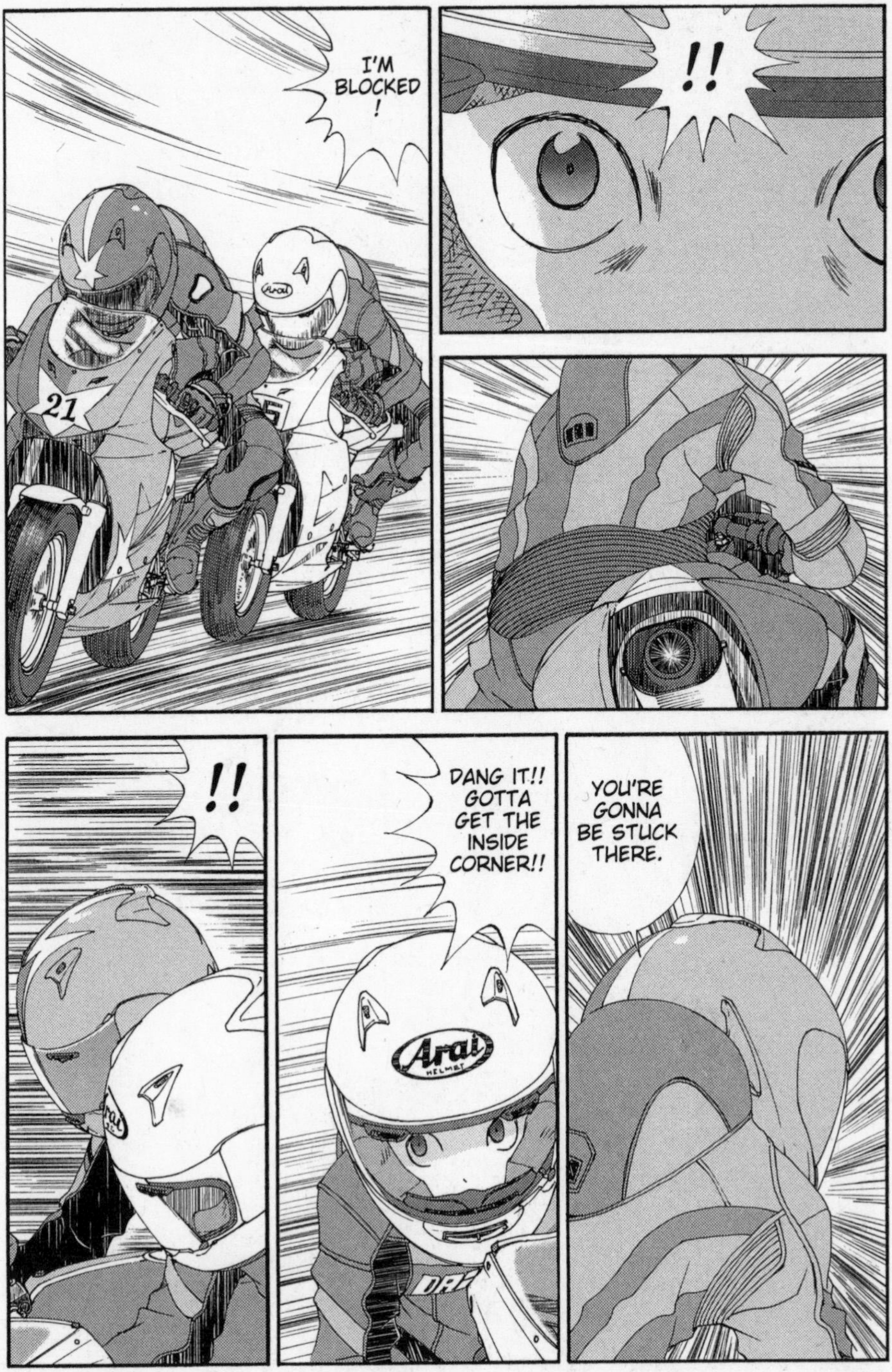
I'M BLOCKED!
!!
!!
DANG IT!! GOTTA GET THE INSIDE CORNER!!
YOU'RE GONNA BE STUCK THERE.

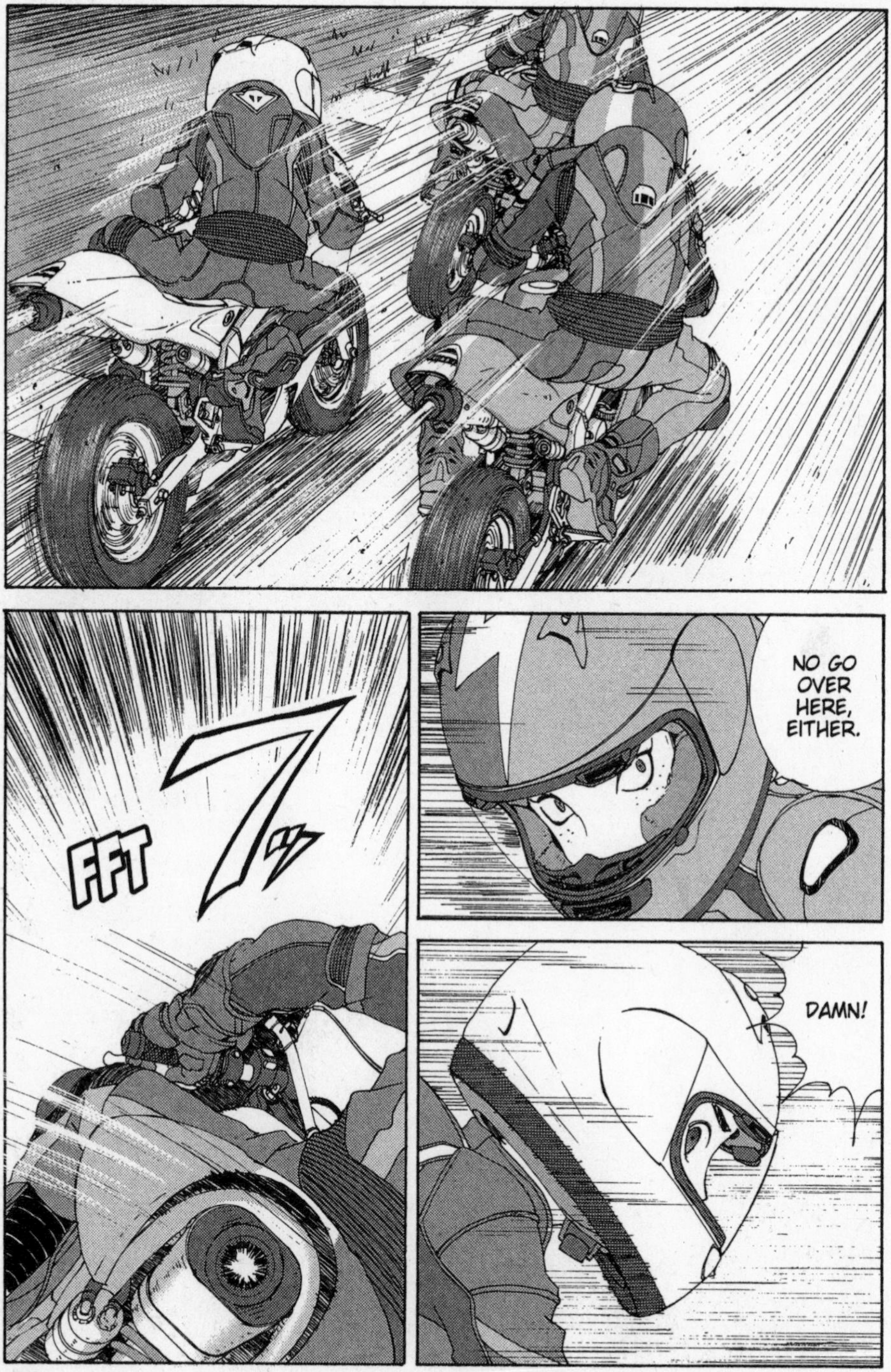
NO GO OVER HERE, EITHER.
FFT
DAMN!

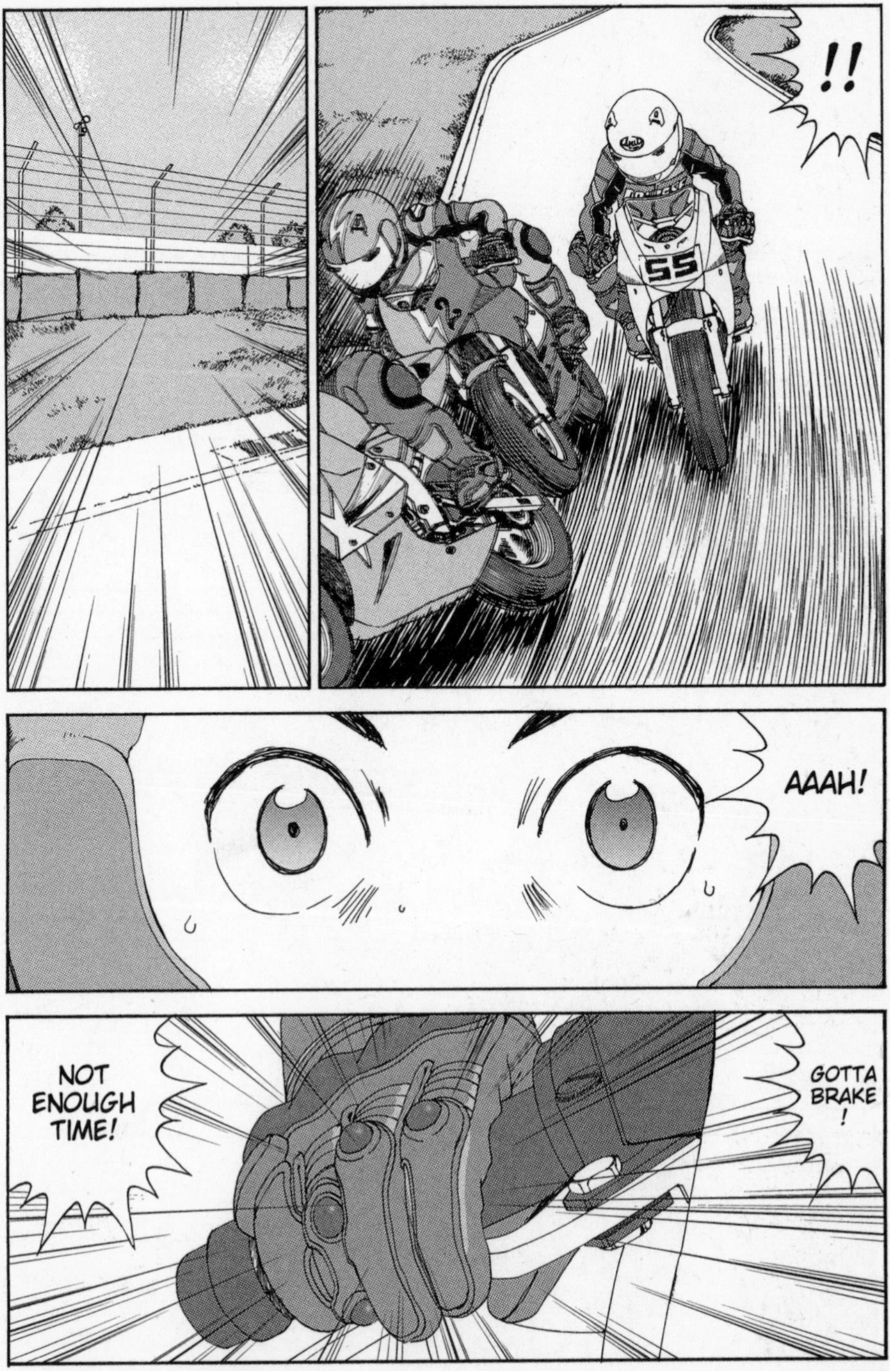
!!
AAAH!
GOTTA BRAKE!
NOT ENOUGH TIME!

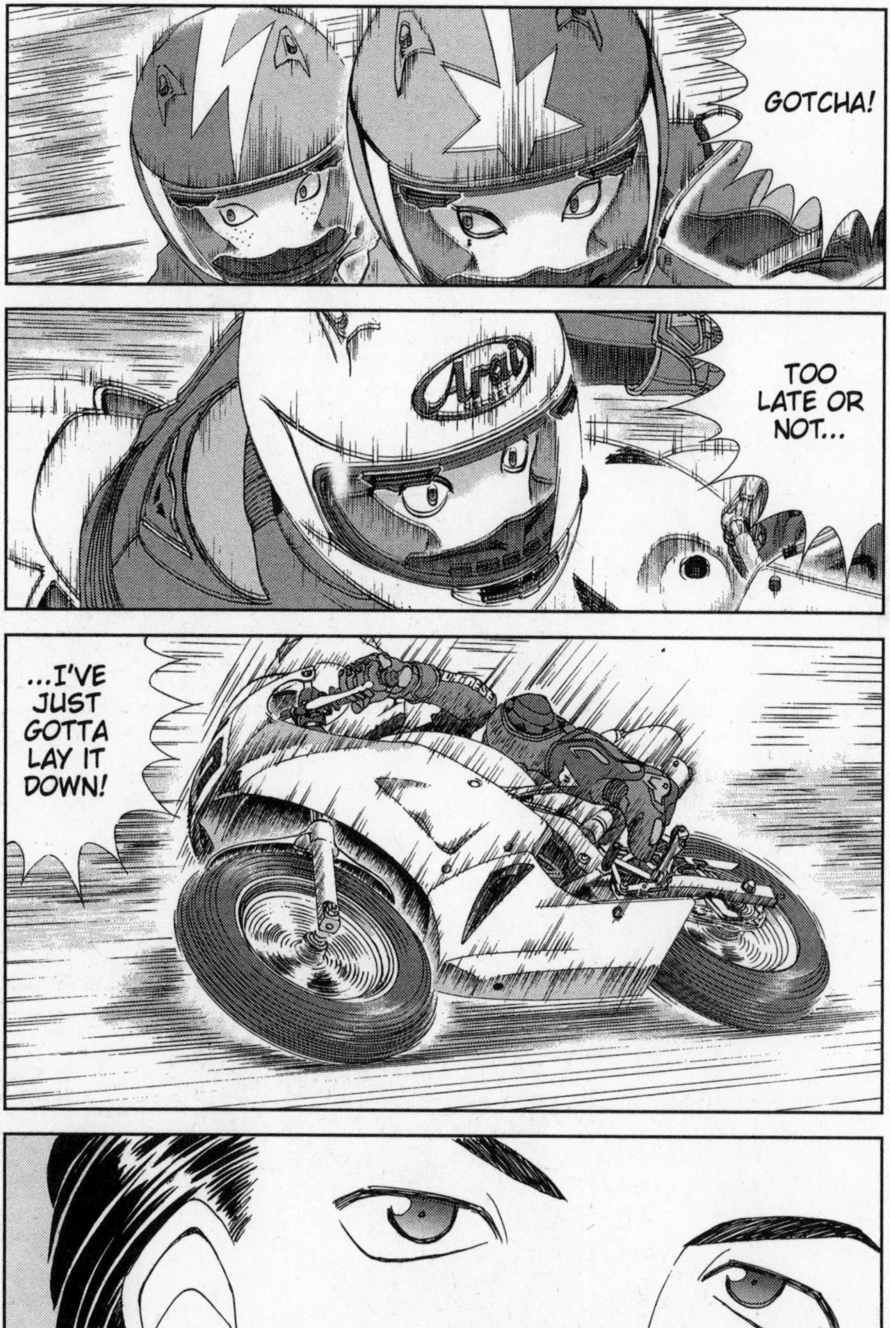
GOTCHA!
TOO LATE OR NOT...
...I'VE JUST GOTTA LAY IT DOWN!

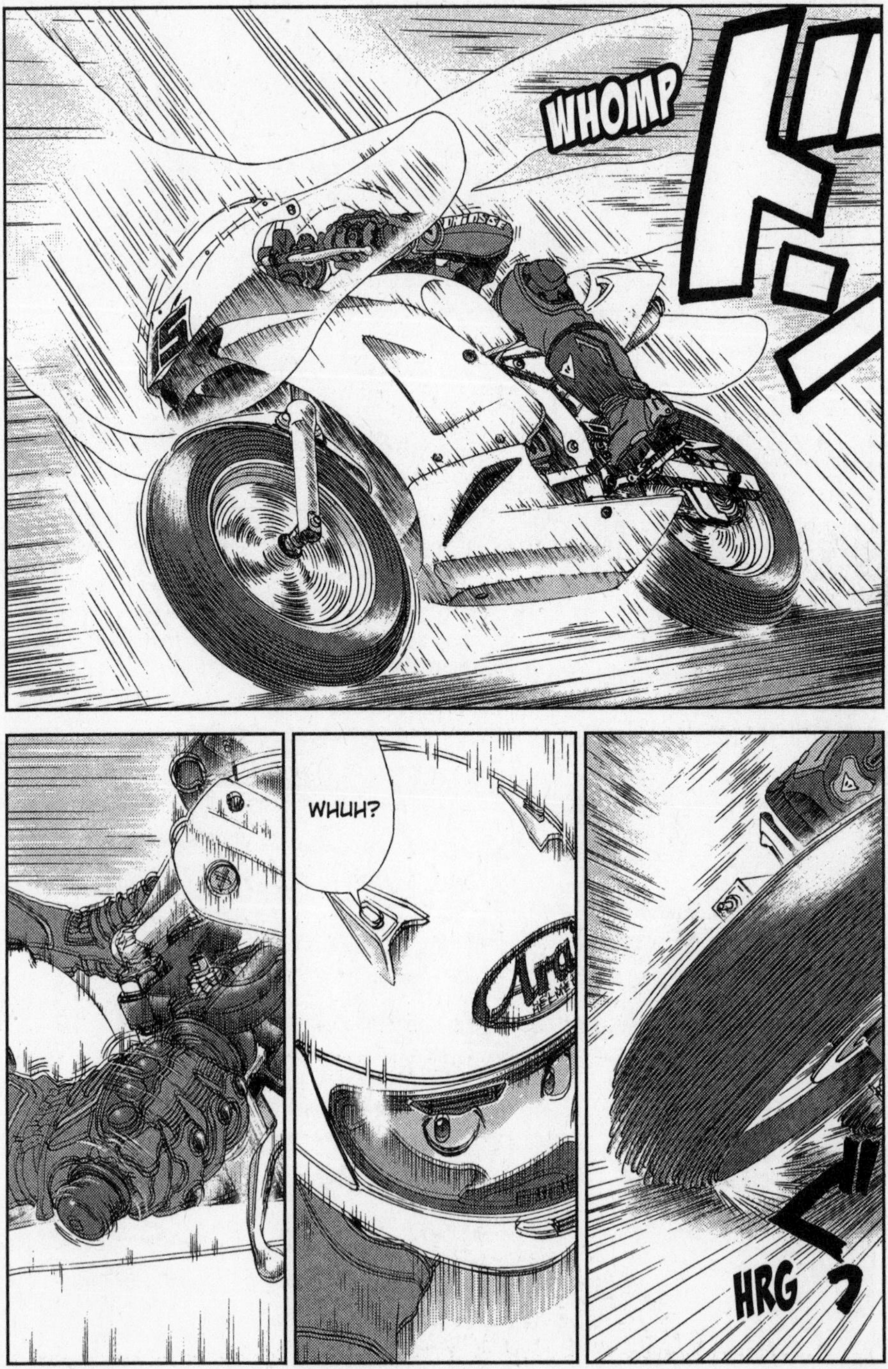
WHOMP
HRG
WHUH?

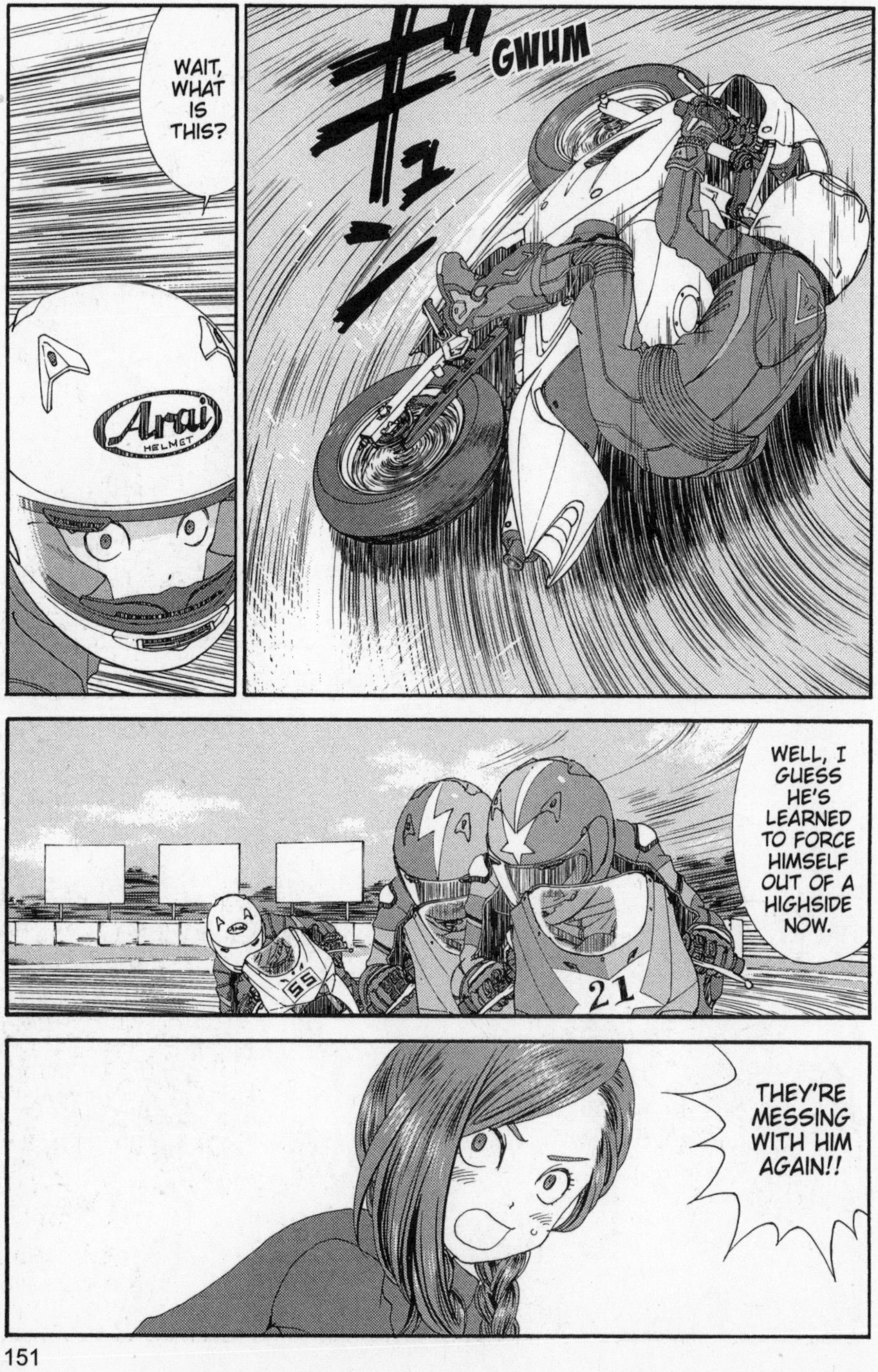
GWUM
WAIT, WHAT IS THIS?
Arai HELMET
WELL, I GUESS HE'S LEARNED TO FORCE HIMSELF OUT OF A HIGHSIDE NOW.
21
55
THEY'RE MESSING WITH HIM AGAIN!!

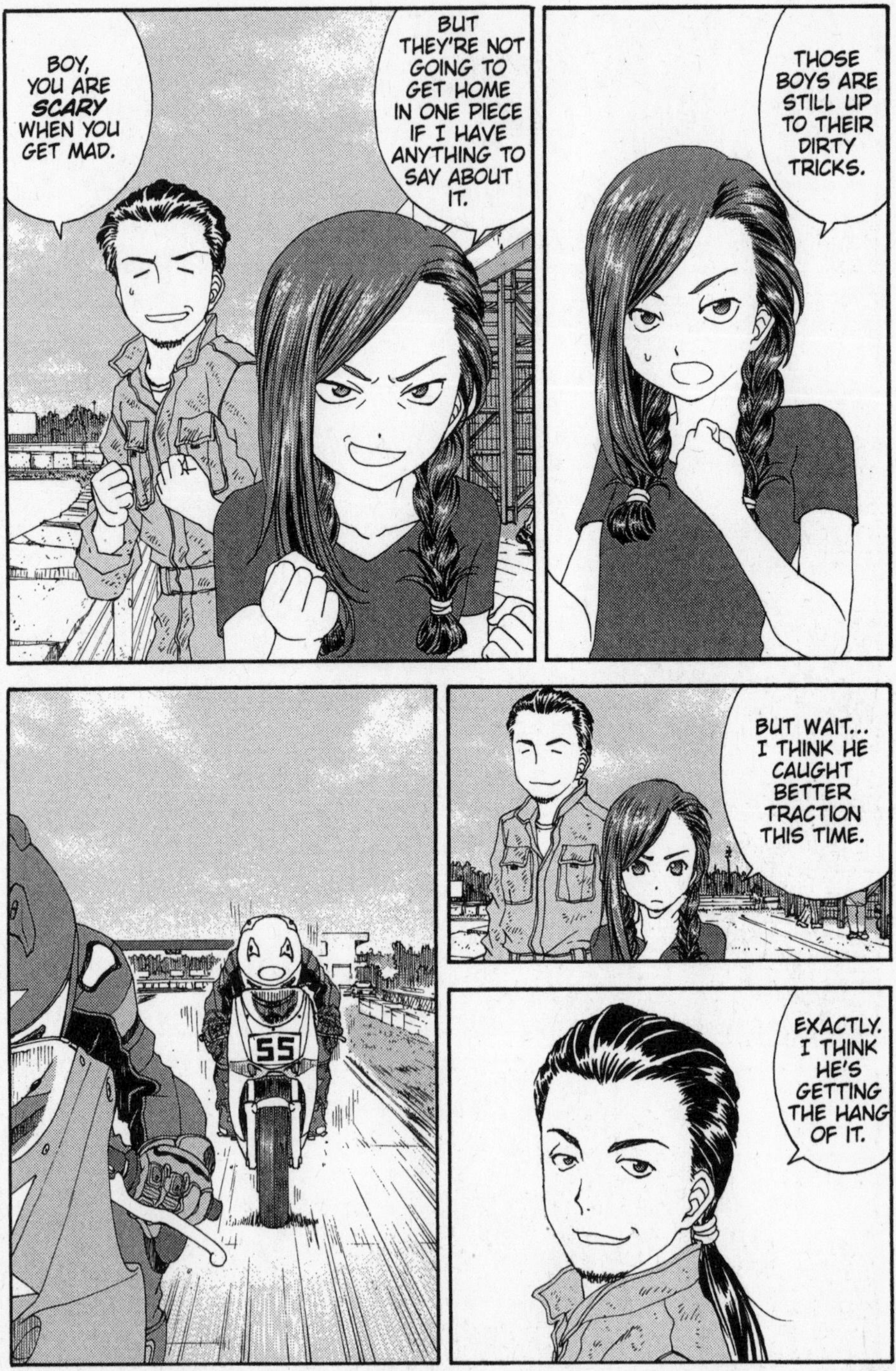
THOSE BOYS ARE STILL UP TO THEIR DIRTY TRICKS.
BUT THEY'RE NOT GOING TO GET HOME IN ONE PIECE IF I HAVE ANYTHING TO SAY ABOUT IT.
BOY, YOU ARE *SCARY* WHEN YOU GET MAD.
BUT WAIT... I THINK HE CAUGHT BETTER TRACTION THIS TIME.
EXACTLY. I THINK HE'S GETTING THE HANG OF IT.
55

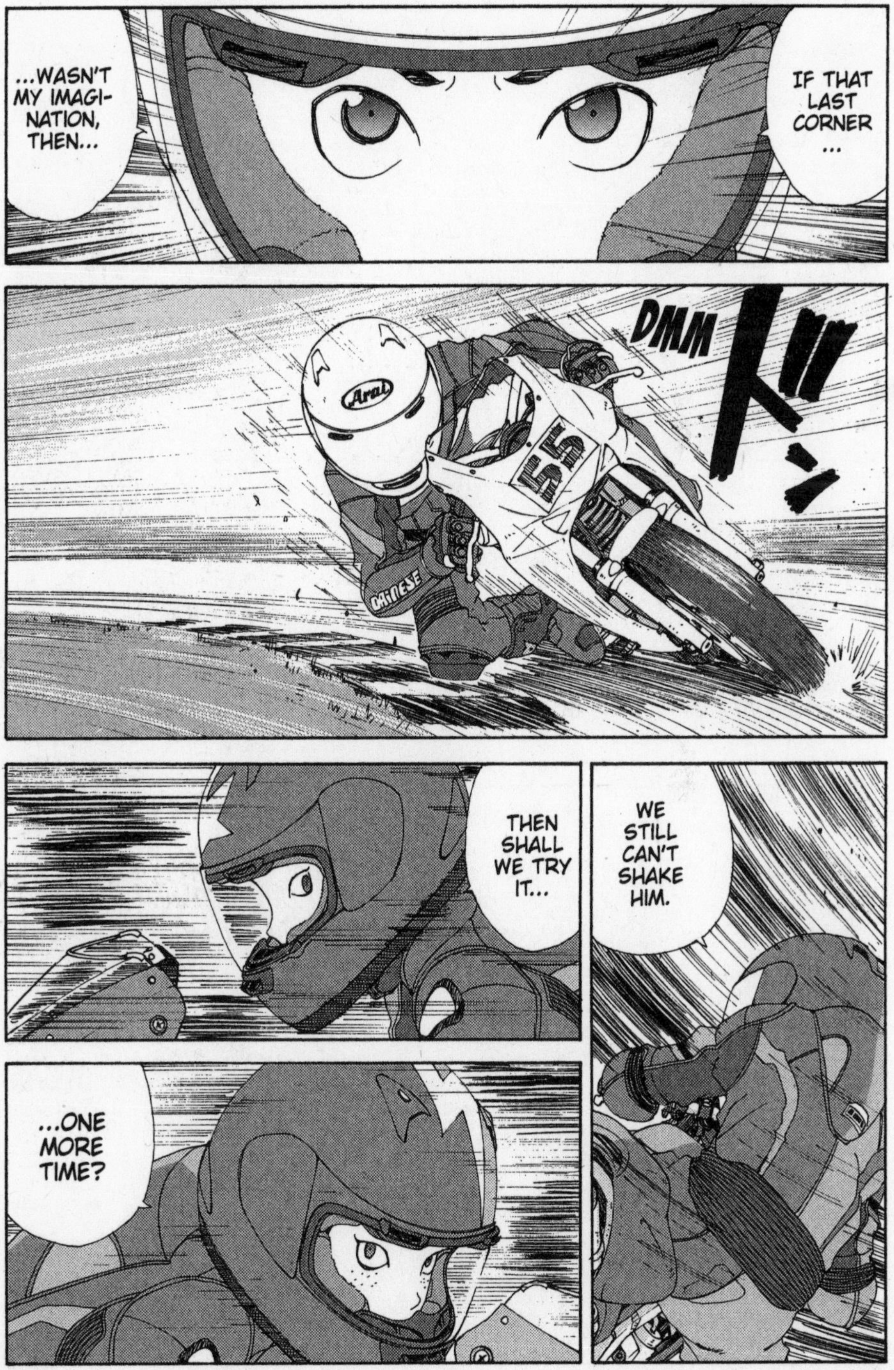
IF THAT LAST CORNER ...
...WASN'T MY IMAGINATION, THEN...
DMM
ドン
WE STILL CAN'T SHAKE HIM.
THEN SHALL WE TRY IT...
...ONE MORE TIME?

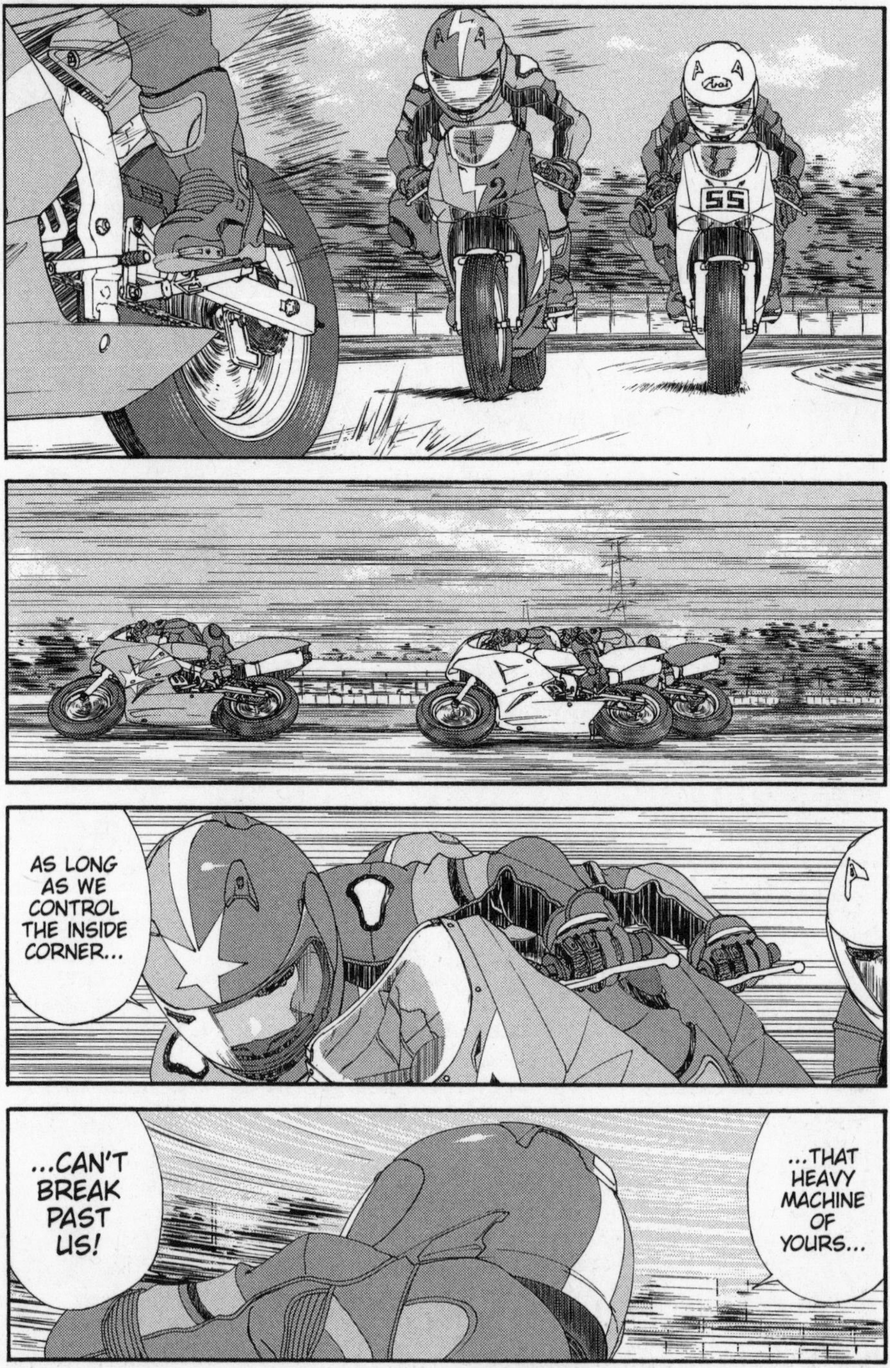
AS LONG AS WE CONTROL THE INSIDE CORNER...
...THAT HEAVY MACHINE OF YOURS...
...CAN'T BREAK PAST US!

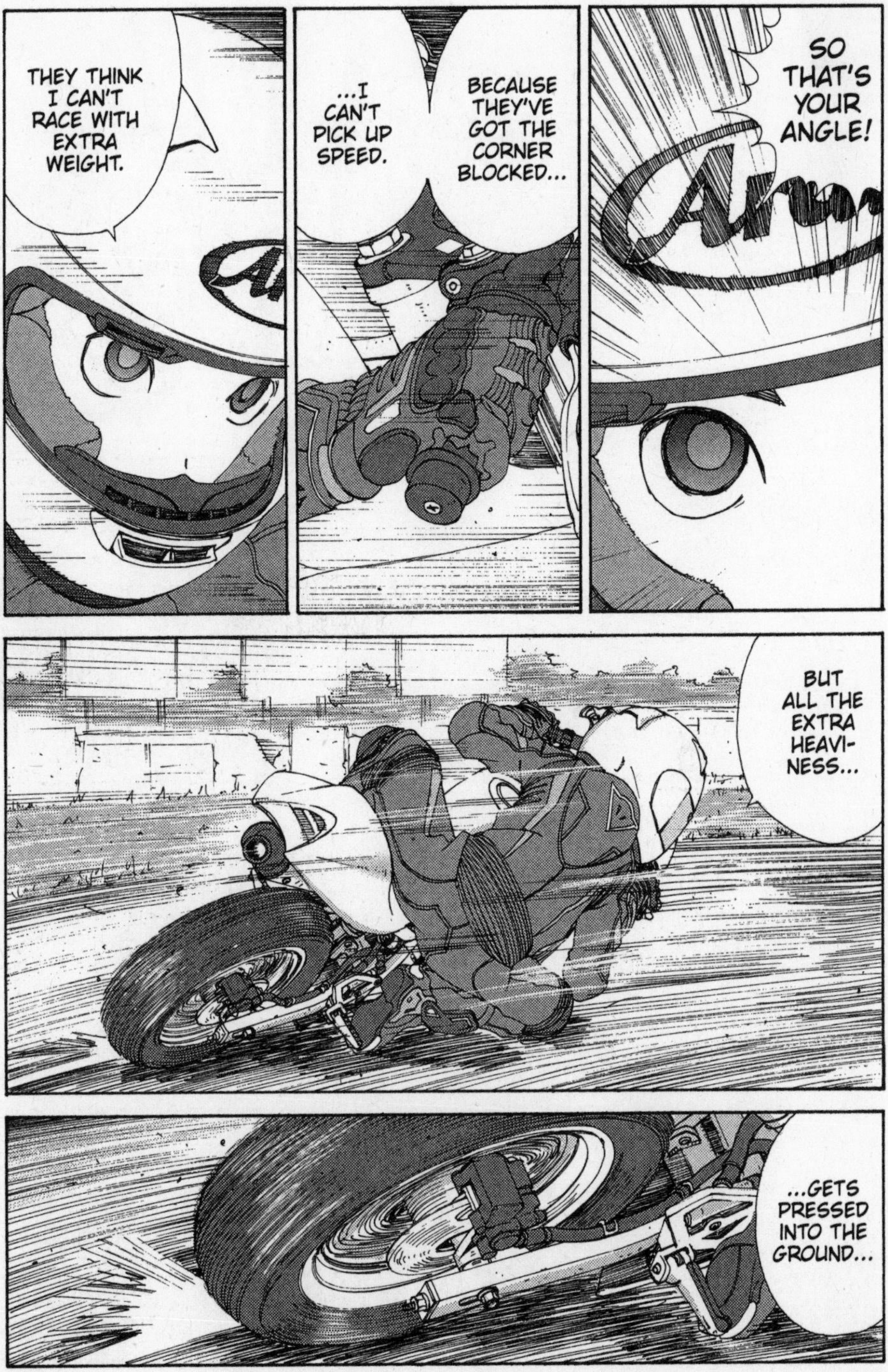
SO THAT'S YOUR ANGLE!
BECAUSE THEY'VE GOT THE CORNER BLOCKED...
...I CAN'T PICK UP SPEED.
THEY THINK I CAN'T RACE WITH EXTRA WEIGHT.
BUT ALL THE EXTRA HEAVINESS...
...GETS PRESSED INTO THE GROUND...

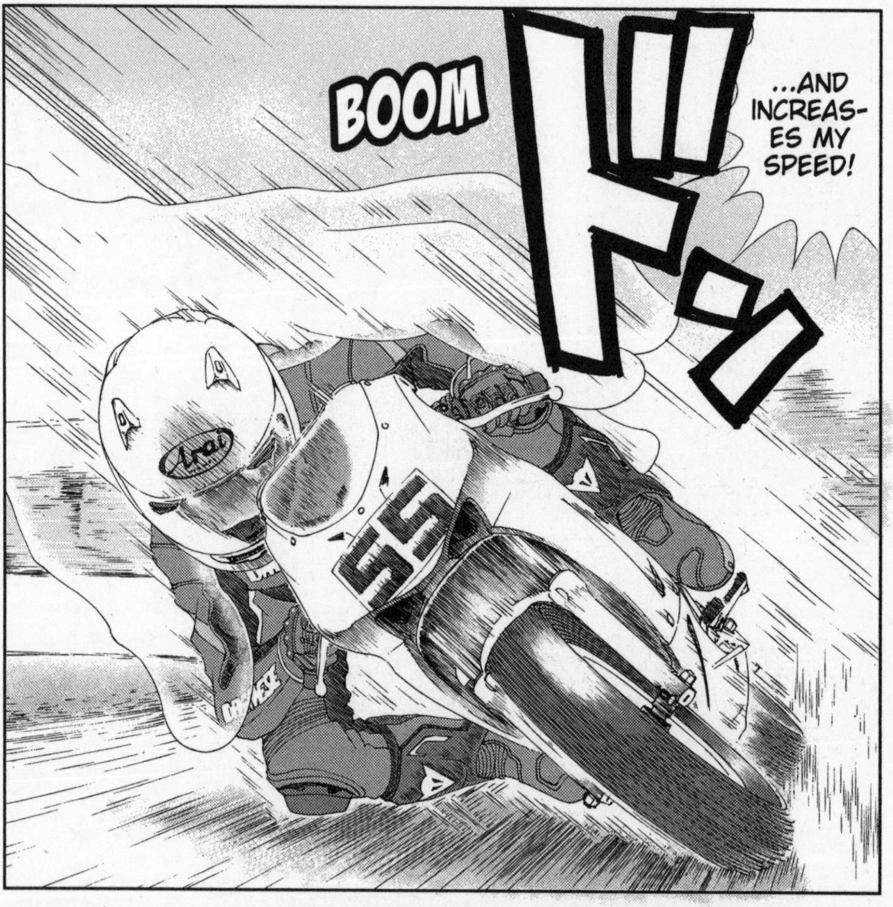
BOOM
...AND INCREASES MY SPEED!
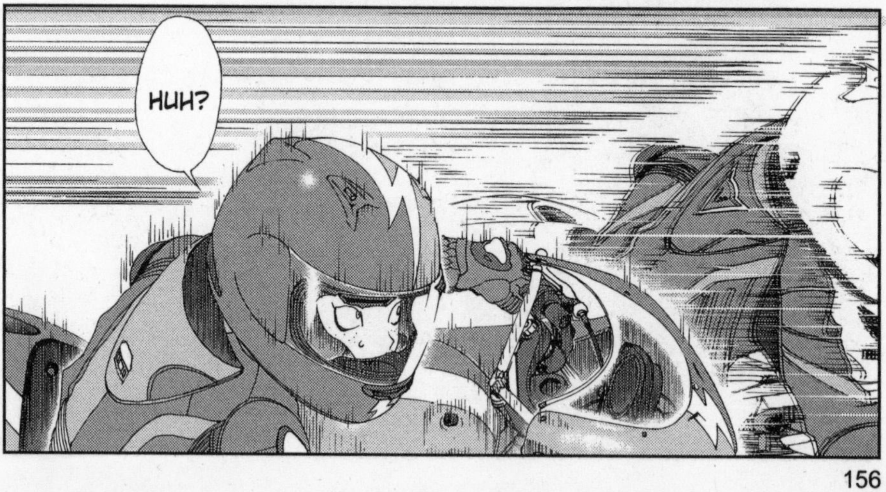
HUH?

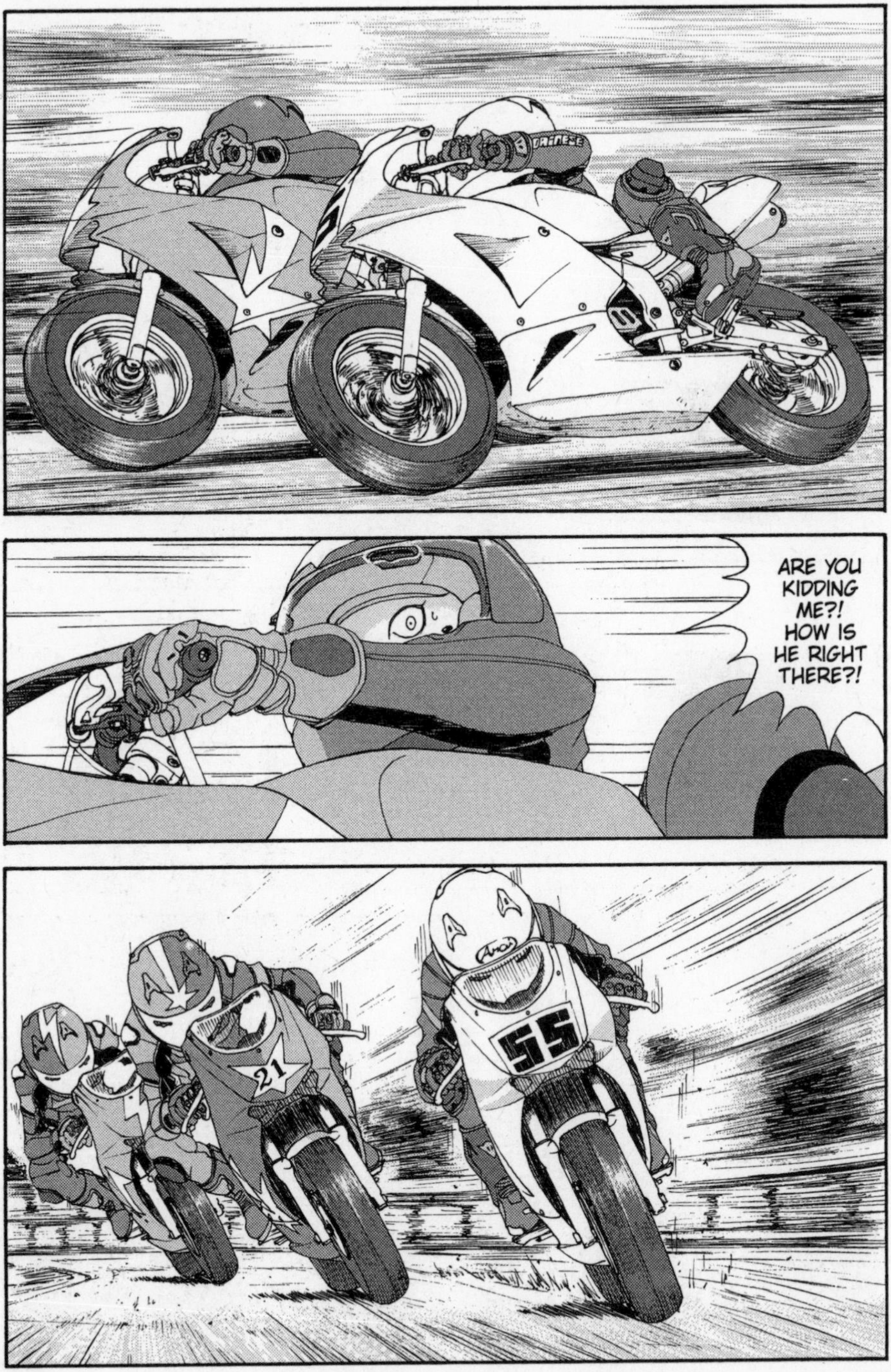
ARE YOU KIDDING ME?! HOW IS HE RIGHT THERE?!

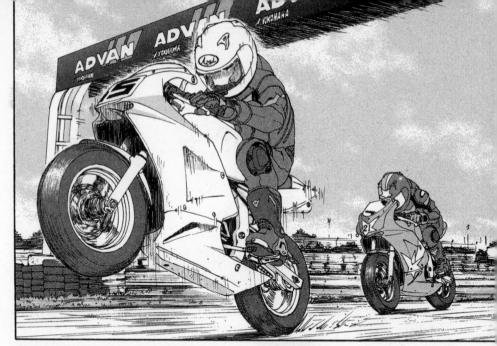

WOW! WOW!

HE DID IT!

OH, RIGHT...

YOU GONNA KISS HIM?

SO...

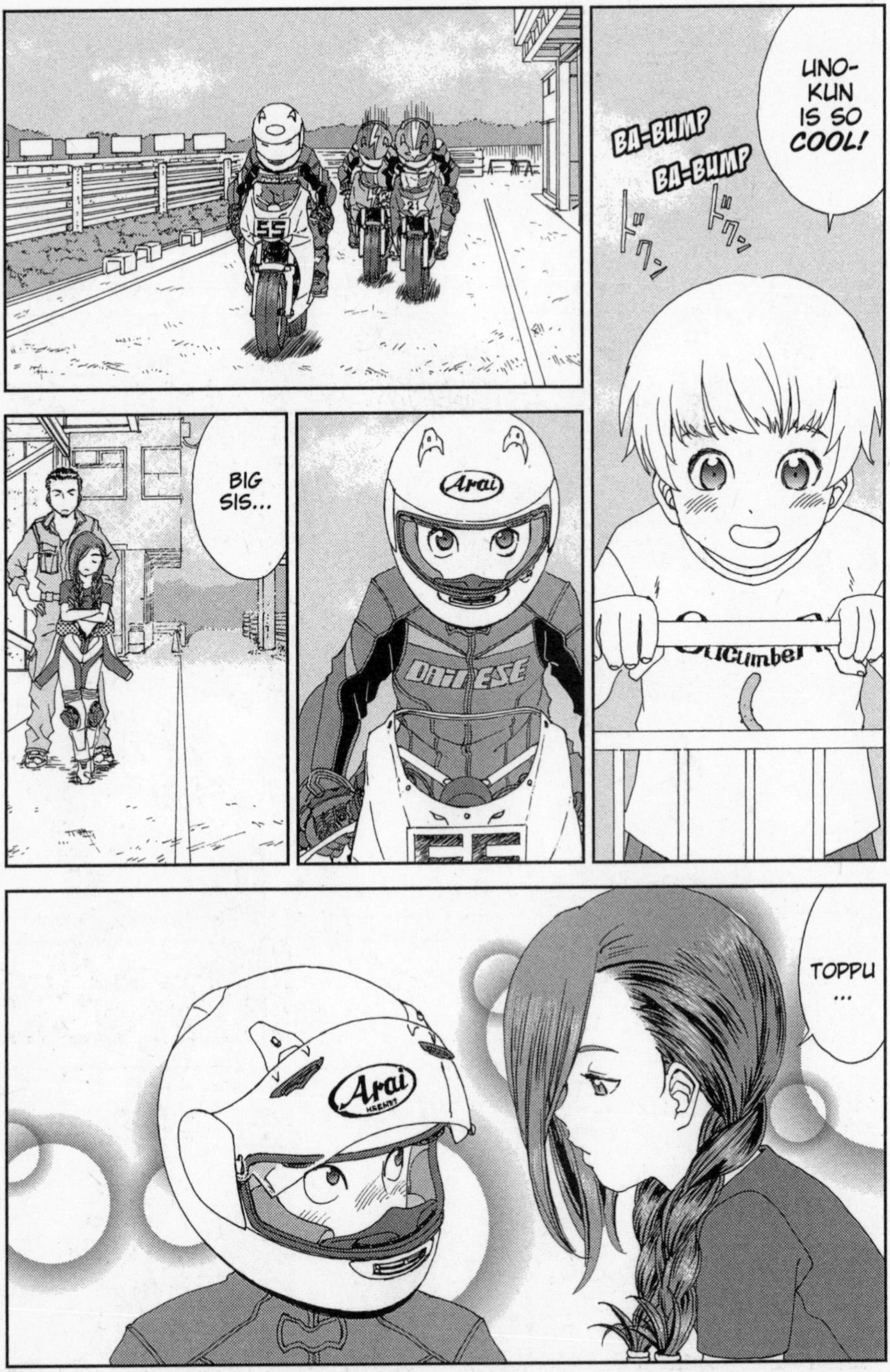
UNO-KUN IS SO COOL!
BA-BUMP
BA-BUMP
ドクン
ドクン
BIG SIS...
TOPPU ...

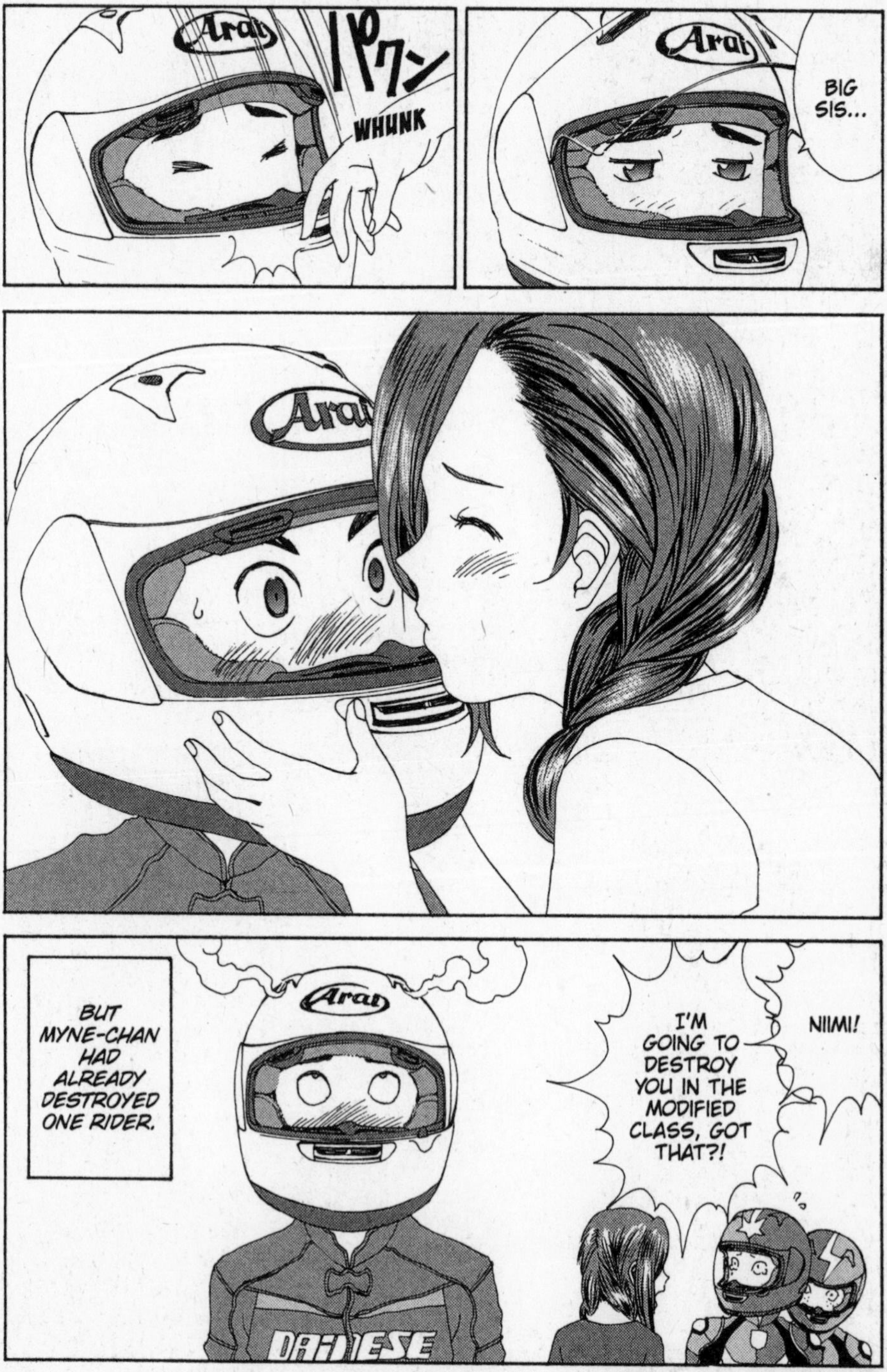
BIG SIS...
パクン
WHUNK
NIIMI!
I'M GOING TO DESTROY YOU IN THE MODIFIED CLASS, GOT THAT?!
BUT MYNE-CHAN HAD ALREADY DESTROYED ONE RIDER.

Lap 6: end

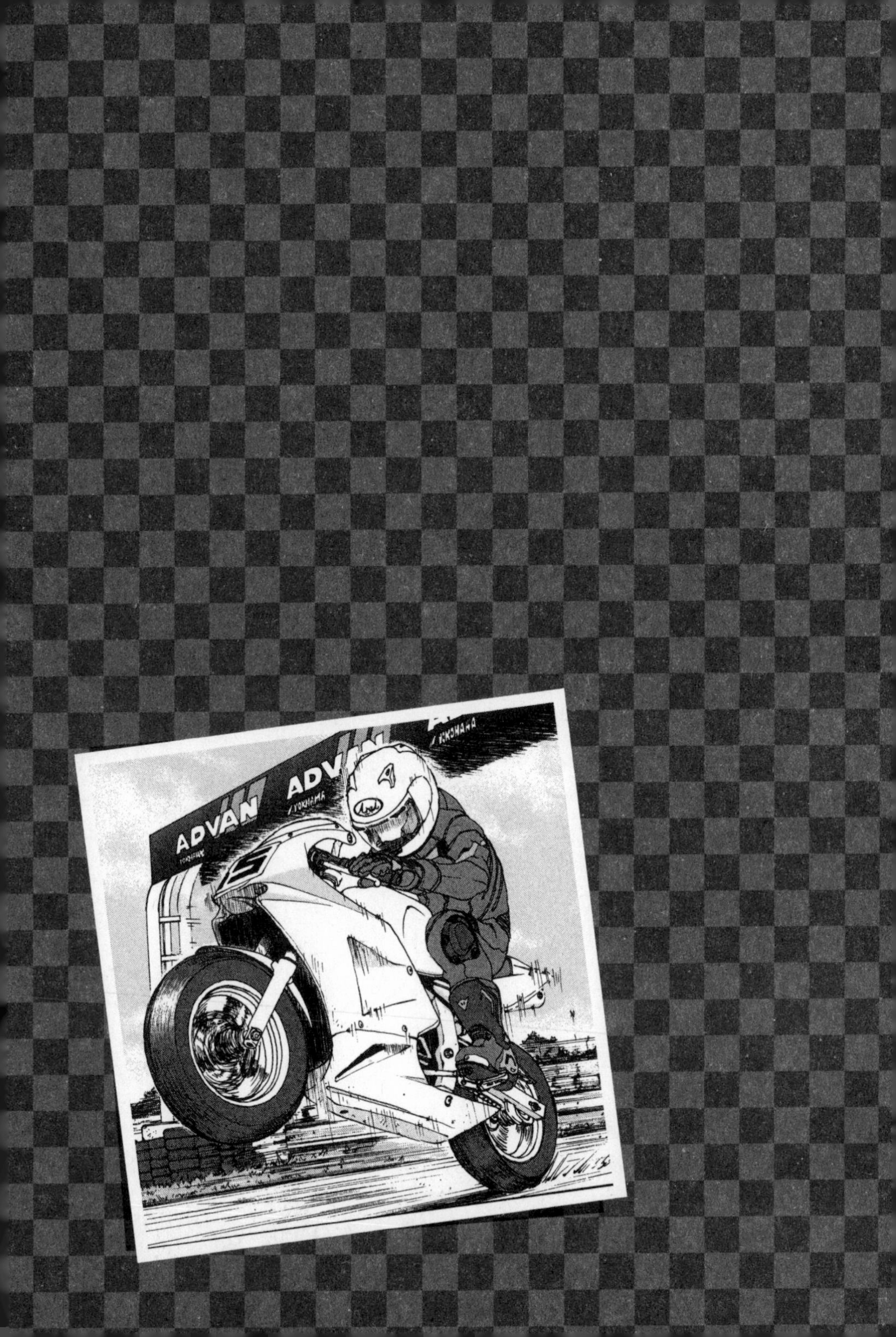
ADVAN
/YOKOHAMA
ADV
/YOKOHAMA
ADVAN

Toppu GP

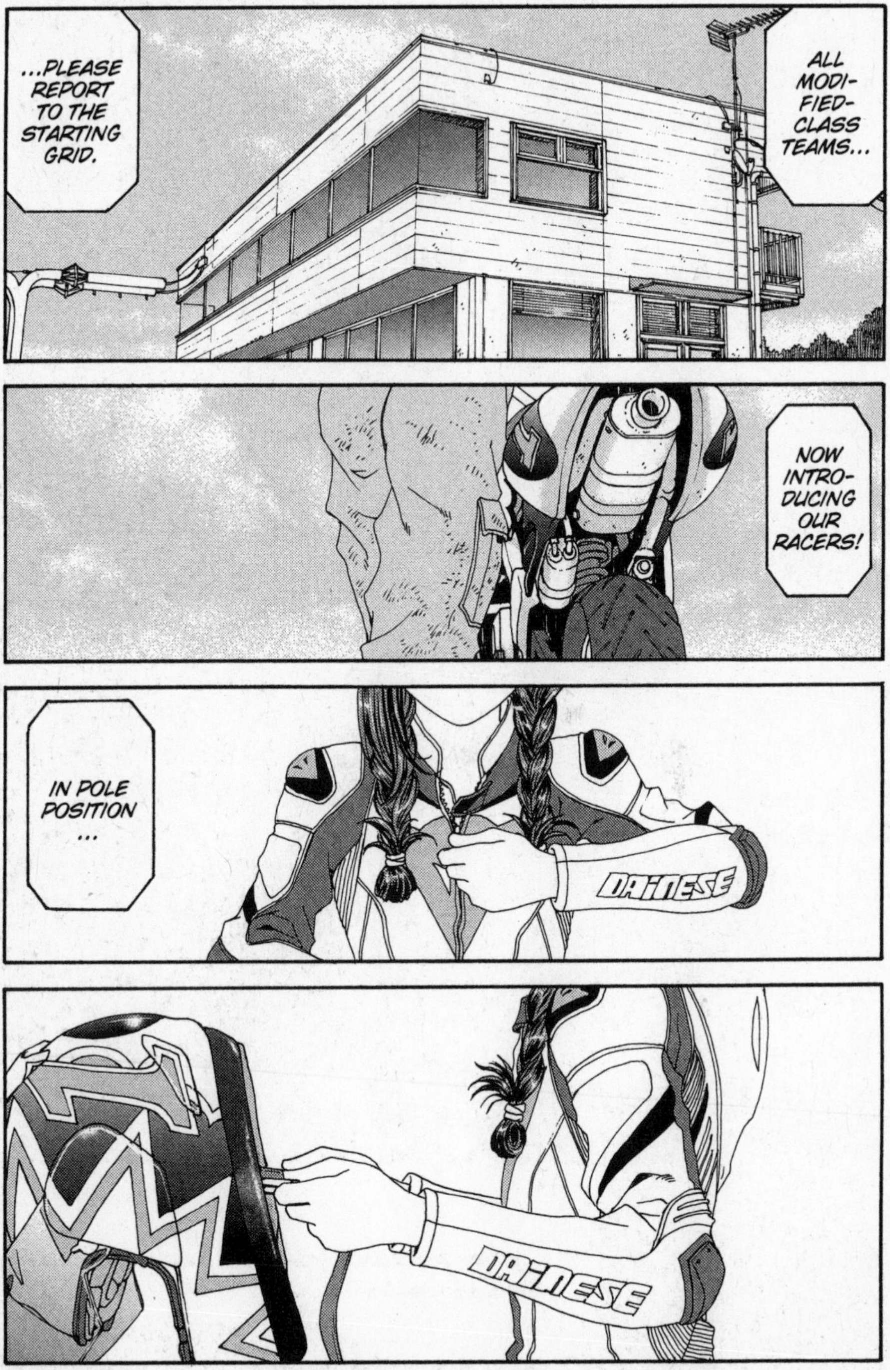
ALL MODIFIED-CLASS TEAMS...
...PLEASE REPORT TO THE STARTING GRID.
NOW INTRODUCING OUR RACERS!
IN POLE POSITION ...
DAINESE
DAINESE

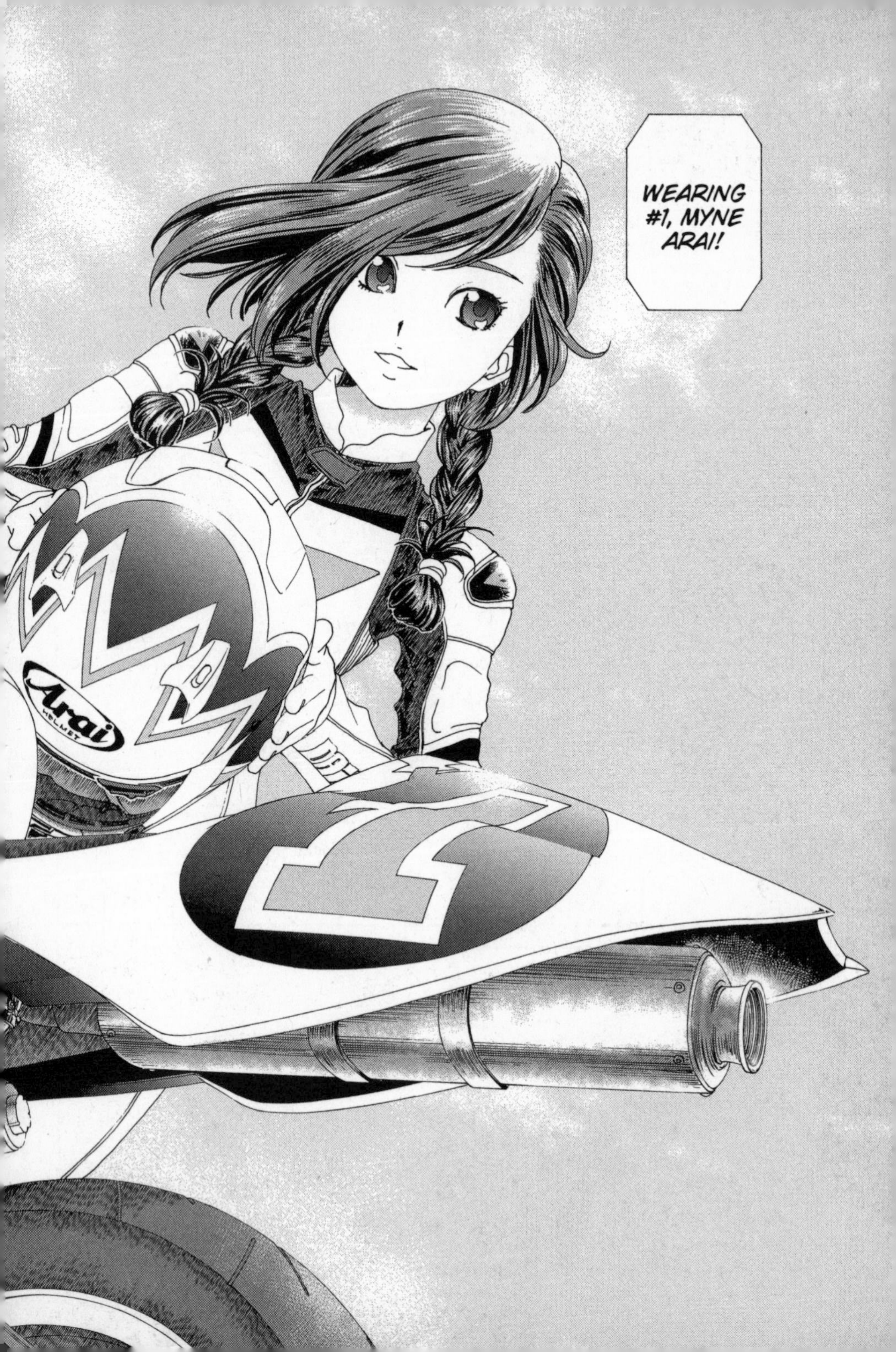
WEARING #1, MYNE ARAI!

Lap 7:
FEMALE RIDER

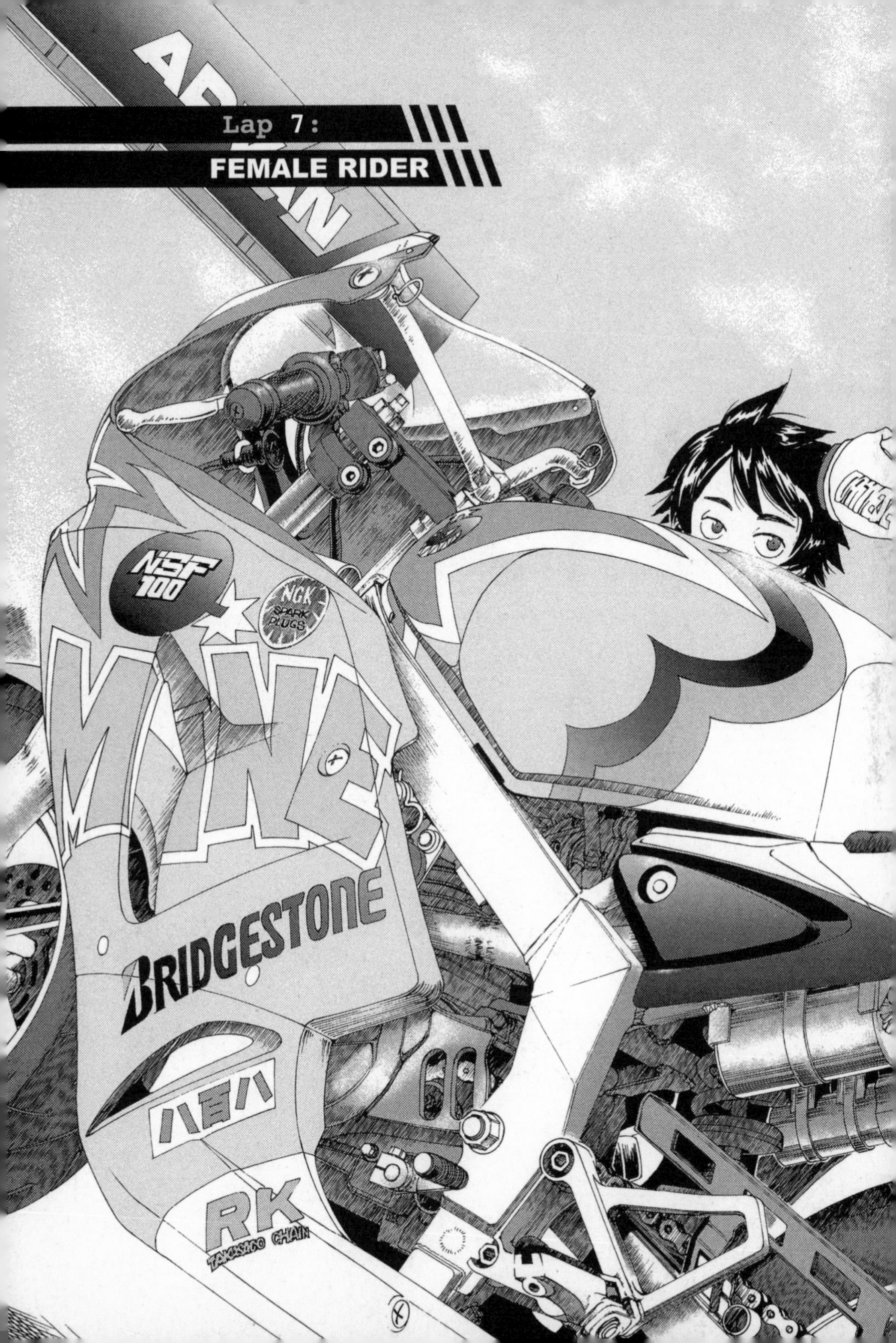
NSF 100
NGK SPARK PLUGS
BRIDGESTONE
八百八
RK
TAKASAGO CHAIN

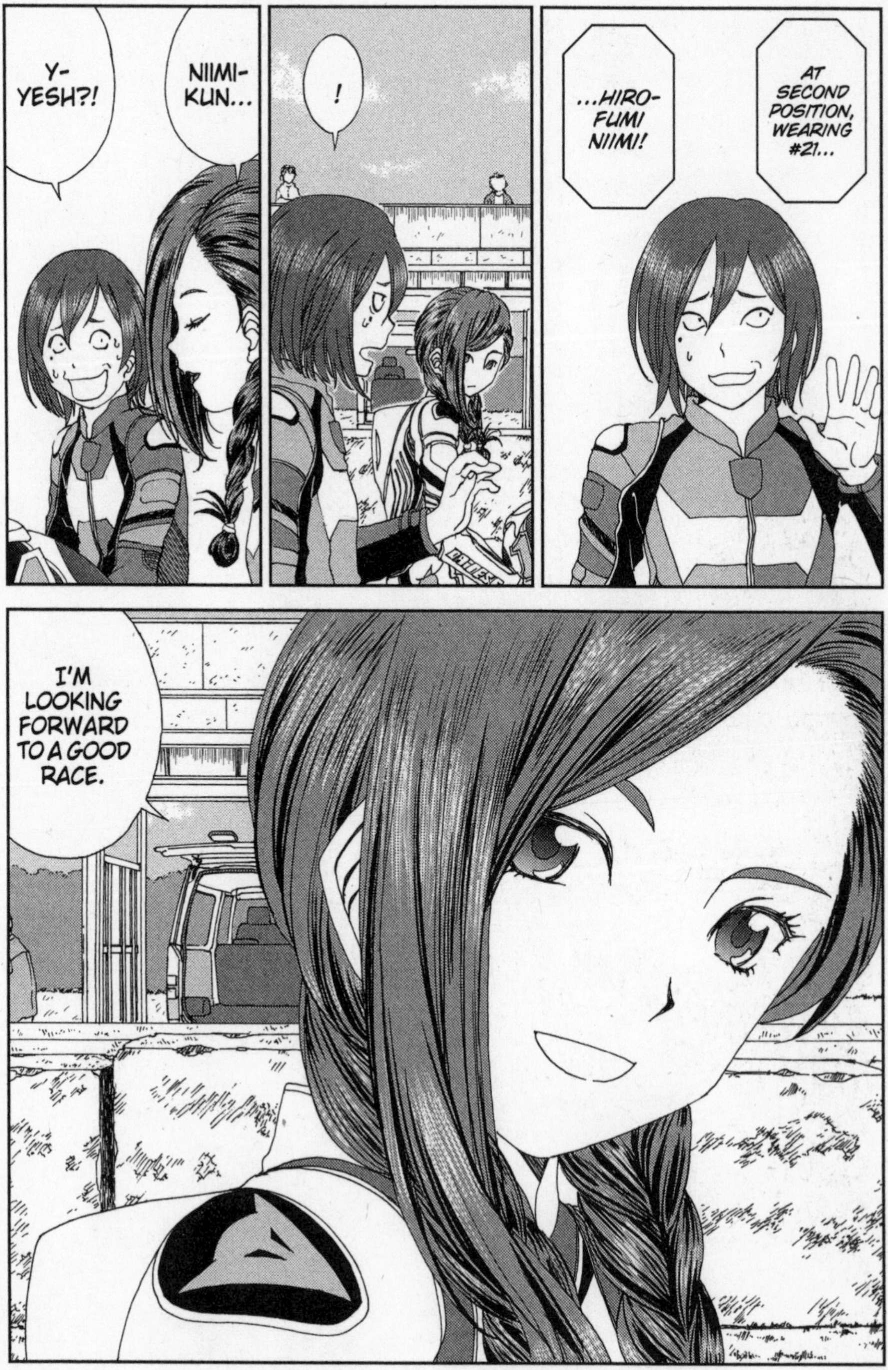
AT SECOND POSITION, WEARING #21...
...HIRO-FUMI NIIMI!
!
NIIMI-KUN...
Y-YESH?!
I'M LOOKING FORWARD TO A GOOD RACE.

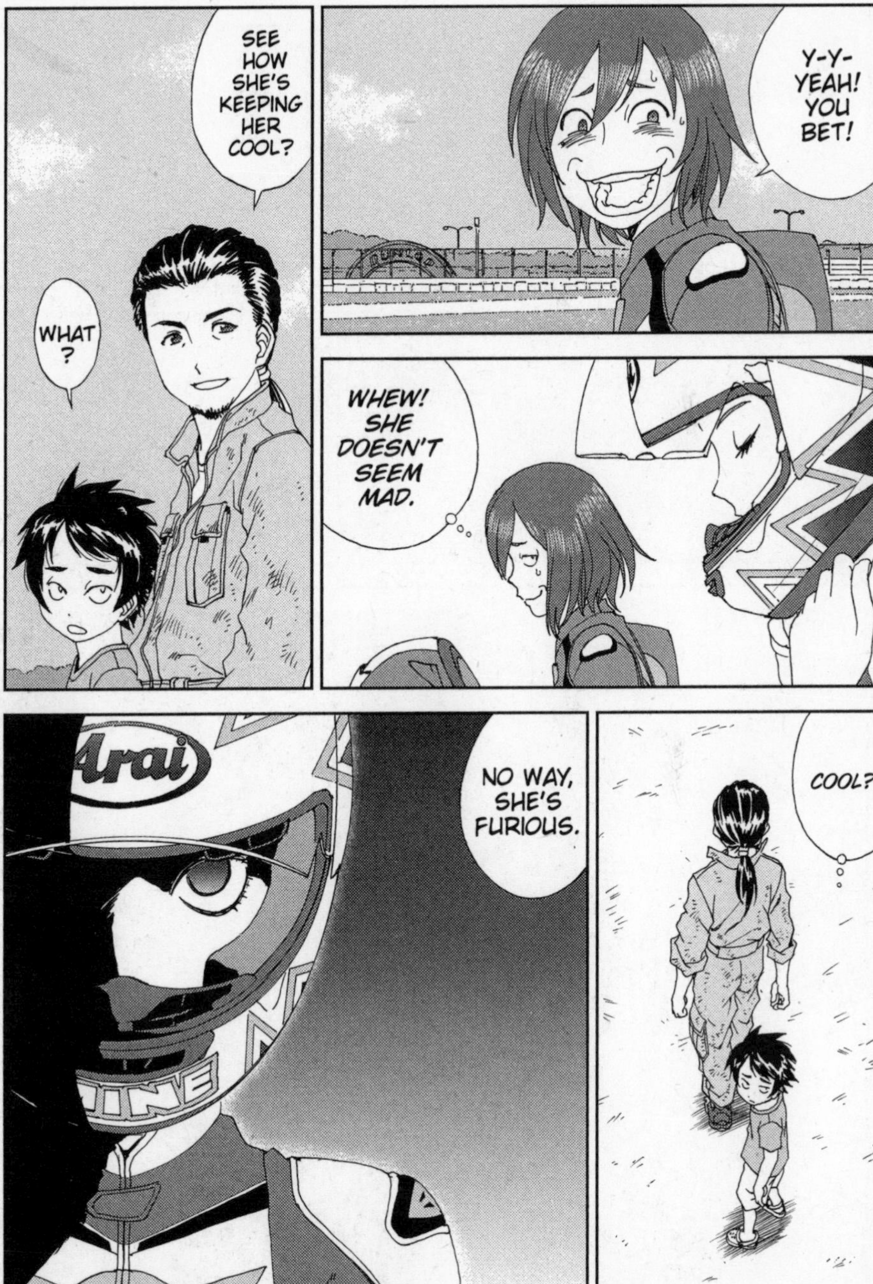
SEE HOW SHE'S KEEPING HER COOL?
WHAT?
Y-Y-YEAH! YOU BET!
WHEW! SHE DOESN'T SEEM MAD.
NO WAY, SHE'S FURIOUS.
COOL?

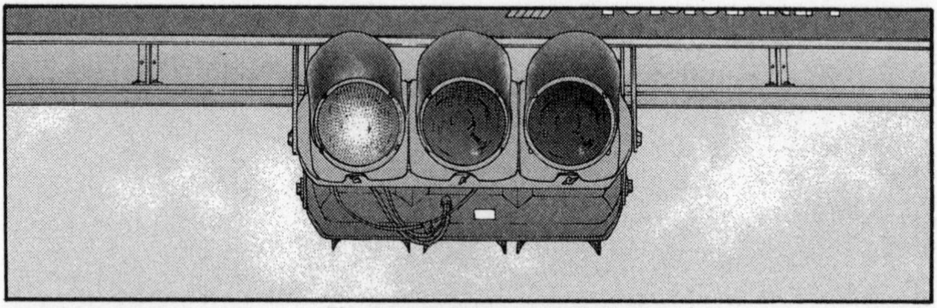

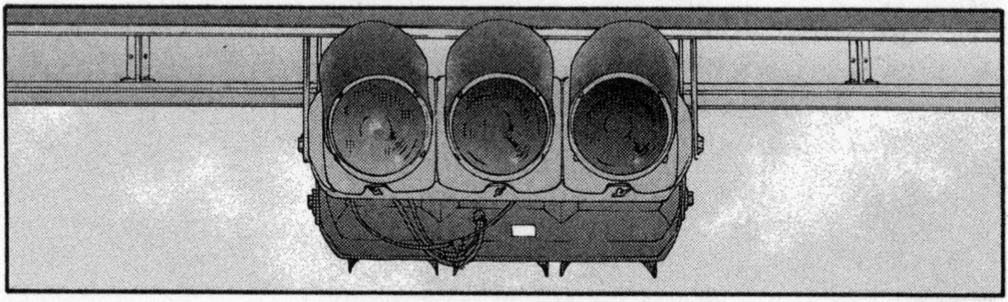

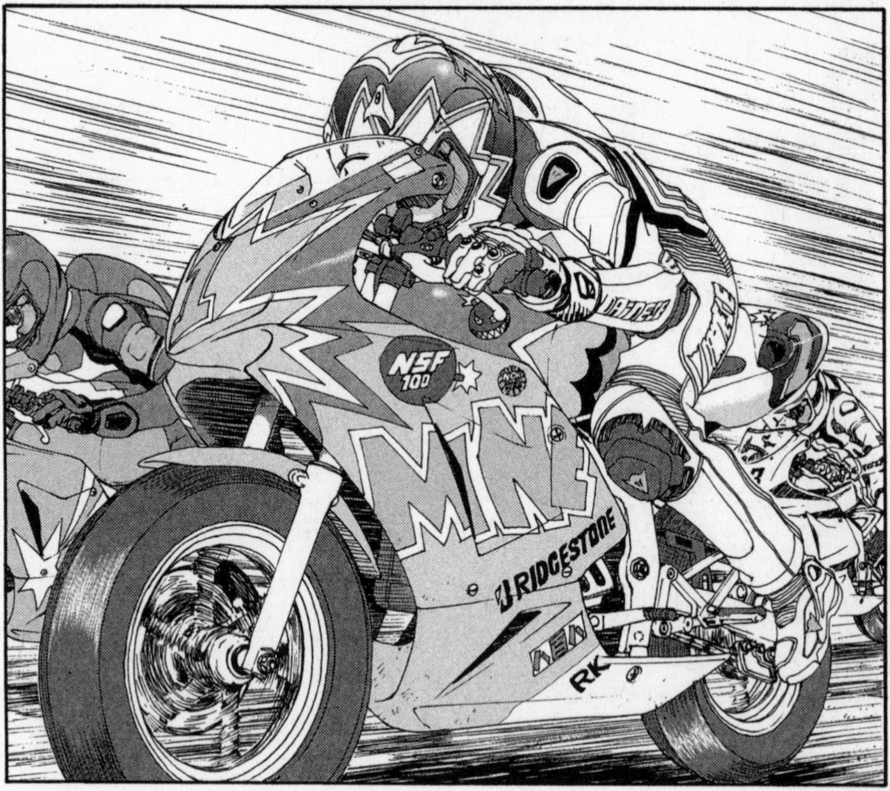
NSF
100
BRIDGESTONE
RK

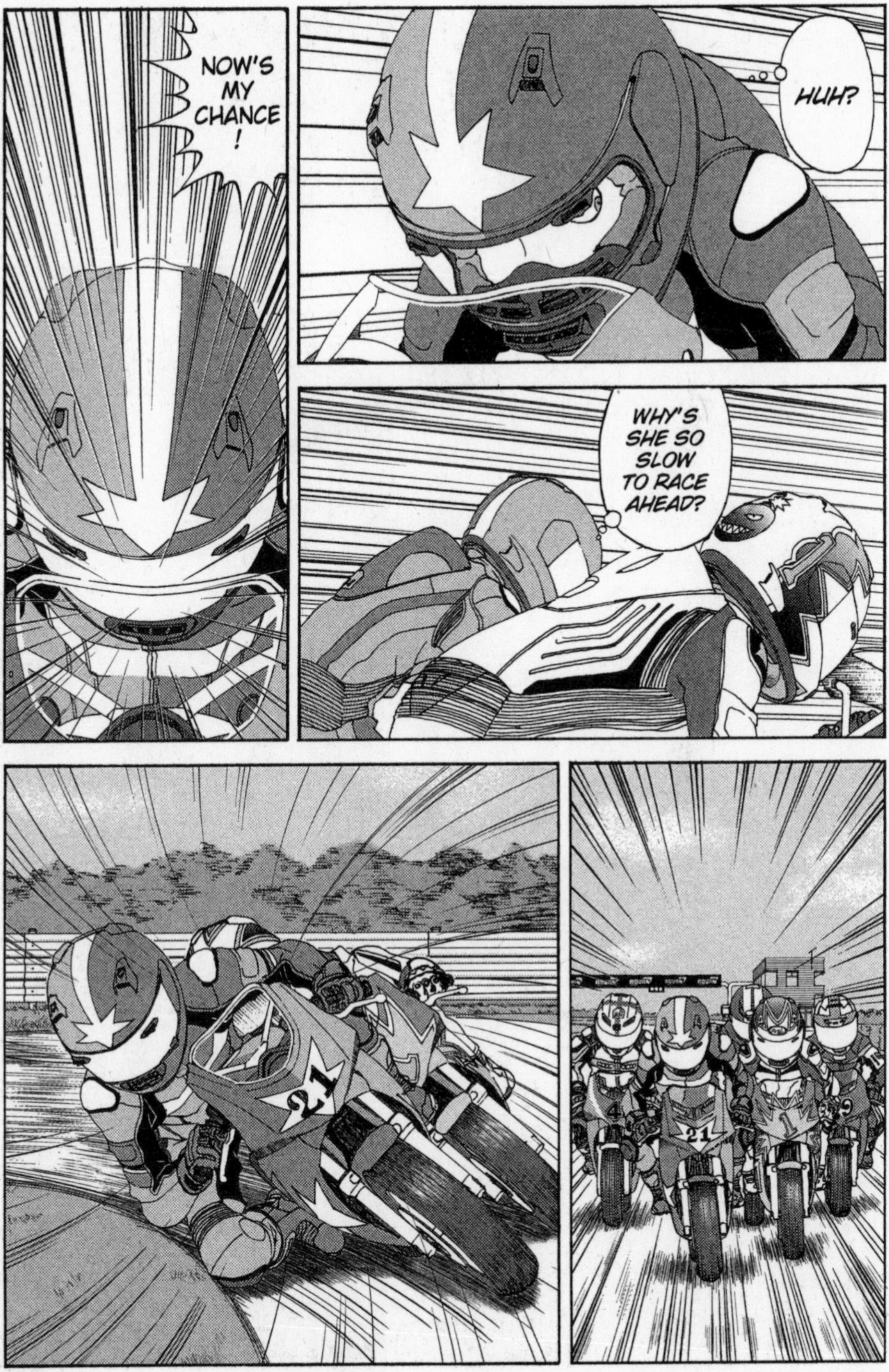
HUH?
WHY'S SHE SO SLOW TO RACE AHEAD?
NOW'S MY CHANCE!

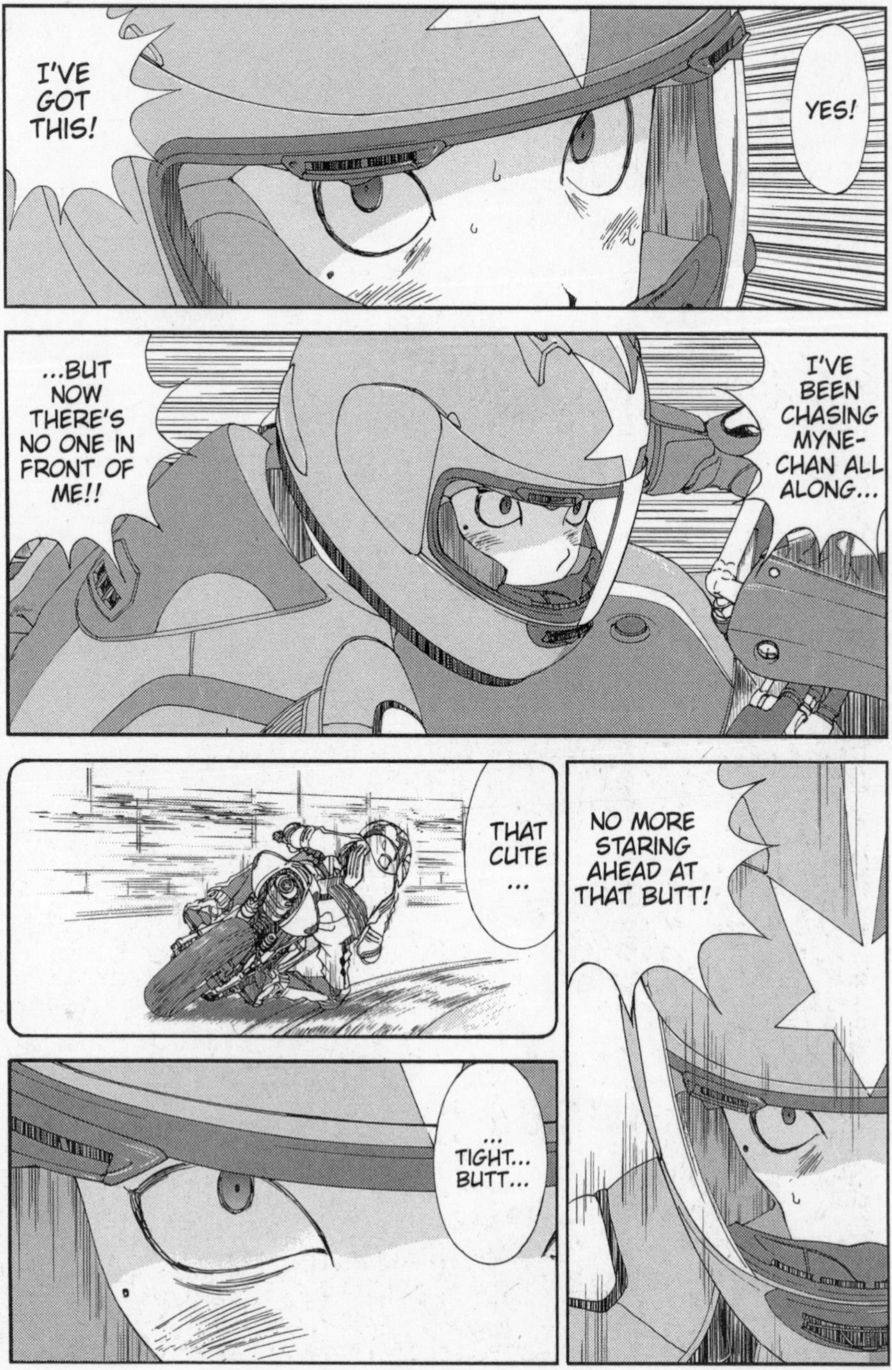
YES!
I'VE GOT THIS!
I'VE BEEN CHASING MYNE-CHAN ALL ALONG...
...BUT NOW THERE'S NO ONE IN FRONT OF ME!!
NO MORE STARING AHEAD AT THAT BUTT!
THAT CUTE ...
... TIGHT... BUTT...

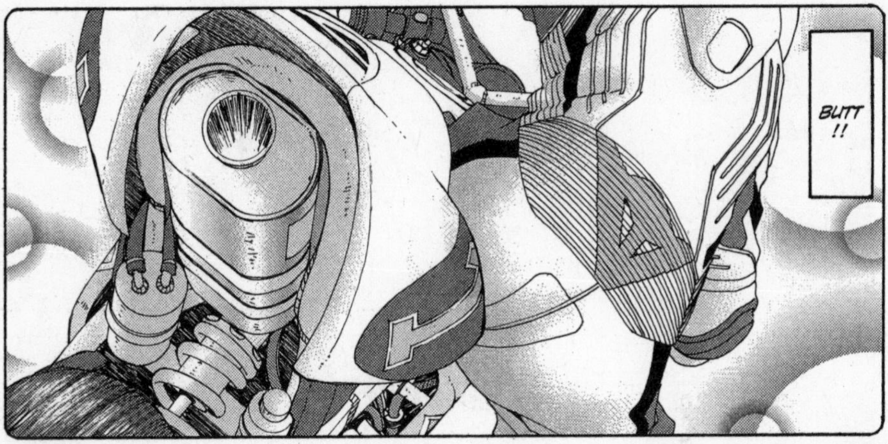
BUTT
!!
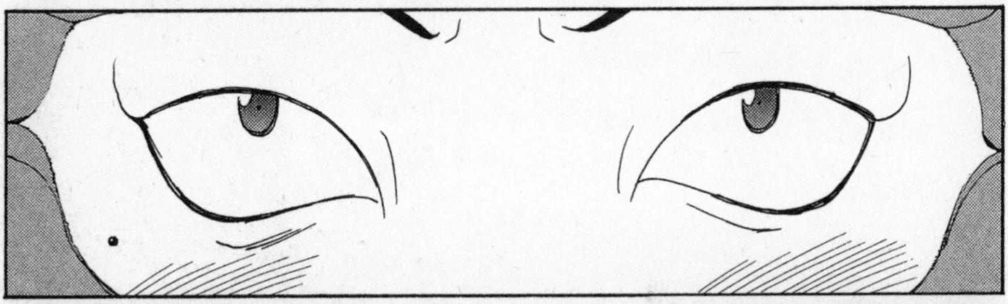
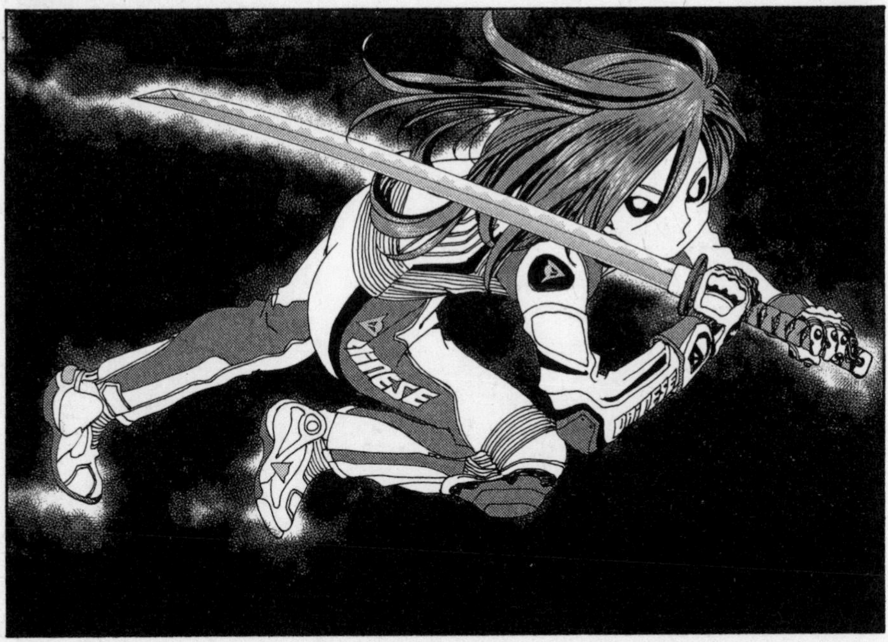

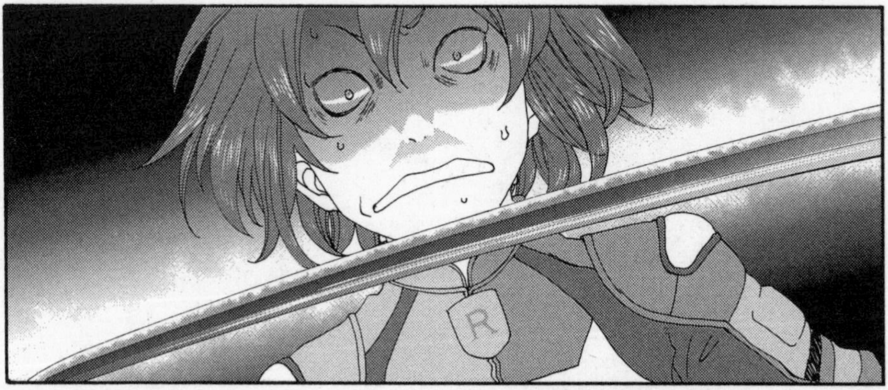

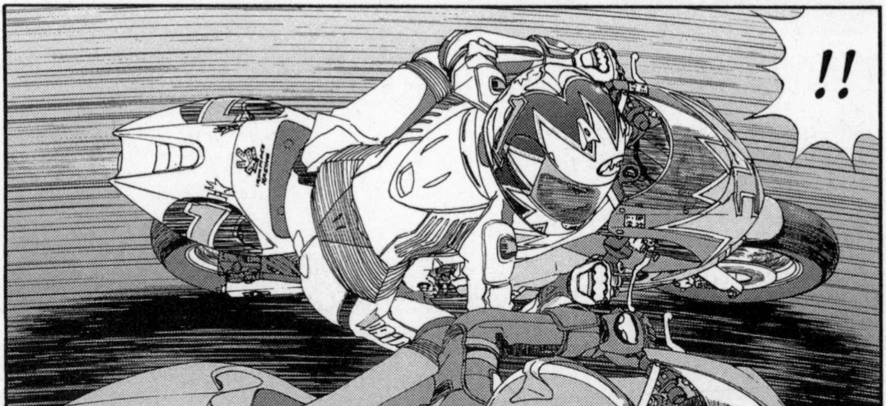
!!

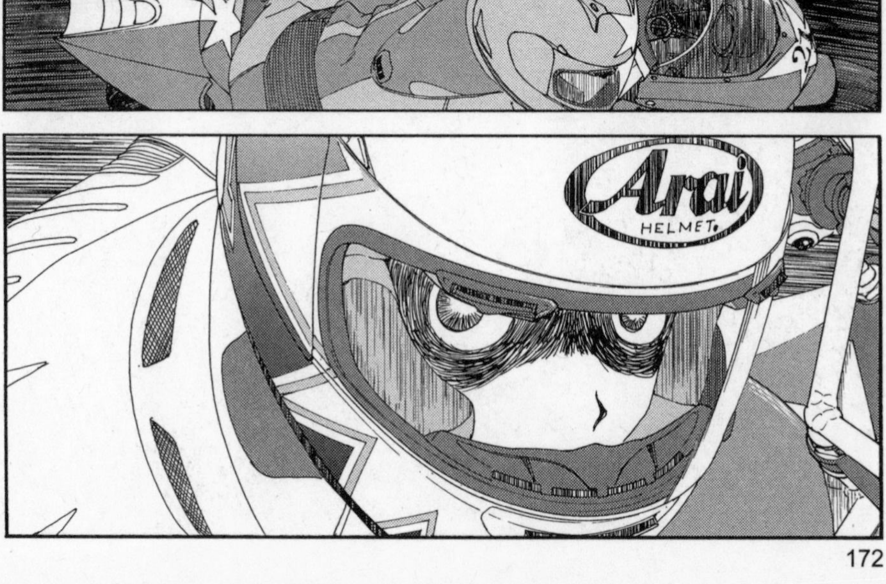
Arai
HELMET

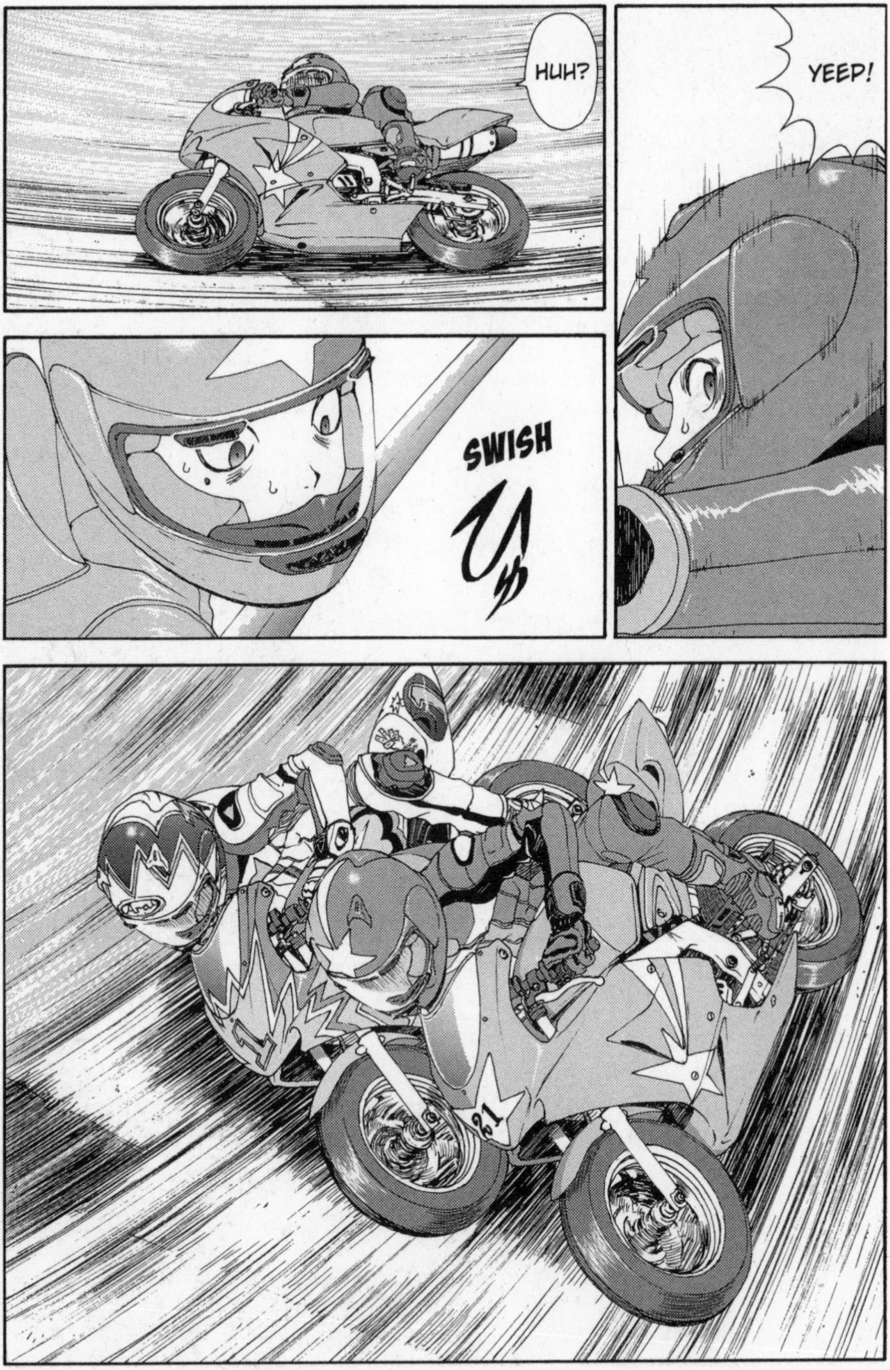
YEEP!
HUH?
SWISH

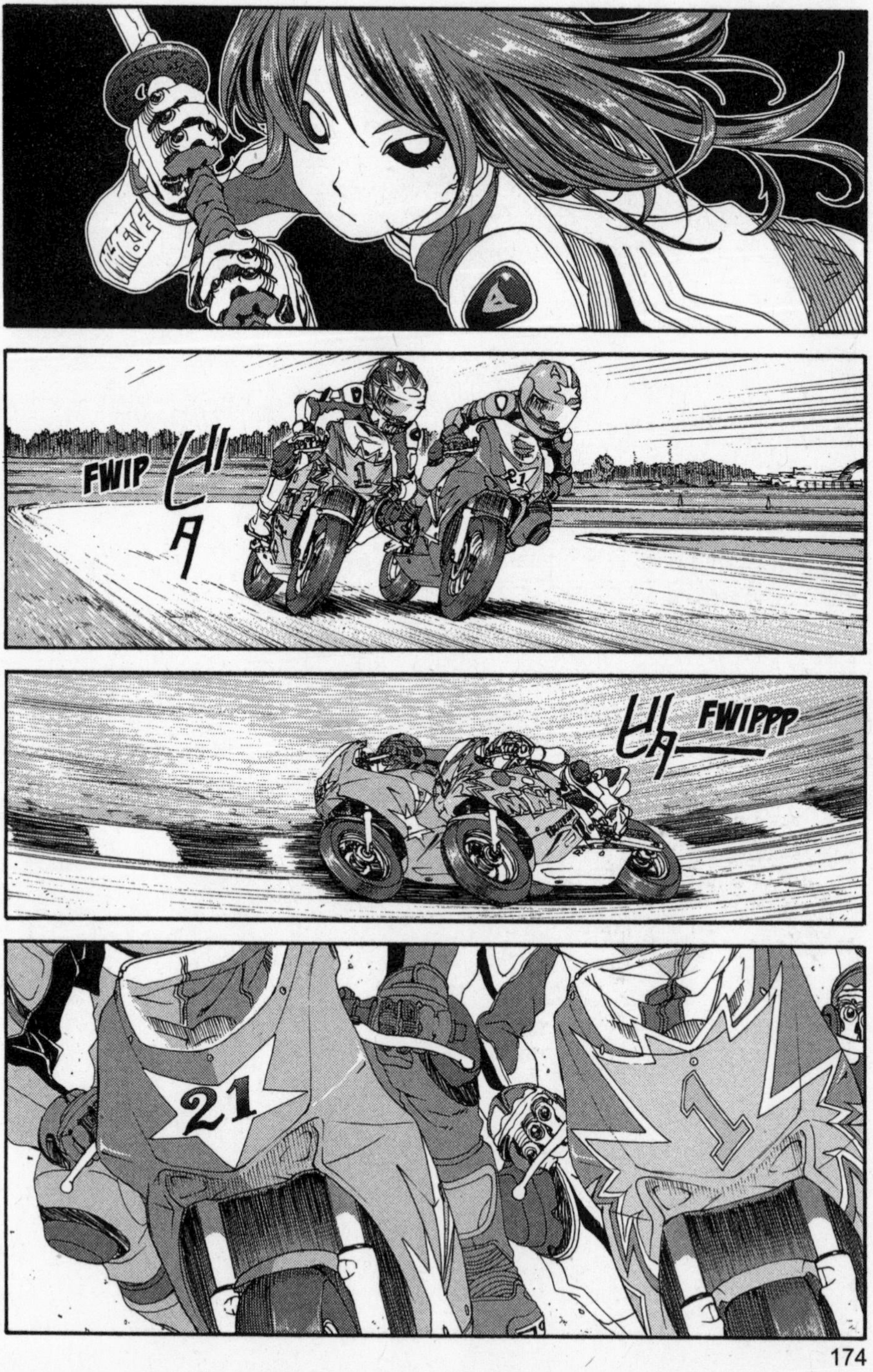
ピタ
FWIP
ピタ―
FWIPPP

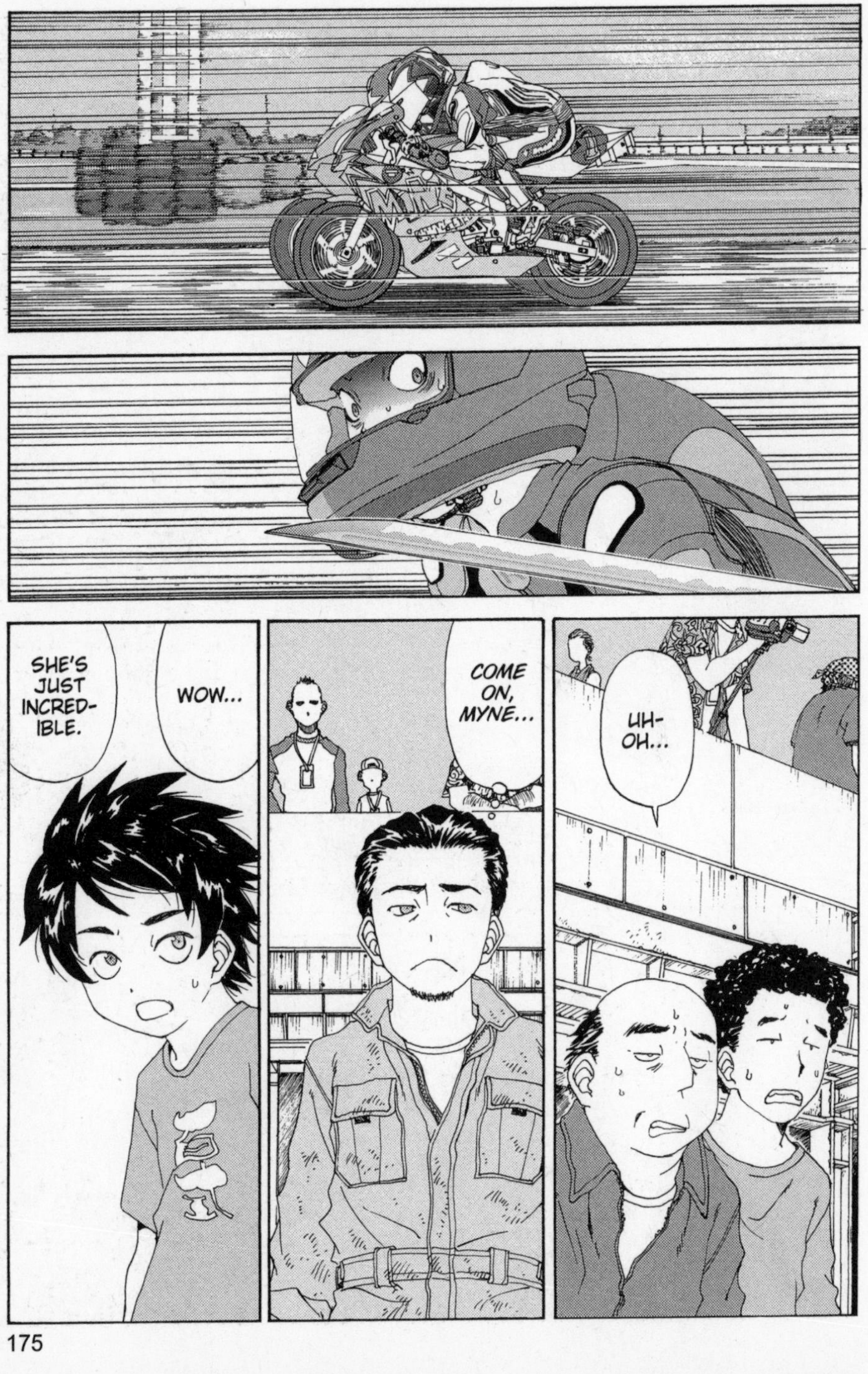
UH-OH...
COME ON, MYNE...
WOW...
SHE'S JUST INCRED-IBLE.

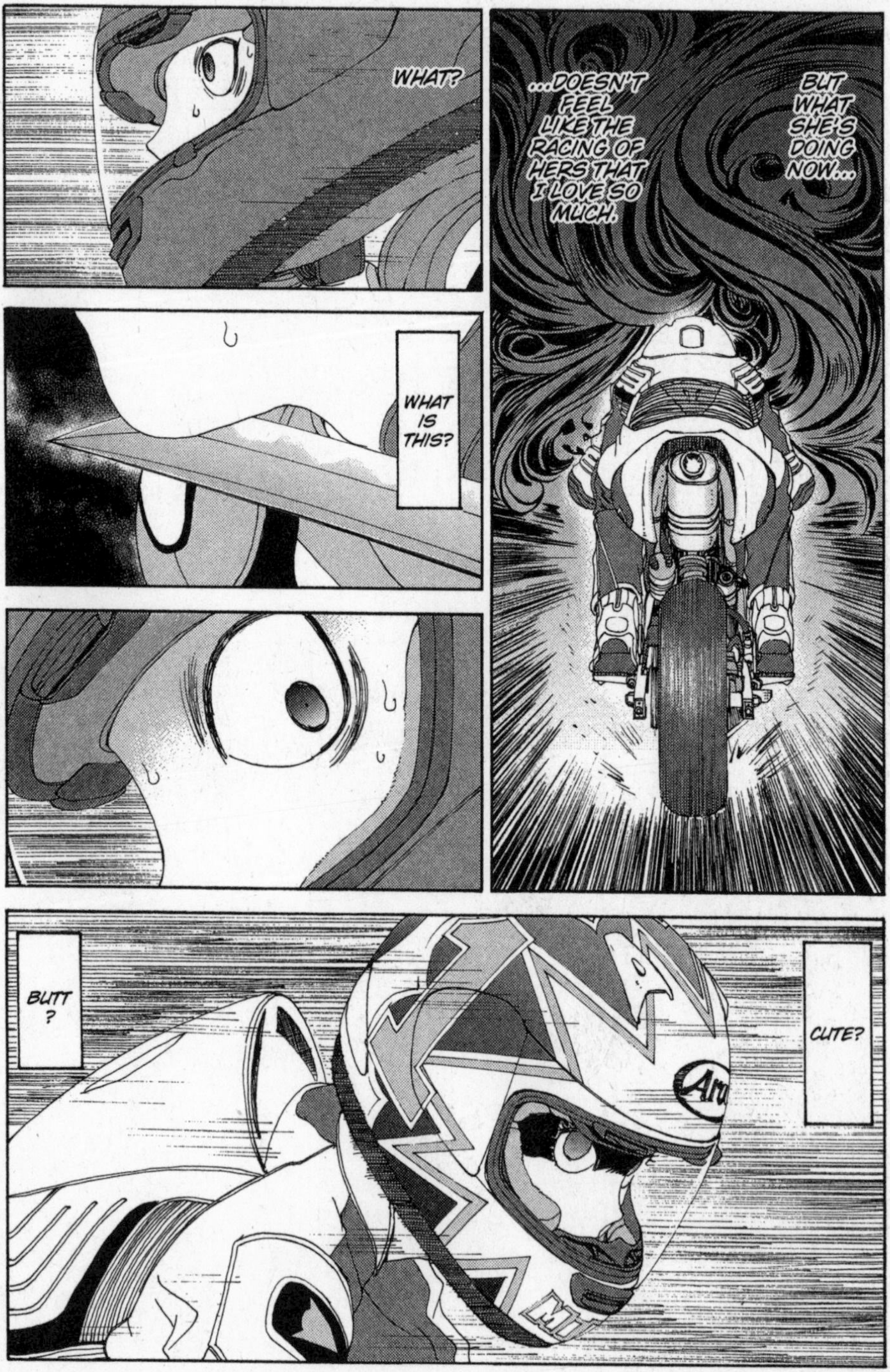
BUT WHAT SHE'S DOING NOW...
...DOESN'T FEEL LIKE THE RACING OF HERS THAT I LOVE SO MUCH.
WHAT?
WHAT IS THIS?
CUTE?
BUTT ?

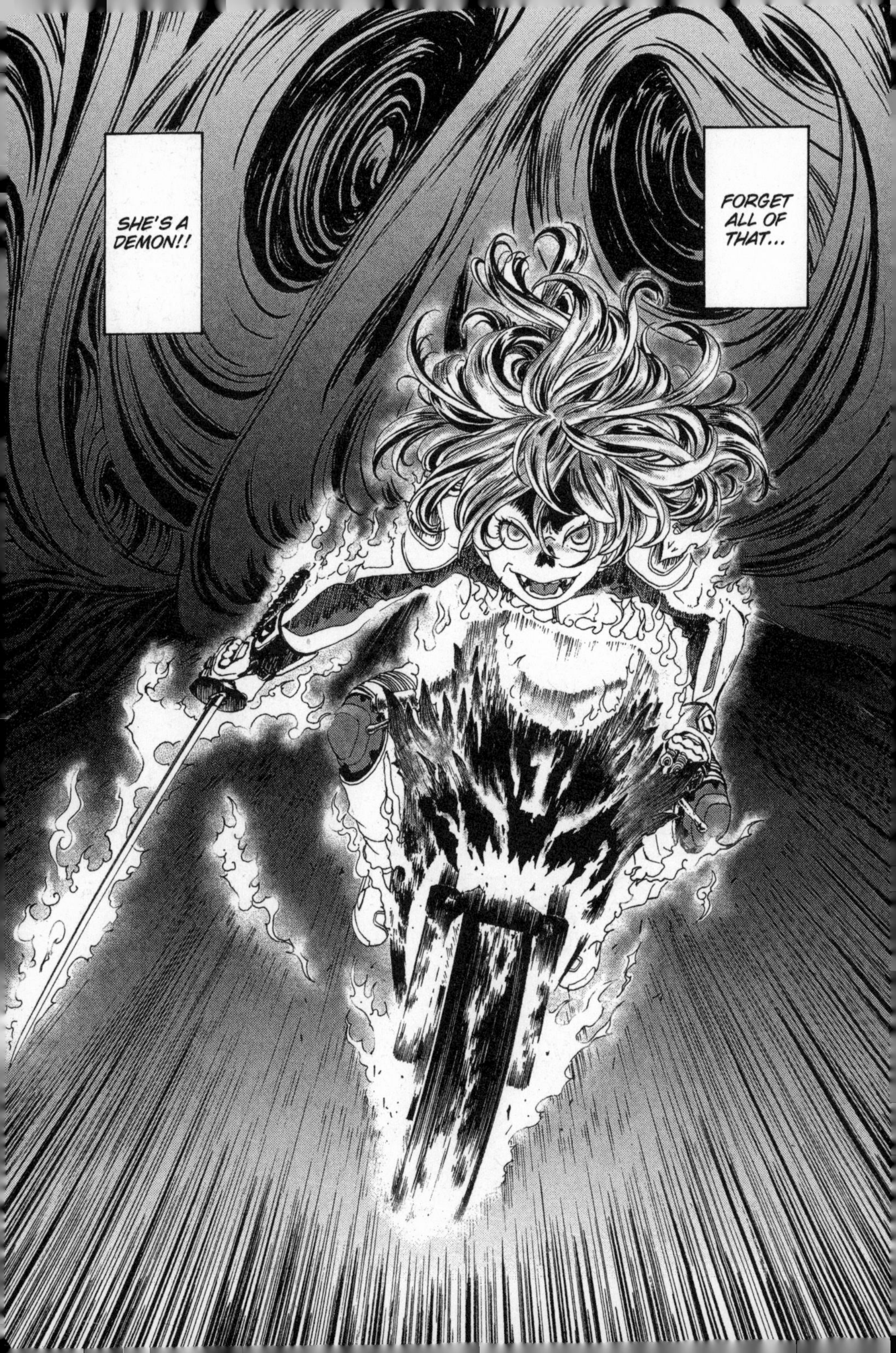
FORGET ALL OF THAT...
SHE'S A DEMON!!

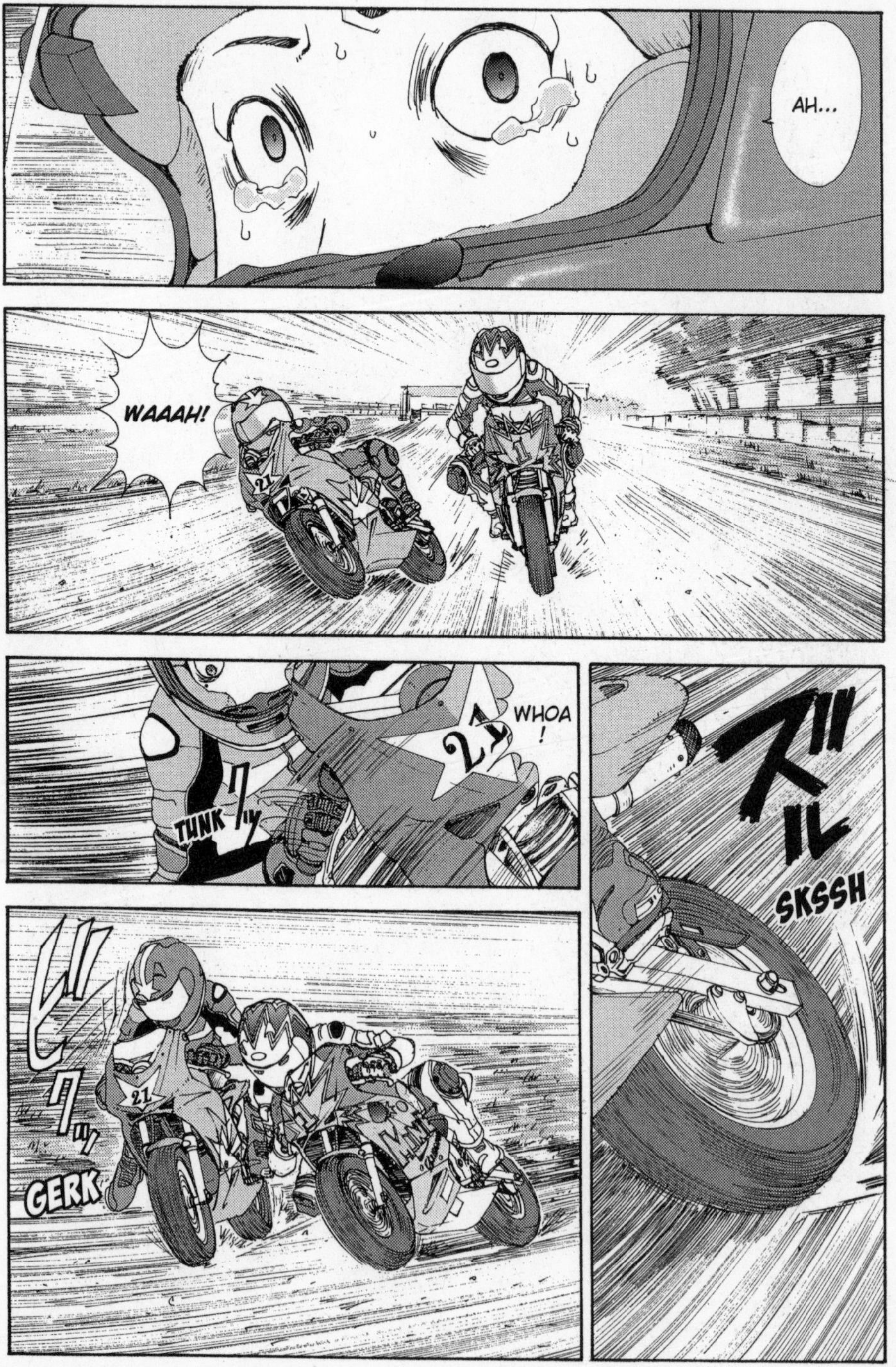
AH...
WAAAH!
ズル
SKSSH
WHOA!
TUNK
GERK

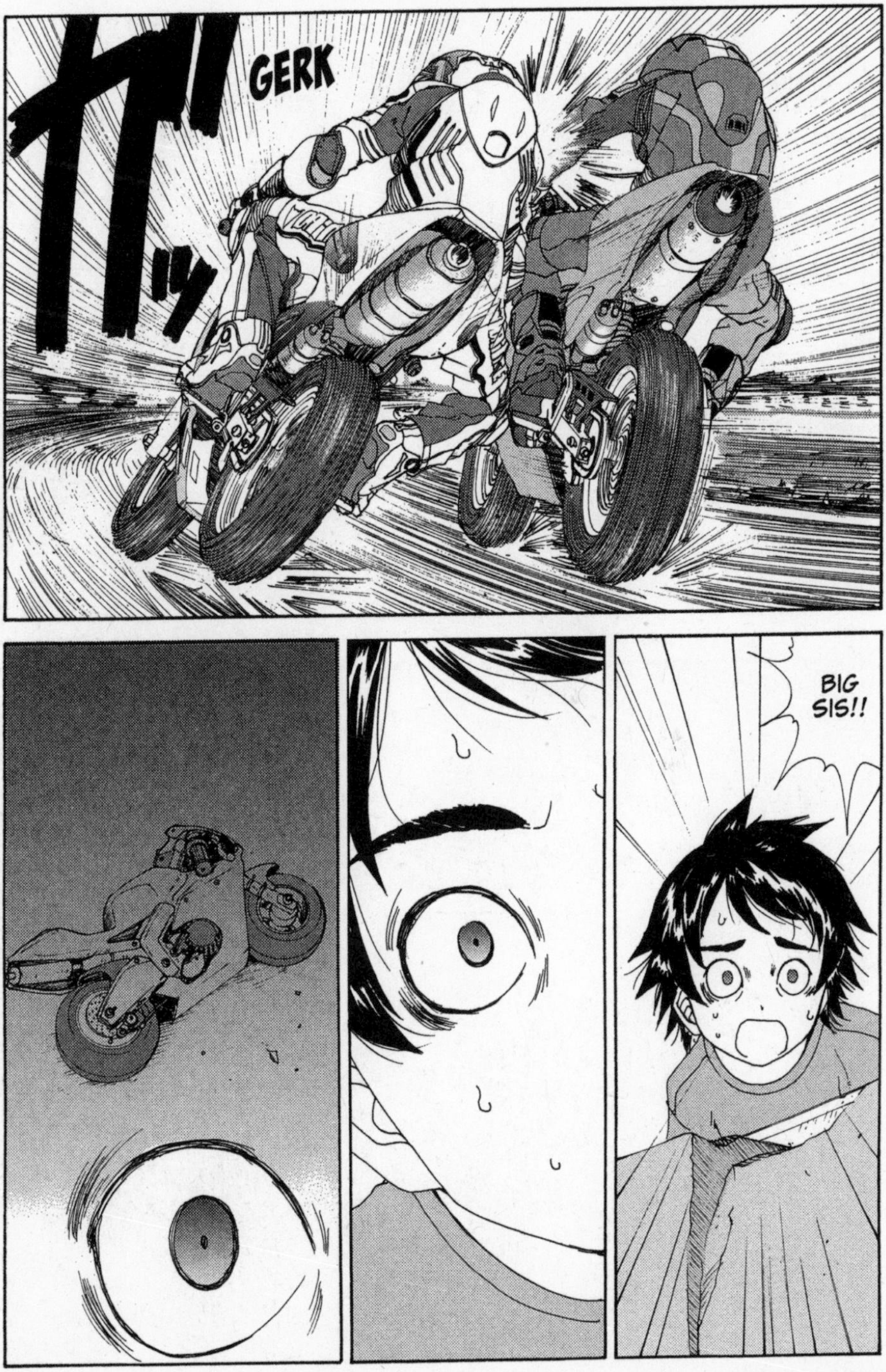
GERK
BIG SIS!!

WHAT'S GOING ON?

WHAT WAS THAT?

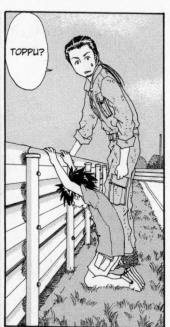

TOPPU?

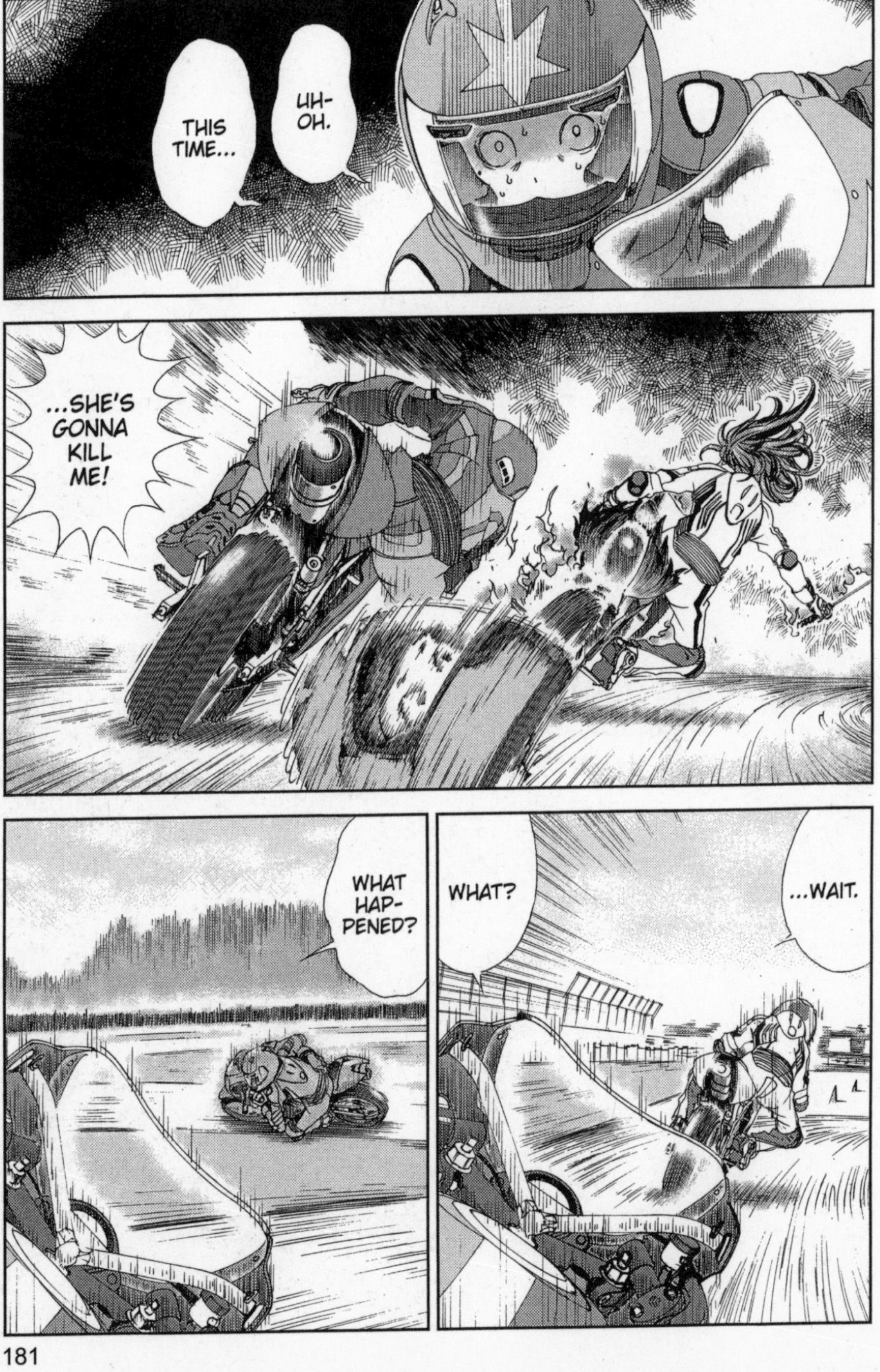
UH-OH.
THIS TIME...
...SHE'S GONNA KILL ME!
...WAIT.
WHAT?
WHAT HAP-PENED?

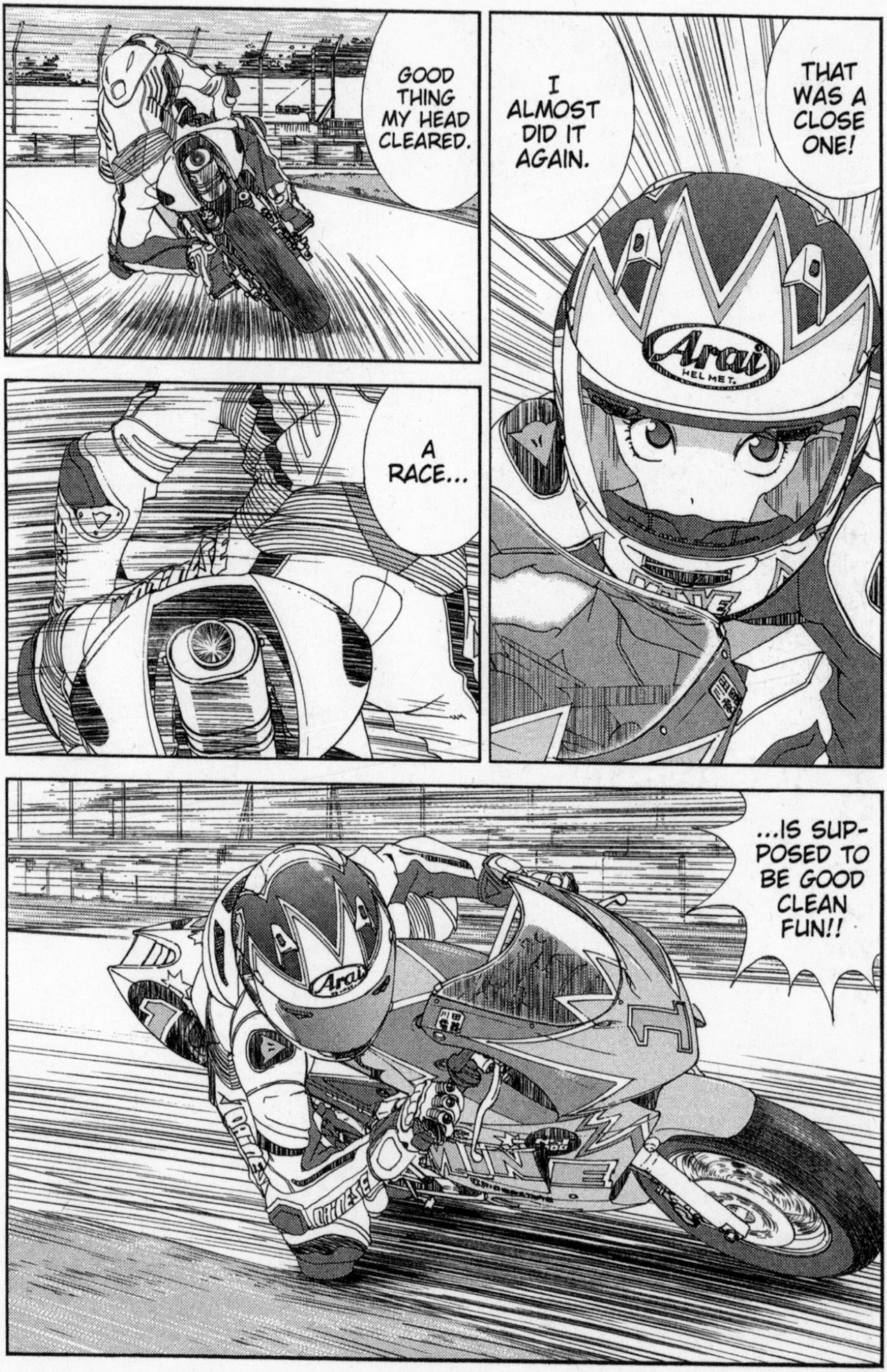
THAT WAS A CLOSE ONE!
I ALMOST DID IT AGAIN.
GOOD THING MY HEAD CLEARED.
A RACE...
...IS SUP-POSED TO BE GOOD CLEAN FUN!!

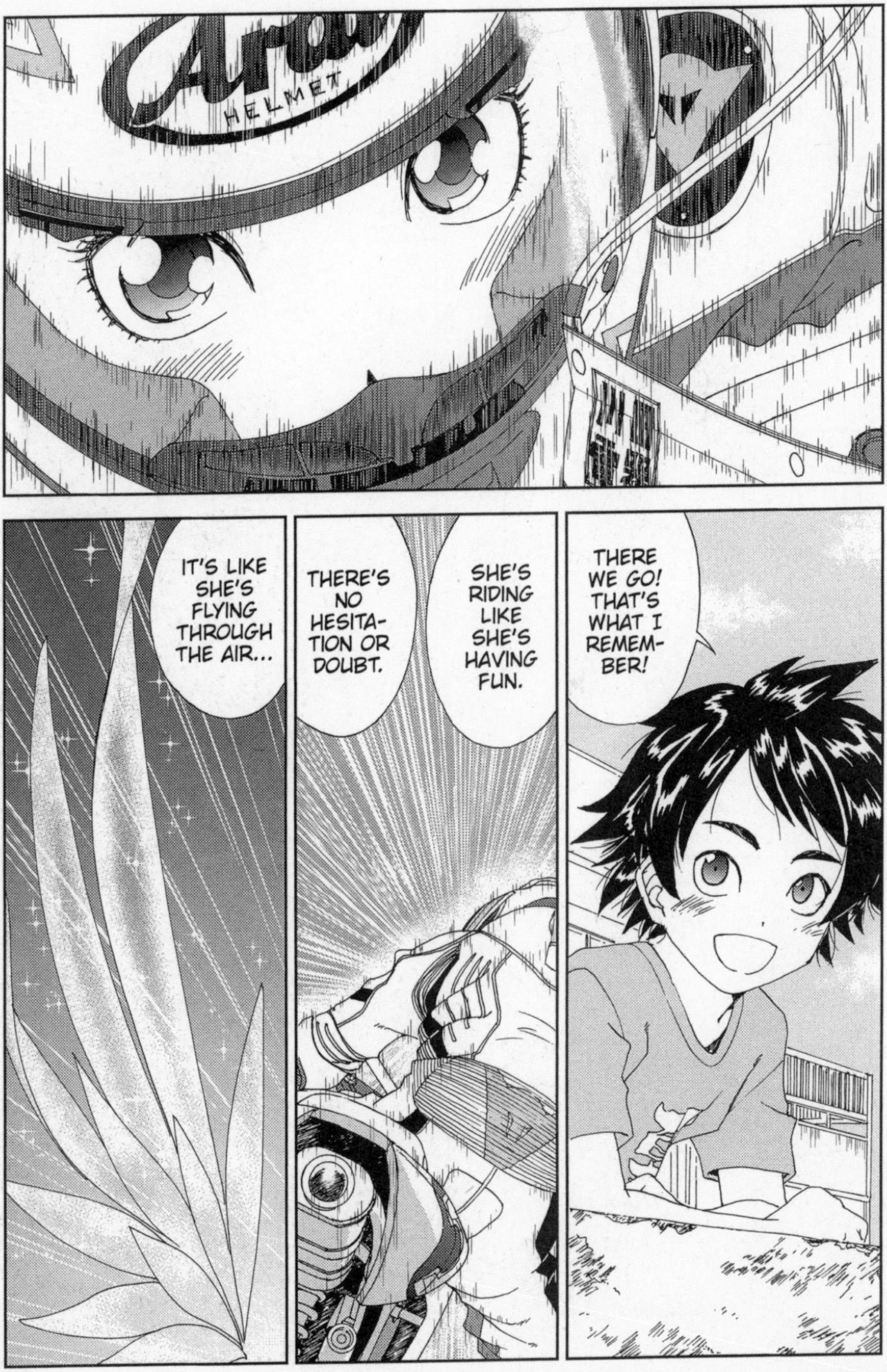
HELMET
THERE WE GO! THAT'S WHAT I REMEMBER!
SHE'S RIDING LIKE SHE'S HAVING FUN.
THERE'S NO HESITATION OR DOUBT.
IT'S LIKE SHE'S FLYING THROUGH THE AIR...

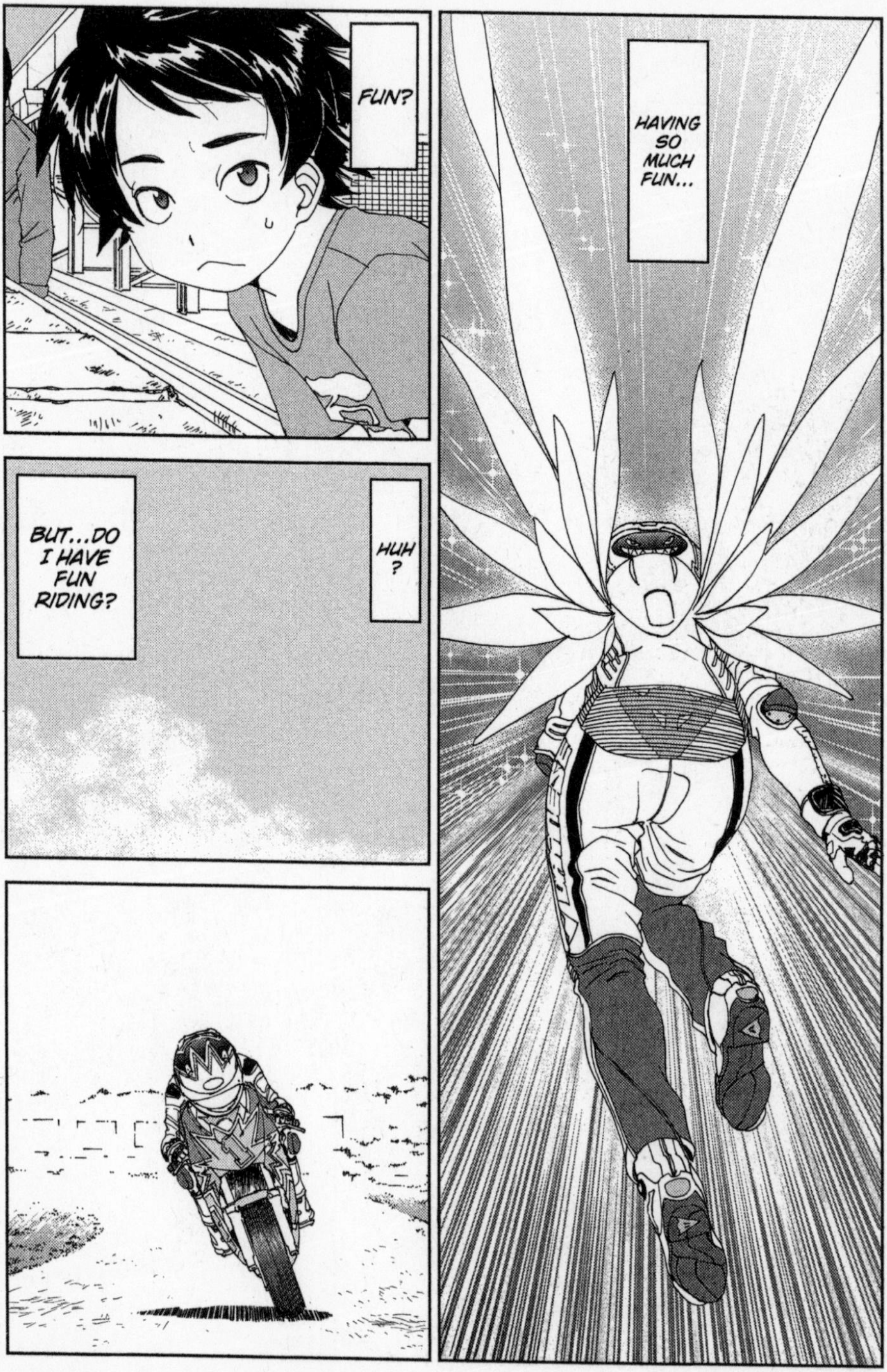
HAVING SO MUCH FUN...
FUN?
HUH?
BUT...DO I HAVE FUN RIDING?

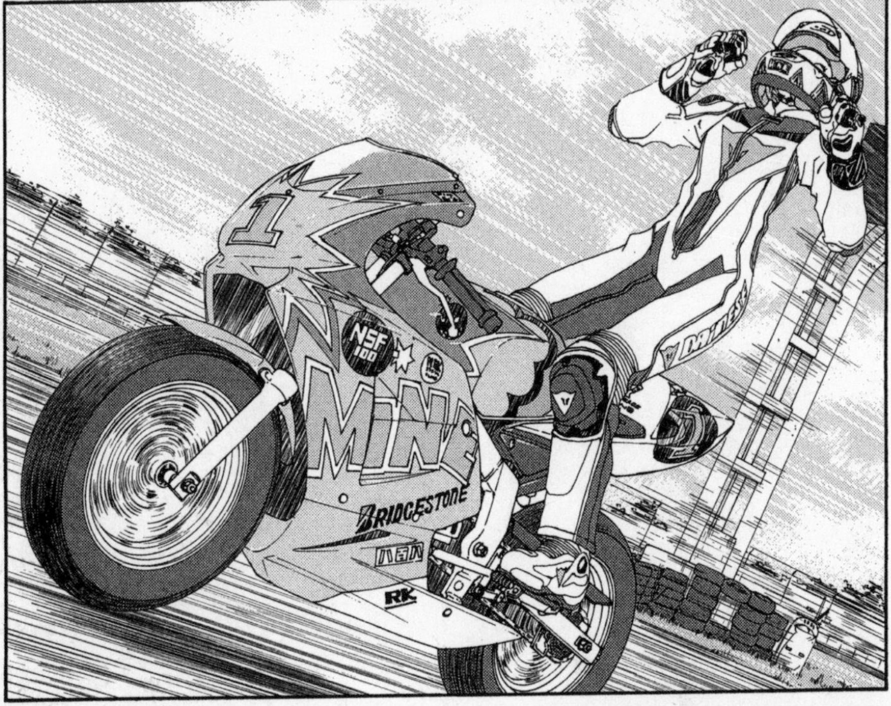
NSF 100
BRIDGESTONE

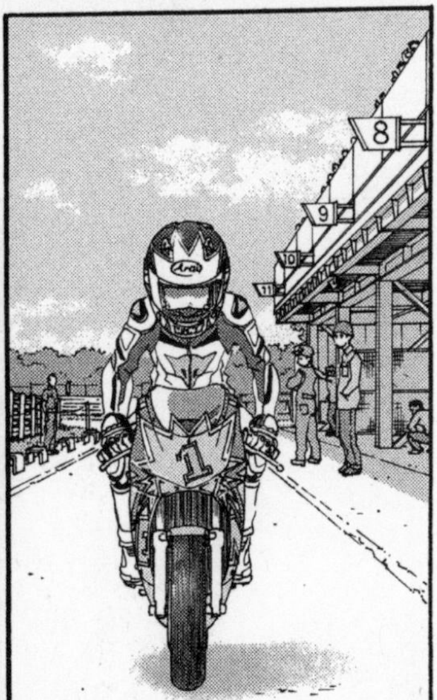
8
9

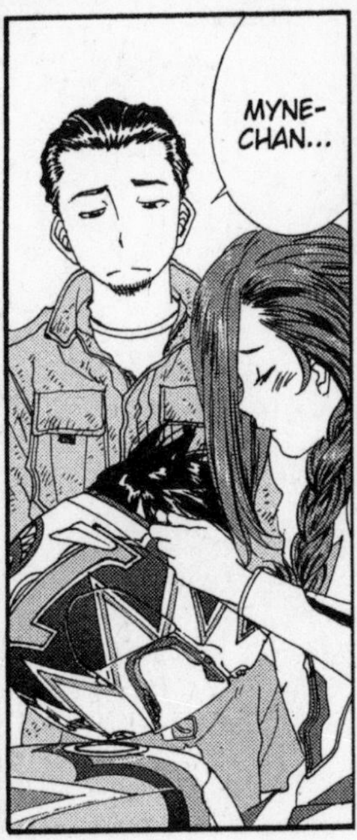
MYNE-CHAN...

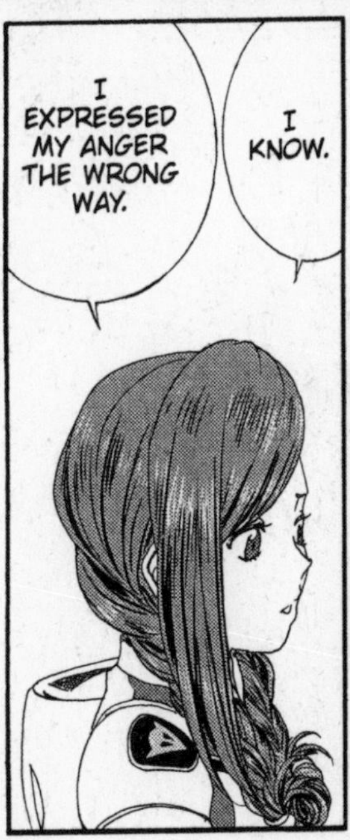
I KNOW.
I EXPRESSED MY ANGER THE WRONG WAY.

I'M SORRY, TOPPU.
I THINK ...
...I OUGHT TO HAVE SET AN EXAMPLE TO YOU FOR HOW TO RACE INSTEAD.
BUT I WAS THE ONE MAKING A MOCKERY OF IT.
UH...
NO, IT'S OKAY ...
I THOUGHT YOUR RIDING WAS SCARY AT FIRST...
...BUT BY THE END, IT WAS REALLY COOL.
YOU WERE MAD ABOUT WHAT HAPPENED TO ME, WEREN'T YOU?

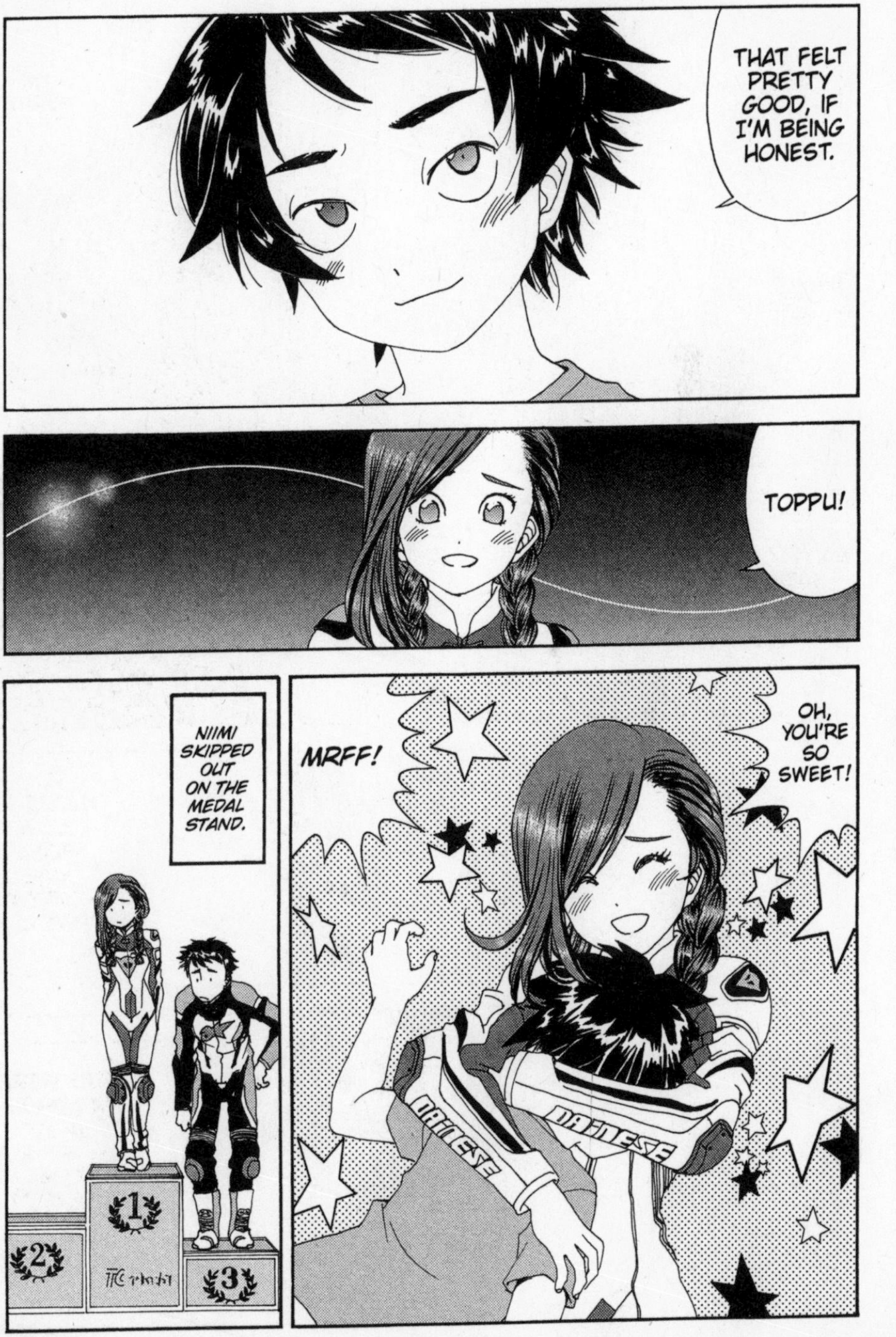
THAT FELT PRETTY GOOD, IF I'M BEING HONEST.
TOPPU!
OH, YOU'RE SO SWEET!
MRFF!
NIIMI SKIPPED OUT ON THE MEDAL STAND.

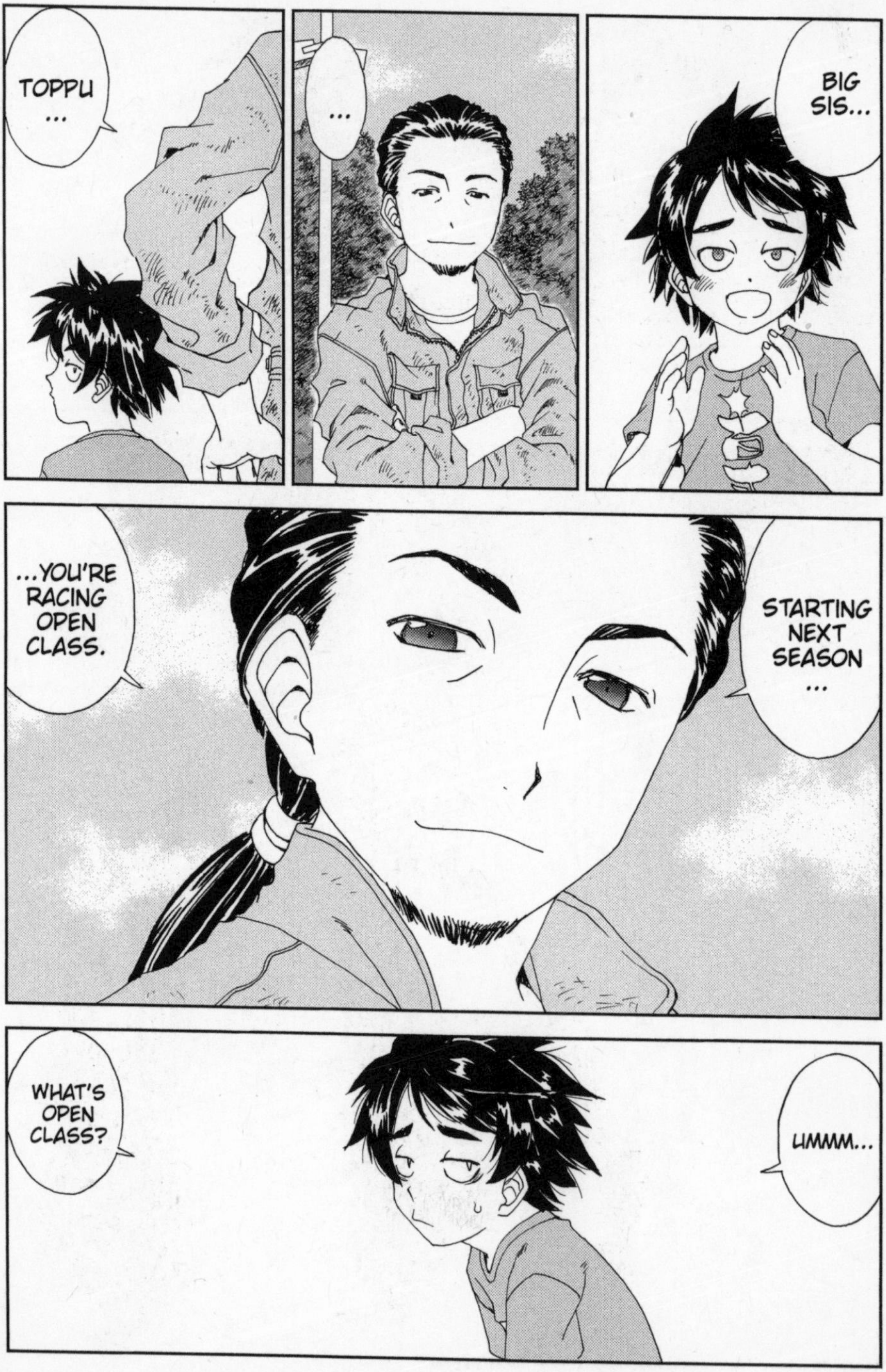
BIG SIS...
...
TOPPU ...
STARTING NEXT SEASON ...
...YOU'RE RACING OPEN CLASS.
UMMM...
WHAT'S OPEN CLASS?

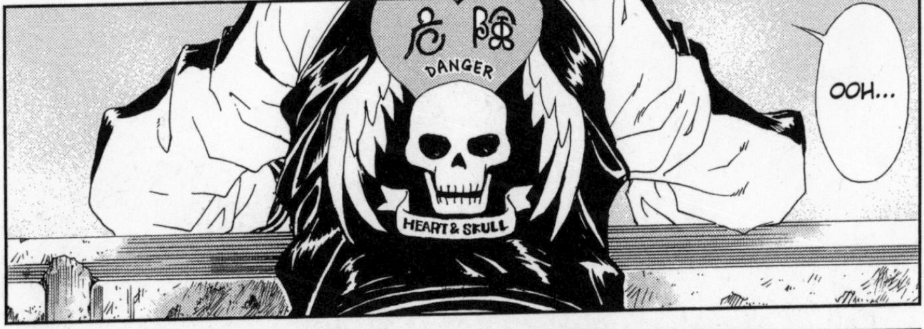
OOH...
危険
DANGER
HEART & SKULL

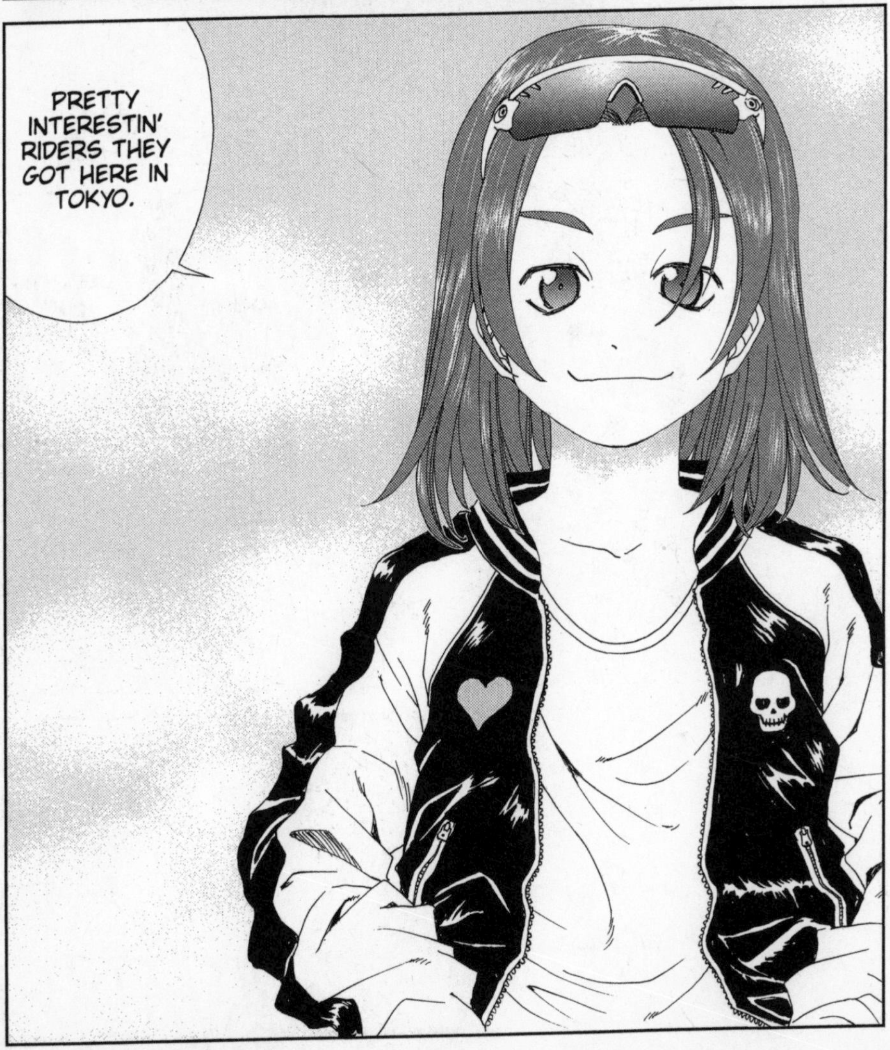
PRETTY INTERESTIN' RIDERS THEY GOT HERE IN TOKYO.

Lap 7: end

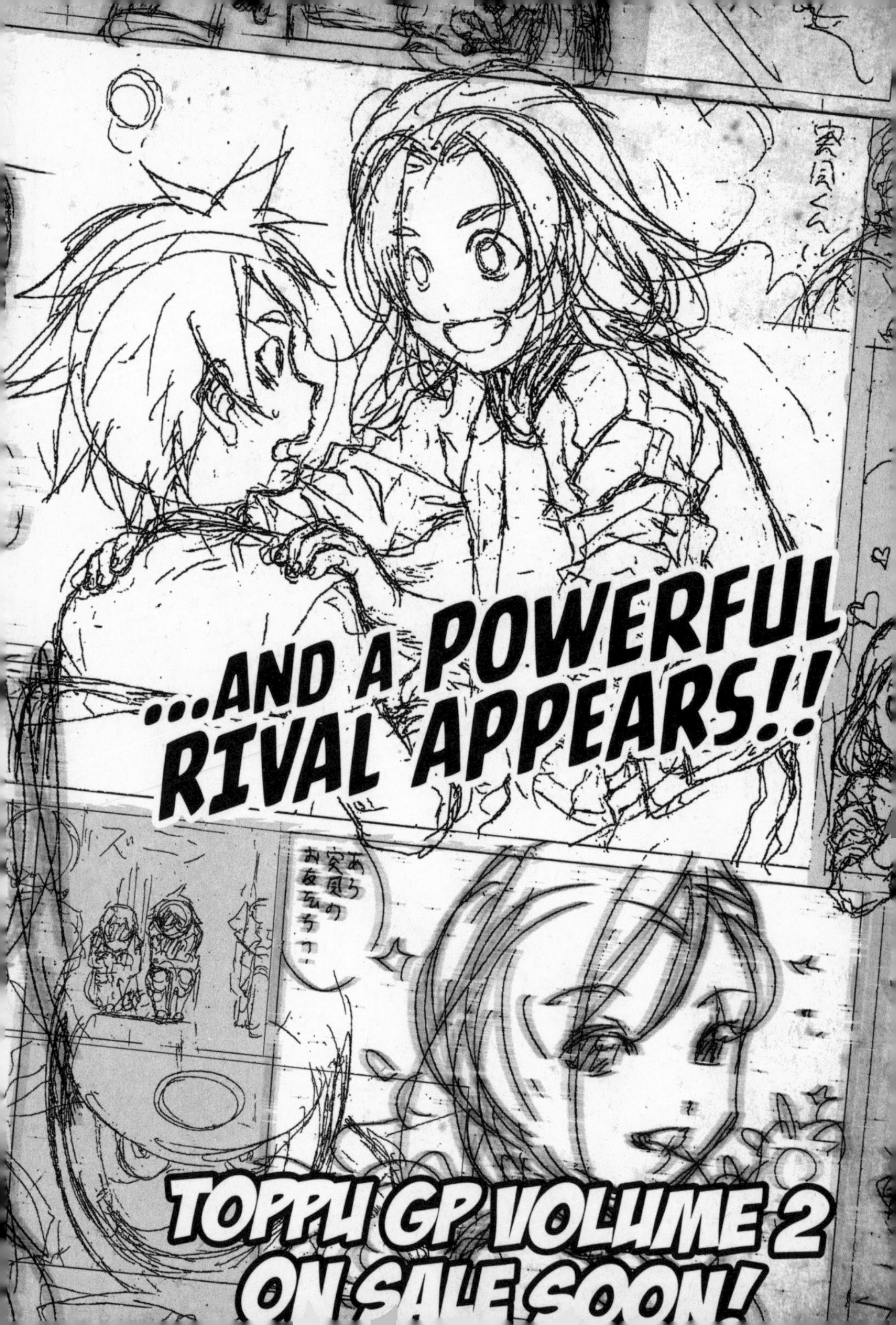
...AND A POWERFUL RIVAL APPEARS!!
TOPPU GP VOLUME 2 ON SALE SOON!

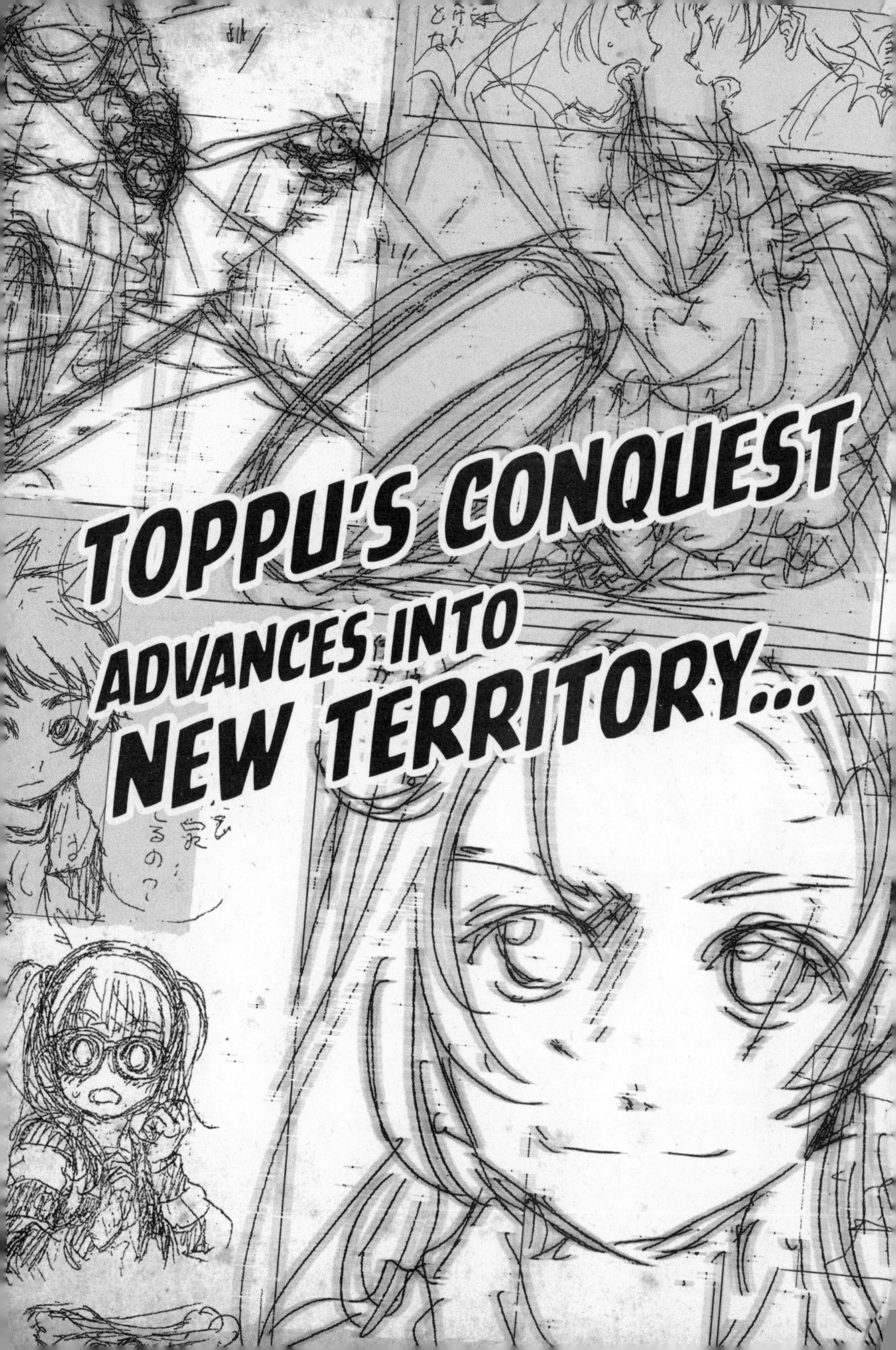
TOPPU'S CONQUEST
ADVANCES INTO
NEW TERRITORY...

Toppu GP Volume 1 is a work of fiction. Names, characters, places, and incidents are the products of the author's imagination or are used fictitiously. Any resemblance to actual events, locales, or persons, living or dead, is entirely coincidental.

A Kodansha Comics Trade Paperback Original.

Published in the United States by Kodansha Comics,
an imprint of Kodansha USA Publishing, LLC, New York.

Publication rights for this English edition arranged through Kodansha Ltd., Tokyo.

First published in Japan in 2016 by Kodansha Ltd., Tokyo, as *Toppu GP* volume 1.

ISBN 978-1-63236-451-7

Printed in the United States of America.

www.kodanshacomics.com

9 8 7 6 5 4 3 2 1

Translation: Stephen Paul
Lettering: Lorina Mapa
Editing: Paul Starr
Kodansha Comics edition cover design: Phil Balsman